Alternatives within the Mainstream II

Alternatives within the Mainstream II
Queer Theatres in post-war Britain

Edited by

Dimple Godiwala

CAMBRIDGE SCHOLARS PUBLISHING

Alternatives within the Mainstream II: Queer Theatres in post-war Britain, edited by Dimple Godiwala

This book first published 2007 by

Cambridge Scholars Publishing

15 Angerton Gardens, Newcastle, NE5 2JA, UK

British Library Cataloguing in Publication Data
A catalogue record for this book is available from the British Library

ISBN 1-84718-306-9; ISBN 13: 9781847183064

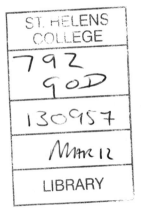

TABLE OF CONTENTS

Acknowledgements vii

Chapter One.. 1
Introduction: Queer Theatres in Post-war Britain
Dimple Godiwala

**Section I: Alternatives within the Mainstream: Gay, Lesbian
and Other Queer Theatre**

Chapter Two 12
The Trouble with Queers: Gays in Plays 1945-1968
Ian Spiby

Chapter Three 36
Tears, Tiaras and Transgressives: Queer Drama in the 1960s
Kate Dorney

Chapter Four... 59
Loving Angels Instead: The Influence of Tony Kushner's
Angels in America on 1990s Confrontational Drama
Paul T. Davies

Chapter Five 83
Did AIDS Paranoia Close *La Cage aux Folles*?
Simon O'Corra

Chapter Six 98
Days Gone By: Tracking AIDS Theatre and Queer Performance
Paul T. Davies

Chapter Seven.. 124
Fear of the Queer Citizen: From Canonization to Curriculum
in the Plays of Mark Ravenhill
Sarah Jane Dickenson

Chapter Eight 142
The Fluidity of Bodies, Gender, Identity and Structure in the plays
of Sarah Kane
Selina Busby and Stephen Farrier

Chapter Nine 160
Transgendered Masculinities in Performance: Subcultural Narratives
Laid Bare
Catherine McNamara

Chapter Ten 180
'The Dialectics of Desire': *Aunt Mary* and Transgendered Representations
Dimple Godiwala

Chapter Eleven 189
Notes on Cheryl Moch's *Cinderella, The Real True Story*
Dimple Godiwala

Chapter Twelve 192
Through the Looking Glass with Sarah Daniels
Dimple Godiwala

Chapter Thirteen 219
Soap, Sexual Identity and Mid-life Crisis: Lesbian Drama
between Essentialism and Gender Trouble
Kathleen Starck

Chapter Fourteen 239
We Sinful Dykes: Lesbian Sexuality and Racial Politics
in Valerie Mason-John's *Sin Dykes*
Ashley Tellis

Chapter Fifteen 248
Impermanence and Displacement in *Weldon Rising, The Strip*
and *Never Land* by Phyllis Nagy
Kathy McKean

Section II: Queer Television

Chapter Sixteen 272
Non-heterosexual Characters in post-war Television Drama: From Covert
Identity and Stereotyping, Towards Reflexivity and Social Change
Christopher Pullen

Chapter Seventeen 298
The Queer Subjects of Twenty-First Century Television Drama in Britain
Tony Purvis

Section III: Theatres of Difference

Chapter Eighteen 322
Grey Silhouettes: Black Queer Theatre on the post-war British Stage
Victor Ukaegbu

Chapter Nineteen 339
A Visitor's Guide to Glasgay!
Deirdre Heddon

Contributors 362

ACKNOWLEDGEMENTS

I am grateful to Paul T. Davies for reading and commenting on the MS. My husband, Stephen Michael McGowan (thankfully always curious to read what I have been working on) was kind enough to comment on the introduction.

Thanks are also due to Doug Pye (University of Reading) for reminding me to re-visit the term 'post-war theatre'.

I am grateful to Peter Lang, publishers of my monograph *Breaking the Bounds: British Feminist Dramatists Writing in the Mainstream since c. 1980* (2003; University of Oxford 2001) for the permission to reproduce materials published in the 2001 and 2003 publications of the book. The photo on the cover is from *Lovers* by Nina Rapi, West End Shorts, Gielgud Theatre, Nov 2001. Photo by Heide Martin.

I would like to extend my acknowledgements to Andy Nercessian, Carol Koulikourdi, Amanda Millar, Vlatka Kolic and the team at CSP for their efforts in bringing these two volumes into publication.

For the support, encouragement and time required to complete this book I am grateful to my husband, Stephen Michael McGowan.

This book is dedicated to the Labour government under the leadership of Anthony Blair for bringing in the Civil Partnerships Act.

CHAPTER ONE

INTRODUCTION:
QUEER THEATRES IN POST-WAR BRITAIN

DIMPLE GODIWALA

Critics of the English theatre have severally analysed post-war drama in terms of the new class egalitarianism that Clement Attlee's Labour government brought in, in the wake of the values of the Welfare State which brought about equal University access. These critics have charted 1956 as the watershed year in the English theatre, a year which ushers in the new egalitarian values as reflected on the British stage.

1956 is also the year the Berliner Ensemble first toured to Britain. It must be pointed out that this year of Brecht's death also was the year in which began the undoubtedly strong influences of Bertolt Brecht's theatre and his theories of the theatre which contributed to the new class consciousness of the stage.

As I have noted elsewhere, in terms of gendered writing for the stage, the watershed year is 1958 with Joan Littlewood's production of Shelagh Delaney's classic *A Taste of Honey,* a play which brings to the stage all four of the most significant issues that the post-war British stage has grappled with: class, gender, race as well as alternative sexuality.

This book traces one of the most pertinent issues to haunt British society and its stage since at least the Wilde trials: alternative sexuality. Tracing the drama which takes the stage in the post-war years to the present day when another Labour Government – under the leadership of Tony Blair – has made Civil Partnerships legal in continuing the party's long tradition of egalitarianism, this book begins with a period in living memory when it was still a criminal offence to be gay, a period in which lesbians were not legally visible, to a present moment which is celebratory in its legal acceptance of homosexual partnerships, signalling the beginning of another era of official and legal egalitarianism in British society.

Centuries of English drama have portrayed gay men in negative and stereotyped images. The criminalisation of gay sexuality, an offence partly repealed by the 1967 Sexual Offences Act which made legal homosexual acts in private between adult males in England and Wales paralleled the 1969 Stonewall bar incident (Osment 1989: xii). The latter half of the twentieth century was a period of rising awareness of discrimination in the gay community, preceded by the American Black movement and the women's movement in Britain and America. In Britain the Gay Liberation Front (GLF) met regularly, making themselves visible through demonstrations and marches. Inevitably, the ideology and politics of the GLF were to affect the theatre. Bette Bourne formed *Bloolips* and Alan Pope and Drew Griffiths were to found *Gay Sweatshop* (Osment 1989: xiii). It was the latter company which was to prove 'the power of theatre as a force of change and enlightenment' (Drew Griffiths in Osment 1989: xxiv) through the country.

The twentieth and the twenty-first centuries have seen a sea-change in attitudes and laws pertaining to the practice of homosexuality in Britain. The history of post-war gay theatre in Britain which this book, in part, sets to chart out, is paralleled by a critical and analytical discourse called Queer theory which addresses the role of gays and lesbians in history. Queer theory comes to the fore in the 1990s with British critic Alan Sinfield's prolific theorizing, with Americans such as Eve Kosofsky Sedgewick following closely on his heels. The precursors of queer theory are feminist/lesbian theory such as that of Monique Wittig and Hélène Cixous (of Jewish-Algerian heritage), later followed by Judith Butler's seminal work on the performativity of gender. In this introduction I would like to briefly chart out some thoughts on gender and sexuality and the flux of oppositions which makes for as many categories of sexuality as there are, possibly, individual subjects-of-desire.

Sexuality and gender

i. the Other

Although I have, on occasion, used the term 'Other' as feminist and postcolonial critics do, to designate gendered or racialized identity, and although it is often used in this way to denote the oppositional relations of man/woman, black/white, whilst attempting to trace the fluidity of the boundaries of sexuality the term ceases to be representational.

It must be pointed out that Sartre, speaking of the ontological relations of consciousness, stressed that 'Other' was *non-being*, the 'object' was perceived to be non-consciousness itself. (Sartre [1943] 1992: 241). Thus when a feminist casts herself as an Other, or a person of race is termed Other, what is being articulated, in Sartrean terms, is a non-being of non-*consciousness*. Thus the act of such a non-being possessing the consciousness of a subject with agency, when for example, fighting for suffrage or black rights or writing about topics such as queer theory is an act of the negation of self when self is perceived as Other.

Other denotes a category separate from the Self. In identifying with our Others we see them as similar to or the same as ourselves. This leads to an acceptance of those we perceive to be most unlike ourselves, especially in terms of race, class, gender or sexuality.

In this first decade of the twenty-first century, it is fallacious to assume the British mainstream (in any sense of the term) is white, middle-class and heterosexual. In terms of the representation of race, class and sexuality we can find spaces in the mainstream which are alternatives to what has passed as normative.

ii. perception

In terms of the consciousness of occupying a place on the continuum of homosexuality, the ontological positions of gay, les, bi, trans cannot be perceived as oppositional in terms of conventional western binaries.

Instead, these identities must be seen as fluid and continually shifting; and even as they locate themselves on the continuum of homosexuality, they constitute in that space a continuum of their own. These internal spaces can be seen conventionally, as a gay man can be described as 'camp' or 'straight-acting'; lesbians can be 'butch', 'dyke', 'femme'. Persons sharing a triadic arrangement or partnership can occupy any of the positions on the homosexual continuum. However, each space on the homosexual continuum, whether gay or les or any other, unfolds an ever shifting space of newly-named identities which reveal homosexual subjects as infinitely various in their subject positions of sexual identity.

Queer identities are fluid and always in a state of flux, defying definitions and binary oppositions. When my lesbian friends see me as 'butch' and my male dates insist I am the acme of femininity, it is not I who has changed but their perceptions which impose on me apparently contradictory definitions.

It is social perception which makes an Other. A human being can be the object-of-consciousness only through the mode of perception. The being of consciousness *perceives* another human being as an object: non-being; non-consciousness.

The self is composed of male-ness and female-ness in a yin/yang mode of inseparability, a polarised beingness we all inhabit. To be gay, les, bi or trans is in essence a freeing of a *normative* repressiveness which defines us as heterosexual and strictly 'male' or 'female'.

To realise we are all 'queer' is a recognition of what is introduced as 'Shadow' in Nina Rapi's 1989 play *Ithaka*.

> Shadow: All extremes contain within them their opposites and can easily transform into each other.
> Sula: Who are you?
> Shadow: I am the one you can't run away from. I'm Shadow.
> Sula: Tell me what Shadow is.
> Shadow: Shadow is the edge of time, is the crack of dawn. Shadow is a depth where you can only hang suspended, never reaching the end.
> Shadow is thoughts never formed in words, dreams that won't go away, poems that refuse to be moulded. Shadow is the law of desire and passion, the Realm of the Underworld, the world of misfits, outcasts and rebels. Shadow is the time when every moment reveals a new possibility. Is the darkness that defines light, the hell that heaven is marked with.
> Shadow is the eyes that couldn't see, the lives that couldn't be, the chains that were never broken. [Nina Rapi, *Ithaka*]

Shadow is where we begin to recognise the depths of sexuality (and otherness) we all possess. Shadow reveals normative repressiveness as obscurity, an opacity which casts us in a socially acceptable sexual role. To invite an introspection which rests on the shadowed self we need to recognise that our sexualities, however they may have been moulded are based on a certain opacity of self.

Alan Sinfield's extension of Freud in his dissident models of male sexuality (and Sinfield is right about the gay models pertaining also to female sexuality) are relevant here in that desire-to-be ('a *relative* matter') and desire-for (the person who confirms one's own identity as our other) determine the sexuality of the individual subject (See Sinfield 2002). One can be formulated to desire-to-be A (androgynous), F (female or feminine), M (male or masculine) or B which I define as a certain fluidity of self where one is M, F or A in various roles or situations or circumstances. I would add to Sinfield's theorizing that desire-to-be M is based on *a certain opacity of the capacity to be* F, and vice versa. A would denote a blurring of boundaries which is typically represented by a physical self which blurs the divide between M and F. However, the physicality of the body-self need not determine the desire-to-be A. The representation of the typical physical A-self is merely a stereotype or indeed can be seen as *symbolic* of the consciousness of being-A.

Herbert Bless, Klaus Fiedler and Fritz Strack point out that in the construction of social reality, human beings strive for a consistency of perception (2004: 17). This is what has possibly led to the binary division in the perception of man/woman. Physically perceived differently, man is thought to be different from woman as a human subject. The traditional roles played by men and women have inevitably led to the genders being regarded as usually two (in some ancient cultures such as India, at least three). The encoding of knowledge ('I am a woman') leads to the behavioural responses deemed appropriate for the gender which leads in turn to the birth of stereotypes or *social categories* of gender and the idea that behavioural responses are gendered. Thus we possess prior beliefs about groups, such as men and women.

iii. transgendered identities

When the materiality of the physical body is in conflict with the subject's perceived gender or, when the subject's gender is not clearly defined in the materiality of the physical body (the *interstitially-gendered* body) there is an attempt to transform into what is perceived as another gender. The other gender is usually the perceived opposite of or different from the materiality of the physical self.

iv. social identities

In societies which continue to divide genders into two, where a physical deviancy is unmentionable and hidden, human perception and behaviour will gravitate subjects to conform to the occupancy of one or another gender category, i.e., man/woman. For the well-being of the human subject, the behavioural response in social groups must coincide with self-definition which is achieved in relativity as a response to the other/s. (See, e.g., Brewer and Hewstone 2004: 278 ff). Brewer and Hewstone point out that self-categorization theorists have suggested distinguishing between two basic forms of self-definition: the individual self (personal identity) and the collective self (social identity) (279). In terms of the consistency of perception we have spoken of, the individual self must need be consistent with the binary divide of gender in the collective group to establish the subject's definition of a collective self.

The Civil Partnership Act 2004

Paul T. Davies wrote to me on 29 January 2006 to say he could not attend my National Theatre Platform talk with Pam Gems on 07 April as he was tying the knot with his partner Neville Edrich the next morning. Contributor Ian Spiby likewise emailed and said he had entered into a Civil Partnership. During the making of this book, like some of the contributors, hundreds of same-sex couples across the country were getting married. Although not termed strictly a marriage, the Civil Partnership Act 2004 which came into force on 5 December 2005 enabled same-sex couples to obtain legal recognition of their relationships. Same-sex couples are now 'civil partners' in a civil partnership.

Emerging mainstream social groups

With the Civil Partnership Act of 2004-5, homosexuality becomes recognised in its broadest sense of legality and thus enters mainstream discourse. At the current time, negative attitudes to homosexuality will linger in the social consciousness even as these newly recognised social groups emerge to take their place alongside the mainstream of heterosexuality to establish and determine new, equal status, inter-group relations.

The legalization of same-sex relations has long been a subject of debate and discussion in same-sex theory which is divided into the camps that insist that legalization is an assimilation into the normativity of heterosexual ideals whereas others insist it is a 'vital stepping stone toward civil rights and state recognition' (See, e.g., Bernstein and Schaffner 2005: xi). However, I see legalization as most importantly a step toward *the social acceptance of groups considered minorities* (low-status groups with low self-esteem and increased inter-group anxiety; see Brewer and Hewstone 2004: 287-288). Low-status groups which have been without *a recognised* voice or agency and thus far powerless to exert an influence except on the fringes of social acceptance need legal and state recognition to live in a society of freedom, tolerance and equal rights.

Undoing repression and the evolution of desire

We are all born bisexual. It is the self-same repression which underlies the unconscious constructions of individual minds and bodies determining whether individuals are gay or heterosexual. The heterosexual has had the gay/lesbian side repressed; the homosexual has repressed the impulse attracting him or her to what is conventionally referred to as the opposite sex. Monogamous individuals must of necessity have suppressed one side as they forge intimate relationships with another, whether male or female.

Undoing repression consists of at least two responses to one's constructed sexuality: firstly individuals must be able to embody and express positive behaviour traits conventionally regarded as strictly male and female; a kind of *unisexuality*. In this respect western contemporary popular culture is beginning to recognize that human subjects are not binarily divided: for example, boys *can* cry. Secondly, individuals must be able to desire another in terms of affective emotions rather than gendered sexuality; in effect, an *evolution of desire* is necessary in terms of ability to bond and share with another human being rather than a particular sexed gender. This would lead to desire for another human being rather than same-sex desire or opposite-sex desire, a kind of unisexuality rather than bisexuality or heterosexuality.

Although the British Civil Partnership act is an acknowledgement of queer sexualities, the bisexuality or (usually) repressed desire inherent in each and every human subject could only possibly be answered by the formation of dyads freed-from-gender-stereotyped behaviour patterns, or triads or, perhaps, quartets.

If the individual is freed from the repression of desiring the same sex (gay and lesbian) or the other sex (heterosexuality), a marriage or partnership could be one of more than the heterosexually arranged conventional dyad. Two men and two women could meet the needs of same and other sexual partners (in this regard see my chapter on *Aunt Mary* and triadic arrangements amongst queers).

Of course, free or freed individuals could meet each others' need *in dyads* if the masculine and feminine selves could be free to be expressed in individual subjects. This would entail a non-stereotyped self which performs (in terms of the performativity of gender) the same as well as the other gender-as-constructed. These are, of course, theoretical answers to the unconscious mechanisms which govern repressiveness that heterosexuality and same-sex partnerships are both based upon, but, as in the Pam Gems play, *Aunt Mary,* could possibly work in terms of permanent partnerships as opposed to the experimental communal living attempted (largely unsuccessfully) in 60s and 70s Britain.

With a planet-wide population explosion, the need to 'go forth and multiply' may have itself worked its way to completion, and reproductive behaviour need not determine the seeking of sexual partnerships. The theoretically ideal answer is a kind of unisexuality which would lead the individual to find a partnership based on mutual love, trust, bonding and sharing regardless of gender. This would make the still stereotypical categories still in play – heterosexual, gay, lesbian, bisexual, queer – redundant and obsolete as individuals and societies strive toward a sharing based on affective bonding behaviour rather than sexually gendered responses to individuals. Exploring the shadows in the repressed constructions of our sexualities may lead to a freeing of individual minds and bodies as we accept an other sexually, regardless of gender and also the other factors that sometimes determine sexual bonding: for example, a rigid adherence to the preference for the same class and race.

Alternatives within the Mainstream II

This book is an appraisal of queer theatre on the post-war British stage, some notable American influences, with additional chapters on television drama and an overview of Black queer theatre. Each chapter is prefaced by an author's synopsis to aid in an appraisal of the chapter contents. There is some degree of overlap between the first volume *Alternatives Within the Mainstream: British Black and Asian Theatres* (CSP 2006) and this one. For chapters on queer black theatre see, in Vol. I, especially Chapter Nine: 'Black and Female is Some of Who I Am and I Want to Explore It': Black women's plays of the 1980s and 1990s' by Kathleen Starck; Chapter Ten: 'The Search for Identity and the Claim for an Ethnicity of Englishness in Jackie Kay's *Chiaroscuro* and Valerie Mason-John's *Brown Girl in the Ring*' by Dimple Godiwala.

Alternatives Within the Mainstream II follows from the first volume's dedication to a critical appreciation of and a tracing of trajectories of the theatres of our Others on the British stage. The first volume *Alternatives Within the Mainstream: British Black and Asian Theatres* traced a history of Black and Asian British plays, playwrights, theatre companies and theatre voices. The two volumes celebrate the plurality on the post-war British stage in terms of class, gender, race and sexualities.

Alternatives Within the Mainstream II: Queer Theatres in Post-war Britain is aimed as an introductory text which introduces the several plays, playwrights, theatre companies and queer theorists to students and scholars of contemporary queer British theatres.

Works cited

Bernstein, Elizabeth and Laurie Schaffner, eds. *Regulating Sex: The Politics of Intimacy and Identity*, New York & London: Routledge, 2005.

Bless, Herbert, Klaus Fiedler and Fritz Strack, *Social Cognition: How individuals construct social reality,* Hove & New York: Psychology Press, 2004.

Brewer, Marilynn B., and Miles Hewstone, eds. *Self and Social Identity*, Oxford: Blackwell, 2004.

Rapi, Nina, *Ithaka* [1989] in *Seven Plays by Women,* ed. Cheryl Robson, London: Aurora Metro, 1991.

Sartre, Jean-Paul (1943 [1992]), *Being and Nothingness*, trans. Hazel E. Barnes [1956], New York: Gallimard; Washington: Washington Square Press.

Websites

Sinfield, Alan, 'Lesbian and Gay Taxonomies' in *Critical Inquiry,* Volume 29, No. 1, Autumn 2002. See http://criticalinquiry.uchicago.edu/issues/v29/v29n1.sinfield.html. Accessed December 2004.

http://www.direct.gov.uk/RightsAndResponsibilities/RightsAndResponsib ilitiesArticles/fs/. Accessed April 2004.

SECTION I:

ALTERNATIVES WITHIN THE MAINSTREAM: GAY, LESBIAN AND OTHER QUEER THEATRES

CHAPTER TWO

THE TROUBLE WITH QUEERS: GAYS IN PLAYS 1945-1968

IAN SPIBY

Synopsis

The chapter begins with a discussion of ways of thinking about homosexuality during the period 1945-68 and the strict censorship which applied to the theatre, moving on to an interrogation of the idea of secret "codes" supposedly hidden within certain plays to indicate a queer subtext. A number of plays are examined in detail to demonstrate the different ways in which playwrights dealt with queer characters and themes both in the commercial theatre and in the club performances which evaded the strictures of the Lord Chamberlain. It is concluded that while isolated examples of changes in attitude to queers can be cited, their representation on the stage as a whole differed very little from the 1940s to the 1960s.

Introduction

In Cynthia Lennon's book about her former husband, John Lennon, she recounts how in 1963, he had gone on holiday to Spain with his gay manager, Brian Epstein. When he returned he faced a series of 'sly digs, winks and innuendo' which ended in a brawl at a party with a friend who accused him of being queer (2005:154). Earlier in the book she comments on how in those days 'if you were gay, you kept it secret' because you were 'disliked and distrusted' (104). While no one could claim that in contemporary society, homophobia has ceased to exist, the anecdote does indicate the extent to which attitudes have changed. But it also offers a timely warning that in studying the drama of the earlier time we need to be aware of the very different ways of thinking that were current. For reasons that will become clear, in viewing the plays that were written between 1945 and 1968, it is not easy to assess the extent of the virulent homophobia that existed or to appreciate fully the way in which the idea of homosexuality itself was regarded. A collection of essays published in 1955 under the title, *They Stand Apart: a Critical Study of the Problems of Homosexuality* offers some insight. Routinely throughout the book, homosexuals are referred to either as perverts or inverts and the 'problem' of the title is that homosexuality is a medical condition which needs to be addressed. Indeed W. Lindesay Neustatter, a consultant psychiatrist, who contributes the chapter 'The Medical Aspects', categorises it as a psychological disorder alongside depression, schizophrenia and psychopathy. While he attempts a survey of possible causes of homosexuality, Viscount Hailsham, the author of the second chapter, 'Homosexuality and Society' is in no doubt. '[M]ale homosexuals are made and not born' (21) - and they are made by older men preying on young men or adolescents and infecting them with the disease:

> No doubt homosexual acts between mature males do take place, just as other acts of extraordinary sexual perversity take place in other ways. But the normal attraction of the adult male homosexual is to the young adolescent or young male adult to the exclusion of others (28)

This attitude is one which, while plainly absurd to present-day sensibilities, found favour among the authorities of the time. When the actor John Gielgud was fined for importuning in a public lavatory in 1953, the magistrate, E.R. Guest ordered him to see a doctor and take whatever advice he had to offer 'because this conduct is dangerous to other men, particularly young men...' (Brandreth 2000:96).

Homosexuality, or more precisely, homosexual acts, either public or private were of course, illegal, and Lord Hailsham argues strongly for the retention of legal sanctions. In support of this, he cites the fact, 'beyond dispute', that '[M]ale homosexual practices known to the police are running at a rate between four and five times that of 1938' (1955: 21). Other commentators, nearer to our own time testify to the fact that there was considerable alarm not only by this apparent explosion but about homosexuality itself. The Kinsey Report, which had been published in 1948, stated that a larger number of men than had hitherto been dreamed of, had had homosexual experiences. Moreover the spectacular defection to Russia of the apparently respectable and 'normal' civil servants, Guy Burgess and Donald Maclean served to increase the unease felt about the whole question: 'Who's queer and who isn't'. Dan Reballato refers to the series of articles entitled 'Evil Men' (1999: 157) published by the *Sunday*

Pictorial which attempted to expose this disease at the very core of society while Nicholas de Jongh quotes from a report on Tennessee Williams' play *Suddenly Last Summer* by the Lord Chamberlain's office:

'There was a great fuss in New York about the references to cannibalism at the end of the play, but the Lord Chamberlain will find more objectionable the indications that the dead man was a homosexual' (2000: 82)

It is clear then, that the seismic shift in attitude that was to occur over the next half century was beginning to happen during this time. Homosexuals could no longer be placed neatly in an easily-recognised, effeminate stereotype as the sort of man you would 'meet ... one day in Piccadilly with a painted face' (Shairp, 1984: 92). They were ubiquitous and hidden (the term 'hidden menace' was often used) and that fact had to be faced.

The Lord Chamberlain

As far as the theatre was concerned, any open discussion of queer issues was hampered by the Lord Chamberlain's establishment. This representative of the Royal household, apart from his other duties acted as the official censor and was responsible for licensing all plays before they could be performed publicly. Both the journalist, Nicholas de Jongh and John Johnston, a former member of the Lord Chamberlain's office, have written detailed and full length accounts of how the institution worked and the effect it had upon the theatre of the time. A number of factors have a significant bearing on our discussion. Firstly, until 1958, the Lord Chamberlain disallowed completely any play which contained homosexuals or dealt with homosexual subjects. After the Wolfenden Report was published in 1957 which recommended the legalising of relations between consenting adults, he allowed restricted representation of gays on stage as long as they were necessary to the action, there was no violence, that there were no embraces between them and the plays dealt seriously with the subject (Johnston 1990: 172). So while in a sense there was a move towards liberalisation, he nevertheless kept a tight grip on the limitations of what he would permit, which in its turn led to many tussles with theatre managers. One method of circumventing censorship (and it was a way which had been used for decades) was to present plays in private theatre clubs to members of that club only, membership having to be sought some time before a ticket was sold. In certain highly publicised cases, West End theatres were 'converted' into clubs for the run of a play which would otherwise have been banned. Club presentation, however, limited the number of people who could actually see the piece and was therefore only used by commercial managers occasionally. Furthermore, theatre clubs had to take seriously the threat of prosecution if they overstepped the line – made even more difficult by the fact that the line was unspecified. The Lord Chamberlain made it clear that while he approved of *bona fide* clubs, he was opposed to what he saw as the flouting of the law when legitimate theatres were turned into clubs for particular plays (Johnston 1990: 210-217). Both the censorship of plays and the threat of prosecution then, led to playwrights being circumspect in dealing with queer themes which in turn leads to the question of codes.

The Question of Codes

Most commentators on Queer Drama in the 1940s and 1950s claim that the plays contained codes that were discernible to any gays in the audience but which would be undetected by the average theatre goer. This notion however, presents certain difficulties, not least because the word has different meanings according to who is writing. The idea of the secret code known only to the initiated is an attractive one – indeed it has been the subject of more than one best-selling novel but whether it stands up to scrutiny is another matter. Polari, the queer cant of the time, made popular in the BBC Radio series' *Beyond our Ken* and *Round the Horne* is often cited in support of the argument. Words such as lallies (legs), varda (look) or trolling (cruising) are used to great comic effect by the characters Julian and Sandy. In this instance, however, the idea of a code is undermined by the fact that instantaneous translations are frequently provided for the audience by Kenneth Horne (who always took part in the sketches) and by the fact that both Julian and Sandy, in their language and behaviour conform to the stereotype of the effeminate homosexual.

Alan Sinfield has misgivings about such codes. Taking the word 'Bunbury' from Oscar Wilde's *The Importance of Being Earnest*, he interrogates the assertion made by Patricia Flanagan Behrendt that it was a term for 'promiscuous sodomite', by Linda Gertner Zatlin that it stands for a 'homosexual pickup' and by Joel Fineman that it means a 'male brothel' and a 'desire to bury in the bun'. He finds all of these explanations wanting (1990:27) and far more sensibly locates such interpretations in the minds of the audience and their ability to negotiate meanings from their engagement with the text. An example of this occurs in Michael Wilcox's book, *Benjamin Britten's Operas*, (1997). In the chapter on *Albert Herring*, first performed at Glyndebourne in 1947, Wilcox seeks to demonstrate that along with Swan Vesta matches in the opera, references to whistles and the jingling of such items as keys show that 'beyond all doubt, Albert is homosexual' (42). His argument is based on the claim that such signals were used at that time by queer men for picking one another up in the dark. However, he glosses over the fact that the whistles in the opera are very firmly linked to the courting couple, Sid and Nancy – Sid whistles for her and Nancy responds. Albert, watching them go off together, makes up his mind that he wants to do what they are doing, practises a whistle of his own and goes off in search of someone, after first muffling, not jingling the shop door bell. Instead of Wilcox's notion that he will spend the night in the arms of a shepherd lad, a more straightforward and less tortuous reading has him going off in search of a girl (Herbert 1989: 161).

Knowing the strictures under which playwrights were operating, it seems that rather than putting in secret codes, their plays contain intimations and omissions. Gay characters and gay issues are hinted at but mostly it is what is not said that provides the information, rather in the way that sex scenes in popular novels of the time were often indicated by three dots. The audience is left to work it out for themselves and they will do this according to how well aware they are of the conventions under which the author is operating. This is not new of course; in Ibsen's *Ghosts*, nowhere is the word 'syphilis' mentioned, yet the critics in the audience of the first London production were sufficiently attuned for the newspapers to greet it the following day with howls of disgust.

Playwrights could also call upon a long tradition of signifying queer characters through stereotypes. The effeminate homosexual already referred to is an obvious example but there were many other more subtle representations. Sensitive or artistic men, anyone with long hair or wearing flamboyant clothes, men belonging to certain professions such as interior designers or hairdressers could all be placed within a context which would signal to an audience that they were queer. Alan Sinfield cites Dodie Smith's 1935 play *Call It a Day* in this respect (1999:21) where the character, Roger is keen to put an end to his seventeen-year old son Martin's friendship with twenty-year old Alistair. Alistair is perfectly presentable, respectable and amiable but for one thing – he is an interior decorator, which makes him an unsuitable companion for the teenager. In addition to stereotypes, Nicholas de Jongh (1992) also refers to a whole series of hints available to the playwright to indicate queer goings-on. Fingers touching briefly but held a second too long, one man stroking another's hair, a hand held on the shoulder and eyes meeting are all signs which can be used. And because they are non-verbal they were more difficult to censor.

Now Barabbas

William Douglas Home's play *Now Barabbas* provides us with a text book example. First presented at a commercial theatre in London in 1947 it is set in a prison and while there is a subplot concerning a condemned prisoner who during the course of the action is hanged, the concern of the main plot is the queer relationships between a group of the inmates. Paddy, a 33-year-old 'tall, thick-set, rough-featured Irishman' (24) is in prison for terrorist activities. He is married and misses his wife greatly. Medworth, '60, thin hair, horn-rimmed glasses, small pointed beard, well spoken' (25) is an ex-schoolmaster and his crime is unspecified although it becomes clear fairly early on through hints and inferences that it was for homosexual activities. He is unmarried. Neither of these two conforms to a homosexual stereotype, particularly Paddy; nor does the first newcomer, Roberts, 'young, fresh, good-looking, Scotch', (24) in prison for embezzlement and engaged to a young woman, Kitty. The second newcomer, Richards, however is a fully-fledged effeminate queer. He is 'tall, very long hair elaborately arranged, theatrical gestures' and 'speaks with a precious accent' (27). His occupation is 'choruses' and 'a bit of ballet dancing' (41). It is his first time inside although his crime is never referred to – presumably it is too obvious to mention. From his first entrance he attracts both mockery and insults from the other inmates but does not moderate his manner of speaking and fairly quickly they accept him, awarding him the rather affectionate nickname, Polly.

From the beginning, both Medworth and Paddy are attracted to Roberts. Paddy's first remark to him dictates in a stage direction that before speaking, he has been 'looking' at him (25) while to Richards, on the other hand, he says '[t]hey ought to hang the likes of you.' (28). Medworth cultivates Roberts' friendship, playing draughts with him and encouraging him to talk. His queerness is signalled by his reference to the 'lovely eyes' (52) of another prisoner and his telling him the 'beautiful' story of David and Jonathan who 'loved each other very much'. These overtures are lost on the other man who responds in a jocular fashion but Medworth begins to read his hand, telling him his girl will let him down and that he will need 'love and friendship then … like sunshine to a flower' (55). Paddy, who has entered and heard the end of this, interrupts them violently and sends Medworth off and while Roberts is packing away the draughts, he looks at him hard.

Meanwhile, after his initial reaction, Paddy has forged a

relationship with Richards. In one episode which if it were between a man and a woman would almost constitute a conventional falling-in-love scene, Richards is combing out his hair while the other man talks about his wife and how he came to be in prison. At one point Richards sits down close to Paddy and after one of his angry remarks about England, gently puts his hand over the other man's mouth. Later on Paddy walks over to Richards and looks down at him; he then takes the comb and pulls it through the other one's hair before turning away and asking him 'Why don't you break it up – and find a girl?' Richards, after declaring that he doesn't like women, relates something of his miserable childhood and Paddy ends the scene by giving him cigarettes, a present which it has been emphasised earlier, amounts to gold in prison.

The action then, concerns the relationships between these four characters and in particular, the bitter, jealous rivalry between Paddy and Medworth. The climax of the play occurs when Medworth denounces Paddy and Richards to the prison governor, who arranges to have Richards moved to a local prison where, it has been made plain, conditions will be much harsher. Later, Roberts is left devastated when his fiancée, Kitty throws him over, and at the same time, Medworth leaves the prison, having come to the end of his sentence. In the last scene, Paddy commiserates with Roberts and, standing behind him, looks down at his hair. 'His hand steals out towards it, but he checks himself' (p 109) He then gives him cigarettes and, after putting his arm through Roberts', they go off to exercise together.

Seeing the plot described in such a bald fashion, a reader might be justified in asking how it was able to escape censorship and the answer lies in the fact that Douglas Home makes skilful use of ambiguity. Even the final act of walking off arm in arm could be interpreted as innocent friendship – it was fairly common at the time for two men to do just that without the implications which would accrue in a twenty-first century setting. Within the context however, it is easy to see that it signifies the start of a queer relationship, particularly after Paddy has reached out to touch Roberts' hair and Roberts has accepted his cigarettes, the same seduction technique which had been used with the blatantly queer Richards earlier.

In Medworth's denunciation to the prison governor an equally fine line is trodden. Medworth begins by saying 'I've - tried very hard to start again since I've been here … I want to start afresh. And help others to – as well' (73) which immediately focuses the audience on the fact that we are talking about homosexuality. He then, after many hesitations, accuses Richards of having an 'evil influence' on O'Brien (Paddy). In the subsequent interview with Paddy, the Governor talks about his 'friendship' with Richards and asks him to 'cut out this lad … give him up' - when he chooses a friend it should be a 'good one. Not a rotten little - ' (75). Paddy's interruption prevents him from completing the insult but the Irishman's refusal to comply with this order results in Richards being sent to another prison. Once again on the surface it could be interpreted as an innocent befriending of a young man by an older one, but with the hair touching and lingering looks elsewhere in the play, the meaning is clear for those who wish to see it.

The attitudes to queerness portrayed in the play range from suspicion to antagonism, particularly from those in authority although they are largely tempered with compassion. Even Richards' dismissal to a local prison by the Governor is done without harshness while his treatment of Paddy is positively sympathetic. And as mentioned earlier, the use of Richards' nickname 'Polly' by the other prisoners is more affectionate than hostile.

Tea and Sympathy

Matters are very different in Robert Anderson's play, *Tea and Sympathy*, written in 1953 but presented in London in 1957 under club conditions to avoid the censor, after a considerable commercial success in New York. The setting is an all-male establishment, but this time a boy's boarding school and the plot concerns the hounding of a seventeen-year old pupil, Tom, because of a suspicion that he is homosexual. His schoolfellows ostracize him and taunt him with the nickname 'Grace' refusing to shower with him and putting pressure on his roommate to move out. Everyone is involved in this harassment including the teachers and his father - the words 'queer' and 'fairy' are used freely in connection with him - and he is only saved from believing himself to be queer when his housemaster's wife, Laura takes him to bed.

A number of attitudes can be discerned in the play, some overt, some hidden. Firstly, and probably most importantly, while there is a strong case made by the author for tolerance and the avoidance of prejudice, it does not extend to an actual acceptance of homosexuality - even Laura regards that as a 'terrible thing' (251). Rather as if Tom had been charged with being a thief or an embezzler, Anderson's main concern is that he has been accused wrongly without evidence and on the basis of appearance alone – the crime itself is not condoned. Tom is thought to be queer because he is not like the other boys – an 'off horse'. He wears his hair long rather than in a crew cut, he walks 'sort of light', (276) his musical tastes are different from the others and most condemningly of all, he has played women's roles in the school plays. Interestingly, although he doesn't like sports such as football or baseball he excels at tennis and is not only the school champion but also the champion of his club at home. But this is not enough to redeem him. His father, Herb complains that he doesn't 'play tennis like a regular fellow. No hard drives and cannon-ball serves. He's a cut artist. He can put more damn twists on that ball' (257). So it is more important to be a 'regular fellow' than to win. What Anderson does is to link masculinity firmly with heterosexuality and femininity (long hair, artistic tastes, subtle tennis playing) with homosexuality. In the final analysis, however, Tom, after first failing disastrously with a local good-time girl, Ellie, and trying to commit suicide, is proved to be straight because he has sex with Laura.

Cat on a Hot Tin Roof

There is a hint that things may be more complicated in that at the end of the play Laura accuses her ultra-masculine husband, Bill of repressing the queer side of his nature whose reaction to her outburst is to say that he expects her to be gone when he returns – the marriage is over. In Tennessee Williams' *Cat on a Hot Tin Roof*, the main character, Brick's response is similar except that when his wife Maggie refuses to leave, he takes to drink. The play appeared in London in 1958, once again under club conditions and while it is more complex than *Tea and Sympathy* with an intertwining of several themes there are a number of resonances between the two. During the play we are told that Brick had been a professional football player and together with his best friend and team mate, Skipper, had achieved some success. Maggie recounts that after their marriage she noticed that the relationship between her husband and Skipper was more than just friendship and after she confronted the latter with it, he made a 'pitiful, ineffectual little attempt' (135) to prove that it wasn't true by making love to her. Later, he confessed his true feelings to Brick over the telephone and afterwards killed himself. The links with Tom in the earlier play are clear. Accepted wisdom of the time it seems, dictates two imperatives: the only way to prove you are not queer is by sleeping with a woman and if that doesn't work, commit suicide. But the central dilemma and the one that Williams probes relentlessly is the reason for Brick's moral and emotional deterioration, starting at the point where Anderson left off with his character, Bill.

Brick is crippled, physically by a sporting accident, mentally by alcoholism and emotionally by Skipper's confession and suicide. In the first confrontation with his wife, where she recounts the circumstances leading to his friend's death, he is both defensive and violent. He claims that the 'one great, good, true thing' in his life was his friendship with Skipper and she is 'naming it dirty' (134). Reciting conventional understanding, he asks 'Why would I marry you, Maggie, if I was - ?' but she cuts in, saying at first that it was only Skipper who 'harboured even any *unconscious* desire for anything not perfectly pure between you two' (author's italics) but afterwards saying that 'something was not right ... between you' (135). He throws his crutch at her, causing him to collapse on the floor and shortly afterwards the first act ends. In Act Two, however, the attack on his defences is renewed, this time by his father, Big Daddy. In a brilliantly constructed scene, the conversation moves round and round until Big Daddy closes in, noting that Brick only started drinking after Skipper died and suggesting that there was something not 'normal' in the their relationship (p 167).

Unlike Tom's father in the earlier play, Big Daddy treats the idea of such associations lightly, implying that he engaged in them in his youth. But Brick violently protests his innocence, describing how he and others had forced a queer student to leave when he was at university. The crunch comes when Big Daddy wrests the truth about Skipper's phone call from his son and then delivers his final blow: '*You!* – dug the grave of your friend and kicked him in it! – before you'd face truth with him!' (173) Brick's response is '*His* truth, not *mine!*' but in revenge tells his father the truth about his (Big Daddy's) terminal cancer and the play veers off in another direction.

At the beginning of this final altercation, a detailed stage direction begins:

> *Brick's detachment is at last broken through. His heart is accelerated; his forehead sweat-beaded; his breath becomes more rapid and his voice hoarse.*

Quoting from a contemporary book entitled *Homosexuality*, Nicholas de Jongh demonstrates that these were the symptoms which were thought to be characteristic of 'repressed homosexual inclinations' and from this argues that the playwright is indicating that Brick is indeed a latent homosexual (1992: 75). However, later in the same stage direction, Williams states that '*some mystery should be left in the revelation of character in a play*' which should '*steer [the playwright] away from 'pat' conclusions, facile definitions which make a play just a play, not a snare for the truth of human experience.*' (1957:167-8). So Brick may not be the victim of 'repressed homosexual inclinations' but be consumed by guilt and remorse at his part in the death of his closest friend. It is plain, though, that Williams is examining both the notion of queerness as well as conventional and unconventional reactions to it. Skipper is a football player, not 'artistic' like Tom, yet he desired Brick. Brick's disgusted reaction causes him to lose the friend he loved as well as setting him on the road to self-destruction while Big Daddy who has not only 'bummed around' in his youth but spent a considerable portion of his life working for the two gay owners of the property he has now inherited, does not regard queerness as such a big deal. Williams may be making a plea for tolerance and covering some of the same ground as Anderson, but he does it in an infinitely more subtle and complex way.

Quaint Honour

In contrast to such pleas, *Quaint Honour* by Roger Gellert reads almost as a manifesto for the overthrow of traditional ideas and an acceptance of queerness on its own terms. Presented yet again under club conditions in 1958 despite the relaxation of the Lord Chamberlain's strictures we return once more to the all-male establishment of a public school, albeit this time in England. Tully, an eighteen year old prefect sleeps regularly with, among others, fifteen year old Turner, who persuades him to seduce the innocent and 'dreary' Hamilton, also fifteen, for a laugh. Against all expectations, they fall for one another and when the affair is discovered, Hamilton proves to have wisdom and maturity beyond his years. Tully is expelled, but not before delivering excoriating attacks on conventional morality and religion and defending his queerness with spirit. All three boys are portrayed without effeminacy; Tully and Turner are keen and vigorous sportsmen while Hamilton is studious and naïve rather than that most damning of descriptions - artistic.

The central scene in the play is where Tully seduces Hamilton, not just to persuade him into his bed but to bring him from mouthing conventional platitudes to a state where he starts to think for himself. Sex is something pleasurable between them, something shared on equal terms and he later rejects his housemaster, Hallowes' accusation that he forced Hamilton to take the part of a woman for his personal gratification (89)

> Why do you assume that every sexual act must have a male and a female to it … if you want to know, when Hamilton and I lie together, there's no submitting, there's no top dog and substitute bitch - (89)

Hallowes' depiction of homosexuals as 'pathetic half men … with painted faces and womanish gestures' is seen to be hopelessly fuddy-duddy in the face of the evidence before the viewer. Queerness is not a pale reflection of heterosexual relationships; it is something quite distinctive in its own right. Monogamy is not seen as the norm; Turner actively encourages Tully to seduce Hamilton and it is made clear in the play that he himself sleeps with other boys. Sex is fun and the aim is to have as much of it as possible. In *Quaint Honour,* then, we gain a glimpse of the social revolution that was beginning to happen elsewhere in the Fifties.

Queer Posing as Straight

While plays with queer themes were emerging during this time it could be deduced that they were for the most part confined to club performances while the major proportion of the commercial theatre was unavailable to them. But this was not strictly the case. Hugh (Binkie) Beaumont, head of the theatre empire, H.M.Tennant was the most powerful theatre producer in London and it was he, for example, who provided a challenge to the Lord Chamberlain when he turned his Comedy Theatre into the New Watergate Club for the presentation of both *Tea and Sympathy* and *Cat on a Hot Tin Roof.* As Richard Huggett (1989) makes clear in his biography, Beaumont was extraordinarily adept at 'fixing' things and his support would go a long way to enable a play to be presented in the West End. Two of Beaumont's coterie of gay writers, Noel Coward and Terence Rattigan, were arguably the most popular playwrights of the time and therefore between them they comprised a formidable trio. All three, however, were concerned to keep their sexuality secret and in the case of the playwrights, this meant writing plays with heterosexual characters and themes.

By 1945, all of Coward's memorable pieces had been written: nevertheless much has been made of the supposed queer subtexts in them. Most of these interpretations teeter on the edge of absurdity and Alan Sinfield, for example, treats them with ironic scepticism (1999:98). In only one late play, *A Song at Twilight* is there an overtly queer theme – the plot concerns an elderly homosexual writer at the end of his career – but Coward, who played the main part, took pains to let it be known that it was not autobiographical but based on Somerset Maugham (O'Connor 1998: 104). What he did do, however, was to play a large part in making the word 'gay' synonymous with 'homosexual' (Sinfield 1999:109-113).

More interesting perhaps, in terms of actual homosexual themes given a heterosexual gloss can be found in three of Rattigan's plays: *The Deep Blue Sea, Separate Tables* and *Variations on a Theme. The Deep*

Blue Sea was first presented at the Duchess Theatre, London in 1952 by H.M. Tennent. The main character, Hester Collyer is a middle-class woman in her thirties who has left her husband (a judge) to live with a younger man, Freddie Page, an out-of-work pilot. They live together in a somewhat down-at-heel flat in a 'gloomy Victorian mansion' in north-west London. At the beginning of the play Hester is discovered lying very close to an unlit gas fire with a rug over her head. She has taken twelve aspirin and attempted suicide but has been saved by the fact that the money in the gas meter has run out.

At least three of Rattigan's biographers testify to the fact that the play was based on an incident in his own life where a former lover Kenneth Morgan had left him to live with a younger man, Alec Ross and after six months had committed suicide by swallowing pills, covering his head with a towel and turning on the tap of a gas ring. Michael Darlow asserts that in an early version of the play, the character of Hester was in fact a man, Hector, thus bringing it directly into line with the playwright's own experience. This is disputed by Geoffrey Wansell who bases his argument among other things on a conversation he had with the original director, Frith Banbury, himself gay, who maintains that if there had been such an original version he would have known about it. Furthermore, both Rattigan and Beaumont would have realised that there was no chance of such an overt homosexual theme being permitted by the Lord Chamberlain. Nevertheless, some years later, writing to the playwright John Osborne about the change in theatrical climate which would now permit homosexuality on stage, he says:

'Perhaps I should rewrite *The Deep Blue Sea* as it really was meant to be, but after twenty years I just can't remember why I made all that fuss.' (Wansell 1995: 218)

While it is possible to argue that the character of Hester is the successful portrayal of a woman and that her relationship with Freddie rings true, even so there are a number of features which may give us pause for reflection. Firstly, Rattigan, gives us a stark portrayal of female sexual passion, which was uncommon at the time at which it was written. It is of course, couched in decorous terms with suitable hints and omissions but nonetheless it is made clear that Hester's problem is her (largely unfulfilled) burning desire for Freddie. She wants to have sex with him ('Shall we call it love? It saves a lot of trouble' (313)) but he is only prepared to oblige 'from time to time'. Moreover, he appears to be happier playing golf or drinking with his male companions than being with her. While several decades later, this may be a legitimate situation for stage presentation, it was unusual at a time when conventional representations of female desire were very different. And it is at this point that we may be able to discern a gay subtext if we are able to show that Rattigan is actually depicting his relationship with Kenneth Morgan. The facts supplied by his biographers appear to support the notion. Morgan, in common with other long-term lovers such as Michael Franklin who superseded him, was kept on the fringes of Rattigan's social high-life. Moreover the playwright had a constant stream of casual sexual liaisons. It is therefore possible to hypothesise that sex between them had become routine and even dwindled to a situation where it happened only 'from time to time' leaving Morgan, in Hester's words, with feelings of 'anger, hatred and shame – in about equal parts' (311).

The character of Freddie Page may also give cause for reflection. Depicted as a former hero fighter pilot and in a relationship of ten months standing he claims throughout the play to be in love with Hester and yet is uninterested in having sex with her. Furthermore, there is definitely no other woman. He rather uncomfortably explains to his drinking pal that this situation has existed from the beginning of their relationship and concludes with the excuse: 'Damn it, Jackie, you know me. I can't be a ruddy Romeo all the time' (323). This is unsatisfactory at a number of levels. Clearly, from a dramaturgical point of view, Rattigan would not want Freddie to have another woman: it would weaken, and even trivialise Hester's situation - the dilemma of a woman whose partner has a mistress is commonplace. On the other hand, neither the Lord Chamberlain nor the commercially-minded Beaumont would have permitted Freddie to be gay and therefore his male companions have to be merely boozing and sporting pals. But the result is that the audience is left without a sense of completion and we can only speculate why the playwright left it as it was. One supposition could be that he projects his own feelings onto the situation – how he might react as a gay man if he found himself in a relationship with a woman such as Hester – or taking it one step further, how he behaved in his relationship with Morgan in the months before the younger man left him.

One more character in the play is worth a mention. Mr Miller, who lives upstairs has in the past been a doctor but has been struck off the register for an un-named offence. His role is to provide both practical, and more importantly, philosophical help to Hester in order for her to face life rather than commit suicide at the end of the play. Michael Darlow (2000:279) refers to the fact that in an earlier draft, the reason for his striking off is because he is homosexual - so the playwright conceives a queer character and then takes steps to hide the fact, leaving the audience to draw their own conclusions. He does this more systematically in the next play to be considered: *Table Number Seven*.

First presented at the St James's Theatre, London in 1954, *Table Number Seven* is the second of two linked one-act plays under the collective title of *Separate Tables*. The plot is straightforward. The residents of a Bournemouth hotel discover that one of their number, Major Pollock has been convicted in a local magistrates court of 'insulting behaviour'. He had 'persistently nudged [a woman] in the arm and later attempted to take other liberties' (166) Led by one of the residents, Mrs Railton-Bell, they petition the manager of the hotel, Miss Cooper to have him evicted. This she refuses to do and even encourages Pollock, who has decided to leave anyway, to stay and face it out. He does so and one by one, with the exception of Mrs Railton-Bell, the residents speak to him, including, significantly, her downtrodden daughter Sibyl.

The play enjoyed considerable success in London and for its transfer to New York, Geoffrey Wansell recounts how Rattigan wished to institute a simple but important change to the character of Major Pollock. He re-wrote the passage where Pollock's offence is described in the newspaper. Instead of his original offence, the report tells how he approached a series of men on the Esplanade, asking for a light for his cigarette and then making a 'certain suggestion' (1995:277). There was a great deal of opposition to the idea both from the Broadway producer and the actor playing Pollock and so it was dropped. But it reveals a great deal more than the simple notion that Rattigan had second thoughts about the piece and wanted to tinker with it. Looking at the revised passage within its context and the subsequent reaction of the various characters to the crime (not least, Pollock himself), it becomes clear that the Major was originally conceived as a queer character and his crime changed to involve women rather than men at some stage before the London production. Looking at it in this way also explains some of the things that either don't quite ring true in the received version or simply make more sense if his crime is male rather than female-related.

In describing a minor criminal prosecution which results in disgrace and ostracism for the accused, Rattigan was picking up on the fear that assailed every gay man who pursued any sexual liaison, however private and discreet. In recent memory was the highly publicised case of John Gielgud, already referred to, whose conviction very nearly ruined his career. Looking at the text of the play, when the residents are discussing the Major's court appearance, Mrs Railton-Bell refers to 'this dreadful vice that's going on all over the country' (p 176). Few people in the audience could take seriously the belief that there was an epidemic of elbow-nudging in cinemas but they were warned regularly by the popular newspapers that the 'vice' of homosexuality was on the increase. Charles Stratton, the only resident who will not condemn Pollock comments that 'The Major presumably understands my form of lovemaking. I *should* therefore understand his' (173 author's italics), again a remark that makes much more sense when referring to gay sex. Furthermore, when he says that Senator McCarthy could use Mrs Railton-Bell's talents the audience would be likely to recall that the two main targets for that politician's witch-hunt were Communists and homosexuals.

When Pollock talks about the situation to Sibyl Railton-Bell he gives as a reason for his behaviour the fact that he has always been afraid of women, he was shy and timid as a child and his father despised him. All of these were, and still are in many respects, popular, if misconceived explanations for homosexuality. Moreover, when contemplating where he will go if he leaves the hotel, he tells her he has a friend in London but does not want to stay with him because 'it's rather a case of birds of a feather' (183) Once again it makes more sense if he fears they would accompany one another to clubs or other gay haunts, providing mutual encouragement and support in an illegal and therefore risky enterprise rather than going together to a cinema to engage in what would seem to be a very private activity. In the character of Sibyl, he returns briefly to the theme of women's sexuality although in her case she is repressed and totally 'scared of – well – shall we call it life' (p.182). She does achieve some kind of breakthrough, firstly by being able to utter the word 'sex', then by defying her mother and finally by accepting Pollock and his difference in sexual proclivities.

Rattigan returned to the topic four years later with *Variations on a Theme,* produced in London at the Globe Theatre and which received an overwhelmingly hostile critical reception. The plot is loosely based on *La Dame aux Camellias* by Victor Hugo and concerns the consumptive Rose Fish, living in the South of France among the high-class drinking and gambling set, who has married and divorced four wealthy husbands and is about to take her fifth, Kurt. She falls in love with a younger man, the ballet dancer Ron Vale and after a brief affair drops him in favour of Kurt only to take him up again when she discovers that he 'needs' her. Yet faced with the reality of living a life of (relative) poverty with her young dancer, she once again takes up with Kurt. After a further dramatic appeal from Ron, and knowing that unless she spends the winter in a sanatorium she will die, she chooses to go off with him for a last three months of cigarettes, alcohol and gambling. More than once in the play she says she loves Ron more than life and in this action she is acting on her word.

Another character, Sam, the choreographer of the ballets in which Ron has starred is clearly queer and in the first scene of the play, Ron explains the situation to Rose:

> 'All right –so he lets me drive his car. All right, so I live in his villa at Monte. All right, if you like, so for all I know he may be – but that doesn't make *me* does it?' (213)

Sam later explains to Rose his interest in the younger man as that of a father figure.

The portrayal of an overt gay character, even when expressed in such tentative terms was probably Rattigan's response to The Wolfenden Report and the Lord Chamberlain's decision to allow homosexuality to be represented (within limits) on stage. Indeed Sam refers to Rose's 'Wolfenden-conscious mind' (268). But this did not stop the critics from accusing the playwright of dishonesty - Alan Brien in the *Spectator* openly stated that 'The subject should be a homosexual relationship between a bored and aging rentier and a sharp, oily male tart' (Wansell 1995:296) However, B.A Young (1986:148-9) attests to the fact that *Variations on a Theme* was written for and about Rattigan's close friend, the actress Margaret Leighton who had married a younger actor, Laurence Harvey. Alan Sinfield provides the added information that before his marriage, Harvey had been kept and promoted by a male film producer (1999:163).

In a way that was not possible at the time, it is probably feasible for us now to see that Rattigan has produced a genuine examination of the relationship between an older woman and a younger man – a relationship which he was able to observe close at hand. Kenneth Tynan (1964:72) and others were justified in pointing out the weaknesses of plot and characterisation but that does not take away from the fact that the play contains a genuine examination of love, despite the brittle life-style of the characters and the society in which they move.

A Taste of Honey

In 1958, however, the mood of the times was largely unsympathetic to such a portrayal. In particular, and widely cited, the 19 year old Shelagh Delaney, seeing *Variations on a Theme* during its pre-London tour and disgusted by what she regarded as a mealy-mouthed representation of queer characters, wrote her first play, *A Taste of Honey* as a response. It was taken up by Joan Littlewood and presented at her theatre in Stratford East on May 27 1958, only nineteen days after the London opening of the Rattigan play. The contrast between the two could not be more marked.

Delaney's setting is a seedy Manchester flat. Jo, a teenage girl is abandoned by her mother Helen, who goes off with her latest 'fancy man' and Jo herself has a brief affair with a black sailor who leaves her pregnant. Jo is befriended by a young queer art student, Geoff who looks after her through her pregnancy. At the end of the play, Helen returns and quickly sends him packing.

Although Delaney does not spell it out in so many words, Geoff is meant to be recognisably queer and in the stereotyping of the time that appears to mean that he behaves in an effeminate manner. Certainly, that is how Murray Melvin, who played the role and whose performance is captured on film, portrayed him. Peter, the 'fancy man' recognises him for what he is as soon as he sees him, with the oath 'Oh Christ, no!' (65) and Helen, when told his occupation says, 'An art student, I might have known' (67). Moreover he is exposed to various levels of insult by all the characters with whom he has contact. Even Jo treats him to remarks such as 'You're like a big sister to me' (54) and 'You'd make somebody a wonderful wife' although they are said in an affectionate, good-humoured way. Not so Helen or Peter; Helen calls him a 'pansified little freak' (63) and tells him to take his 'simpering little face out of it' (63) while Peter calls him by female names ('Lana' and 'Mary') and mutters that he can't stand such 'fruitcake parcels' at any price (68). In every case, Geoff's response is one of complete passivity.

Interestingly, Jo makes a reflective remark at the end of the play which throws light on contemporary thinking about queers. She says:

> 'I used to think you were such an interesting, immoral character before I knew you. I thought you were like that …for one thing. You're just like an old woman really. You just unfold your bed, kiss me good night and sing me to sleep' (72)

She was attracted to his company because she thought they were both 'degenerates' – something exciting, dangerous and rebellious but then discovers the reality as she sees it: that he is actually tame and sexless.

Joe Orton

If Delaney reflects contemporary mainstream thinking about gays, Joe Orton is nearer to the proselytising attitudes expressed in *Quaint Honour* - but with one crucial difference. While Roger Gellert sets his play in a public school (and all that that implies in terms of class) Orton's settings and characters are at the opposite end of the social scale. And unlike Gellert he is concerned to challenge taboos and traditional moral codes on a wider scale - so not only do his young male characters treat queerness as simply one of a number of pleasurable activities which include sex with women, they also indulge quite casually in violence, robbery and murder. Hal and Dennis in *Loot* for example, have sex together, but Dennis is also rampant in his desire for girls, something which Hal encourages. They also of course, have been involved in a bank robbery and at the end of the play conspire together in the murder of Hal's father, McCleavy before heading off to a (female) brothel together.

Entertaining Mr Sloane, however, is the play where queerness is central to the plot. It was presented by a commercial management at the New Arts Theatre in 1964, transferring after a few weeks to the larger Wyndhams Theatre. Because it had to pass through the Lord Chamberlain's office, Orton makes more use of ambiguity in the queer action than plays already discussed which had been put on as club performances but the meaning, nevertheless, is quite clear. Sloane is taken into Kath's house as a lodger and very quickly he is sleeping with her on a regular basis. He also begins to work for her brother Ed as a chauffeur, who dresses him in leather and engages in a long-term seduction. After he murders their father, Kemp, they blackmail him into staying and servicing each of them on a six-monthly basis.

As an Orton character, Sloane belongs in the same category as Dennis in *Loot* and Nick in *What the Butler Saw* and the playwright describes him quite plainly in a letter to the American director, Alan Schneider:

> Sloane knows Eddie wants him. He has absolutely no qualms about surrendering his body. None. He's done it many, many times. Sloane is no virgin. He's been in bed with men and women in the past. But he isn't going to give in until he has to. And while he can get away with … riding around in cars, just fucking Kath a couple of times a week, getting paid a good salary, why should he give up his trump card. Eddie, naturally, doesn't know how amoral Sloane is. He imagines that he has a virgin on his hands. He thinks he can get Sloane. Sure he can. But it may take a bit of time – cause Sloane is such a nice kid (Lahr 1980:178).

So Sloane is an attractive but dangerous figure who uses sex as a weapon in the game of survival that takes place in a dog-eat-dog world. Ed on the other hand is a more conventional gay figure – the older man attracted to teenage boys who enjoys the process of a slow seduction. His first encounter with Sloane is illuminating because it reveals in close detail the pick-up process where each party is sizing up the other before coming to a mutual understanding – a method drawn no doubt from Orton's cornucopia of sexual encounters described in his Diaries (Lahr 1986).

Ed has come to Kath's house having heard she has taken a lodger who he is determined must be evicted. When Sloane comes into the room, Ed is at the window and turns to face him. His first word 'I' is followed by a pause as he takes in the picture before him; then obviously changing what he was going to say, he begins asking Sloane about his days in the orphanage, enquiring whether it was single sex, how many boys there were to a room and were their ages mixed. When told that there were older boys in the same room, his reply is 'Oh well, you had compensations then' [84], with the slightest hint that there may have been sex between them. Sloane is wary at this stage, giving only monosyllabic answers but he clearly suspects the path that Ed is treading, for all of them are what the older man wants to hear. Sloane says he likes soldiers, he isn't married nor does he have girlfriends. Then Ed begins to show his hand by offering Sloane a present 'within reason ... no ... Jags (*Laughs.*) ... no sports cars. I'm not going as far as that' (85). The pauses and hesitancy indicate how Ed is feeling his way in the exchange. At this point, a stage direction indicates that Sloane relaxes as he replies 'I was going to suggest an Aston Martin' to which Ed replies, 'I wish I could give you one, boy. I wish I could.' (85). Both of them now are sure what game is being played and Ed's use of the term 'boy' is a further showing of his hand. They then discuss outdoor sports and Sloane talks more freely now, saying how he enjoys swimming, soccer, running, discus and shot-putting, all of which information Ed receives with increasing enthusiasm. But then Sloane steps too far, too quickly. When he says, 'Yes. Yes. I'm an all rounder. A great all rounder. In anything you care to mention. Even in life', Ed '*lifts up a warning finger*'. Sloane apparently retracts, finishing with '... yes I like a good work out now and then', a phrase, which, depending on how it is spoken, carries a double meaning (86). Now Ed becomes bolder, asking if he strips when he does body building and whether he wrestles as well as boxes. Sloane, leading him on, talks about his own body, his full chest and narrow hips but Ed, following an obvious fantasy, interrupts and asks whether he ever wears 'leather... next to the skin? Leather jeans, say? Without ... ah...' When Sloane replies, 'Pants?' the other man laughs and says 'Get away!' (87) but the understanding between them is complete. The episode ends with Ed warning Sloane against women and ascertaining that he has no designs on his sister. In exchanges such as these, then, there is an element of authenticity, Orton using the restrictions placed upon him by the Lord Chamberlain to replicate the societal restrictions on gays in the game of establishing whether there is mutual attraction between them.

A Patriot for Me

The following year in 1965, John Osborne attempted to take this authenticity further in his play *A Patriot for Me* which deals with a queer officer in the Austrian army at the turn of the century, operating within limitations far more severe than those imposed in Britain of the Sixties. We follow the fortunes of Alfred Redl, who rises through sheer hard work and discipline to a senior army position only to be blackmailed into spying for the Russians, the discovery of which leads to his suicide.

During the first act we see Redl attempting to deny his sexuality. In two sexual encounters with women, Hilde a prostitute and the Countess Sophia, matters are not right. The sex has not been satisfactory with Hilde and she thinks that it is her fault - Redl doesn't like her. She comments on the fact that he grinds his teeth while he is asleep. With the Countess, the affair is more sustained but there is something wrong. Redl insists on having the light out when they make love and he weeps while he is asleep. He refuses to reveal what the cause is. Osborne gives the impression of a man attempting to be heterosexual by sheer force of will and later in the play another character describes the lengths Redl went to achieve this – 'Resolutions, vows, religion, medical advice, self-exhaustion' (p 69), all to no avail.

In Act Two, we discover that the majority of male characters in the play are in fact secretly homosexual and a picture of the gay society of the time emerges. But it is at this point that Osborne falls back on old stereotypes. The first scene of the act is a drag ball and whereas some of the older men (including Redl) have male clothing, all the young man are dressed as women and for the most part are giggly and effeminate. The talk among the older men centres round the attractiveness or otherwise of the younger ones, putting us in mind of Lord Hailsham's statement, quoted earlier, that homosexual men are only attracted to the young. A significant point also, is that Redl, when he relaxes (and is observed to do so by the others) drops his masculine demeanour and becomes giggly like the young men he is talking to – revealing his true nature? Exceptionally, the young Lieutenant who accompanies Redl to the ball is not effeminate and further on in the play we are introduced to others similar to him. In all cases however, they turn out to be heterosexual, the implication being that Redl has seduced them into queer practices - with one man, Mischa, he has even been instrumental in his nervous breakdown. Those he does not seduce, he pays for in one way or another. In two scenes we see him in bed with a casual pick-up and both times they rob him, the first one violently but in the case of the second, several years later, he treats it with world-weary acceptance. The playwright sees his queer milieu as a vicious one, where everyone is out for what he can get and the strong prey upon the weak. To be fair to Osborne though, he does succeed in conveying the intolerable pressure that gay men were under at the turn of the century, which provided resonances for the time he was writing. In the character of Dr Schoepfer, he also encapsulates the prejudice against homosexuals and provides the psychological explanations, now largely discredited, for the so-called 'causes' - prejudices that were still very much alive in the Sixties.

The End of Censorship

The play became something of a *cause célèbre* and could be said to have contributed to the abolishment of stage censorship three years later. Because it could only be licensed for public performance with wholesale cuts which would have mutilated it beyond recognition, the English Stage Society decided to turn the Royal Court Theatre into a club for the duration of the run. This had been done before of course, on other occasions and with other theatres but in this instance, the Lord Chamberlain felt that the law had been breached. He informed the Director of Public prosecutions, who after many delays and circumlocutions involving discussions with the government of the day, decided to take no action. But a process had been started. Several months later, a prosecution for similar reasons was achieved with Edward Bond's play *Saved*, again presented by the English Stage Society under club conditions which led to the setting up of a parliamentary joint committee to review stage censorship. This in turn resulted in the 1968 Theatres Act abolishing the powers of the Lord Chamberlain.

In reviewing the plays with queer themes over the period, it would be elegant to be able to say that there was a growing awareness and gradual liberalisation of attitudes but unfortunately no such straightforward solution presents itself. On the one hand the Lord Chamberlain did relax his opposition to the discussion of homosexuality on stage a little but on the other, similar stereotypes appear at the end of the period as they did at the beginning and earlier. In all the plays, it is difficult to find a happy homosexual – only Turner in *Quaint Honour* comes near it. All too often queerness is associated with degeneracy, mental deficiency, illness or criminality. Queers have a problem and it is one to which there is no obvious solution. But overriding all this is a confusion about masculinity and homosexuality – the two cannot exist in the same person. If you are homosexual, then you are somehow less of a man than if you are heterosexual. Once again, the characters in *Quaint Honour* buck this trend but the overall tendency of playwrights is to make their queer characters effeminate, even if they manage to hide it for some of the time. Joe Orton could be said to be an exception although his thug-like queers, having sex with men and women alike, obsessed with material gain and fighting to get to the top of the dung heap, tend to be in a class of their own. It would take playwrights of the period following the end of the Lord Chamberlain to begin to find a way through these difficulties and to present a more authentic picture of queer men and their lives.

Works Cited

Anderson, Robert, 'Tea and Sympathy' in Strasberg, Lee (ed.), *Famous American Plays of the 1950s*, New York: Dell Publishing Co, 1962.

Brandreth Gyles, *John Gielgud: An Actor's Life*, Stroud, Gloucestershire: Sutton Publishing, 2000.

Darlow, Michael, *Terence Rattigan. The Man and his Work*, London: Quartet Books, 2000.

De Jongh, Nicholas, *Not in Front of the Audience. Homosexuality on Stage,* London and New York: Routledge, 1992.

—. *Politics, Prudery and Perversions. The Censoring of the English Stage 1901 – 1968,* London: Methuen, 2000.

Delaney, Shelagh, *A Taste of Honey,* London: Methuen Publishing Ltd, 2000.

Douglas Home, William, *The Plays of William Douglas Home*, Melbourne, London, Toronto: Heinemann, 1958.

Gellert, Roger, *Quaint Honour. A play in three acts,* London: Secker and Warburg, 1958.

Hailsham, Viscount, 'Homosexuality and Society' in Rees, J. Tudor, Harley V. Usill, (eds), *They Stand Apart. A Critical Survey of the Problems of Homosexuality,* Melbourne, London, Toronto: William Heinemann Ltd, 1955.

Herbert, D (ed), *The Operas of Benjamin Britten,* London: Herbert Press, 1989.

Johnston, John, *The Lord Chamberlain's Blue Pencil,* London, Sydney, Auckland, Toronto: Hodder & Stoughton, 1990.

Huggett, Richard, *Binkie Beaumont: Eminence Grise of the West End Theatre 1933 -73*, London: Hodder and Stoughton, 1989.

Lahr, John, *Prick up your Ears*: *The Biography of Joe Orton*, Harmondsworth: Penguin, 1980.

—. (ed), *The Orton Diaries*. London: Methuen, 1986.

Lennon, Cynthia, *John,* London, Sydney, Auckland, Toronto: Hodder & Stoughton, 2005.

Neustatter, W.Lindsay, 'Homosexuality: The Medical Aspects' in Rees, J. Tudor, Harley V. Usill, (eds), *They Stand Apart. A Critical Survey of the Problems of Homosexuality,* Melbourne, London, Toronto: William Heinemann Ltd, 1955.

O'Connor, Sean, *Straight Acting. Popular Gay Drama from Wilde to Rattigan*, London and Washington: Cassell, 1998.

Orton, Joe, *Orton: The Complete Plays*, London: Eyre Methuen, 1976.

Osborne, John, *A Patriot for Me*, London: Faber and Faber, 1966.

Rattigan, Terence, 'The Deep Blue Sea' in *The Collected Plays of Terence Rattigan, Vol. Two,* London: Hamish Hamilton, 1953.

Rattigan, Terence, 'Separate Tables' and 'Variation on a Theme' in *The Collected Plays of Terence Rattigan, Vol. Three,* London: Hamish Hamilton, 1964.

Rebellato, Dan, *1956 and all that. The making of modern British drama,* London and New York: Routledge, 1999.

Rees, J. Tudor, Harley V. Usill, (eds), *They Stand Apart. A Critical Survey of the Problems of Homosexuality,* Melbourne, London, Toronto: William Heinemann, 1955.

Shairp, Mordaunt , 'The Green Bay Tree' in Wilcox, Michael, *Gay Plays,* A Methuen Theatrefile, London and New York: Methuen, 1984.

Sinfield, Alan, *Out on Stage. Lesbian and Gay Theatre in the Twentieth Century,* New Haven and London: Yale University Press, 1999.

Tynan, Kenneth, *Tynan on Theatre*, Harmondsworth: Penguin, 1964.

Wansell, Geoffrey, *Terence Rattigan. A Biography,* London: Fourth Estate, 1995.

Wilcox, Michael, *Benjamin Britten,* Bath: Absolute Press, 1997.

Williams, Tennessee, *Cat on a Hot Tin Roof,* Harmondsworth: Penguin, 1957.

Young, B.A., *The Rattigan Version. Sir Terence Rattigan and the theatre of character,* London: Hamish Hamilton, 1986.

CHAPTER THREE

TEARS, TIARAS AND TRANSGRESSIVES:
QUEER DRAMA IN THE 1960S

KATE DORNEY

Synopsis

This chapter examines the impact of the social, political and cultural contexts on queer drama in the 1950s and into the 1960s from the Wolfenden Report to the proscriptions of the Lord Chamberlain's Office. It traces the development of queer characters from the stereotypes of the tearful neurotic and farce queen (tears) through John Osborne's A Patriot for Me which mixed tears with tiaras quite literally in the characters of Redl and Baron von Epp to the unapologetic and untroubled queer agenda of Joe Orton's plays with their transgressive attitudes to gender, sexuality and social hierarchies.

*****

In 1967 playwright Joe Orton advised his friend Kenneth Williams to 'reject all the normal values of society. And enjoy sex. When you're dead you'll regret not having fun with your genital organs' (Orton 1986: 251). Unlike Orton, Williams, an actor whose camp performances on radio, film and television had made him a household name, was tortured with guilt about his sexuality, and never achieved his friend's easy acceptance and enjoyment of sex. In this respect he resembles many of the queer characters who appeared on stage before the 1970s. Orton, on the other hand, eschewed camp and anguish and opted for the guilt-free anti-authoritarian stance with which he imbued most of his characters. As with Oscar Wilde, much is made of Orton's sexuality and its part in his downfall and death (details of his promiscuity and his troubled relationship with his partner provided courtesy of his diaries and biography have all contributed to his iconic queer status). Despite this relatively little attention has been paid to the construction and performance of sexual identity in Orton's plays. Written at a time when homosexuality was not only illegal, but when references to 'the forbidden subject' were also carefully regulated by the Lord Chamberlain in his capacity as stage censor, the frank depiction of sexuality in the plays is remarkable. Even more remarkable is the fact that none of his characters are troubled by their queerness, that they display a decidedly masculine side (a refreshing change from the usual queer signifier of the stereotypical camp queen) and, with very few exceptions, will have sex with anyone if it promises an easy life or a way out of trouble (a socially, morally and sexually transgressive stance in the dark days before the Sixties started swinging). Usually the only way to get queer characters past the Lord Chamberlain's keen scrutiny was to portray them as unhappy sufferers who, more often than not, do the decent thing and commit suicide or practice celibacy, as Kenneth Williams did. Into this restrained and restraining milieu Orton thrust a series of amoral characters both male and female who regard queerness as unremarkable. His characters reflect a shift in the use of the word 'queer' from its pre-1960s sense as outlined by Sinfield: 'up to the 1960s, 'queer' is appropriate because it includes that obscure sense of something 'not quite right' which so often accompanied dawning or partial awareness of same-sex passion' (Sinfield 1999: 5-6), but also in the sense that Shepherd uses in his discussion of Orton's life and times:

> I am using the word 'queer' quite consciously in the book: I mean to denote, historically, a *pre-gay* homosexual identity and culture; but also I think that, in principle, the fact of being queer, bent, different, should be celebrated as a positive alternative to the exploitation and brutality that underlie the notions of 'normal' and 'straight' in this world. (Shepherd 1989: 8-9)

This chapter examines Orton's characters in the light of their forerunners in British theatre of the 1950s and 1960s and posits Orton as one of the first writers to put openly and happily queer characters on the British stage.

The Queer Challenge

'In a book on the life of Dame Sybil Thorndike there was a photograph of her [dressed as Edith Cavell] sitting on a chair in a room, but a picture of a man's torso had been pasted in front of her face to show her looking at the

man' A glance at the dust jacket shows she's not looking generally at the
man but specifically at male genitals (Shepherd 1989: 13)

Allegedly outraged because their local library did not have a copy of
Gibbons *Decline and Fall*, but had plenty of popular novels, Orton and
Halliwell began a sustained attack on books beloved of middle-England
and, by implication, on the readership of those books. They began in a low
key way by typing what the judge later described as 'mildly obscene'
blurbs on the back inside covers of best-selling authors such as Dorothy L
Sayers and subtly altering the title and contents of a variety of books
(ranging from a collected edition of John Betjeman to the *Collins Book of
Roses*). The first volume of Emlyn Williams' collected plays, after Orton
and Halliwell had finished with it, read as: 'Knickers Must Fall', 'Up the
Front', 'Up the Back', 'Olivia Prude', 'He Was Born Grey', 'Mr Winifred'
and 'Fucked by Monty' (Lahr 1978: 95). The Sybil Thorndike example
above was accompanied by the caption: 'During the Second World War, I
was working from dusk to dawn to serve the many thousands of sailors,
soldiers and airmen. American GIs came in shoals to my surgery and
some had very peculiar orders for me' (Lahr 1978: 95). *Because We're
Queers*, Simon Shepherd's 1989 reappraisal of Orton and his work, took
as its title Orton's alleged response to the punitive sentence he and
Halliwell received for defacing the library books. Shepherd's study of
Orton and Halliwell's 'crime' is a fitting place to start this consideration of
the queer trajectory of British drama through the 1960s because it
encapsulates precisely the discomfort that queer work and queer writers
apparently provoked in the Establishment and the public at large. Whether
it be the distaste, bafflement, or plain obtuseness that the staff of the Lord
Chamberlain's office displayed in their reading of queer plays or, as they
more often seemed to find, queer themes and characters in otherwise
'normal' plays, or the reaction of critics and the general public to these
plays, one thing is certain: queer plays troubled people. Orton's drama
continued the assault on the sensibility and morals of the general public
started by his and Halliwell's alterations to the books from Islington
Central Library, and introduced a queer sensibility to the British stage in
its insistence on questioning and ridiculing governing notions of sexuality,
morality and the social order. In Orton's dramatic universe norms are
subverted: a family is joyously reunited at the end of *What the Butler Saw*
through a series of incestuous sexual assaults in a parody of *The
Importance of Being Earnest*; in *Ruffian on the Stair*, Wilson tries to
provoke his brother's killer to murder him to so that they can be reunited
in their idyllically incestuous relationship; *The Erpingham Camp* ends in a
Bacchanalian frenzy as the polite facades of straight society come off

during a series of 'entertainments' at a family orientated holiday camp.

Orton's work draws on influences as diverse as Firbank, Genet, Pinter, Greek drama and Whitehall farce. He encapsulated this fusion of farce and tragedy, structure and anarchy with the comment: 'I always say that the theatre is the Temple of Dionysus, and not Apollo. You do the Dionysus thing on your typewriter, and then you allow a little Apollo in, just a little to shape and guide it' (Orton 1964). The publication of Orton's diary after his death and the revelations of his enjoyment of cruising, cottaging and casual sex have allowed many critics and his major biographer John Lahr to dwell on the similarities between, on the one hand, Orton's sense of mischievous fun and his interest in, and frank enjoyment of, sex ,with Dionysiac frenzies and his bloody death at the hands of Halliwell (initially his mentor as well as his lover) on the other. His early and sensational death has ensured that Orton's image is crystallized in the public imagination as young, beautiful and daring (helped by his decision to have himself sketched nude for the program of *Crimes of Passion*, and to be photographed bare-chested, and on one occasion, mimicking Christine Keeler's iconic pose, naked on a chair), and his relatively small oeuvre is regarded as the peak of black farce perfection with a radical new queer twist on the traditional sex comedy. He achieved this by inverting Society's accepted moral structure, so that outrageous behaviour is greeted with equanimity, while the mundane attracts comment. *The Ruffian on the Stair* opens with a husband telling his wife about his appointment with a man in the toilets at Kings Cross station. She replies, 'You always go to such interesting places' as if this were a perfectly normal place to meet and conduct business (Orton 1993: 33).

The Background

At the beginning of the 1960s British theatre was enjoying the post-coital flush of the 'angry' movement of the 1950s which had dared to depict life as it actually, or more accurately, allegedly, was. The stage was peopled with 'real' characters: from John Osborne's angry young man ranting about the Sunday papers and the hypocrisy of the upper classes, Wesker's national servicemen unhappy with their lot, Pinter's confused/depressed/terrorised and terrorising working class men through to Ann Jellicoe's juvenile delinquents and Shelagh Delaney's plucky working-class heroines. For the first time, so the myth goes, the British public were seeing people who experienced the same highs and lows, hopes and fears as they did. Unless you were queer, in which case you had Rattigan's tortured and closeted middle-class men, Coward's luvvies,

Geof from *A Taste of Honey* (1958), who really wanted to be a woman anyway, neurotic Clive from *Five Finger Exercise* (1958) and the menacingly camp Harold in *Black Comedy* (1965). Depictions of happy queers were rare both because procuring or performing homosexual acts was illegal until 1966 but also because the Lord Chamberlain's office, the instrument of theatre censorship in Britain until 1968, did not lift their complete ban on mentioning homosexuality in plays until 1958, the year after the Wolfenden Report on Homosexual Offences and Prostitution was published; and even then there were strict guidelines proscribing its representation. The result of these restrictions was, unsurprisingly, an unbalanced and on the whole dismal representation of queer life and queer people, somewhat paradoxical considering that a sizeable proportion of British theatre at the time, and particularly West End theatre, was populated by queers. In *Still Acting Gay*, John M Clum sums up pre-1968 queer British theatre as 'cautiously showing what could not be said':

> By both suggesting and denying the existence of homosexuals, the plays of this period dramatise and maintain the closet. Such 'closet dramas' could be written by heterosexuals exploiting the potentially sensational subject matter, or, in the case of Harold Pinter, toying with the very restrictions involved in presenting homosexuality at all. Or they could be written by gay playwrights like Noel Coward, dependent on the popularity and rewards of commercial success, or Joe Orton, desiring success like Coward's but wanting as well to place homoerotic desire at the centre of his plays (Clum 2000: 71).

What he does not mention is the very real fear felt by the officers of censorship that queerness, thought by some to be contagious, might be learned or caught from the depiction of queers on stage. One of the results of this is that the Lord Chamberlain's office had less trouble passing plays about unhappy queers than happy ones as they represented a salutary lesson on the dangers of 'unnatural' vice. Depending on whether the play inclined toward comedy or tragedy, they tended to rely on two stereotypes. Tragedy usually showed the tortured unhappy queer who realised their 'perversion', or was discovered and rejected by their family and loved ones; either way, downfall and disgrace were inevitable. *Staircase* (1966), *A Patriot for Me* (1965), *Five Finger Exercise* (1958), *A Taste of Honey* (1958) *Third Person* (1951) and *Surface* (1945) are all examples of this tendency. At the lighter end of the spectrum was the camp queen, a mainstay of British comedy for more than thirty years. Clum describes the appeal of this stock character:

> The safety offered by the farce queen is that of instant, reassuring recognisability. This is what gay people are like. They exist only in beauty

parlours, antique stores, and, on occasion, in the men's clothing section of department stores. But since they have such identifiable characteristics, one is in no danger. Moreover, they aren't in the least erotically provocative (Clum 2000: 98).

The work of Orton and the queer writers and companies that followed him, Gay Sweatshop in particular, were to challenge that notion. Orton wanted his audience to understand the sexual attraction his characters felt for his 'sexy hooligans' (as Shepherd describes them, 1989: 99) and was always very clear in his instructions to actors and directors about the casting and playing of queer roles in his plays. In his diary, he records the fact that he wanted the actor playing Sloane in the television film version of the play to be 'someone you'd like to fuck silly' (Orton 1986: 79), and when Alan Schneider was directing the play in the USA, Orton cautioned him:

> In German, Ed was the central pivot of the play. His stalking of the boy's arse was as funny and wildly alarming as Kath's stalking of his cock. Unless this is so – you're in trouble (Lahr 1987: 186).

As in Orton's plays, syntax is the key to understanding the world-view proposed here: Ed's desire is posited is the norm, and Kath's as the exception. Her expression of her sexuality is 'wildly alarming' and comic, and the comedy in the play is that for once, so is the queer desire.

The Wolfenden Report and the depiction of homosexuality on stage: 1950s-1960

> Illegality, isolation and pity all had their effects on the way individual homosexuals regarded themselves. A young homosexual man would have to work hard not to learn that his sexuality was unnatural and sick. Homosexuals who were regularly told that their sexuality was anti-social, dangerous and criminal would be inclined to develop a sense of guilt. Pushed into furtive sex and vulnerable blackmail, the homosexual learned to connect his sexuality with insecurity. And always underlying these attitudes and ideas were the very real activities of a police force that hounded and exposed homosexuals. (Shepherd 1989: 15)

The 1950s were a punitive decade in terms of the regulation of sexual desire. Sir Theobald Matthew, Director of Public Prosecutions from 1944-64 was among those who felt homosexuality was a pernicious and tenacious disease, and that the only way to prevent infection was to stamp it out. As a consequence he was determined to prosecute homosexuals from all echelons of society and encouraged a media frenzy which saw constant reportings on the 'scandalous' behaviour of homosexuals, coverage of homosexual cases and general scaremongering. The convictions for 'indecent offences between males' peaked in 1955 at over 4000, and had virtually increased year on year since the 1940s. This did not so much reflect a rise in the number of homosexual acts taking place, as the police's redoubled efforts to stamp out such 'immoral' behaviour, and, perhaps more pertinently, a new method of calculating the number of offences. As De Jongh notes 'the change in the method of compiling statistics after 1949, counting offences on the basis of charges not convictions, bolstered the view that Britain was beset by moral decline' (De Jongh 2001: 89). This view was endorsed by most of the newspapers and the combined scandals of the Montagu and Wildblood trials and the arrest of Sir John Gielgud in 1953 allowed the Establishment to reaffirm their view that every man and boy in the country was at risk from queer contamination. The press were at particular pains to alert the general public to the fact that queers were not necessarily effeminate (two of the accused were airmen, and airmen were national heroes after the Battle of Britain), delicately built, or easily identifiable by their sibiliant consonants (early cherished notions about the markers of queerness), and vigilance was needed in all areas of life. The Montagu and Wildblood trials also marked a departure inasmuch as the men were prosecuted for acts committed in private rather than in public. Wildblood commented that 'we always supposed – and the cases reported in the newspapers appeared to bear this out – that if we behaved ourselves in public, the police would leave us alone' (Wildblood 1955: 26). That this was evidently no longer the case, and that now all members of society from peers, famous actors and journalists to the 'man in the street' were vulnerable, only served to oppress queers even more. No-one and nowhere was immune from prosecution, and this feeling runs through queer accounts right up to the decriminalisation of 'homosexual acts' in 1966. Everyone was on their guard against queer behaviour, the Lords Chamberlain and his readers especially, and yet, as many commentators have pointed out, it was still possible for queers, or manifestations of queer behaviour, to appear on stage.

The Wolfenden Committee on Homosexual Offences and Prostitution (or Huntleys and Palmers to those in the committee in order to preserve the innocence of the clerical workers typing up the notes) first met in 1954 to discuss and deal with the 'problem' of homosexuality. With the advent of Freudian theories and the increasing secularisation of the country after the war, homosexuality had moved from being exclusively regarded as a sin, to being a 'social' problem in the same way that prostitutes, unmarried mothers and latch key children were. The report that resulted from the committee's investigations, published in 1957 was punitive in regard to its recommendations on prostitution, and less progressive regarding homosexuality than is sometimes supposed. The Report recommended the decriminalisation of homosexual acts between consenting adults (over the age of 21) *in private*, and this recommendation was eventually made law in the 1966 Sexual Offences Act. In the time it took for the Report's recommendations to be made law, the Lord Chamberlain, ahead of his time for once, decided that on the basis of the Report he would lift the total ban on homosexuality and issued a memorandum to his staff to that effect in October 1958. Examples of queer representation from either side of this watershed, Shaffer's *Five Finger Exercise* and Pinter's *The Collection* demonstrate how slow the percolation of the new 'liberal' stance was.

Five Finger Exercise premiered in the West End in July 1958. The play is an excellent example of the closeted, coded approach to queers described by Clum and Rebellato. Written and directed by queers (Peter Shaffer and John Gielgud), *Five Finger Exercise* adheres to the tradition of the tortured, implied, homosexual. The play unpicks the troubled relationships in the Harrington family which are brought to a head by the presence of German tutor Walter. Mr Harrington is a bluff man of industry, Mrs Harrington an interior designer, their son Clive is, to the sophisticated audience member, plainly queer. He is close to his mother. Also, like his mother, Clive has 'taste', while his father does not. Clive has joined the Dramatic Society at Cambridge but none of the sporting clubs, although he is thinking about taking up fencing as it tones the muscles. After inquiring about the sort of friends he has, Clive's father warns him: 'People still judge a man by the company he keeps. You go around with a lot of drifters and arty boys, and you'll be judged as one of them' (1976, 36). He has never had a girlfriend, asks Walter to go away with him for Christmas, and for the really obtuse, in case all these signals had not made Clive's queerness apparent, his father accuses his mother of turning him into a 'snivelling little neurotic. A mother's boy' (77). In the final confrontation, even Clive's mother begins to accuse him:

> LOUISE [*rounding on him, her face terrible*]. D'you think you're the only one can ask terrible questions? Supposing I ask a few. Supposing I ask them…! You ought to be glad Walter's going, but you're not. Why not? Why aren't you glad? You want him to stay, don't you? You want him to stay very much. Why?
> CLIVE [in a panic, he rises from the floor: LOUISE drives him to the sofa]. Maman! (Shaffer 93)

Before the watershed, plays allude to queerness in the merest terms and the hints are picked up by both the characters and, it is fair to assume, the audience themselves. The guidelines the Lord Chamberlain laid down for his readers, reproduced here, would make no difference to the representation of queerness in *Five Finger Exercise*: the playwright has censored himself, in common with many other queer plays and playwrights of the period. The lassitude was there, to an admittedly limited extent, but no one chose to exploit it. The Lord Chamberlain's memorandum begins with an assertion that '*Licences will continue to be refused for plays which are exploitations of the subject* rather than contributions to the problem [note problem rather than vice]; and similarly references to the subject which are unnecessary or have merely an exploitation value will be disallowed', before going on to outline his notions of acceptability in more detail:

(a) Every play will continue to be judged on its merits. The difference will be that the plays will be passed which deal seriously with the subject.
(b) We would not pass a play that was violently pro-homosexual.
(c) We would not allow a homosexual character to be included if there were no need for such inclusion.
(d) We would not allow any 'funny' innuendos or jokes on the subject.
(e) We will allow the word 'pansy' but not the word 'bugger'.
(f) *We will not allow embraces between males or practical demonstrations of love.*
(g) We will allow criticism of the present Homosexual Laws, though plays obviously written for propaganda purposes will fall to be judged on their merits
(h) We will not allow embarrassing display by male prostitutes.
(Shellard, Nicholson and Handley 2004: plate 18)

These recommendations offer a barometer of the depiction of queer life in plays in the 1940s and 1950s, for it hints usefully at the tenor of those plays submitted to the Chamberlain's Office but not licensed; it also makes the licensing of Orton's plays even more miraculous, given that they abound in 'funny innuendos' and have been read for generations as 'violently pro-homosexual'. But before considering Orton's plays in all their queer glory, it instructive to look at some queer behaviour from a more unlikely source, Harold Pinter's *The Collection*, first performed in 1962. *The Collection* was able to take advantage of both the relaxation in the Censor's regulations concerning homosexuality, but also of the fact that the play had been broadast on television first (and television allowed considerably more freedom). The play is about a possible one-night stand between fashion designers Bill and Stella and the attempts of Stella's husband James to find out the truth. Reading through and with the typical Pinteresque obfuscation there are lots of hints that Bill is queer: he lives with a man called Harry who treats him as a cross between a pet and a child. When James initially challenges him, Bill responds:

> BILL. I was nowhere near Leeds last week, old chap. Nowhere near your wife either, I'm quite sure of that. Apart from that, *I...just don't do such things.* Not in my book.
> *Pause*
> I wouldn't dream of it.
> (Pinter 1991:118, my italics)

Bill then immediately changes his mind and admits to the affair, but as the play moves on, it becomes increasingly difficult to work out who is lying and who (if anyone) is telling the truth. An exchange between James and Stella midway through the play even suggests that James too might be 'hypnotised' by Bill:

> He [Bill] reminds me of a bloke I went to school with. Hawkins. Honestly, he reminded me of Hawkins. *Hawkins was an opera fan, too.* Always kept it a dead secret. I might go along with your bloke to the opera one night. He says he can always get free seats. *He knows quite a few of that crowd.* Maybe I can track old Hawkins down and take him along, too. *He's a very cultivated bloke, your bloke, quite a considerable intelligence at work there, I thought.* He's got a collection of Chinese pots stuck on a wall, must have cost at least fifteen hundred a piece. Well, you can't help noticing that sort of thing. I mean, *you couldn't say he wasn't a man of taste. He's brimming over with it.* Well, I suppose he must have struck you the same way. No, really, I think I should thank you, rather than anything else. *After two years of marriage it looks as though, by accident, you've opened up a whole new world for me.* (132, my italics)

Queerer and queerer, it would seem. Not only has Bill possibly had an affair with Stella and is possibly having one with Harry, he seems to be leading James from the path of righteousness too. All the old clues are here, indicated by my italics: a love of opera, friends in the world of opera, taste in interior decoration, and a clothes designer to boot. Ever alert to the artistic challenges posed by censorship, it seems that theatre continued to get queers on stage without making a serious contribution to the 'problem of homosexuality', and even managed to suggest queers literally queering the path of straight marriage.

Queering family life: *Entertaining Mr Sloane*

Queering the path of straight (in every sense of the word) life was
something that Orton excelled at. From his interventions into the world of
genteel readers via his 'creative rearrangement' of library books, through
to alter ego Edna Welthorpe's interventions in the moral fabric of society
and theatre in national newspapers and in private correspondence, Orton
aimed at unsettling and satirising the conventional. In *Entertaining Mr
Sloane* (1964), Orton's first performed stage play, he makes his assault on
family values by blowing apart a dysfunctional nuclear family whose
house is situated in the middle of a tip and reassembling the household as
a merry sexual *ménage a trois*. The catalyst for this explosion is the
young and beautiful Mr Sloane who ends up being blackmailed to remain
as the shared sexual plaything of brother Ed and sister Kath after he
murders their father. Unsurprisingly, the Lord Chamberlain's office took
exception to much of the content and stage business of the play and
requested the removal of many of the straight seduction scenes and
'practical demonstrations of love' between Sloane and Kath. The 'thread
of homosexuality which runs strongly through the play' however, is left in,
even though, in the opinion of the Reader, 'there is no attempt to deal with
the subject of homosexuality in a serious manner' (LCP CORR:
1964/4267). As Orton himself noted, the result was that 'he cut all the
heterosexual bits and kept all the homosexual bits' (Orton in interview
with Barry Hanson, quoted in Lahr 1978: 191). Ed and Sloane's first
meeting is a victory of Orton's attuned innuendo, Ed's conversation with
Kath immediately preceding the meeting suggests that Sloane will have to
leave immediately to stop him taking advantage of Kath and preying on
her kind nature. Once he begins talking to Sloane however, his resolve
weakens:

ED (*turns, faces Sloane*). I ... my sister was telling me about you.
Pause
My sister was telling about you being an orphan, Mr Sloane.
SLOANE (*smiling*). Oh, yes?
ED. Must be a rotten life for a kid. You look well on it though.
SLOANE. Yes.
ED. I could never get used to sleeping in cubicles. Was it a mixed home?
SLOANE. Just boys.
ED. Ideal. How many to a room?
SLOANE. Eight.
ED. Really? Same age were they? Or older?
SLOANE. The ages varied by a year or two.
ED. Oh well, you had your compensation then. Keep you out of mischief,

eh? (*Laughs*)
(Orton 1993: 84)

Ed then begins to make Sloane the offer of a 'gift' to ameliorate the loss of the room - not the sports car that Sloane jokingly asks for, although Ed admits 'I wish I could give you one, boy. I wish I could' - when Sloane discloses his love of fresh air and exercise. This leads to a verbal display of such naked lust that the fact that it made it passed the censors is little short of miraculous and hilarious, particularly given the relatively innocuous material in other plays that was banned:

SLOANE. We had a nice little gym at the orphanage. Put me in all the teams they did. Relays...
ED looks interested.
... soccer ...
ED nods.
...pole vault, ... long distance ...
ED opens his mouth.
100 yeards, discus, putting the shot.
ED rubs his hands together.
Yes. Yes. I'm an all rounder. A great all rounder. In anything you care to mention. Even in life.
ED lifts up a warning finger.
... yes I like a good work out now and then.
ED. I used to do a lot of that at one time. With my mate ... we used to do all what you've just said. (*Pause*). We were young . Innocent too. (*Shrugs. Pats his pocket. Takes out a packet of cigarettes. Smokes.*) All over now. (*Pause.*) Developing your muscles, eh? And character. (*Pause.*) ... Well, well, well. (*Breathless.*) A little bodybuilder are you? I bet you are ... (*Slowly*) ... do you ... (*Shy*) exercise regular?
SLOANE. As clockwork.
ED. Good, good. Stripped?
SLOANE. Fully.
ED. Complete. (*Striding to the window*). How invigorating.
SLOANE. And I box. I'm a bit of a boxer.
ED. Ever done any wrestling?
SLOANE. On occasions.
ED. So, so.
SLOANE. I've got a full chest. Narrow hips. My biceps are –
ED. Do you wear leather ... next to the skin? Leather jeans, say? Without ... aah ...
SLOANE. Pants?
ED. (*laughs*) Get away! (*Pause*). The question is are you clean living? You may as well know I set great store by morals. Too much of this casual bunking up nowdays. Too many lads being ruined by birds. I don't

want you messing about with my sister.
SLOANE. I wouldn't. [...]
ED: I've a certain amount of influence. [...] I've two cars. Judge for
yourself. I generally spend my holidays in places where the bints have got
rings through their noses. (*Pause.*) Women are like banks, boy, breaking
and entering is a serious business. Give me your word you're not
vaginalatrous? (86-88)

In the 1970 film, this scene is further sexualised. Sloane lies on
the bed in his underpants and runs his hands over his body as he talks,
while Ed struggles to remain in control of himself. Interestingly, Ed is one
of Orton's only exclusively gay characters. Sloane himself, and the
characters in the subsequent plays are all cheerfully bisexual, sleeping
with whoever they please or whoever is most advantageous to them, but
Ed only likes men. Orton was careful to make him as far from the
stereotypical farce queen as possible, and strenuously resisted efforts to
portray the character that way in production:

> In *Sloane* I wrote a man who was interested in having sex with boys. I
> wanted him played as if he was the most ordinary man in the world, and
> not as if the moment you wanted sex with boys, you had to put on earrings
> and scent. I hope that now homosexuality is allowed people aren't going
> to continue doing the conventional portraits there have been in the past. I
> think that the portrait of the queer in Peter Shaffer's *Black Comedy* is very
> funny, but it's an awfully conventional portrait. It's compartmentalisation
> again. Audiences love it, of course, because they're safe. But one
> shouldn't pander to audiences (Orton in an interview with Barry Hanson
> quoted in Lahr 1987: 187).

And true to his word, Orton never did, constantly challenging the
audience and denying them the conventional patterns of action and
behaviour his plays initially suggest. To fully appreciate how radical
Orton's depiction of queer desire was, we can compare it to John
Osborne's *A Patriot for Me*, the play credited with bringing down
censorship alongside Edward Bond's *Saved*, but in which queer desire it
still portrayed as an inevitable source of misery and embarrassment.

The Pansies Charter

In 1965 the English Stage Company sent John Osborne's new
play, *A Patriot for Me*, to the Lord Chamberlain's office. Osborne, the
figurehead of the 'angry young man' movement and the playwright who
had brought Laurence Olivier high-kicking and snarling into the modern

age with the role of Archie Rice in *The Entertainer*, was (despite his status as a confirmed misogynist and homophobe) to strike a fatal blow at theatre censorship with a seriously queer piece of drama. The play charts the career of Alfred Redl, an officer in the Austro-Hungarian army, through his early success as an intelligence officer and sophisticate to his eventual suicide after being exposed as a queer Jewish spy of inferior birth. Redl is hardly a role model for queers and confirms every prejudice held by the public at large about the unstable and duplicitous nature of 'perverts'. In fact, in some ways the play can be seen as confirming Field Marshal Montgomery's reasons for opposing the decriminalisation of homosexuality. In a speech given in the House of Lords in 1965 he asserted:

> If these unnatural practices are made legal a blow is struck at the discipline of the British armed forces at a time when we need the very highest standards of moral and discipline with these forces serving throughout the world .... Take a large aircraft carrier with 2000 men cooped up in a small area. Imagine, what would happen in a ship of that sort if these practices crept in (quoted in Dollimore 1983: 53).

Imagine indeed. If Osborne's account of life in the armed forces presented here is to be believed, the men would swing between workaholic avoidance, sybaritic capitulation and treachery. Not the sort of patriot Montgomery and the House of Lords had in mind at all. As in most plays of the period, we discover Redl's queerness by degrees. Initially he is a model officer and human being, as Osborne rather clumsily conveys through a report read out by his commanding officers:

> German – excellent. Polish, French – fair. Punctilious knowledge military and international matters. Seems to know Franco Prussian campaign better than anyone who actually took part. Learned. All the qualities of a first class field officer and an unmistakable flair for intelligence. No. Wait a minute, there's more yet. Upright, discreet, frank and open, painstaking, marked ability to anticipate, as well as initiate instructions, without being reckless, keen judgement, cool under pressure – (Osborne 1998: 97)

Yet almost as soon as this exchange finishes, doubts are subtly introduced. Redl is reprimanded for being the second of Siczynski (a Jew) in a duel that ended in the latter's death and then closely questioned about the dead man and his relationship to him. Redl starts by saying he hardly knew him and then '*realises quickly he needs to provide more than this*' and goes on to criticise him as 'hyper-critical, over-sceptical' about army life and traditions, and, more damningly still, he reveals, 'I never thought

of him, no one seemed to, as a ladies man' (98). Yet, as the Lieutenant-
Colonel points out, he was an attractive man, and so, we assume from the
tone of the rest of the conversation, the only possible explanation for the
lack of women in his life must be that he was queer. Following on from
this, Redl is questioned about his own intentions regarding marriage (he
has no plans to marry soon), in what is almost a reverse parody of the
exchange between Sloane and Ed discussed above. The signs start to flow
thick and fast after this: in a brothel with a brother officer to celebrate
passing their war college exams Redl faints when left alone with a whore;
Redl wakes weeping every night when he stays with his lover the
Countess; Redl stops seeing the Countess; a strange man in a café flirts
with him and when he fails to respond tells him, 'I know what *you're*
looking for' provoking Redl into a violent outburst (130). Then in the
next scene, we see two figures in bed in the dark; Redl exclaims 'why did
I wait - so long' and we find out that the other figure is a man (131).
Queer at last. And meted out the traditional punishment: Redl's lover lets
four more soldiers into the room, they rob him and beat him up, and as
they leave, Redl's first male lover tells him, 'Don't be too upset love.
You'll get used to it.' (131). This fatalistic advice could be the theme of
the whole play: violence, shame and degradation are the inevitable result
of acting queer.
    Even in the famous transvestite ball scene which opens Act Two,
violence is the result of queer pleasure, in this case, Redl, who has
internalised all of the Establishment's horror of homosexuality, is the
perpetrator rather than victim. Osborne's stage description of the ball,
hosted by Baron von Epp, is as revealing of his attitude to queers as the
Lord Chamberlain's memo was of his. Yet whereas the Chamberlain
expresses fear and a desire to control, Osborne appears to be torn between
fascination and pity and he describes the participants in a way that
suggests more sympathy than his public persona might suggest:

Note: *At any drag ball as stylish and private as this one the guests can be
seen to belong to entirely different and very distinctive categories.*

1.   *The paid bum boys whose annual occasion it is – they wait for it from
      one year to the next and spend between 3 and 6 months preparing an
      elaborate and possibly bizarre costume. This is the market place
      where in all probability they will manage to acquire a meal ticket for
      months ahead. They tend to do either tremendously careful, totally
      feminine clothes – or the ultimate in revelation – e.g. Lady Godiva,
      except that he/she might think, instead of a gold lame jockstrap, that a*

gold chastity belt with a large and obvious gold key on a chain round his/her neck, be better.

2. *The discreet drag queens. Like the Baron/Queen Alexandra, and the Tsarina – their clothes, specifically made for the occasion by a trusted dressmaker, as the night becomes wilder are usually found to have a removable skirt revealing stockings, suspenders, jewelled garters, and diamond buckles on their shoes. But even despite this mild strip tease, they still remain in absolutely perfect taste.*

3. *The more self-conscious rich queens, who, though in drag, tend to masculine drag, and end up looking like lesbians. Someone tells me they saw one once in [a] marvellously cut black riding habit – frilled white jabot and cuffs, long skirt and boots – top hat with veil. Also in this category are the ones who go out of their way to turn themselves into absolute grotesques, and quite often arrive in a gaggle. They make a regal entry enjoying having their disguise penetrated or not as they case may be. If, for instance, the theme of the ball were theatrical they would probably choose to come as the witches from Macbeth. But marvellously theatrically thought out in every detail.*

4. *Another category of rich, discreet queens, who don't want us to offend their host by making no effort at all but who baulk at dressing up; for them full and impeccable evening dress with sash orders and neck decorations and elaborately over made-up faces. They usually look more frightening than any of the others – with middle aged decadent faces, painted like whores.*

5. *There are the men who positively dislike women and only put on drag in order to traduce them and make them appear as odious, immoral and unattractive as possible.*

6. *Finally, the ones who don't even make that effort but wear, like Redl, full dress uniform and decorations – or evening dress. It's not inconceivable that some of the bum boys would dress as pampered children.* (133-34)

Unsurprisingly, the Lord Chamberlain refused to allow the ball scene, not just because of the drag impersonation of Queen Alexandra and the inclusion of lots of 'unnecessary' homosexual characters, but also perhaps because some of the most well-adjusted queers appear in this scene, Baron von Epp in particular, who raises some particularly frightening notions for a moral guardian determined to keep the general public safe from queers. Near the beginning of the ball, the Baron describes the event as: 'the celebration of the individual against the rest, the us's and the them's, the free and the constricted, the gay and the dreary, the lonely and the mob

(139). Then later, even more alarming to the authorities, he suggests:

> Instead of all joining together, you know, one Empire of sixty million
> Germans, like they're always going on about. What about an Empire of
> *us*. Ex million queens. (143)

An anonymous memo in the Lord Chamberlain's correspondence
describes the play as 'the Pansies Charter for Freedom', yet despite these
revolutionary words Osborne's queers remain closeted but for this one
occasion a year, and remain firmly within a stereotypical field of reference
which transcends the historical period of the play. The tearful and
troubled queer, albeit wearing a tiara once a year, is still the norm. A state
of affairs reinforced by Charles Dyer's *Staircase* performed the following
year. Also originally hailed as revolutionary because it focuses on a queer
'marriage', *Staircase* concerns the miserable plight of Charlie and Harry, a
couple of hairdressers and, in Charlie's case, 'resting' female
impersonator. Harry is troubled by the prospect of his daughter (from his
previous marriage) coming to visit and seeing Charlie, while Charlie is
worried about his recent arrest for 'importuning in female attire' and
whether or not this will be taken any further. Hardly a challenge to the
farce queen stereotype - except in their evident misery which aligns them
with the tragic stereotype discussed above.

The Freaks Roll Call: *Loot* and *What the Butler Saw*

> I don't want there to be anything queer or camp or odd about the
> relationship of Hal and Dennis. Americans see homosexuality in terms of
> fag and drag. This isn't my vision of the universal brotherhood. They
> must be perfectly ordinary boys who happen to be fucking each other.
> Nothing could be more natural (Orton, US production note, quoted in
> Lahr 1978: 248).

Orton's use of 'natural' in this context signals his refusal to be
ruled by the prevailing queer stereotypes. In *Loot* (first performed 1965
then successfully restaged in 1966), as in *Sloane*, perceptions of natural
and conventional are inverted on all levels. Hal and Dennis' relationship
is a given rather than a shock to the other characters in the play, with the
exception of Mr McLeavy, the ultra-conventional, ultra-religious suburban
rose grower, who is rewarded for his virtue by being framed for his wife's
murder and a bankrobbery carried out by his son. Hal and Dennis'
sexuality is fluid and undefined, they 'happen to be fucking each other',
but they also happen to be fucking lots of other people. Their primary
objective is enjoyment, and this is what was so shocking to the Lord

Chamberlain and to the play's first audiences. Interestingly, Ifan Kyrle Fletcher, who read the play for the Lord Chamberlain's office, interpreted Hal and Dennis' relationship as a homosexual one, despite the fact that their bisexuality is referred to on almost every page (see LCP CORR:1966/4614). This exchange between Fay, Mrs McLeavy's nurse, and Hal is typical of the subversive tone of the play:

> FAY. The priest at St Kilda's has asked me to speak to you. He's very worried. He says you spend your time thieving from slot machines and deflowering the daughters of better men than yourself. Is this a fact?
> HAL. Yes.
> FAY. And even the sex into which you were born isn't safe from your own marauding. Father Mac is popular for the remission of sins, as you know. But clearing up after you is full-time job. He simply cannot be in the confessional 24 hours a day. That's reasonable isn't it? You do see his point?
> HAL. Yes.
> FAY. What are you going to do about this dreadful state of affairs?
> HAL. I'm going abroad.
> FAY. That will please the Fathers. Who are you going with?
> HAL. A mate of mine. Dennis. A very luxurious type of lad. At present employed by an undertaker. And doing very well in the profession.
> FAY. Have you known him long?
> HAL. We shared the same cradle.
> FAY. Was that economy or malpractice?
> HAL. We were too young to practise and economics still defeats us.
> FAY. You've confirmed my worst fears. You have no job. No prospects. And now you're to elope to the Continent with a casual acquaintance and not even a baby as justification. Where will you end? Not respected by the world at large like your father. Most people of any influence will ignore you. You'll be forced to associate with young men like yourself. Does that prospect please you?
> HAL. I'm not sure. (200)

Hal and Dennis embody every popular fear about young men in the 1960s: they are criminal, sexually indiscriminate and, as Orton advised Kenneth Williams, they reject all normal values of society and so cannot be controlled. In the second, successful production of the play directed by Charles Marowitz, Hal and Dennis were dressed as mods, thus tapping into contemporary fears about young men and their desire to live for kicks. The equanimity with which everyone assumes that Hal and Dennis are lovers is just a part of Orton's inverted universe, but it does at least offer a more progressive vision for queer audiences than the tortured figures who populated the stage before. Hal is tortured, but not by his

sexuality or his criminality, it is his inability to lie which causes him so
much anxiety. In *Loot*, queerness is accepted even though the nearest Hal
and Dennis come to expressing desire for each other, is the fact that Hal
refers to Dennis as 'baby'. When they are alone together, they talk about
brothels, women and money; both are accused of fathering unwanted
children, and yet everyone also assumes that they are lovers.   When
questioning Hal and Dennis about their movements and learning that both
of them claimed to be in bed asleep on the night of the robbery, Truscott
appeals to Fay:

> TRUSCOTT: What a coincidence, miss. Don't you agree? Two young
> men who know each other very well, spend their nights in separate beds.
> Asleep. It sounds highly unlikely to me. (233)

Loot queers and challenges all the normal values of society.   It
constantly foregrounds queerness and queer desire while also affronting
the nation's morality through the defiling of corpses, slurs on the Catholic
Church and the Police Force, and showing promiscuity and crime
triumphing over religiosity and upright citizens.   And it won the *Evening
Standard* Award for play of the year.   The times were changing:
homosexual acts were between adults in private were decriminalised in
1966 and in 1968 the Theatres Act ended pre-censorship of British theatre.
Theatre could now be officially queer. Orton lived to see the legalisation
of homosexuality, but not the end of censorship and his dramatic response
to the former was to produce another play in which the characters are not
overtly queer, but the universe which they inhabit regards queerness as the
norm.

What the Butler Saw (1969) is the pinnacle of Orton's crusade
against Society's pretensions.   Set in a mental hospital on a set designed
for farce (French windows, multiple doors, windows and cupboards), the
play deals with lunacy, incest, adultery, malpractice and sexuality.
Inverting the idea that the 'lunatics are taking over the asylum', Orton
posits the much simpler, 'the lunatics already run the asylum' to allow us
to question notions of madness, sanity and normality. Employing all the
standard farce conventions of cross-dressing, infidelity and mistaken
identity, *What the Butler Saw* allows Orton to make a point about the
extent to which sexuality and sexual identity is ever 'natural' or 'normal'.
In the scene below, for example, Dr Prentice is being questioned by Match
about his alleged harassment of Geraldine, but because she is dressed as a
man, Match understandably misinterprets Prentice's 'crime':

MATCH. Have you anything to say, sir?
PRENTICE. Yes. What this young woman claims is a tissue of lies.
SERGEANT MATCH *scratches his head.*
MATCH *(pause)*. This is a boy, sir. Not a girl. If you're baffled by the difference it might be as well to approach both with caution. (*To* GERALDINE.) Let's hear what you've got to say for yourself.
GERALDINE. I came here for a job. On some pretext the doctor got me to remove my clothes. Afterwards he behaved in a strange manner.
MATCH. What did he ask you to do?
GERALDINE. He asked me to lie on that couch.
SERGEANT MATCH *glances at* DR PRENTICE *in disapproval.* DR PRENTICE *drinks whisky.* MATCH *turns to* GERALDINE
MATCH *(quietly)*. Did he, at any time, attempt to interfere with you?
PRENTICE *(putting the glass down)*. You'll be disappointed, sergeant, if you imagine that boy has lost his virginity.
MATCH. I hope he'll be considerably more experienced before he loses that, sir. What reason had you for taking off his clothes?
PRENTICE. I wished to assure myself of his unquestioning obedience. I give a prize each year. I hope ultimately to tie it in with the Duke of Edinburgh's Award scheme.
MATCH. I'd prefer not to have Royalty mentioned in this context, sir. Have you been in trouble of this kind before?
PRENTICE. I'm not in trouble.
MATCH. You must realise this boy is bringing a serious charge against you?
PRENTICE. Yes, it's ridiculous. I'm a married man.
MATCH. Marriage excuses no one the freaks' roll-call. (408-409)

The norms of society and sexuality are challenged by one of the most stable heteronormative forms. Farce always turns on secrets, near misses, marital infidelity, and the occasional stereotypical farce queen thrown in for good measure. But in *What the Butler Saw*, the farce staples of disguise and mistaken identity open up a new performative field, and proclaiming marriage to be proof of heterosexuality becomes as questionable as proclaiming being married as proof of the sanctity of marriage. Mrs Prentice, by contrast, is an honorary member of a lesbian club: 'I myself am exempt from the rule because you count as a woman' (369). Even the certifiable Inspector of Madness Dr Rance refuses to recognise such outdated notions, reproving Dr Prentice's protestations of heterosexuality: 'I wish you wouldn't use these Chaucerian words. It's most confusing' (411). Employing the euphemism 'Chaucerian' in conjunction with heterosexuality makes us aware that this is a context in which heterosexuality is seen as a dirty word. Orton pushes this point further through the device of cross-dressing to present queer as the norm and straight as 'a gross violation of the natural order'. Rance, struggling to explain 'unnatural behaviour' to Nick (who is dressed as Geraldine), presents the following scenario:

> RANCE: Suppose I made an indecent suggestion to you. If you agreed something might occur which, by and large, would be regarded as natural. If, on the other hand, I approached this child (*he smiles at Geraldine* [who is dressed as Nick]) – my action could only result in a gross violation of the order of things. (416)

Rance, the mouthpiece of the Establishment, is manipulated by Orton into a pro-queer stance. 'Naturalness' and 'unnaturalness' are exposed as entirely arbitrary, a matter of appearance, rather than fact and, as such, subject to change.

As subversive as Orton's work is, one must be wary of claiming too liberated a stance for him. Orton was comfortable with his own queerness, but as Shepherd, Sinfield and Clum have pointed out, his liberation had its limitations. In his diary he records his relief at not being exposed as queer at the *Evening Standard* Drama Awards:

> the lunch was announced. On the board it said 'Mr and Mrs Orton'. Peggy laughed. 'I'll be your wife for the afternoon,' she said. All I could think of was how embarrassing, if, as I'd originally planned, I'd taken Kenneth. (Orton 1986: 57)

and in an early interview with Barry Hanson for *Plays and Players*, he mentions a (fictitious) marriage that broke up before he went to prison. So in life, he was not as boldly anarchic as his characters, an inevitable consequence, one could argue, of coming of age in a time of anti-queer hysteria. In the next decade, Gay Sweatshop were able to achieve a much more cohesive and confrontational queer style, but it was to be nearly another decade, when they turned down Martin Sherman's *Bent*, in the belief that the play deserved a wider audience, that such an unapologetic description of queer life and desire made its way onto the mainstream stage of British theatre.

Works cited

A Patriot for Me, Royal Court Theatre, London, 1966. Theatre Museum Archive Production File; V&A Theatre Musuem.
Clum. J.M, *Still Acting Gay*, New York: St Martins Press, 2000.
The Collection, Aldwych Theatre, 1962. Theatre Museum Archive Production File; V&A Theatre Musuem.

Crimes of Passion Royal Court Theatre, London, 1967. Theatre Museum Archive Production File; V&A Theatre Musuem

De Jongh, Nicholas, *Not In Front of the Audience: Homosexuality on Stage*, London: Routledge, 1993.

— . *Politics, Prudery and Perversion*, London: Methuen, 2001.

Dollimore. J., 'The Challenge of Sexuality' in *Society and Literature 1945-70*, (ed), Alan Sinfield, London: Methuen, 1983.

Dyer C., *Staircase*, London: Harmondsworth, 1966.

Entertaining Mr Sloane, Arts Theatre, 1964. Theatre Museum Archive Production File; V&A Theatre Musuem.

Entertaining Mr Sloane Lord Chamberlain's Reader Report, LCP CORR: 1964/4267, British Library.

Hall Carpenter Archives, *Walking After Midnight: Gay Men's Life Stories*, London: Routledge, 1989.

Hampton, C., *When Did You Last See My Mother?*, London: Faber, 1967.

Higgins. P (ed), *A Queer Reader*, London: Fourth Estate, 1993.

Johnston, J., *The Lord Chamberlain's Blue Pencil*, London: Hodder and Stoughton, 1990.

Lahr. J., *Prick Up Your Ears*, London: Harmondsworth, 1978.

Loot, Jeanetta Cochrane Theatre, 1966. Theatre Museum Archive Production File; V&A Theatre Musuem.

Loot Lord Chamberlain Reader's Report LCP CORR:1966/4614, British Library.

O'Connor, S., *Straight Acting*, London: Cassell, 1998.

Orton. Joe, Interview with Alan Brien, BBC Radio 4, 14 July 1964.

—. *The Orton Diaries*, ed. Lahr, London: Methuen, 1986.

—. *The Complete Plays*, London: Methuen, 1993.

Osment, Philip, *Gay Sweatshop: Four Plays and A Company*, London: Methuen, 1989.

Osborne, John, *A Patriot for Me* in *Collected Plays Three*, London: Faber and Faber, 1998.

Pinter Harold, *The Collection*, *Plays Two*, London: Faber and Faber, 1991.

Porter K and Weeks G (eds), *Between the Acts*, London: Routledge, 1991.

Rebellato, Dan, *1956 and All That*, London: Routledge, 1999.

Shaffer, Peter, *Five Finger Exercise* in *Three Plays*, London: Harmondsworth, 1976.

Shellard D, Nicholson S and Handley, M., *The Lord Chamberlain Regrets*, London: British Library Publications, 2004.

Shepherd, S., *Because We're Queers. The Life and Crimes of Joe Orton and Kenneth Halliwell*, London: Gay Men's Press, 1989.

Sinfield, Alan, *Out on Stage*, London and New Haven, Yale University

Press, 1999.
—. *The Wilde Century*, London: Cassell, 1994.
What the Butler Saw Production File, Queens Theatre 1969. Theatre Musuem Archive
Wildblood, P, *Against the Law*: London: Wiedenfield, 1955.
Williams, K, *The Diaries of Kenneth Williams* ed. Davies, London: Harper Collins, 1993.
—. *The Kenneth Williams Letters* ed. Davies, London: Harper Collins, 1993.

CHAPTER FOUR

LOVING ANGELS INSTEAD: THE INFLUENCE OF TONY KUSHNER'S '*ANGELS IN AMERICA*' ON 1990'S BRITISH DRAMA

PAUL T. DAVIES

Synopsis

This chapter begins with an analysis of the American playwright Tony Kushner's *Angels In America*, and then continues to examine its influence on British playwrights throughout the 1990s. These playwrights form the core of the 'In-Yer-Face' movement, in particular Anthony Neilson, Sarah Kane and Mark Ravenhill, but I will also illustrate how earlier Queer constructions staged by Robert Chesley established a clearer presence in British drama.

Angels In America

Gay and lesbian theory argued for the deconstruction of binary oppositions, the complete separation of all forms of sexual behaviour from any kinds of moral judgements. Dualism, as well as binaries, continue to be adopted in queer theatrical representation, and this is illustrated in Tony Kushner's epic *Angels In America* (1992/94). The play brought aspects of Queer theory and performance out of the 'alternative' scene, and placed them centre stage in mainstream, national theatres. Having a broader aim than earlier AIDS drama, and the sweep of the play covers themes and concerns beyond the disease itself. Kushner wanted to write about three things - AIDS, Mormons and Roy Cohn, a right-wing homophobic politician 'outed' and killed by the HIV virus. Other subject matters, spirituality, loss of identity and self, the weakening ozone layer, addiction, truth and democracy create a universality of concerns between all people.

Kushner constructs a gay gaze, the aim of which is for audiences to employ and view the work through that gaze. Kushner's "gay fantasia on national themes", presents a world seen entirely from Queer and gay viewpoints and its success within mainstream drama encourages heterosexual audience members to adopt that gaze; similarly Elyot presents the male nude body as an object of desire for all members of his audience. Both playwrights, by their very location within mainstream success, are not playing for the exclusive male gaze, as in Chesley's audience, or presenting heavily melodramatic structures for a traditionally melodramatically trained audience as Kramer does in *The Normal Heart*. Both playwrights place gay issues, bodies, humour and tragedy at the centre of their dramaturgy, and as the focus of the gaze. Both playwrights construct what I refer to as the Queer Pause, which support the gay gaze. It also echoes notions of Genet analysis discussed earlier.

Angels In America (Part One *Millennium Approaches,* Part Two: *Perestroika),* has a combined playing time of over seven hours, and a variety of theatrical devices are employed. Scenes shift between reality and fantasy, mythology and naturalism, mimetic structures and physical encounters, direct address to the audience, in other words a range of performative structures. Kushner appropriates elements of expressionism, Brechtian epic theatre, poetic drama, popular cultural theatricalism and historical thematic traditions. The juxtaposition of codes and media within post-modern practice allows him to explore new identities, such as the Person With AIDS, and queer performativity, without being tied to traditional forms such as melodrama. A changing social order and a crumbling of faith in society are explored, HIV itself causing characters to take account of their lives and belief systems.

The influence of Brecht is profound, and ever present in Kushner's work, in particular his Lehrstücke, or learning plays. Kushner is fascinated by "the painful dismantling, as a revolutionary necessity, of the individual ego" (Kushner 1995: 35). His socialist politics are never far from the surface of his work, and Fisher defines Kushner's new brand of socialist 'progressivism', or 'socialism of the skin, one that honours the values and traditions of the past without a slavish adherence to belief systems whose traditions have excluded or oppressed diversity in culture, sexual orientation and politics.' (Fisher 2002: 4). Kushner sees the oppression of gays as part of a wider system of oppression.

The metaphor of the Angel serves many purposes, not least to bridge the gap between the demands of naturalism and the fantasia/fantastic aspects. But the angel also has a philosophical grounding, an image derived from Paul Klee's painting *Angelus Novus*, which Benjamin discusses in his *Thesis on the Philosophy on History*. Benjamin wrote that people have to be 'constantly looking back at the rubble of history. The most dangerous thing is to become set upon some notion of the future that isn't rooted in the bleakest, most terrifying idea of what's piled up behind you.' (Fisher 2002: 21). Thus the angel provides the strong metaphorical grounding for Kushner's work. The Klee painting;

> shows an angel looking as if he is about to move away from something he is fixedly contemplating. His eyes are staring, his mouth is open, his wings are spread. This is how one pictures the angel of history. His face is turned toward the past. Where we perceive a chain of events, he sees one single catastrophe which keeps piling wreckage upon wreckage and hurls it in front of his feet. The angel would like to stay, awaken the dead, and make whole what has been smashed. But a storm is blowing from Paradise; it has got caught in his wings with such violence that the angel can no longer close them. This storm irresistibly propels him into the future to which his back is turned, while the pile of debris before him grows skyward. This storm is what we call progress. (Benjamin 1955: 249).

The angel, a sign of purity, of a blissful state achieved in the after-life, generally asexual, angels as messengers of hope and peace, achieve an ironic representation, as they are connected strongly to People with AIDS, particularly the character of Prior. The characters also have to battle with their personal good and bad angels.

One of the play's main strengths is in its characterisations, and in particular the character of Roy Cohn. He was Joe McCarthy's aide-de-camp, and he helped to prosecute the Rosenbergs, who were accused of passing secret material about the atom bomb to the Russians in the 1950s. In the play, it is made evident that Cohn was instrumental in achieving Ethel Rosenberg's execution, and he is therefore haunted by her ghost, particularly when he faces his AIDS- related death in Part Two. A self-hating gay man, Cohn is the person that the gay community would be reluctant to acknowledge as a 'brother', a closeted homosexual with the political power to harm other gay men. Kushner himself has said, 'I don't know why lesbians and gay men aren't all as twisted and wrecked inside as Roy Cohn was.' (Kushner 1995: 52).

The most effective aspect of his portrayal is that his is the only AIDS- related death that the audience witness. This hateful, vile character, who even refuses to acknowledge his sexuality, is depicted in graphic pain, rather than the characters who have aroused audience sympathy and support. Kushner, in his subtitle of gay themes, is prepared to encompass the closeted homosexual. As a group, they are often targeted by other gay men as traitors to the gay community. Larry Kramer's attitude, accusing closet gays of eroding gay solidarity and contributing to the spread of HIV, is in contrast to Kushner's, who gives voice to this aspect of gay life. Kushner dramatises closetry twice, the second time in the character of Joseph Porter Pitt.

The Angel imagery also allows Kushner to connect with the Mormon faith, itself based on an angelic vision, and developed strongly through the character of Joseph, fascinated as a boy by a picture of Jacob and the angel, and a fascination tinged with homoeroticism;

> Jacob is young and strong. The angel is...a beautiful man with golden hair and wings, of course. I still dream about it. Many nights. I'm...it's me. In that struggle. Fierce and unfair. The angel is not human, and it holds nothing back, so how could anyone human win, what kind of a fight is that? (Kushner 1992: II, ii. 34).

Named after Joseph Smith, the Mormon prophet to whom the revelation was made, and belonging to a religion that does not acknowledge homosexuality, the angel, represents Joseph's struggle with his gayness. Joseph is a favourite employee of Roy's, and Cohn's homosexual interest in Joseph is made clear. Essentially a good man, Joe's conflict is between his Mormon faith and belief in the politics of Reaganism, and his homosexuality. He cruises the Rambles in Central Park, then the liveliest outdoor gay pick-up area in New York. His wife, Harper, also a Mormon, has a valium addiction, and her pill-induced fantasies initially introduce the 'Fantasia' element to the play.

Louis Ironson is Jewish, a word-processor for the Second Circuit Court of Appeals. His lover, Prior Walter, is diagnosed with AIDS, and, unable to cope with this, Louis eventually leaves Prior. Angst-ridden, self-pitying, *human*, Louis spends much of his stage time seeking forgiveness for his leaving Prior. It is left to the audience to decide whether this is betrayal or bravery. Prior plainly sees this as betrayal. An openly proud gay man, formally into drag, the enjoyment of which he rediscovers in the second play, trying to deal with his illness, Prior's angels manifest themselves on stage as the medication he takes leads him to hallucinate, in particular to hearing the voice of the Angel. She appears to him at the end of Part One, and convinces him he is a Prophet early on in Part Two. Prior refuses to die, and thus begins his battle with his angel, a struggle for his own life, and this reflects the Biblical Jacob's struggle with the angel. In *Perestroika*, Prior eventually has to ascend to Heaven to bargain for his own life. His body, like Cohn's, is a site for the representation of AIDS. However, the appearance of the Angel also points toward other manifestations, that of Divine Bodies and Spiritual Bodies. An angel has reached the perfect state, an afterlife that involves no pain or disease, a higher plane that Prior can reach if he gives up his life.

Sedgewick's observation that the crisis of homo/heterosexual definition has affected our culture through its use of the binary categories, which include: '... secrecy/ disclosure, knowledge/ ignorance, private/ public, masculine/ feminine, majority/ minority, innocence/ initiation, natural/ artificial, new/ old, health/ illness, same/ different, passive/ active', (Sedgewick 1990: 11), clearly applies to *Angels In America*. In the play, of course, the largest binary is set in the two characters of Prior and Roy Cohn, the 'Angel' and the 'Devil', The process of the plays see the binaries reverse, with the seemingly strong Cohn weakening and the undervalued Prior gaining strength.

Hannah Pitt, Joseph's mother, begins the play with unswerving Mormon faith, and she moves from Salt Lake City to New York after Joseph 'comes out' to her during a clumsy, drunken telephone call. Her appearance initially presents her as the voice of reason and authority, her beliefs may be unshifting, unsympathetic to the alternative life styles of the other characters. However, as her role increases in Part Two, so does her compassion, as she learns to deal with the shifting times. She befriends the sick Prior, becoming his ally, and ends the play with a more balanced outlook. Prior even shows her his KS lesion, the same one he shows to Louis in Part One of the play, as they discuss Biblical visions. Her faith helps her to accept Prior's evangelical visions more than the other characters. Indeed, she witnesses the Angel herself in the second part of the play.

Belize is the sole black character/actor in the production, a former drag queen and ex-lover of Prior. A registered nurse, his name was originally Norman Arriaga, Belize being a drag name that stuck. Therefore, he has already shifted his identity, constructed a life more suitable to him, has refined his Queer Performance, and has adapted to cope with the age of AIDS. That he is a black male nurse, places him firmly outside the white, middle-class structure that dominates the rest of the play and societal ideology. Oppositionally to Hannah, his advice makes more sense to those in the gay world, as he refuses to compromise his sexuality or beliefs. As a drag queen, appearing in some scenes in full drag, he joins Cohn in Kushner's embrace of all aspects of gay sexuality. He embodies, along with the closet homosexual, another aspect of gay life that some gay men are uncomfortable with, that of public, flaunting drag. From Queer perspectives, however, to deny the drag queen is to distance oneself from Radical Drag, 'a way of inverting the effeminate stigma attached to being gay and wearing it as a badge of pride.' (Baker 1994:

238). Drag has always had an uncomfortable relationship with gay politics. The 'masculine' response to this, of course, is to make fetishistic aspects of hyper-masculinity/ patriarchy, and create a leather drag, or the "clone" image, returning us to the 'Village People' look and representations in Chesley, and, in *Angels In America,* the Rambles 'pick-up' scene, to be discussed shortly.

Belize's campness, and his drag, are essential components of Kushner's representation. Kushner pushes the stereotype, first by celebrating it, and secondly by making his characters *active* and political, they do not fall into victimhood. By being Queer, they challenge the notion of a sexuality based solely on sexual *behaviour.* Like Chesley's dramaturgy, homosexuality and sexual behaviour are centre stage, but Kushner's characters, like Chesley's, are camp *and* strong, Queer *and* loving. When Belize and Prior drag up for a memorial service, they are creating a Queer performance, not just as a way to cope with the death toll, but also as an ongoing stance that celebrates who they *are.* They can discard this aspect of themselves as soon as the funeral is over, they adopt drag in much the same way as the Leatherman in the park adopts his leather drag, it is a performance. Whilst drag on stage, of course, is far from being new, mainstream audiences, for the first time, are seeing drag that is motivated by the urgency of the AIDS crisis, presented with a Queer activeness.

Louis leaves Prior, and his guilt at being unable to support his sick lover, and his denial, leads Louis to seek anonymous sex with other men. In a landmark scene, in which Kushner borrows elements of Chesley's work and adapts it for a mainstream audience, Louis is picked up in Central Park

> (Louis and a MAN in the Rambles in Central Park...Louis and the MAN are eyeing each other, each alternating interest and indifference.) (Kushner 1992: II, iii. 37-42).

Louis, upset, angry and guilty, seeks 'no strings' casual sex, and to be punished for his feelings of inadequacy. He seeks to play out his own deathwish.

In the London production, the actors were on either side of the stage, not placed together, or in physical contact, although the script itself does not specify there should be distance between the two actors. As the representation is of outdoor, quick casual sex, neither actor is naked. There is no call for romantic imagery. The MAN is a stranger to Louis, and the actor is in black leather gear, from a peaked cap down to his boots. He wears shades and a moustache, he is as 'cloned'as possible. He is fetishised.

MAN: What do you want?
LOUIS: I want you to fuck me, hurt me, make me bleed.
MAN: I want to-
LOUIS: Yeah.
MAN: I want to hurt you.
LOUIS: Fuck me.
MAN: Yeah?
LOUIS: Hard.
MAN: Yeah? You been a bad boy? (Kushner 1992: II, iii. 39).

The language is full of gay sexual codes and meaning, an understanding to the gay audience of the SM potential of this encounter, and for Louis this is not his usual *play,* he is seeking pain, blood and punishment. Offence to members of the audience not versed in encounters of this nature was diluted by the staging, the physical and theatrical distancing between the performers. The moral and aesthetic boundary was clearly laid out by the distance between the actors. Another, separate, scene between Joseph and Cohn, took place centre stage, running simultaneously with this one. Both actors playing Louis and The Man were fully clothed, the anonymity of the encounter emphasised by them both looking out at the audience, not making eye contact with each other. Within the script, the sexual nature is also tempered by humour, as the encounter falls apart as the scene develops. The men can't go back to Louis's place because of Prior, and the MAN lives with his parents. Louis's tart response of 'Oh' to this drew a strong laugh from the audience:

MAN: Here then.
LOUIS: I...Do you have a rubber?
MAN: I don't use rubbers.
LOUIS: You should. (*He takes one from his coat pocket*)
Here.
MAN : I don't use them.
LOUIS: Forget it then.
MAN: No wait. Put it on me. Boy. (Kushner 1992: II, iii. 41).

The humour here develops as the roles reverse. The tough Macho Leather Man pleads for Louis to stay and let him fuck him. The act of fucking was mimed, the actors still apart, Louis bending over, the Man thrusting aggressively, sex talk and groaning. During the sex, as it gets rougher, the condom breaks:

> MAN: I think it broke. The rubber. You want me to pull out?
> LOUIS: Keep...Keep going. Inject me. I don't care. I don't care.
> (*Pause. The MAN pulls out.*)
> MAN: I...um, look I'm sorry, but I think I want to go.
> LOUIS: Yeah-give my love to Mom and Dad.
> (*The MAN slaps him.*)
> LOUIS: Ow!
> (*They stare at each other.*)
> LOUIS: It was a joke. (Kushner 1992: II, iii. 41).

Note that the pain actually does hurt when the characters have stepped outside of the sexual script. The black humour here, tinged with anger, places the emphasis less on the representation of fucking, and more on the unsafe sex aspect. The risks these characters seem prepared to take are what could cause offence, not the act of male anal sex. Kushner dramatises a difficult dilemma for the gay man, that of 'survivor's guilt', and challenges the detractors of gay sex who insisted on abstinence as the best policy. Safer sex is presented as a good option, initially, at least, as a sexy option. Kushner seemed to be acknowledging Kramer when he pointed out:

> When the epidemic first hit, the first reaction, especially among many gay men, was a complete repudiation of sex: saying we've made a terrible mistake, we should never have been screwing around as much as we were and now we're paying the price. They adopted the response of the Right. (Croft 1992: 8).

What the distance between the men does, however, is distance the audience, enabling them to look at the scene objectively, to consider the layers of issues present in such a short stage time, Louis's guilt leading him to seek anonymous sex and punishment, the MAN's reluctance to engage in safer sex, the humour of the scene, the farce of an urgent, casual pick up. Taken in isolation, it is a Lehrstck, the scene is a learning play, the dismantling of the individual ego, the dismantling often figured as death, or the presence of the threat of death via infection in this case.

There is another Queer Pause in Part Two. Joseph and Louis have begun their affair, and are in bed together, in fact they spend days in bed making love. Developing from the 'pick-up' scene, Louis now appears to have found love and stability. In the production, both actors walked on stage during a scene change. They were both naked, and faced the audience, presenting their bodies, not acknowledging the audience, but inviting the gaze, displaying the focus of gay male desire, a double icon. Both actors had well developed, muscular bodies, one smooth, one hairy, fitting into the 'perfectible body' ideal, attractive to many male and female members of the audience. This created a Queer pause, a moment or two of reflection, but one directed exclusively toward the male body and the penis. When they go to bed, they simulate acts of gay sex, following the stage directions such as 'they start to fuck'. The audience has already adopted the gay gaze, in the sense that entire stage world has been presented through Queer lives, and see the following discussions from a gay standpoint. Their acts of closeness contrast with their dialogue, in which they have many a philosophical discussion about gay repression, religion and beliefs. Here, the two religions explored in the play, Judaism and Mormonism, are in bed together. Both religions are traditionally not supportive of homosexuality, and thus fail to ultimately provide comfort for the two characters. Their affair ends with a fight, fulfilling Louis's desire for self-punishment.

There is much discussion in the play of the 'National' themes of Justice and freedom. These emerge as AIDS shows the limitations of tolerance, in much the same way as Ibsen uses syphilis in *Ghosts* to break down the fragile structure of Mrs Alving's world. The central characters are aware, and discuss the fact that they belong to 'lines of oppression'. Black, gay, Mormons, they are outside the majority, and search for freedom in the Land of the Free. They are restricted by limitations of freedom imposed by the system they operate within and live in. Even Roy Cohn recognises that 'the worst thing about being sick in America...is that you are booted out of the parade. Americans have no use for sick.' (Kushner 1992: 36).

At the end of Part One, *Millennium Approaches,* an Angel comes crashing through Prior's ceiling, announcing that she is the messenger and he is a Prophet. It is theatrically a stunning stage picture and moment, carefully crafted to provide an original, amusing and gripping climax to Part One, which Prior comments as, 'Very Steven Speilberg'. (Kushner, 1992: III, viii. 90). The Angel also distils Kushner's own definition of Queerness, and added to the moments when the naked male body is shown to the audience, and through the camp theatricality inherent in the text, she symbolises Fabulousness. Kushner's definition of it, as it relates to art, and homosexual history and sociology, is illuminating:

> Irony. Tragic history. Defiance. Gender- Fuck. Glitter. Drama. It's not butch. It is not hot - the cathexis surrounding the fabulousness is not necessarily erotic. Fabulousness is not determined by age or beauty. Style has a dialectical relationship to physical reality. The body is the Real.

Style is Theatre. The raw materials are reworked into illusion. For style to
be truly fabulous, one must   completely   triumph over tragedy, age,
physical insufficiencies, and just as important, one's audiences must be
aware of the degree of transcendence, of triumph; must see both the
triumph and that over which the triumph has been made. In this the magic
of the fabulous is the magic of the theatre. The wires show. The illusion is
always incomplete, inadequate; the work behind the magic is meant to be
appreciated. (Fisher 2002: 69).

The orgasm that Prior experiences as the Angel approaches, the
intense sexual feeling, ensures his body is the centre of the drama, of the
literal climax. The first time we see Prior in Part Two, the ceiling is intact,
he awakes as from a nightmare, pulls back the bed covers and comments:
'First orgasm in months and I slept through it.' (Kushner 1994: I, v. 8).
Memories of his encounter with the angel return though. The theatrical
'magic' Kushner says the angel must own is, however, sacrificed in Part
Two as she is developed into more of a comic turn, there is an abdication
of the Fabulous, a demystification of the angel.

The final scene is optimistic, leaping five years and reflecting
1990s attitudes to *surviving* AIDS. It is an under-played scene as Prior,
Hannah (now his biggest supporter), Belize and Louis sit on a bench in
Central Park, close to a statue of the Bethesda Angel at the Bethesda
Fountain. The Angel is an iconic presence above them all. A kind of truce
has been reached in their relationships with each other, they are now an
alternative 'family', and Prior delivers his direct address to the audience.
His speech reflects the strength needed to cope: 'I have been living with
AIDS for five years now', emphasising that death is not an immediate
certainty upon HIV diagnosis. The strength of *Angels In America* lies in its
treatment of the personal impact of AIDS and the world it has created. In
1992, its messages needed to be heard by gay and straight alike, and the
play is a landmark of AIDS representation. Kushner managed to escape
the easy sentimentalism and domestic melodrama of many AIDS dramas,
such as *The Normal Heart*, while retaining some important theatrical
devices that had been established in particular by Chesley. The body of
Prior is also the site of struggle, of hope, fear, illness, health and survival.
This utopianism and sentimentality of the body has, of course, been
present in the works by Chesley, and in *Angels in America* the importance
of the gay male sexual 'ill' body is presented to a more mainstream
audience. The Queer pauses that Kushner creates, brings the full audience
attention onto the male body, whether clothed as in the Park pick up scene,
or naked.

The Influence of Angels In America

In a sense, in *Angels In America,* the naked gay body becomes *established* in gay mainstream AIDS drama, as it is the site for struggle, survival, memory and pleasure. It is also the focus for anxiety as well as celebration, and those Brechtian pauses I can now term Queer pauses. Like Chesley, and developing from the sexual textuality set by him, Kushner is showing the *Fabulousness* of the naked body in those moments when the body is presented. (The 2003 HBO film of *Angels In America,* naturally, edited these Queer pauses, as they are exclusively theatrical in construction and execution. For example, the pick-up scene was shortened, with the actors more naturally closer together.)

However, just as representations of gay sexuality were being portrayed by Kushner to mainstream audiences in a more positive light, one aspect of gay sex, that of anal penetration, was hijacked by the British 'New Laddism' of the 1990s. Ironically, the Queer theatricality established by Chesley, Elyot and Kushner were adopted by heterosexual playwrights. The unavoidable fact of AIDS drama is, of course, that illness and death is ever present, and that unprotected anal sex is the highest risk activity. Although the pick-up scene in Central Park carries the presence of risk and the dangers of transmitting the disease, Kushner also later in the play shows men enjoying sex with each other. He brings onto his stage some of the pride in gay sex, including anal sex, that is central to Chesley's work. Men are shown being gentle and loving with each other in the midst of an epidemic.

Elsewhere the act of anal penetration became used throughout the decade as a shock tactic, by a number of writers who used anal rape as a metaphor for wider issues and as a form of violence that, ultimately, underlined anxieties surrounding anal penetration. It became, when all other scenes of violence had been exhausted, the ultimate threat. The following discussion is a necessary diversion into theatrical representation throughout the 1990s, as I wish to posit the argument that Queer theory and Queer stage constructions developed more radical representations of sexuality, sex acts and, in particular male nudity and relationships between men. Heterosexist notions of the anal sex act, for example, incorporated Queer constructions to present the other side of that binary opposition of homo/heterosexuality.

The 'In-Yer-Face' playwrights, Sarah Kane, Anthony Neilson and Mark Ravenhill, pushed the boundaries of representations of violence and sex on stage. Many of the most successful and acclaimed plays of the Nineties used male rape as a metaphor to represent many of the issues they were exploring. The naked body can be a defiant one, can be celebratory, yet in these plays the body being attacked was often laden with significance of vulnerability, as one male character used rape to gain control over another male character. Male rape became the last act that could finally shock the audience, exposing human fragility, vulnerability and mortality. All the anxieties of anal penetration are brought to the fore, the dramatists are replicating some anxieties surrounding penetration, ultimately leading to a hijacking of anal sex being represented as a loving, committed act.

Penetrator

This metaphorically occurs in Neilson's 1993 play *Penetrator,* which explores the relationship between three male friends. Max and Alan share a crummy bedsit, and just as anal sex becomes a lazy device for power signification, two young men in a filthy bedsit, smoking dope, drinking beer and talking about sex swiftly became a metaphor for Thatcher's 'lost' generation. The arrival of Tadge, possibly on the run from the army, opens up fissures between the friendship of the other two. The play begins with a porn fantasy, foregrounding from the outset extreme heterosexual private imagining, speaking in the language of cheap soft core scripting, bringing it into the public arena.

The scene cuts to Max in the flat masturbating over a porn magazine, and after he is finished, Alan arrives and the friends take drugs, play cards, and, for losing the game, Max's beloved teddies are arranged into positions of fucking. Tadge, Max's childhood friend, arrives, AWOL, and acting weirdly, claiming Norman Schwarzkopf, Commander-In-Chief of Gulf War One, is his father, but more significantly claims he has been locked in a dark room and tortured by a gang of Penetrators. Before they could rape him with a wooden pole, he escaped, and, using Alan as a foil, demonstrates that escape. Whilst the other two debate how to deal with Tadge, and feel that something very terrible has happened to him in the army, Tadge's fear and fascination with the Penetrators grows. Accusing Alan of being a Penetrator, he produces a huge knife, 'the knife to end all knives', proclaiming 'I took it off one of them. He was going to stab me up the arse with it.' (Neilson, *Penetrator,* 1999: *vi.* 101). He savagely disembowels one of the teddies, threatens Alan, and Max's revelation that he knows Alan has betrayed him by sleeping with his ex-girlfriend, causes Alan to leave and the childhood friends remain. Tadge's obsession, the attraction of the Penetrators, is derived from a childhood memory, an intimacy between him and Max that they accidentally discovered.

MAX: You *know* what happened.
TADGE: *Tell* me!
MAX: You took my trousers down.
TADGE: And then?
MAX: My pants.
Long Pause.
I lay down on the leaves. *(Pause)* You pulled my shirt up. You listened to my heart.
TADGE: It was cold.
MAX: It was cold, yes.
TADGE: And I touched you.
MAX: Yes.
TADGE: Where did I touch you?
MAX: You touched my balls. You asked me to cough. You turned me over and spread my arse.
TADGE: Do you remember the smell of me?
MAX: Yes.
TADGE: I remember the smell of you.
(Neilson 1999: vi. 112).

Although Tadge mainly speaks in the language of pornography, and constantly refers to anal sex both as a threat (to Alan), and a punishment, (by the Penetrators), this is not a homophobic play. Neilson is more concerned with the dehumanisation of a man by military/masculine enforcement of patriarchy and by porn. The memory is conveyed in intimate, tender language. Neilson claims that Tadge is based on a friend of his, whose father was in the police force, brought up in a very macho environment, and went into the army to prove himself a man. He had homosexual leanings and 'the pull between those two things, and also perhaps the more ambiguous things that happen in an all male environment, just set him off.' (Sierz, 2000: 77).

Whilst Tadge communicates through pornographic imaginings and violent fantasies about the Penetrators, he wants more than a sexual experience, as conveyed in the play's conclusion. Tadge, after describing extreme violence and sexual acts that he claims are shown in porn shown at the Barracks, he ends up screaming "cock" and "cunt" over and over again. It is Max who calms him down, and the final lines return to childhood, with Tadge saying, 'I used to like coming to your house'. (Neilson 1999: vi. 117) This is a play about lost childhood, lost opportunities, and intimacy between male friends, the destruction of the teddy symbolising the end of childhood. Neilson is using heterosexual fear of penetration as a device for exploring relationships between men.

Blasted

Perhaps the most notorious of Nineties plays was Sarah Kanes's *Blasted*, (Royal Court Theatre, 1995.) Much has been written about the furore surrounding the play, in particular the critical response to the depiction of male and female rape, eyes being sucked out and eaten, cannibalism, the eating of a baby's corpse, and onstage defecation. *Blasted* is set in a hotel room in Leeds where a middle-aged journalist, Ian, has brought a naive young woman, Cate. Ian, recovering from lung cancer, smokes and coughs heavily, Cate sucks her thumb, stutters when stressed and is prone to epileptic fits. Ian wants to have sex with her, and during one of her fits rubs himself against her. He masturbates frequently throughout the play, particularly in the first section. The initial clue to the situation outside is that he has a gun in a shoulder holster, and talks about working undercover, and gradually we become aware that there is a war taking place.

The situation in the room intensifies. Ian rapes Cate, and she gives him a blow job and bites his penis, she turns the gun on him but is unable to shoot. The situation outside the room has also intensified, and when a nameless soldier gets into the room, Cate escapes. The power game now occurs between the man and the man who has the bigger gun. The soldier has been reduced by his experiences to animalistic needs and survival, focusing on major, basic instincts, food, sex and survival. Following *Penetrator*, he is an extreme representation of Tadge, a development of that kind of hyper- masculinity. The soldier urinates on the bed, and then the hotel is blasted apart by a bomb. In the debris of the room, the soldier recounts some of his war experiences, of Bosnian levels of atrocity.

With his rifle pointed at the back of Ian's head, the soldier rapes him, and during the course of the rape the soldier begins to cry out. But these are not cries of orgasm, the soldier breaks down until gradually he is grieving at the moment that he ejaculates. Afterwards, the soldier asks Ian if he has ever been fucked by a man before, and when Ian says no, the soldier diminishes Ian even more:

> Didn't think so. It's nothing. Saw thousands of people packing into trucks like pigs trying to leave town. Women threw their babies on board hoping someone would look after them. Crushing each other to death. Insides of people's heads come out of their eyes. Saw a child, most of his face blown off, young girl I fucked hand up inside her trying to claw my liquid out, starving man eating his dead wife's leg. Gun was born here and won't die. Can't get tragic about your arse. Don't think your Welsh arse is different

to any other arse I fucked. Sure you haven't got any more food, I'm starving. (Kane, *Blasted,* 2001: iv. 50).

The soldier then sucks Ian's eyes out, and in the next scene he has shot himself. Cate returns with a crying baby, which, when it dies, she buries it under the floor boards. The blind Ian is left alone, and subsequent scenes show him crying, masturbating, trying to shit, and eventually digging up the baby's corpse and eating it. He then clambers under the floorboards and the rain falls on him as Cate returns with food, and blood pouring down her legs. She, a vegetarian at the beginning of the play, feeds sausage to Ian before she eats it herself. His final words are 'Thank you.'

The stage imagery created by Kane makes a powerful and lasting impression. Of course, some of her devices are not new to theatrical representation, the eye gouging being endured by audiences of *King Lear* for centuries. Her use of rape as metaphor for power, of invasion and forced occupation of another person and space was staged in scene three of Howard Brenton's *The Romans In Britain* in 1980. (The moral panic that surrounded this play has also become legendary.) The attempted rape of a young Celt by a Roman soldier disturbed many not so much by the how the rape was represented, but, as Brenton said, 'What is so hard to take is the flippancy of the soldiers.' (Sierz 2000: 27) This brings us to Kane's soldier emphasising the irrelevance of Ian's arse in the theatre of civil war. The indelible image is of anal penetration as an act of war, connected with power and violence, and, ultimately, despair as shown in the soldier breaking down as he rapes Ian. There are no angels and prophecies in *Blasted.*

You'll Have Had Your Hole

The use of male rape as a device to symbolise power and terror finds its apotheosis in Irvine Welsh's *You'll Have Had Your Hole* (West Yorkshire Playhouse, 1998.) (The title is a colloquialism for having sex.) The play concentrates almost totally on torture, both mental and physical. Dex, a small-time gangster, has been kidnapped by Docksey and Jinks, two other gangsters, in revenge for Dex's double crossing of Docksey in the past. Whilst Laney, Dex's girlfriend, waits to hear from him, the two keep Dex imprisoned in a sound-proofed, disused, recording studio. Whilst Docksey visits Laney, and begins to gain her trust, Dex is left mainly in the hands of Jinks who from the outset uses his homosexuality to scare and threaten Dex.

Here Jinks is a literal representation of a Penetrator. There is another level to the threat however, and it is made clear to the audience, and then to Dex, that Jinks is HIV positive, and shows early AIDS symptoms, and deliberately intends to infect Dex. His threat to rape Dex is ever present, and the terror for Dex reaches new heights when Jinx reveals his HIV status after he has raped him. For the first time on stage, AIDS is now *deliberately* transmitted by a sick (mentally and physically), gay man, and all the early fears of AIDS, all the demonising of gay men are now personified in the character of Jinx. He uses poppers (amyl nitrate) to give them both a 'high' as he carries out the attack, thus bringing a gay representation, (the use of poppers), into the scene. Hard man Dex is completely broken by the rape, but more is to come. Two syringes are brought on by Docksey, one to stun Dex, the other to kill him. Feeling betrayed because Docksey intends to start a new life with Laney, Jinks 'accidentally' injects the killer syringe into Dex and stuns Docksey. The play concludes with Docksey chained up as Dex had been, with Jinks cradling his body.

Drummers

By the time we get to Simon Bennett's *Drummers* (Out of Joint, 1999), audiences appear to have become almost irritated by portrayals of male rape. A 'drummer' is a house-breaker, and Bennett's play concentrates on Ray, just out of prison who returns to drumming, along with his younger brother, Barry. Both battle drug addiction, but resentments between the brothers increase when they are out 'drumming' together, and when Barry steals from Ray, he exacts his revenge not just by simply beating up his brother, but by raping him. Even in the provincial Mercury Theatre in Colchester, in front of a fairly young audience, the rape scene was greeted with irritation. It may have been because theatrically the rape comes out of nowhere, is so obviously just a shock tactic, or it may have been that the hip young crowd had, by now, seen it all before. Whatever the reason, power within families, particularly among siblings, was now represented by rape, anal penetration once again used as a weapon.

Overshadowed by illness, and carrying with it historical and sociological constructions of 'perversity', anal sex was always going to be uncomfortable for many people to see portrayed. Yet as part of a loving relationship, and as a safe way for men to enjoy sex with other men, there was the opportunity for intercourse between men to be staged as an act of love. By the end of the 1990s, however, audiences were more used to seeing men abuse and rape other men than seeing them love each other.

In-Yer-Face-Theatre played into all the heterosexual *and* homosexual anxieties and fears regarding anal penetration, and used rape to once again, as Welsh did, demonise the Person With Aids. This faced audiences away from Kushner's claim that we will be citizens, and confirmd that loving relationships between men would continue to be ghettoised onstage and off. Before this happened, however, there was the opportunity for another form of representation, as shown by the Queer pauses.

As is now clear, the most influential AIDS drama emerged in the early years of the epidemic, when urgent responses created scripts and visuality that have remained emotionally and theatrically important. If *Angels In America* widened mainstream representations of Queer performance, theatre since 1993 has seen the fading of those representations within AIDS drama. Combination therapy, the emphasis on 'living' with the disease, and indeed the possible limitations of theatrical representation, meant that the HIV positive body became less central in 1990s drama as the decade progressed. The Queer male 'ill' body began to move back into alternative representations (see Ron Athey), as Queer representation itself became more firmly established. Mainstream theatre appeared to 'catch up' with some of the underground representations of Queer and AIDS drama.

Ravenhill's Queer Constructions

Mark Ravenhill, in particular, took the representational space bequeathed to him by earlier playwrights and used Queer performitivity to explore his overall and ongoing thesis of the dehumanising effects of capitalism. In Ravenhill's work, everything can be bought or sold, always at the cost of meaningful relationships. His anal gang rape and anal knifing at the end of *Shopping and Fucking* echoes *Night Sweat,* where Richard's threesome with two hunky men is due to end with a knife being plunged into his neck. Richard has *paid* for his death in much the same way that Gary pays for his (assumed) death in *Shopping and Fucking.* Richard, however, is saved from death by the intervention of the safer sex drag nun in Chesley's fable, whereas Gary is assumed to have concluded his death transaction successfully at the end of Ravenhill's.

Shopping and Fucking

Shopping and Fucking begins with Lulu and Robbie trying to get Mark to eat some takeaway food. All the food they eat is either pre-packed or takeaway. Their attempts at self-improvement are shown to be futile in

a series of quick scenes. Mark books into a clinic to try and cure his drug
addiction, but is quickly thrown out when he has sex with a fellow addict.
On the streets he meets Gary, a teenage rent boy, and falls for him. Lulu's
attempt to get a job involves stripping for middle-aged Brian, the only
character with any power (as he has the money and the market), and he
tests her by giving her 300 Ecstasy tablets to sell. Her flatmate Robbie,
however, stoned and idealistic, gives the tablets away in a club. Brian
threatens them with torture, and the two now have to raise the money for
him. They sell telephone sex, and the strands of shopping and fucking
come together when sex becomes a commodity that has to be sold urgently
to save themselves from harm. In an earlier scene, Lulu has witnessed the
stabbing of a female shop assistant in the local newsagent. As she does
phone sex with a punter, she realises he is watching and masturbating to
the CCTV recording of the stabbing, copies of which have quickly found
its way onto the market. It is when Mark brings Gary to the flat to meet the
others, that a game of truth and dare brings to the surface the issue that
anything can be bought and sold.

It is in the character of Gary, the teenage rent boy, that the
extremes of the market are demonstrated. Ravenhill must be credited with
bringing rimming (licking of the arsehole), onto the mainstream stage. In
desperation, Mark buys this from Gary:

> Just a few minutes OK? Thirty quid.
> Just get my tongue up, wriggle it about...
> This isn't a personal thing. It's a transaction, OK?
> (Ravenhill, *Shopping and Fucking,* 2001: v. 26).

When Mark lifts his face from Gary's arse though, there is blood
around (and in) his mouth. Gary's response is to say 'Didn't think that
happened anymore... Thought I'd healed, OK? I'm not infected, OK?'
(Ravenhill: page 24) In scene six, the two become close when Gary tells of
the abuse he endured from his stepfather, hence the bleeding. Gary needs a
Dad, and Mark partially fulfils this role. At the climax of the play, in the
game of truth and dare, Gary reveals his need for abuse. Ravenhill is
careful to make this consensual, Gary asks to be abused. Robbie spits on
his dick and fucks him, then Mark does the same. However, this does not
provide enough for Gary, he wants Mark to be his Dad. And in his fantasy,
Gary is not only blindfolded and fucked by his Dad, his Dad doesn't use
his dick. Gary has won money from the fruit machines, and offers to pay
off their debts if they will penetrate him with a knife, give him a 'good
hurt'. Mark agrees to carry out the transaction, and Gary says:

Are you gonna do it? I want you to do it. Come on. You can do it.
Because he's not out there.
I've got this unhappiness. This big swelling like it's gonna burst.
I'm sick and I'm never gonna be well.
I want it over. And there's only one ending.
He's got no face in the story. But I want to put a face to him. Your face.
Do it. Do it and I'll say I Love You.
(Ravenhill 2001: xiv. 85).

Thus both get what they need from the transaction, Gary using the ultimate bribe of love. At the end of the play, order is restored, as Brian settles his account with Lulu and Robbie, and, inspired by the film *The Lion King*, pronounces his philosophy that 'Money is civilisation'. The play ends with Lulu, Robbie and Mark feeding each other a takeaway, the audience assumes Gary is dead. Here anal sex has become a transaction, and for Ravenhill the extreme transaction, a teenager paying for abuse/death, and a man prepared to do it because that is the only way the object of his affection will tell him he loves him. The characters understand fully the market forces behind this, and whatever pleasure or result they may get from it, they cannot buy feelings, love, fidelity or joy. Anal sex is graphically equated with death at the end of the play, or at the very least with abuse.

Handbag

In *Handbag* (1998), there is an extensive sex scene that not only recalls Chesley, but also takes the black comedy and sexual representation from the pick-up scene in *Angels In America* further. The following exchange echoes a Chesleyesque world, where comedy, sex, and commercial exchange combine in a Queer performance that is inherited from the earlier drama:

Under a bridge. Phil is fucking David. Phil pulls away.
DAVID: No. Don't stop. Don't stop.
PHIL: Fifty quid.
DAVID: I don't   think I... I think you've had... Luncheon vouchers? AMEX?
PHIL: Gotta be cash.
David finds some money.
DAVID: It's all I've got left.
PHIL: ...Alright then.
He carries on fucking David. David's mobile rings.
You gonna get that?

They continue fucking.
I think you'd better get it.
David answers the mobile.
DAVID: Hello? Oh. Hi... I'm sorry that ...I'm busy OK?- Fuck (*To Phil.*)
Don't stop. Don't stop. Oh fuck it. Fuck it.
DAVID: My kid's been born.
More fucking.
PHIL: Yeah?
More fucking.
Boy or girl?
David stops. Pushes last number re-dial.
DAVID: Hi. Me. Boy or girl?
(Ravenhill 1998: *Handbag*, vi.172).

Here we see clearly the extension of the pick-up scene in Kushner's epic, here the fucking is more prolonged and presented more explicitly. The same notions of mutual need are explored, both Phil and David need to achieve something from the transaction, i.e. money and sex, and the phone call adds the layer of comedy that was also present in Kushner's scene. Gay and queer drama paved the way for later playwrights to extend and make more explicit sexual imagery and representation. Again, Ravenhill's characters only feel something is 'real' for them if they can buy it, if a transaction is made. This is developed further in *Some Explicit Polaroids* (Out of Joint, 1999.)

Some Explicit Polaroids

Nick, released from prison after serving fifteen years for a savage attack on Jonathan, a capitalist entrepreneur, finds a society much changed from the one he was excluded from in 1984. His former partner and fellow revolutionary, Helen, is now a New Labour councillor with ambitions to be an MP. As Nick wanders the city he encounters Nadia, a lapdancer who lives by self-help clichés that fail to protect her from her abusive ex-boyfriend, and Tim, an HIV positive man whose boyfriend is Victor, who Tim has 'downloaded' from the Internet, and bought, therefore he owns him to use as he pleases. None of the characters, particularly the younger ones, behave in the way that Nick expects them to. Nadia fails to get angry at her ex- boyfriend for the violent and increasingly frequent attacks he makes on her, instead she clings onto her faith in thinking and acting positively.   Hedonism is central to their lives, Nick feels unable to join in with their frantic and desperate partying. Their claims and insistence that they have 'happy lives' are empty against the realities of domestic violence and HIV infection that confront them. Of interest here is the relationship between Tim and Victor, who has a 'fucking amazing body', and who Tim has bought on condition that no feelings or emotions ever come into their relationship with each other. Victor, who wears a fashionable SM dog collar, is addicted to trash, and when we first see them, it is at the airport where Tim has gone to collect his property. Nadia informs Victor that Tim is ill, and Victor says he doesn't want to be near ill, ugly bodies as he watches Tim take his pills:

> VICTOR: I could be in any country in the world with any guy.
> TIM: But I paid for you. I own you.
> VICTOR: Please. What is it like to be ill?
> TIM: Are you feeling sorry for me?
> VICTOR: No.
> TIM: So what are you feeling?
> VICTOR: Nothing.
> TIM: Good boy, because I warn you, you feel anything, you're out okay? And you pay your own way home.
> (Ravenhill 2001: *Some Explicit Polaroids,* ii. 245).

The negation of feelings is the major aspect of the transaction, to be involved on an emotional level, to indulge in pure hedonism, to have fun. In a later scene, Nick goes to Nadia's flat to find Tim and Victor there. Victor is high on speed, and they have incorporated the combination therapy into their Father/child relationship:

> TIM: Now these are something you wouldn't have seen in nineteen ninety four. These are new. You wouldn't have seen these in nineteen eighty four.
> NICK: What are they?
> TIM: In nineteen eighty four you were calling it a plague, weren't you?
> VICTOR: Yes. Gay plague. Honey. Chug, chug, chug.
> TIM: The story's got a happy ending. That's something you've got to get used to. We've reached 'They all lived happy ever after' and we've gone past it and we're still carrying on. Nobody's ever written that bit before but we're doing it. This is the happy world.
> VICTOR: Yes, happy world.
> (Ravenhill 2001: v. 268).

Here Ravenhill appears to be signing off the effectiveness of HIV as a dramatic device, and with this exchange he wishes to draw a line under AIDS as effective drama, and to explore the other issues that concern him. His preoccupations, always, are with love and consumerism, and throughout his plays he posits the notion that gays have so commodified and trivialised sex that they have rendered it loveless.

Throughout his work, up to and including *Mother Clap's Molly House,* (2001), Ravenhill suggests, from his left-wing perspective, that consumerism and self- indulgence have infected and corrupted the capacity to love.

However, there is an emotional intensity to *Some Explicit Polaroids* that is explored as the desire to be happy and to pursue hedonism begins to feel empty. Tim, feeling that he needs to gain some sort of control over his body, stops taking his medication and is hospitalised. Scene Seven shows Victor caring for Tim, urging him to take his medication, and Nadia and Victor tell Tim that they love him. The only way to persuade him to take his pills is to begin having sex with each other until Tim feels excluded enough to take his medication. In Scene Nine, however, Tim is dead, and Victor rages against him, hitting the body until the ghost of Tim now talks to him. In a sequence that has refrains of Chesley, Tim persuades Victor to masturbate the corpse. The grim humour of this scene is underlined by the tragic sense of loss, and once more contains the ultimate bribe, that of love:

> VICTOR: Please say that you love me. I don't care whether it's true or not. I don't care whether you're lying to me. Please. I just want you to say it.
> TIM: You don't care if it's true?
> VICTOR: A lie is okay. So long as I hear it.
> TIM: That's... pathetic.
> VICTOR: I know.
> TIM: I love you.
> VICTOR: Thank you...
> TIM: ...Move your hand down... Well of   course you're disgusted. But you love me... Maybe I need you or I need someone. To stop me being alone. Alone with this. (*He indicates his erection.*) But don't confuse that with love.
> *Victor starts to masturbate Tim, crying as he does.*
> (Ravenhill 2001: v. 269).

Tim can only admit he loves Victor when Victor can no longer hear him, an admission that arrives too late, and says he will haunt him, 'stalk him.' It is a death scene that avoids the sentimentality and melodramatic devices employed in *The Normal Heart,* yet still achieves emotional intensity. What we see clearly illustrated here is that stage representation of AIDS and gay sexuality created by the Eighties gay playwrights has given Nineties gay playwrights like Ravenhill the opportunity to push that representation.

Faust Is Dead

In his loose adaptation of the Faust legend, *Faust Is Dead* (Actor's Touring Company, tour 1997), Ravenhill explores the relationship between Alain, a high powered academic who quits his university post, and Pete, the disenchanted son of a computer magnate called Bill, a possible reference to Mr Gates. Alain is based on Foucault, and in the play he and Pete journey into the Californian desert, and indulge in sex and drugs, as 'when Foucault was in the States', says Ravenhill, 'he drove to Death Valley with a student and they took LSD and had sex'. (Sierz 2000:.135). Pete introduces Alain to the Internet, and he becomes seduced by it. The play explores the difference between those who intellectualise and those who are studied, or as Ravenhill puts it, 'the meeting of somebody with a very chic notion of violence with people for whom violence is real.' (Ravenhill 2001: 135). Through the Internet they meet Donny, a disturbed boy who cuts himself online for voyeurs. When the three meet, a competition emerges between Donny and Pete as to who has the most scars. As they compete in cutting themselves, filmed by Alain throughout, Donny again is unable to fully appreciate the reality of his position and, intent on winning, he cuts his jugular and dies in front of the other two. Ravenhill here is, obviously, concerned very much with self- mutilation: 'In LA, they told me that cutting has almost taken over from anorexia. People who are powerless find the only thing they can control is their bodies, however perversely'. (Sierz, 2000: 137). But here he is parodying performance art that has actually become a potent form of Queer representation. He continues to say that:

> There's a lot of rather trendy performance art in which people cut themselves,' says Ravenhill, but I find it repulsive.' He is sceptical about 'academic writing about the body and the fascination with piercing', and criticises the attitude that people cutting themselves are somehow 'interesting': usually, 'it just means that there's something deeply wrong. (Sierz 2001: 137).

In particular, Ravenhill is providing a counter-commentary to the intellectualism of performance art theory. However, whilst his opinion may have some relevance regarding the limitations of performance art, his statement may say more about his prejudices towards the genre rather than engaging with the uses of performance art. After all, Ravenhill is a playwright, working within different structures and fields, creating specific narratives. In *Faust Is Dead*, he is bringing alternative representations into mainstream theatrical spaces, and parodying them, but it is in the work of Ron Athey, as I have discussed, that these Queer alternative acts take place, and are culturally relevant.

Works cited

Baker, Roger, *Drag,* London: Cassell, 1994.

Benjamin, Walter, *Illuminations,* London: Fontana Press, 1955.

Bennett, Simon, *Drummers,* London: Nick Hern Books, 1999.

Brenton, Howard, *Plays: Two,* including *The Romans In Britain,* London: Methuen, 1989.

Croft, Giles, *Platform Papers 2: On Angels In America,* London: National Theatre, 1992.

Fisher, James, *The Theatre of Tony Kushner,* New York and London: Routledge, 2002.

Kane, Sarah, *The Complete Plays,* including *Blasted,* London: Methuen, 2001.

Kramer, Larry, *The Normal Heart,* London: Nick Hern Books, 1985.

Kushner, Tony, *Angels In America Part One: Millennium Approaches,* London: Nick Hern Books, 1992.

—. *Angels In America Part Two: Perestroika,* London: Nick Hern Books, 1994.

—. *Thinking About the Longstanding Problems of Virtue and Happiness,* London: Nick Hern Books, 1995.

Neilson, Anthony, *Plays One,* including *Penetrator,* London: Methuen, 1999.

Ravenhill, Mark, *Plays One, Shopping and Fucking, Faust Is Dead, Handbag, Some Explicit Polaroids,* London: Methuen, 2001.

—. *Mother Clap's Molly House,* London: Nick Hern Books, 2001.

Sedgewick, Eve Kosofsky, *Epistemology of the Closet,* New York: Penguin, 1990.

Sierz, Aleks, *In-Yer-Face-Theatre,* London: Faber and Faber, 2000.

Welsh, Irvine, *You'll Have Had your Hole,* London: Methuen, 1998.

CHAPTER FIVE

DID AIDS PARANOIA CLOSE
LA CAGE AUX FOLLES?

SIMON O'CORRA

Synopsis

This chapter will introduce and detail the play 'La Cage aux Folles' and the possible reasons for its closure in 1987. The use of fear and scaremongering about AIDS to socially and sexually control the population will be explored using examples of contemporary media coverage and prior legal theatre censorship cases. It is generally accepted that AIDS paranoia closed La Cage and what is clear is that AIDS became the signifying vehicle by which the dominant culture could transmit its control. However, it was not necessarily the real or only reason for closing the show. Were there other reasons at play? This paper explores some of those other possibilities using camp, queer and transvestite theory.

*****

The philosophy 'Life's not worth a damn till you can say hey I am what I am' has wrought upon this planet a self-inflicted pestilence in which the innocent will perish with the guilty. It is fortunate that the vast majority of the British public remain normal, solid and orthodox and regards sexual deviation as abhorrent.

The Olivier panel has obviously reflected this view and deserves every praise for having the guts to reject *La Cage* from the nominations. *La Cage* is based on a totally unsavoury premise and the sooner it ends the better (The Stage 1986).

La Cage aux Folles is about a long-standing monogamous gay relationship set against the lavish surroundings of a Riviera drag nightclub.

The story is complicated by the arrival of the son of one of the main characters who is intending to marry the daughter of the Deputy Minister for Morality, who at a subsequent visit to the flat above the drag club to meet the boy's parents witnesses a delicious downplaying of the mother by Albin, the male partner of the boys father and a drag artiste. The upshot of the Deputy Minister's visit is that he has to don drag in order to escape the journalists and photographers who have been tipped off that he is at the club. Fundamentally it is a extravagant musical comedy bordering at times on farce. As he did in *Torch Song Trilogy*, Harvey Fierstein – who has adapted the book from Jean Poiret's play – pleads for tolerance towards homosexuals, but here it comes across in such a sweet sugary mixture that no one will take offence. (London Weekly Diary of Social Events 1986).

This chapter is not an exhaustive study as the show operates on so many levels it would be impossible to encompass all elements that contributed to its closure in the space of one chapter. So why choose *La Cage aux Folles*? This multi-faceted show is a crucible through which one can examine what is going on in society. It raises many questions about what is 'normal' and what is 'abnormal' and successfully blurs the boundaries between the two in its form and content.

The Birdcage, a 1996 remake of the 1978 film *La Cage aux Folles*, which garnered mixed reviews from both the mainstream and gay media, may at least have contributed to the revival of the play on Broadway in 2004, where it received rave reviews again. *La Cage aux Folles* was a successful play on Broadway garnering awards there and running for four years.

Upon its transfer to the West End in London it could have fully expected a repeat of the accolades heaped upon it in the States. Also on 17 April 1986 'the La Cage producers had also relented to a Gay Switchboard request for a gay night on 2nd May' (The Stage 1986). This is at least a tacit acknowledgment of the plays importance to the gay community. Therefore there were strong contra-indicators to the shows closure. Yet close the London production did and after less than a year.

La Cage aux Folles is based on a French film hit born of a long-running French farce about the troubles of two middle aged homosexuals. The critics described it as a slick, carefully-packed musical designed to offend no one willing to pay up to 45 dollars for a ticket. (Evening Post 1983).

However, it has been suggested that there was very practical reason for the show's closure in the UK. Europe including the United Kingdom was passing through a phase of anti-Americanism occasioned by Ronald Reagan's clumsy and petulant response to Europe's refusal to agree to the sanctions he wished to impose on Libya. Mr Reagan dissuaded Americans from going to Europe on the pretext that it was unsafe to do so. This meant that the shows profitability could have been affected. La Cage was abandoned ostensibly because of a fall in takings in the early part of 1987 and because of the AIDS Crisis according to its producer. In the case of La Cage its producers were businessmen and any risk to profitability had to be scrutinised carefully. Louis Benjamin, the producer of La Cage, in a television interview focussed mainly on falling box-office figures and the AIDS crisis but said interestingly enough that they had had only a few complaints about the show. In contrast in the same television programme one of the Cagelles, a drag chorus character, said that they had had loads of complaints.

So what caused the furore and led to the closure of this show? Well the show was situated within the framework of the dominant hetero-centrist culture and was therefore subject to its rules

> Cultural heterosexism is the stigmatization, denial or denigration of non-heterosexuality in cultural institutions ranging from the church to the courthouse. Psychological heterosexism is a person's internalisation of this worldview, which erupts into antigay prejudice. Here, we define heterosexism as a belief in the superiority of heterosexuals or heterosexuality evidenced in the exclusion, by omission or design, of non-heterosexual persons in the policies, procedures, events or activities. We include in our definition not only lesbians and gay men but other sexual minorities such as bisexuals and transgender persons as well (James T. Sears 1997).

The quote at the beginning of this chapter is ambiguous in that it is not clear whether the correspondent is talking about 'gay lifestyles' or 'AIDS or both as they can be confluent and used as a double discrimination tool against gay men particularly by the Media, itself a tool of the dominant heterosexual culture. From where does such vituperative language spring? Here is venomous AIDS paranoia backed by a hetero-centric certainty and led by an irrational fear.

The correspondent is clear in his language of discrimination that the epidemic (be it AIDS or homosexuality) is in fact a pestilence (plague) of global proportions where no one is safe. Simply said La Cage and gays should not exist. But, if AIDS is purely a gay plague as he seems to think surely his fear of a pestilence feeding on the innocent is nonsense taking into account Alfred Kinsey's spectrum of sexuality and the results of a study undertaken in 1985 and commented on in The Daily Mirror: 'Two in five men "have had gay affairs"' (The Daily Mirror 1985).

AIDS coverage by the media seems to have worked its magic on

Mr. Tunstall and all on such flimsy evidence. He is clearly a victim of the media's success in scaring and controlling populations. Below are just a few of the many headlines that appeared from 1981 to 1986:

Headline	Publication	Date
Scourge of the Gays	Time Out	18/12/81
AIDS: The price of promiscuity?	The Daily Telegraph	26/04/83
Alert over 'gay plague'	Daily Mirror	02/05/83
The 'gay' scene, which has added its share to the total sexual licence of our day, now produces an AIDS situation..........	The Yorkshire Post	07/05/83
Gay bug kills gran	The Sun	14/06/83
Menace that looms in Britain	The Sunday People	24/07/83
Tide of fear	Daily Mirror	18/05/85
AIDS – the horror that threatens us all	Oxford Mail	23/08/86
TOWNS OF TERROR – Everyone is at risk – AIDS, the most feared disease of the 1980's, is out of control	The Sun	04/11/86
AIDS: Cabinet fear violence in the Streets – grim faced ministers emerged from a cabinet meeting yesterday fearful that the killer plague AIDS will spark violence on the street of Britain. The prospect of bloodshed as terrified citizens make 'reprisal' attacks on homosexuals and drug addicts is now seen as a real threat	The Sun	21/11/86
AIDS The Deadly Threat	Daily Record	22/11/86
Halting the Holocaust	Daily Mirror	24/11/86
Maggie's Rap for gay outcasts – Gays and drug addicts were slammed by	The Star	03/12/86

Mrs Thatcher last night. She warned them that their behaviour was no longer socially acceptable.		
Virus victims 'swirling in cesspit of their own making' Spread of AIDS blamed on 'degenerate conduct'	The Daily Telegraph, Speech by James Anderton, Chief Constable of Greater Manchester	12/12/86

So where did the heterosexism and homophobia engendered in the Media of the time come from? The free love and political agitation of the 1960's had led to a need for the State to take control and was backed by a predominantly conservative press baying for blood after the decriminalisation of Homosexuality in the Sexual Offences Act of 1967, the Act had not only benefited gay men but made enormous and to many, unacceptable shifts in British Culture, amounted at this time in an upsurge in the dominance of moralising groups concerned with live theatre and television such as The Viewers and Listeners Association (VALA) founded in 1965 by Mary Whitehouse.

In talking of the arguments over the possible causes of AIDS and the Media/Governments responses to it in the early 1980's Michael Tracey says that

> The media, in so far as they were aware of these arguments, apparently found it nigh on impossible to deal with them. Instead, and partly at the government behest, they adopted a somewhat paradoxical position. On the one hand they were playing off homophobia, and moralising, and suggesting that this was a gay plague. On the other, they were pursuing the line that dominated the education campaigns that we are all at risk. Posters on billboards in Britain urged people not to 'die of ignorance' (Michael Tracey 2001)

Whether the theory that the government of the time was leading an exercise in control or whether it was operating from ignorance about an epidemic the nature of which opposing factions are still arguing, but the effects may be the same.

Enabling non-gay people to point the finger at gay men as the cause of the AIDS epidemic the British media nevertheless continued to hold the whole population in thrall to terror which culminated in the bringing into law of Section 28 of the Local Government Act 1988 which prohibited Local Authorities from intentionally promoting homosexuality in schools.

Mr Tunstall is clearly operating from this newly manufactured cultural norm and the attacks that the mainstream culture faces from every side particularly from the sexual deviant.

Such is the power of heterosexism that even a well known gay playwright can turn on his own when Larry Kramer the writer of The Normal Heart a play about AIDS suggested that

> gay liberation had spawned an overflowing of promiscuity that brought the plague down on the heads of gay men (The Stage 1986).

Proof indeed of the effectiveness of heterosexual mainstream culture in promulgating internalised homophobia. So it seems that even gay men were hoodwinked into believing the sensationalist, reactionary and fatalistic message about AIDS.

Clearly the triumvirate of AIDS, deviant sex and irrational fear that the media uses to sell newspapers and television programming was a more combustible mixture for the detractors of La Cage in 1986/87, than it had been in previous legal cases. This is because the play could not be regarded legally as obscene, a fact which I explain later.

In the twenty first century the view of AIDS is evolving with many experts overturning previously held and entrenched beliefs about the nature of AIDS and its causes. However, back at the beginning of the AIDS epidemic in the early 1980's it was a convenient whipping tool to beat homosexuals with. No one knew enough about AIDS to challenge the narrow view of the Media. These factors led to a heightened level of scaremongering both practiced in the Media and experienced by the whole population at this time. The hysterical paranoia had an effect on the cultural life of gay theatre professionals and theatre going public for a considerable time to come.

> A more recent analysis by Deborah Lupton, in a book published last year concluded: 'AIDS reporting in western nations has invoked imagery associated with homophobia, fear, violence, contamination, invasions, vilification, racism, sexism, deviance, heroicism and xenophobia.' (Michael Tracey 2001).

Most of the words used above by Michael Tracey in quoting from Deborah Lupton's analysis to describe AIDS reporting are reflected in the feelings expressed by the Minister of Morality in La Cage. His character was probably the one with whom the likes of Mr Tunstall et al most closely identified when calling for the show's closure.

During the mid -1980's AIDS became the defining standard of gay life as portrayed in the media. Gay men were judged purely on their ability to infect others with AIDS. The spread of AIDS had been brought about through fact based and, more importantly, moral panic and fear in the minds of the public fed by the media, most of which was aimed at gays as potential carriers of disease. The moral high ground was achieved by the mainstream and heterocentrist culture and as AIDS research was in its infancy there was little opportunity in the gay community and elsewhere to challenge contemporary received knowledge about the disease's provenance and coverage. Therefore heterocentrist culture did what it does best and sermonized about and demonized gay men and their lifestyle from on high.

The comparison between the warm gay family in La Cage and the cold puritanical family epitomised by the staunch moralising factions in British culture is complete. A celebration of gayness, camp, drag, alternative families and a freedom of expression is perhaps what hetero-normative culture fears most even more than AIDS.

Quite a few cases had been brought during the 1970's and early 1980's against theatre productions that had a gay or homo-erotic content. The groups and individuals that brought the cases used various laws to achieve their ends of conservatism and bigotry. However, the law that one may have expected to be used was in fact anti-puritan in its nature, The Theatres Act 1968 which replaced the system of censorship operated by the Lord Chamberlain's office meant that La Cage aux Folles could not be easily challenged in law by bigots just because of its gay but non obscene content

> It is necessary to get the Attorney General's approval before prosecuting under the Theatre's Act, and to date there has been only one such prosecution. (Charlotte Vincent www.lawcf.org/dox_102.pdf)

The Theatre's Act potentially blocks the bigots and moralists route to prosecution. Another way had to be found to close down La Cage as the law was unlikely to favour the bringing of a case purely because a play had two gay characters. Imagine the ease with which La Cage's detractors could have closed the show down had the 1968 Theatres Act not been on the statute books.

Let us look at the precedents for the opprobrium that La Cage faced. Only six years previously in 1980 a new play The Romans in Britain by Howard Brenton commissioned by Peter Hall for the National Theatre and directed by Michael Bogdanov opened to a 'howl of execration' (Sutherland 1982).

The main problem with the play and that which gave rise to the now famous court case instigated by Mary Whitehouse using a loophole in the Sexual Offences Act (1956) was the alleged procuring by Bogdanov of the two actors for an act of gross indecency i.e. simulated buggery and rape. It is interesting to note that the play's main themes were of racism and colonialism, not something that Mrs Whitehouse saw fit to complain about. Mrs Whitehouse was able to bring so many cases to court because there was at the time a great deal of resentment against gays since homosexuality had been decriminalised in 1967. With new gay rights had come new powers and not everyone appreciated that fact.

Another private prosecution for blasphemous libel was brought by Mary Whitehouse against Gay News which had printed a poem by James Kirkup entitled 'The Love that Dares Speak its Name' with an illustration of the dead Christ with 'tuberous cock and balls' being lowered by a Roman soldier.

> Deviant sex and blasphemy was a more combustible mixture than mere obscenity (protected by the 1959 law) mere homosexuality (protected by the 1967 law) or mere blasphemy (protected by the tradition of freethinking dissent against which no British authority had dared take action for 50 years (Sutherland 1982).

It is important to deconstruct in brief the other components that may have had an impact on the dominant culture's decision to victimise this fine piece of traditional musical theatre. It was not only a victim of AIDS paranoia but other factors as well.

To better understand the queer nature and theoretical base of La Cage aux Folles and its closure it is crucial to recognise the nature of the hetero-normative functioning when undertaking research in a culture that has a hetero-sexist bias. It can be hard to get beyond the hetero-centrist nature of the mainstream culture and the tools it uses to sustain its position. Firstly, queer theory was invented only very recently. The Act of Sodomy was criminalised in the latter half of the mid–nineteenth century but the emphasis was subsequently switched from a physical act to a homosexual person. This switch in definition has enabled the dominant culture to reduce gay men to a medical construct where they can define and pathologise them as 'abnormal', thereby reinforcing their 'normality' and continue focussing on them as sexually deviant and confined to pathological models of sexual desire. Despite this philosophical and medical shift the act of sodomy is still assumed to be the only thing that marks out a gay man from a straight man in many people's mind. Mainstream theatre, which reflects heterosexist culture, has used this premise to reinforce the view that heterosexuality extends beyond the bounds of sex acts in a way that homosexuality does not. This effectively keeps gay people in a place of being only 'sexual beings'. Further, if homosexuality is abnormal what hope for gay people to have a gay sensibility and/or culture acknowledged by the mainstream or 'normal' culture?

La Cage aux Folles fundamentally challenges the ideal of a modern nuclear heterosexual family unit, a dogma upheld by Government and Moral Crusaders of the time in the form of the 'chill factor' a way of the Government exercising control by informally extending their legislation relating to pornography to encompass mainstream broadcasting and I believe by inference the performing arts. Much behind the scenes Government pressure was brought to bear on broadcasters who were programming politically and morally sensitive dramas and documentaries. As previously mentioned Mrs Thatcher's public and moralistic jibe against gays and drug addicts in December 1986 was another form of social control without the backing of legislation and came at about the time that the closure of La Cage was announced (Bill Thompson, 1991). The show obviously deeply challenged this doctrine of family values' in an extravagant and forceful way and by countering what Eve Kosofsky Sedgwick (1990) talks of as the 'Open Secret' nature of the 'Closet', that which keeps homosexuals in a perpetual binary of opacity and transparency, a perfect control mechanism and with a resulting cultural effect.

'Gay identity is fundamentally shaped by the dualism of secrecy and disclosure, but since 'telling' is both prohibited and required, queer identity is always an internal contradiction between opacity and transparency, at once hidden and revealed' (Glick 2001: 129-163).

Some of the ways in which La Cage challenges that control mechanism can be found in the fact that it has a gay male character who is not only a father but a good one with a well-rounded and loving son, a family unit along with his male partner which apes the hetero-normative ideal. The partner Albin, a drag artiste revels in and is unapologetic about cross-dressing and role swapping and this challenges the mainstream culture's core beliefs and understandings about what makes a man and a woman. Another confusing and challenging element in the plays content and the mainstream culture's response to it is the depiction of a homonormative monogamous relationship between the two men which exploded the contemporary stereotype that all gay men are promiscuous and disease carriers. The flip side to these challenges is that of the straight-laced and uptight character who as Deputy Minister of Morality is hounded by the media who are baying for blood because of his bosses' death whilst in the company of an underage prostitute, something all 'Family Values' exponents most fear and are in most danger of.

I believe, it may be the form rather than just the content of the show that is of primary importance in understanding the negative reactions of some people who became determined to close the show down. By this I mean its High Camp form which when coupled with the highly subversive content for its time may give an answer to the riddle of why La Cage was closed down.

La Cage it has been said before is a High Camp extravaganza. It is a mix of artifice, frivolity, gentle excess, a kind of naïve middle class pretentiousness and a serious portrayal and exploration of relationships, families and hypocrisy, some of which are key elements of Camp as described by Susan Sontag in 1964, namely that camp is inspired by a sexual fascination expressed by bending genders and unseating the earnest in its lighthearted approach to serious issues and often by celebrating the 'awful'.

La Cage explores gender stereotypes and bending. La Cage has as one of its main characters Albin who is a drag artiste and the play is predominantly set in a Drag club. Carl Jung (Anderson, 2001) maintained that transvestism is the secondary gender expression coming out from a repressed male who has held down his feminine instincts in order to be accepted in his culture. It is not clear why Albin chooses to cross-dress in his performance but it is easy to see how certain audience members would be disturbed by this show if they too have repressed their secondary gender responses. Albin's portrayal is High Camp drag offering a serious idealised portrayal of a diva that makes for a high degree of audience popularity with gay men, some of who may stifle these expressions in themselves but appreciate them in another, and some women. Of course this not necessarily true for heterosexual men, conservative women or feminists. If audiences were challenged about their own gender expression, by a play which used serious High Camp as its vehicle, it is easy to understand why they were so venomous in their attacks on the show at a time when they are being told to be scared of a plague spread by the very kind of people they are witnessing on stage.

La Cage uses an old genre of the comical and unreal stage musical to play with ideas of Camp, Queer and Drag. In doing this it explodes the stultifying views of the conservative, moralizing and controlling institutions peopled by the few in a position of power who seek to control and to maintain their share of the market by creating fear underpinned by cloying dictates about how we should all lead our lives.

The Deputy Minister of Morality exposes his campness when

expounding his limiting and bigoted views and his cross-dressing in order to escape La cage is unexpected and also awful.

Clearly La Cage in its High Camp form does fulfil Baudrillard's (1999) view of cultural forms of expression as being a catalyst for reasoned debate and discussion by the mainstream culture on more than one of its minority groupings and their complexities. However, the High Camp used in La Cage alongside its depiction of a homonormative relationship also challenges members of the heteosoexual mainstream with its unnerving and offbeat dualism of humour and seriousness.

La Cage is a surprise even a shock on many levels and this may have impacted on its premature closure occasioned by 'fear' and 'control' exercised over the rituals of mass culture.

As Foucault says 'If you want to be an equal part of a straight world by proving how ordinary, how 'just-like-you' (but perhaps a bit more sensitive or artistic) you are, it simply won't do to flaunt your more excessive, transgressive desires or relations' (Spargo 1999: 31)

Other shows fell victim to this 'fear' and 'control' including 'The Normal Heart' mentioned earlier and the 'March of the Falsettoes' these closures were due in part to the perception that British audiences were not ready for the show's anti-establishment message and especially in the context of the AIDS paranoia of the time.

La Cage aux Folles is unapologetic about the identities and personalities of two men and with its signature tune 'I am what I am' is 'in one's face' about homosexuality, its expression and the fundamental freedom of choice we have to be who we are. In the telling of these identities too the main protagonists and the producers, writers and directors of the show face a double bind. It is ok to be 'out and proud' but how that information is received is dependent on the mainstream culture's narrow prescriptive view of homosexuals and homosexuality and its place in the dominant hetero-centrist culture. Homosexuals can define themselves as well-rounded human beings but often they are judged primarily on their sex lives rather than the other positive things they bring to the culture as lesbians and gay men. Also non- homosexuals may have a salacious interest in gay sex lives but when gay men tell them they gay this immediately conjure sexual images in their minds e.g. coming out over dinner or on stage in a musical.

Judith Butler explains it further:

> Homosexual conduct, defined as 'a statement that the member is homosexual or bisexual'; in this definition the 'statement' is a form of 'conduct,' .... If the statement is conduct, and it is homosexual conduct, then the statement that one is a homosexual is constructed as

acting homosexually on the person to whom or before whom it is uttered. The statement is in some sense not only an act, but a form of conduct, a ritualistic form of speech that wields the power to be what it says, not a re- presentation of a homosexuality, but a homosexual act and, hence, an offence (Butler 1997 : 112).

Therefore, this 'coming-out' can feel like a sexual act played out in all manner of situations that had previously no or little sexual ambience. Pair this with one aspect of theatre i.e. live performance in front of an audience often made up of strangers that can most frighten individual members of any given audience and you have a recipe for strong reactions to be brought to the fore. So we have content and form of a piece of theatre coupled with the art form itself (another triumvirate). Finally two positive responses can be found one in letter from one of the stars of La Cage aux Folles in response to Mr Tunstall's at the head of this paper and the other in a review

> Your correspondent Mr Tunstall who praises the Laurence Olivier awards panel for excluding La Cage from the nominations because of its homosexual themes has allowed his very natural fear of AIDS to lead him into paranoia and bigotry.
> Firstly it is now surely common knowledge that AIDS is not exclusively a homosexual disease – in Africa for example the proportion of men and women victims is approximately equal. We are all in this here.
> Secondly nowhere does La Cage condone promiscuity on the contrary it strongly advocates fidelity and monogamy and the tolerant loving acceptance of people of differing lifestyles from one's own precisely the human qualities needed at this time or indeed anytime.
> Lastly though it would not be surprising to a read a letter of this crude and vindictive nature in certain areas of the daily press, it is sad to see it given such prominence in a paper with some pretensions to being the house journal of a profession which could scarcely exist without the contribution of the gifted homosexuals who have always been and hopefully always will be among its most brilliant members. It is of course just possible that the jury did not nominate La Cage because they did not consider it to be one of the four best musicals of the year, I am bound to disagree of course but I prefer that interpretation of events to Mr Tunstall's (The Stage 1986).

In addition and from a different angle a report in The Daily Mirror in the previous year presaged what we now know to be true about AIDS in the 21st century, namely that by far the largest number of sufferers of the disease were likely to be heterosexuals.

I have detailed just a few of the possible reasons why La Cage aux

Folles, a successful musical on the West End stage closed after only seven months and on the slim official premise of a fall in box office receipts over the Christmas period 1986, something experienced by most shows at that time. Of course as I have mentioned earlier there may be other political/practical issues at stake here. It seems that moral indignation may have had at least something to do with the closure. AIDS hysteria had been whipped up so much that even a well-rounded and positive portrayal of gay monogamous life such as La Cage was suspect but obviously had no connection to AIDS whatsoever. How can a monogamous gay relationship be associated with the gay plague apparently occasioned by promiscuity? Homophobia may be at play here with its underlying assumption that promiscuity is synonymous with being gay and we all know promiscuity leads to AIDS.

So did AIDS Paranoia close La Cage aux Folles? It would seem to be over simplistic to say so. This paper points towards a possible disingenuous use of AIDS by the Media and perhaps the British government as a pretext to halt the ever burgeoning sexual and gender revolution signposted by a play like La Cage. It is a shame that such a fine piece of theatre was hounded out of the West End at a time when the gay community and the individuals in it needed just one positive celebration of who they were in the midst of the horrors of AIDS and such brutal discrimination. Therefore, the story of the closure of the gay play La Cage aux Folles is shocking.

Postscript

Interestingly La Cage has not been performed in the West End since 1986. Would it be closed down now if it was revived. The show was recently revived on Broadway to excellent reviews and yet more awards. It is possible that what for many years was the acceptable face, in the hetero-centrist culture, of homosexuality i.e. camp, effeminate and drag/gender-bending based, has finally been broken down. This portrayal could also make the show unacceptable to a gay community rushing towards integration into hetero-normative society by accepting the rituals of heterosexuality. This creates a hierarchy within the gay community of those who are civilly partnered and those who are either partnered but not civilly or those who are single. Let's not talk about 'homosexuality' just 'same sex civil partners'. This means there is no room for 'I am what I am' because you can't be who you want to be anymore, you are honorary heterosexuals because you exist within our rules now not yours.

The institutions of middle England, conservative bigots and the conformist and conventional West End theatre scene both had the capacity to exclude and omit those art works that caused too much trouble, risked destroying the status quo or could affect profits. Could such a closure happen now? With the developments in globalization lesbians and gay men can now find a partial acceptance through the increased knowledge base of the world at large and lesbians and gay men in particular. The downside of this upsurge in knowledge dissemination through this 'total' medium is that the State now has yet another way of socially controlling populations and It seems nothing much changes when we consider the 21st century's War on Terror.

However, we now know that AIDS is a killer of more heterosexuals than homosexuals worldwide contrary to the view held in the middle of the 1980's that it was a homosexual plague. But back then a reactionary Media aided by political and moral conservatism played on this assumption to such good effect that La Cage, such a visible expression of 'queerness' inevitably fell prey to bigotry, intolerance and heterosexism.

Acknowledgements

Thanks to Lesbian and Gay Newsmedia Archive, Middlesex University, Cat Hill Campus, Barnet EN4 8HT for the newspaper quotes.

Works cited

Butler, Judith, *Excitable Speech, A Politics of the Performative*. New York & London, Routledge, 1997.

Glick, Elisa, 'The Dialectics of Dandyism' Cultural Critique, 2001.

Horrocks, Chris and Jevtic, Zoran, *Introducing Baudrillard*. USA, Totem Books, 2000.

Kosofsky-Sedgwick, Eve, *The Epistemology of the Closet*, USA, University of California Press, 1990.

London Weekly Diary of Social Events, 1986.

Sears, James. T, *Overcoming Heterosexism and Homophobia, Strategies that work, Thinking Critically/Intervening Effectively about Heterosexism and Homophobia: A twenty-five-year research perspective*, 1997, USA, Colombia University Press, 1997.

Spargo, Tamsin, *Foucault and Queer Theory*. UK, Icon Books Ltd, 1999.

Sutherland, John, Offensive Literature, June 1976: 'The Well Hung Christ' – Gay News, Blasphemy and the Funny Bone of Society. UK Junction Books Ltd, 1982.

—. Offensive Literature, October 1980-March 1982: 'Buggering Celts the

Romans In Britain'.UK Junction Books Ltd, 1982.

Thompson, Bill, *Moral Crusades and Media Censorship*, Libertarian Alliance, London, UK, Sociological Notes No.11, 1991.

Tracey, Michael, 'Mere Smoke of Opinion; AIDS and the making of the public mind', Michael Tracey, Continuum Volume 6/No.3 Summer/Autumn 2001.

Newspaper Reviews

Evening Post, 1983
Evening Standard, 1983
The Daily Mirror, 1985.
The Daily Mirror, 1985
The Stage, 1986, Letter from Mr. Tunstall to the editor.
The Stage, 1986
The Stage, 1986
The Stage, 1986, A letter from Dennis Quilley.
The Stage, 1986
The Stage 1987

Websites

Anderson, Catherine, 2001, Jung's Anima Theory and How it Relates to Crossdressing, Accessed Dec. 2005.

Cathy_L_Anderson@yahoo.com. Accessed Dec 2005.

Charlotte Vincent, (Current), Briefing on current UK laws on Obscenity and Related Areas, Public Policy Analyst, Lawyers' Christian Fellowship, www.lawcf.org/dox_102.pdf. Accessed Dec 2005.

Wikipedia, Sontag, Susan, Notes on Camp, from Partisan Review, 1964. Accessed Dec 2005.

CHAPTER SIX

DAYS GONE BY: TRACKING AIDS THEATRE AND QUEER PERFORMANCE

PAUL T. DAVIES

Synopsis

This chapter begins with an analysis of Robert Chesley, an American queer playwright whose queer discourses made his contribution to the genre of AIDS drama controversial and visionary. I will then discuss non - queer responses to the AIDS crisis, in particular Kramer's The Normal Heart, before illustrating the influence of Chesley's theatre in My Night With Reg by the British playwright Kevin Elyot, Jeffrey by the American Paul Rudnick, and on the work of the American performance artist Ron Athey.

*****

Early stage constructions regarding AIDS, and queer performances, were taking shape before queer theory became established within the Academy at the beginning of the 1990s. These constructions reflected more alternative queer practices, including sexual behaviour, that were part of the homosexual community when AIDS struck. AIDS was the force that galvanised the writing of the drama, particularly to challenge homophobic representations of the 'sick' gay man, and, for queer writers, to place centre stage gay sexuality and its many varieties and to convey educative messages regarding safer sex and gay pride in its concerned community.

Night Sweat

It was against this background that the first full-length American play about AIDS, *Night Sweat,* by Robert Chesley, (1943 - 1990), was produced. Thompson praises Chesley as a visionary playwright who understands the ecstatic, spiritual experience of gay S and M sex. (Thompson 1991: xx). Written in 1983, and in contrast to one act 'message' plays of the period, *Night Sweat* opened at the Shandol Theatre in New York on May 24th 1984, almost a year before Hoffman's *As Is* and Kramer's *The Normal Heart*, plays mistakenly thought of as the first-full length AIDS dramas. That it wasn't duly acknowledged as the first was mainly due to its sexual representation, and Baker notes: 'its subject matter also kept it from the mainstream media attention that the other two plays enjoyed. *Night Sweat* was also more shocking in its sexual content, including several scenes of simulated gay sex.' (Baker 1994: 184).

In *Night Sweat*, gay men join the Coup de Grace Club, paying $10,000 for the privilege to do so. The Club is run by The Director (an obvious theatrical term, and appropriate within the meta-theatrical dimensions of performance within the text), and the men who join have paid to have themselves killed, to have the Ultimate Experience. All the members are HIV positive, or have AIDS, even though the word is unspoken during the course of the play. Each 'Experience' that is performed in front of the audience becomes increasingly graphic in its representation. The play opens with a hanging, the body is described pissing himself as he 'shivers in wonderful spasms.' Chesley's central character, Richard, has joined the Club as he cannot face his death from AIDS. He has seen his lover, Michael, succumb to the disease, and this has numbed Richard's emotions. He cannot use the word love, instead referring to 'passionate relationships' and throughout the play Richard is confused as how best to exit, in essence, reflecting his whole uncertainty about the Club.

The Experiences staged build in explicitness and become increasingly theatrical. The hanging at the play's opening introduces the notion of sexual pleasure in 'watersports' (sex play involving urine), and, with death occurring at the moment of sexual climax, immediately establishes the equation sex = death. There follows a card game in which the loser is strangled and his corpse shot. A Western gunfight in which the bad guy is literally killed deals with the iconography of the cowboy, and is an appropriate analogy as Westerns are based largely around concepts of Otherness. (See Hart, 2005: 15). An episode of *'Ratman and Bobin'* explores the allure of the comic book Superhero, and the bad guy,

Hornetman, is 'really' electrocuted. (The gay man has, of course, cast himself in the role of the bad guy, the outlaw and outsider, aligning homosexuality with Otherness). Moving away from these masculine, 'straight acting' scenarios, the alleged love of opera by the gay men is explored at the climax of *Lucia di Lammermoor*, in which 'she', the homosexual man playing the tragic heroine, 'really' stabs herself. Whilst in the Club, Richard meets Tom, and they spend a night together. As a political activist, Tom has chosen, as his Ultimate Experience, to be queer bashed, to be attacked and murdered on the streets. It is going to be 'so ugly it will get attention', he will be stripped naked and have the word AIDS carved into his body over and over again. The Director has relaxed the 'No Exit' rule to allow this to happen, and it is not depicted on stage. It introduces into the play an element of activism, an acknowledgment that gay men were beginning to group together to take action.

Richard's exit choice is revealed as Terminal Sex, to be murdered whilst enjoying sex with two other men. Prior to this scene, though, Richard's friend Alan has broken into the Club to try and persuade Richard to change his mind. This reveals that Richard secretly wants to live, but Alan fails to rescue him from the belief that death from AIDS is inevitable. For Richard's Experience, a seedy Nightclub is reproduced, and against a background of loud disco music, Richard is seduced by two Hunky Men. The stage directions are explicit and homoerotic. At the (literal) climax of the scene, one of the Hunky Men raises a dagger to murder Richard as he reaches orgasm. Then the whole tone and nature of the play is reversed. Tom has not been queer bashed, but now he and the 'queer bashers' are revealed as gay activists as they burst into the Club, filling the stage with sunlight, all of them dressed as nuns. In this celebration of drag and activism, the pessimism of the inmate's situation is overturned as Richard is saved and Tom delivers a safer sex massage to characters and audience alike.

> Sister wants you to think about what a beautiful thing it is that one man can love another! And think how hard we have fought together so that can be so!...But meanwhile you're going to live! Live until the moment you die! And make love! Make love in every possible, safe and sensible way! Enjoy it all, from the most delicate cruising to the heaviest S and M trips! (Chesley, 1990: *Night Sweat*, II, vii. 66).

However, Chesley does not completely sweeten the play's pill. The final Experience is acted by Bunny, who will disco dance himself to death in the Dance of Death. Interesting to note that the Club goes on, there is no scene depicting its closure. As the music and dancing reach a crescendo, Bunny changes his mind, and the final image is of a young gay man screaming 'I don't want to die!' over and over again at the audience.

The Club becomes a metaphor for society at large, prepared to condemn the men to death, suggesting that death is the only course and option open to gay HIV positive men. Produced in a climate of great despair and fear, not only does this attitude presuppose that there is little hope for the 'ill', the play also challenges taboos of sadomasochism and the so called 'darker' areas of gay sex. Although gay sexuality, sensuality, and the wide variety of gay sex enjoyed by men is what Chesley foregrounds in his plays, sexual gratification is *not* a criteria or a goal in these plays, despite the textual or dramatic content, or in some audience responses.

Chesley finds comparison with another queer outsider and playwright, Genet. Similar, albeit from a different (textual) sexual perspective, to Genet's *The Balcony*, Chesley's script plays with fantasy and reality. Genet creates a world within a brothel where every fantasy is fulfilled, and powerful men, such as The Judge, The Bishop and The Chief of Police, indulge themselves in role play and performing alternative scenarios to their real life roles. The characters make repeated references to the revolution taking place off stage, and as the play progresses, each character performs in fantasy a version of the reality taking place outside. Genet's brothel setting allows the clients the opportunity to act out their fantasies of power, whilst the outside world descends into revolution and chaos. I am not suggesting here that Genet is a polar opposite to Chesley, for, although he depicts a heterosexual brothel, the playwright definitely has a queer worldview, and the linkage of sexuality to power is pertinent. Genet also clearly establishes sexual and political hypocrisy, and there are fascinating parallels between the two writers. *The Balcony* is, essentially, a series of rituals and the then debunking of those rituals, as Genet plays with issues of power and sex, domination and submission, and the power of the state. All this is explored in *Night Sweat*, the state being in Chesley's drama the power of heterosexist society.

The Chief of Police in *The Balcony*, like the Director in *Night Sweat*, is aware that power lies in domination of people's minds, not simply through torture and physical superiority: thus ritual is *essential* to maintain that dominance. Chesley uses ritual in a very similar way to Genet, with 'incantation, magical substitution, and identification... the essential elements of ritual' (Esslin, 1961: p. 233), but develops the 'role play' to a death- fulfilling conclusion for most of his characters. Like *The Balcony*, in many ritualistic scenes in *Night Sweat* there are no characters as such, but are basically the imagery of urges and impulses, particularly in sadomasochistic staging. For Edmund White, Genet reaches the apotheosis of his 'exploration of the sadomasochistic potential of power relationships' in the opening tableau of *The Balcony,* in the "whorehouse enactment's of the judge and the criminal, the bishop and the penitent sinner and the general and his horse (a bridled prostitute).' (White 1993: 423). Devices are similar in *Night Sweat,* the ritualistic scenes are based on 'disguise' and the donning of alternative selves, and the device of a play (let) within a play allows the tragicomedy of unfulfilled desire, (until that is, in Chesley, the moment of death). Like Genet, Chesley explores illusion and authenticity to expose 'the social dynamics of power.' (White 1993: 423). Both create male characters who conform to certain notions of machismo that have long been templates of sexual attraction for many gay men, (the muscled, cropped, hairy, rough, uniformed, I refer particularly here to Genet's film *Un Chant D'amour*), and *Night Sweat* examines these machismo constructions.

In both *The Balcony* and *Night Sweat,* the participants are sometimes confused, as the division between the outside world and their enclosed space is often blurred. Chesley is developing queer notions of performativity explored earlier by Genet, and I find interesting an anecdote from White that Genet, in his re-writing of *The Balcony,* cut a scene involving three handsome young men representing sperm, tears and blood. (White 1993: 417). Chesley represents these fluids constantly, and more graphically, in his drama, the blood and semen being, in most cases, HIV positive.

In *Night Sweat,* each Experience consists of characters 'acting' a part to satisfy another character's fantasy. Workers in, and members of, the Club negotiate together to perform death scenarios chosen by the member, a sort of 'Deathstyle' choice. The issue of the performative is essential here, as the actors perform the characters performing Chesley's queer 'Experiences'. It is significant that the emergence of an interest in the performative developed alongside the issue of AIDS. 'The AIDS context electrifies the depiction of the body and adds an urgency to the need to recognise the diversity of activities and identifications', (Horne and Lewis 1996: 8) ,and this is exactly what Chesley is doing in *Night Sweat,* and he becomes the first queer playwright in the AIDS era to do so. While examining who does what to whom sexually, Chesley also remains realistic in discussing and showing that some sexual activity can save lives, even if, initially, the play seems to take an opposite stance. Within the varied actions in his play, Chesley is illustrating the formation of sexual identities, and the crucial role of representation in those identities, confronting the material directly.

However, the most graphic on-stage Experience enacted is torture, featuring a Grand Inquisitor, a Scribe, and Williams, 'the victim', who confesses to his sins. Here, Chesley powerfully blends black comedy with conspiracy theory, sex with environment, pain with pleasure. The actor playing Williams is stripped naked, bound and restrained, and 'tortured' with red hot irons. The scene begins by placing Williams firmly within American society and gay culture and community. The Inquisitor, introducing the character, asks,

> William Jeptha Williams! Do you confess to being a white, upper-class American male, possessing a good body without disfigurement or disability, not too short and not too fat or fem?...Do you confess to have striven for the American Dream of success? (Chesley: *Night Sweat*: II, v. 56).

Williams has burning rods applied to his feet to enable him to confess to his riches. He lists all his properties and material worth, eventually moving onto his sexual prowess and power. The threat of castration forces his final confession out of him, to reveal the source of his wealth. A corpse is unveiled, with its 'ghastly stare' looking directly and accusingly at William's. This corpse is of a former member of Williams' nightclub. In his death speech, preceded by an 'appalling howl, an orgasm of triumph', Williams confesses that his wealth derives from the ownership of The Sepulchre, a gay club and bath house, where men can meet and have anonymous sex with many other men. These saunas were, and still are, seen as vital meeting places for gay and bisexual men to express their sexuality and sexual freedom unhampered by the constraints of heterosexual society. Williams screams out:

> I killed you all! I betrayed you all! Why didn't you ask me about my silent partners? Why didn't you ask who else owns The Sepulchre? Did you think I could resist the offer they made? Did you think I would care if they experimented with newly engineered viruses at The Sepulchre? I sold you all   down the river! Because you deserve to die faggots!...I chose the money! 'Cause money is a harder and bigger dick than you've ever seen! (II, v. 59).

This play was a remarkable and brave first response to the AIDS crisis. In a time of 'plague' and deep anxiety, with so much unknown about the disease and safer sex, with homosexuality under furious attack, Chesley reaffirms gay sexuality and sensuality. Love and sex, in all its varieties, become acts of defiance. Chesley himself acknowledged the divided responses to the play, 'Some people loved it, but even my closest friends behaved as if I had placed something at their feet which it was best

to step over and politely ignore. My best buddy told me that he wished I
had never written it.' (Chesley, p.10). Kelly Hill, a close friend of Chesley,
and an actor who performed in the San Francisco productions of *Night
Sweat* and Chesley's next play *Jerker*, told me;

> *Night Sweat* was the more difficult to gauge the audience reaction. We
> sold out most performances, the reviews were confusing. Some guys
> argued that it was too dark in mood, that it advocated suicide, but at the
> same time were turned on by its erotic nature. Others loved those very
> qualities and found it very positive in its message. You must remember
> that our production was in 1985 in a very dark period here in San
> Francisco. The fear level was very high. (Hill, 1 May 1997, letter to the
> author.)

Writing for a specifically gay audience, performed in a small, gay
venue and showcase, this is a community member confronting his
audience with uncomfortable truths, and attempting to educate them
through the use of performativity and eroticism, two essential elements of
gay Liberation and Identity. He recreates structures of gay sexual life, such
as the 'cruising' of gay bathhouses for sex, and presents it to his peers,
who then connect with the stage picture. Chesley speaks to his audience of
issues regarding passivity in the face of illness and disease. Williams is
sacrificed to the disease during a representation of the logical conclusion
to S and M activity, death, the Ultimate Trip. Yet Richard is saved as he
climaxes in an orgiastic threesome, demonstrating that sex is an
experience of living, not death, and he comes (pun intended) to realise that
he must live before he dies. Tom's entrance, also pun intended, coincides
with Richard's joyful orgasm, and Eros overcomes Thanatos once more.

Night Sweat operates as a series of performances, and gay/ queer
re-enactments. Using 'metaphorical and surrealist excess', (Romn, 1998:
55), Chesley uses gay iconography to connect with the gay audience
member. The Cowboy, The Site Worker, The Uniformed Guy, The
Leatherman, these images may be part of a 'Village People' iconography
of gay male sexuality for many straight as well as gay people, but the
fetishism of these constructions exists powerfully for gay men. This
iconography developed from late 1970s Gay Liberation, in which, as a
response to the abusive stereotyping, gay men desired to be distinguished
from their straight counterparts by their *more* masculine appearance. Segal
refers to this as the 'butch shift', which celebrated a more conventional
(and more *desired*) masculinity, and a deliberate hyper- masculinity.
(Segal 1990: 149). Within the frames of sexuality, the 'scripting' of sexual
activities and encounters, and within the frames of the theatrical space,
Chesley is setting out for his audience a debate regarding safer sex,

resistance and pride, yet staging it in a recognisable Club environment, in which sexual activity is scripted and performed.

Using his characters to foreground fetishised gender performance, Chesley creates an intertextuality between stage and audience, with many layers of meaning and membership within the theatrical framework. Kelly Hill confirms the connection, that *Night Sweat and Jerker*;

> both involve the audience erotically as was their intention. Robert believed and wrote to the point that there should be no boundary between art and pornography. His work was geared to create an erotic charge between audience and performer. We used to talk daily about what went on during and after the performances and laugh with delight. Both shows certainly cranked up my sex life! (Hill, 1 May 1997.)

This erotic charge meant that real sex was taking place in the auditorium whilst the simulated sex was being acted out on stage, the naked male body and gay sexuality and fantasies are used to connect with the audience member in a queer construction. By using the whole repertoire available, Chesley speaks, at some point, to every gay man watching, from the Opera Queen to the Disco Bunny via the Leatherman.

Nowhere is this demonstrated more graphically than in sadomasochistic scripting and behaviour. Within the context of S M activity, which for gay men is fetishised in leather gear, the central issue is one of surrender. By totally performing the S M Experience, the participants are demonstrating that, 'surrender is one of the most important and necessary elements of their play, a surrender of fear, inhibition, and ego to some deeper, unrecognised state within.' (Thompson 1991: xix). Male SM role playing is considered totally queer, being a 'perversion' that 'strips sexuality of all functionality, whether biological or social', (Silverman 1992: 187), and is the valorisation of non-functional sex, sex purely for self, expression, even more than pleasure.

Queerness acknowledges that, although sexual behaviour is not the determining factor in self-identification, social identities, especially those of gender, are accompanied by public signification. These take the form of specific acts, gestures, embodiments or speech, but should not also rule out those acts that *are* sexual, that are embraced within personal, queer self - identification. Within sadomasochism, and in addition to surrender, there are other clearly identified constructions that need to be present to perform the S and M Experience. Firstly, exhibitionism is an essential element, an external audience, 'witnesses', being structurally necessary. Secondly, suspense is at the centre of S and M play, climax or 'end-pleasure' is delayed due to the prolonging of ritual and preparation, and clearly suspense heightens pain over pleasure.

The male masochist acts out, persistently and repeatedly, however exaggerated, the conditions of cultural subjectivity. He exhibits his humiliation, finds meaning in performing the 'Other', and subverts the social order by revelling in the sacrificial nature of his surrender, layered with the performative, of course, as the masochist is in charge; this is his *game*. In the face of a frightening AIDS epidemic, Chesley takes this cultural subjectivity, which portrays People With AIDS as victims, sufferers and the diseased 'Others', and uses the queer 'ill' male to demonstrate the dangers of losing queer identity to a heterosexual hierarchy. He uses queer acts, performances, gender identity and the male body to 'perform' queerness.

Chesley is portraying the dynamics of domination and submission, exploring the social dynamics of patriarchy, and warning of the consequences should queer men allow themselves to be 'snuffed' by the heterosexual dominant culture. S and M explores the realities of sex and power that are often submerged behind more romantic, idealised, and sanitised representations of sexuality. By focusing on the penis and anus as sites of pleasure within the Experiences in *Night Sweat*, and particularly with Williams, Chesley dismantles romanticism, and concentrates on the queer sexual performance. The absence of kisses and affection allows an objective and clear presentation of the dynamics of power relations.

The male body is the focus of the torture scene. The actor playing Williams is led onto a set decorated as a medieval dungeon. He is escorted by two black-hooded torturers, bare-chested and wearing fetishised items. His nakedness is important as it feeds the binary of exhibitionism/vulnerability that is part of William's desire. On the rack, Williams becomes a passive man, on one level unable to control any action taken against him, but also in full control as he has dictated the scenario. This is an 'ill' AIDS body submitting to death, but choosing that exit, empowering himself and controlling his final moments. This is an AIDS body eroticised, choosing to follow through and complete an S and M Experience, challenging the audience with an aspect of sexuality in which the giving and receiving of pain is an essential component. In his confession, Williams admits to many 'shameful' acts. His confession confronts the audience with not only his, but perhaps their own, sexual behaviour, and their sexual past and present, with acts that some members will find erotic, others 'perverted'. Chesley, in foregrounding these acts, is affirming gay sexuality and liberty, as Williams has chosen this Experience. Strapped to the rack, at the point of his own death, he can only look back on his sexual past, and his confession is also a lament for the sex that went 'Before', that is, before the virus. The combination of pain and eroticism, the suspense, the delay of the 'end-pleasure', are clearly structured by Chesley, working within S and M scripting. Williams has taken control of his own death, by placing himself sexually in the role of 'victim'.

Here Williams the subordinate is submitting to the superordinate presence of AIDS, as indeed all the 'victims' do in *Night Sweat*. Of course, the S and M scene does not provide the only scripts for gay men to work from, there are many scenes, codes and behavioural expectation in life that are explored in *Night Sweat*, opera, for example, being a particularly highly coded experience for the participant. But, of all the activities, SM does provide the strongest scripts for sexual fulfilment within carefully negotiated boundaries. Williams, who had wealth and materialistic pleasures, has placed himself in the totally subservient role to be punished by his self-hatred, his fear, the Executioner and AIDS. By making him the owner of the Sepulchre, Chesley is also confronting his audience with the notion that, although the gay community is where support is likely to come for the HIV positive man, it is also the community from which the virus was more than likely contracted. Politically, the self-hating gay man has colluded with a homophobic process designed to wipe out the community.

Chesley insists in presenting the HIV positive body as a focus of desire, even in the face of a potentially fatal sexually transmitted disease. The erotic, nude body and gay sexual drive, is placed on the public arena of the stage. Williams' naked body is a site for representation that attempts to break taboos, challenges stigma, and confronts issues of denial and grief. Chesley's men are tied up, tortured, hung and electrocuted, all in apparent passivity toward their disease, the inevitability of death and their lives, Tom being the exception. For the S and M player in the audience who is HIV positive, this will push home a strong message about surviving and *living* with the disease. Williams does not have to succumb, he can enjoy many more SM scenes until he dies. He has a choice in the quality of his (sexual) life, and this point is underlined with the rescue of Richard.

His choice of exit, Terminal Sex, is in the form of a threesome, played out in front of an 'audience' of Club members, and, of course, the 'real' audience in the venue. Chesley's celebration of gay sex is, again, not edited or watered down for the audience, the stage directions being very explicit. As this is enacted, the members of the Club begin to simulate playing with their own cocks, now not only there to watch the sex but to participate in it. The scene progresses;

> The First Hunky Man is fucking Richard from behind, while the Second
> Hunky Man is kneeling in front of him, sucking him and reaching up to
> pinch his tits...the lighting suddenly changes to strobe, and we see the First
> Hunky Man raise the dagger high over his head, ready to plunge it into
> Richard's neck at the imminent climax... (Chesley: II, vii. 65).

It is at this point that Tom and his friends burst into the Club, dressed as nuns, to save Richard and deliver the safer sex message, an amusing coitus interruptus which underlines the message that diagnosis does not equal the end of life, and on a practical level, releases tension in the audience. It jolts the audience and performers out of their sexual enjoyment of the scene, and therefore out of the acceptance of the inevitability of Richard's seemingly impending death. Within this enactment of sex, Richard is *enjoying* his Experience, and Sister Tom reminds him that he can continue to do so. At a time of great fear, Chesley's message was extremely important. He, (Chesley/Richard), is gazing at a time Before, a time of Freedom, free from the virus, whilst engaging in sex in the Present. Sister Tom offers a way to survive the Future. The message to adapt to safer sex and enjoy life may appear rather simplistic, but Chesley involves the audience through powerful gay erotica and an enforcement of sexuality. Sister Tom is not the appearance of a parental or authoritarian figure, it is of a peer, who is not saying 'Don't have sex', but is saying 'Have safer sex.' By staging a range of performances, Chesley is being queer in his presentation, before queer even began to develop as a theory. The persistence of the equation of sex and death, and its constant relationship to AIDS, is internalised and eroticised by Chesley's characters. In the early 1980s, its politics were out of sync with the emotional and political needs of many gay men of the time, especially urban New York City audiences, who suffered terrible losses to AIDS. Yet from the standpoint of today, it is clear that Chesley is staging established homosexual behaviour, particularly queer sexual behaviour, to ultimately offer hope for survival. Through using scripts of sexual behaviour, his characters can re-discover pride and re-affirm their queerness. By tapping into the gay psyche, Chesley is offering his audience hope for longer survival, not just of the individual, but of the gay 'community' itself.

The Normal Response

Working within 'alternative' non-mainstream theatre in America, the queer performativity of Chesley took time to influence gay and British drama. Successful AIDS plays of the 1980s tended to operate along more traditional lines of narrative and drama. Many early British AIDS plays such as Kirby's *Compromised Immunity,* (1985), and Kelly's *Anti-Body,* (1985), were 'message' plays, short, almost TIE drama, and more traditional discourses dominated. Focussing on the drama of Larry Kramer, the emphasis moves onto less queer discourses. It is important to present this material, and whilst I do not wish to construct Kramer as the antithesis of all that is queer, the grounds on which I both appreciate his contribution and deprecate his specific failures to address the queer perspective, divert part of this analysis away from queer Theory. One of the profoundest ironies of the AIDS crisis was that sexually transmitted diseases were not viewed as serious in the late 1970s, at the exact period in time when many male homosexuals redefined themselves as a sexually alternative yet minority group, however ghettoised. Part of the distinctive nature of this group was sexual voracity. Fucking was a cornerstone of the Gay Liberation movement, promoted and celebrated by urban gay men, in particular, as a signifier of sexual freedom and Pride. Kramer has many deep and lasting reservations about this 'Liberation', which inform his theoretical and textual construction. Kramer believed that excessive promiscuity was emotionally (not physically) unhealthy, and that there are ways of coming to terms with individual sexuality and sexual behaviour in private, not public.

The Normal Heart

One of the first to speak about AIDS, and to track the emergence of the epidemic in 1982, Kramer co-founded the Gay Men's Health Crisis, and his style of campaigning for justice clashed with fellow GMHC board members. This led to Kramer being voted out of the organisation. The loss of his friends to AIDS, the death of his lover, his fury at official inaction and the internal conflicts within the gay community, make *The Normal Heart* unapologetically autobiographical. The lead character, Ned Weeks, is clearly Kramer, and it dramatises the personal impact of AIDS and the founding of the Gay Men's Health Crisis. The play was a major success, taking the subject matter of AIDS into mainstream theatre. Opening at the New York Shakespeare Festival Public Theatre on 21st April 1985, less than a year after *Night Sweat* opened, the play ran for almost a year, successfully transferred to London, and then played in cities around the world. The approach to the subject matter, the representations of illness and sexuality, was a more traditional construction than Chesley's.

The time period covered runs from July 1981 to May 1984, beginning in the waiting room of Dr Emma Brookner, and fear and concern is immediately established in the gay men waiting to be examined. Kramer almost instantly employs the Kaposi's sarcoma icon, a dark bruise often associated with the appearance of the disease which quickly found its way into theatrical representation, as David, a minor character, talks about his lesions: 'They keep getting bigger and bigger, and they won't go away.' (Kramer, 1985: I, i. 2). The opening scene also establishes the main thrust of the play, the argument that gay men should stop having sex, to prevent further spread of the disease. Initially, Kramer gives this polemic to Dr Brookner, and she is not only a rational, respected member of straight society, but also, for Kramer, an important character in delivering AIDS history and information to the audience, however matriarchal in her construction, stating bluntly: 'Tell gay men to stop having sex...Tell them they're going to die.' (Kramer 1985: I, i. 8). Ned then begins to establish himself as a campaigner, trying to raise funds to set up the organisation that will become GMHC, and meeting Felix, who is to become his lover. Felix works for the *New York Times*, reporting on society events, and is a closeted gay. Afraid of losing his job if he is 'outed', Felix is initially reluctant to write about, or to force the editorial team, to write about AIDS on a larger scale. Kramer's anger is particularly well targeted towards those in authority, but the tone of the play and his anger is shrill, raging against almost everything GMHC tried to set up.

As the GMHC is established, Kramer dramatises the group struggling to cope with the huge demand for information, and to come to terms with their personal and collective grief at the loss of so many friends, lovers and loved ones. Ned's insistence that promiscuity is at the heart of the virus's spread is always central to the dramatisation. The popularity and success of *The Normal Heart* also owes much to its timing (and the misconception that this was the first AIDS play). By 1985, fears were growing both in the United States and Britain that the disease would soon spread to the 'general population', that is, white, heterosexual, non-drug users.

Ned's relationship with Felix is thinly sketched, however. In Act One Scene Four Felix has rung Ned to make a date, and among Ned's speeches about closet gays, AIDS lethargy and Hitler's Final Solution, they manage to kiss and to make a connection. By Scene Seven, the last in Act One, they are intimate enough to be surrounded by pillows eating ice cream. Yet the first act closes with Felix pulling off his sock and showing Ned a purple spot on the sole of his foot. In an echo of David in the first scene, he says 'It keeps getting bigger and bigger Neddie, and it doesn't go away.' (Kramer, I, vi: 36). Thus the KS lesion again makes its appearance as the sign of AIDS. Here, the political becomes even more the personal as Ned feels more inadequate, helpless and angry in the face of his lover's impending death. Although we are shown very little of their lives together and their relationship (and we certainly do not see them naked or having sex), the lesion is an essential dramatic device. Not only does this humanise the portrayal of Ned, it arouses audience sympathy and support of his cause. Sympathy for the lead character is, of course, essential in the genre of melodrama.

Eventually, the tensions between the GMHC board members and Ned become too much, and they remove him from his post as a director of the organisation he helped to found. Now without his organisation, and estranged from his brother, Ned directs his energy even more toward his sick lover and a search for a cure. The stage is thus set for the final death-bed scene. Dr Brookman 'marries' the two men as Felix is about to die:

> Dearly beloved, we are gathered here together in the sight of God to join together these two men. They love each other very much and want to be married somehow in the presence of their family before Felix dies. I can see no objection. This is my hospital, my church. (Kramer: II, xvi. 71).

Felix dies, and Ned chastises himself for not fighting harder, before breaking down and embracing his brother in an ending of reconciliation.

Its traditional style and structure, together with its message, enabled *The Normal Heart* to appeal to a wider audience. Its structure belongs to that of the 'well made play', and its theme of a lone voice speaking out against denial and threat to an established order places the play strongly in a theatrical tradition. Its success also demonstrates that producers, critics, and audiences in general, are more familiar with notions of love than sex, which is constantly centralised in drama. It also underlines the continuing, incurable 'disease' of American drama, that of romanticism, which can be extremely problematic. There is the sustained belief that audiences are unable to connect with anything *other* than strong characters, therefore characters in drama become complex signs of specificity, rather than generality. An audience can grieve for a dead Felix more than they can relate to him as a sign of a class, a group of people affected by the disease. Love individualises and personalises issues being explored (hence Ned's relationship with Felix), and is a more 'accessible' notion than promiscuous gay sex to the majority of viewers. The gay marriage also helps underline that love between two men (not brotherly or 'comrade' love) is a more central theme than freedom or sex, and marriage is, of course, a heterosexual construction.

The play contains no explicit representations of homosexuality, Kramer approaches the topic from an entirely different angle to that of Chesley. This is, in effect, a homosexual play for heterosexuals. Throughout, Ned/Kramer argues his point from an overwhelming need to be part of a heterosexual ideal:

> Mickey, why didn't you fight for the right to get married instead of the right to legitimise promiscuity?...We have fucked ourselves silly for years and years, and sometimes we have done it in the filthiest places...I don't think much of promiscuity...Maybe if they'd let us get married to begin with, none of this would have happened at all. (Kramer: II, ix. 44).

The heat of Kramer's argument ignores the fact that the central problem for many gay men is that marriage is the *only* ideal presented to young homosexuals growing up in a straight world. The lack of, until recently, openly strong gay role models in society, combined with the pressure to conform to a heterosexual ideal of happiness, led and still leads many gay men to 'force' their sexuality underground, to repress open expressions of love and freedom, making anonymous, quick sexual encounters the only option through which they can express their sexual nature.

There is no male nudity in the play. Ned, when examined by Brookner in the first scene, is told to get undressed. He, after some debate, keeps his underwear on, and contact between them is cold, professional and clinical. This is almost reflected in every relationship depicted. Although Felix and Ned do embrace in the play, their closest moments are when Felix is dying, not when he is healthy and living, and the play is framed with a hospital scene. In Kramer's work, the male body is hidden, closeted even, in contrast to Chesley's which are highlighted or displayed. The closest embraces in the play exemplify an heterosexual ideal. In the second act, Ned and Brookner have a heated argument regarding the battles they have had and will have in their lives. They reach a moment when Emma talks about her polio and her childhood struggle to achieve a life for herself. She admits she is too busy to practice walking, and Ned encourages her to try a few steps. She attempts to walk, but quickly stumbles into Ned's arms. He holds her tight and exposes more of his fears regarding Felix. On one level, this is an embrace of alternative representation, that between a gay man and a disabled woman, an embrace not often depicted in drama. Yet the image, a man and a woman embracing at a time of great emotional vulnerability, is inescapably heterosexual. Ned does not even embrace Felix at the point of his death, even the intimacy of death seems to be too private for Ned to express in public.

The other major embrace occurs just before the curtain falls. The play ends, not with the death of Felix, but with an embrace between Ned and his brother Ben, the person who Ned seeks the most approval from. This embrace between two brothers, a reconciliation between gay and straight worlds, displays Ned/Kramer's aching need to be part of a social ideal, with equal rights and status to heterosexuals. It is an embrace between literal, sibling brothers, not members of a gay 'brotherhood', as explored in Chesley's plays. Whilst Chesley celebrates the *difference* of gayness/queerness through his bodies, language and depictions of sexuality, Kramer attempts to place homosexuality within an over-arching culture, fighting for *sameness*. Attempting to make gayness part of a dominant culture is in complete contrast to Chesley's ideology of a spiritual, sexual identity and community: 'Fuck a guy, find his beauty and touch it, share.' (Chesley, *Dog Plays:* 133).

There is only one brief mention of safe sex, occurring late in the play when Felix is examined by Brookner. He says: 'Some gay doctors are saying it's okay if you use rubbers.' To which she replies dismissively: 'I know they are'. (Kramer: II, x. 50). Thus any potential to discuss safer sex as an aid to loving, living sexual connections is quashed. Produced less than a year after *Night Sweat,* this lack of recognition of the advantages of safer sex seem astonishing, even if the play is set at the onset of the disease. It also adds fuel to the criticism that Kramer's own unease with gay sex/promiscuity coloured his representation of life in the time of AIDS. The play's ending is a conclusion that offers little support to the gay (HIV positive or negative) man in the audience. As Clum says: 'Kramer gives Felix a death bed scene that Dumas or Giuseppe Verdi would have admired...There can be no love relationship, only a deathbed marriage. Gay men are once again doomed to be alone.' (Clum 2000: 63).

The construction of the sick or HIV positive man being sexually active as a *triumphant* exchange is absent from Kramer's work. And it is no coincidence that the pity his victimisation provoked was beginning to be reflected in society at large. Whilst Chesley resists overpowering genres, and foregrounds instead the sexually active 'ill' gay body and his own sexual identity, Kramer, in his need to spread his message, uses a particular form of *romantic* melodrama to construct his narrative. Kramer is not only appealing to the gay audience, he is also trying to recruit a new audience, possibly the *mothers* of the gay ill men. To elicit tears as a response to the crisis is a worthy strategy when applied to a political incentive, which Kramer does in *The Normal Heart.* Unlike Chesley,

however, tears will be the only body fluids we will see secreted. Even
then, these tears will only fall as the tragedy completely overwhelms the
protagonist, the withholding of public displays of intimacy either denied
by a disapproving society, or self-denied by the author/director,
hero/heroine. Felix is a wholly romantic construction, his purpose to
finally bring love into Ned's life, albeit briefly, and to humanise Ned and
arouse sympathy for him as his (brief) happiness is destroyed.

Kramer is tied to the narrative and families of straight, domestic,
American drama. What Kramer is promoting here, in complete contrast to
Chesley, is, insidiously, the notion of *behavioural change,* from
homosexual to over- arching heterosexual modes and acceptances.
Kramer also uses another emotion available to us, that of anger, and this is
correctly targeted in places at officialdom and poor response from those in
authority. The play can also be read as a gay call for help from the
heterosexual community with romantic melodramatic notions the
mouthpiece for that call to be made. In contrast, Chesley employs
eroticism and a celebration of gay sexuality in all its forms as options
available to the viewer/reader. Ned/Kramer is bound to the illusion of
love. Erotic love, with its insistence on the body, is immaterial because of
its temporary nature. The melodramatic/sentimental model gives love
value by negating the erotic and projecting societal ideals and the hopes
that *romantic* love, or even platonic love, will not only transcend the body,
but will fulfil and redeem. However, for Kramer, theatre does have its
limitations, and subsequent plays never reached the success or impact of
The Normal Heart.

Perfect and Imperfect Bodies

Influences of Chesley's queer constructions appeared in the
mainstream drama in Kushner's *Angels In America* (1992/94), see my
previous chapter, and Elyot's *My Night With Reg.* (1994). There was
much debate surrounding *My Night With Reg,* that a gay play, with AIDS
as a central theme, achieved good reviews, excellent box office and won
awards. In actual fact, there is little about the play itself that is ground-
breaking. Although the play runs without an interval, and there are subtle
time leaps between each act, its popularity may have more to do with the
nature of the comedy of the piece. The subtle yet close relationship
between comedy and pain, traditional in British comedy and finding its
apotheosis in playwrights such as Alan Bennett (see in particular *Talking
Heads*) and Alan Ayckbourn, for example, is utilised fully in *My Night
With Reg.* Jokes are made at moments of great, personal revelation,

laughter and self-deprecation are used as defence mechanisms to combat fear. However, the play does construct what I term the queer 'pause'.

My Night With Reg

The play concentrates on a group of six gay male friends, whose lives have, in some way, been affected by the Reg of the title. Like Godot, Reg never appears, yet has a strong hold on the actions and thoughts of the characters. By the second act, Reg has died of AIDS- related illnesses, and it transpires that it is possible that at least five of the six characters had sex with Reg at some point in their lives. Their relationship to Reg, their relationships with each other, and with AIDS, forms the play. For mainstream, West End British theatregoers, the comedy approach to the AIDS issue made the play unusual, and simultaneously acceptable. Comedy is nothing new in AIDS drama, but with its suppressed emotions, mistaken understandings, double meanings and presence of tragedy, *My Night With Reg* has a more recognisable form and content to a British (middle class) audience.

The central character is Guy, a copywriter, excellent cook, knitter, friend and supporter to all the other characters, the one they all confide in. He has been carrying unrequited love (which dare not speak its name) for John for years, ever since their University days. However, he feels, and it seems he is, destined to be on his own. Daniel is the camp outrageous tart, and the partner of Reg at the beginning of the play. Bernie and Benny are a couple, with clearly defined 'masculine' and 'feminine' roles and expectations. They are working class, one works in a factory making paper cups, and the other drives a bus. Eric is eighteen, his role underlining innocence. He is waiting to meet Mr. Right, despite the attentions of the other characters. John is perhaps the least stereotypical of the characters for a heterosexual audience. He is a former rugby player, living off his father's inheritance, and the gay community would probably label him 'straight acting'. Guy's obsessive love for John derives from their University Drama Society production of *The Bacchae,* in which John played Dionysus, and Guy, the director, made him perform in a jockstrap from which his 'balls kept falling out.' Whilst the love remains unrequited, Guy has held on to the jockstrap. Not only is this an icon of the 'straight acting' rugby playing John, his performance as Dionysus would have been a queer performance, garlanded only in the jockstrap, a performance that allows him to display his body and sexuality more freely within the allowance of text and performance.

The seventh character is Reg, and the main information given about this absent character is his promiscuity. As a representation of AIDS and its spread, the reports of Reg and the effect he has on the lives of the on stage characters, could already feed into an entrenched view of the predatory homosexual. He is unselective in his sexual contacts, and it is implied that he had little regard for his health and the health of the men that he has had sex with. As Guy points out;

> I can't help feeling that Reg was having his cake and eating it...What the hell was he playing at? It was all so irresponsible... even the vicar told me what a good fuck he was outside the crematorium. (Elyot, 1994: *My Night With Reg,* II. 59).

As the above quotation shows, anger and pain are often diluted with pithy one-liners. The characters may appear stereotypical, but five of the six are middle-aged gay men, not classically beautiful, two working class, and they are a group still under-represented on gay stage and film. The non-appearance of Reg means he is not given a voice to defend himself with, and his arrival could have given the play a much needed sense of anger. He is the Patient Zero of the piece, the individual who can be traced back as the source of HIV infection amongst the play's community. Bernie, Bennie and John all confide their nights with Reg to Guy. Yet it is Guy, who only has telephone sex, and has adopted safer sex to such a degree that he 'masturbates in Marigolds', who dies of AIDS at the end of the second act. We learn that he told his friends that he contracted the virus after an episode of unprotected anal sex (against his will), whilst on holiday, referred to at the beginning of the play. It remains unclear to the audience whether Guy might have actually had sex with Reg, but Elyot makes the connection between Reg, the virus and the characters so strongly, that little doubt remains.

Elyot employs two devices to represent the virus. One is the second movement of Ravel's Piano Concerto in G Minor, played to signify the passing of time with each act. It is also Reg's favourite piece of music, so, to the audience, it comes to represent the disease itself. It is a slow, romantic, moving piece of music, and the writer fuses this with the second device, the iconic male body itself, in the bridge between the second and third acts. Here we see a link to Chesley's queer performances as Eric strips to the music. Watching this representation of a young healthy body, the audience connect Eric to Reg through the piece of music. Later in the act, Eric tells John that he slept with a special man, whose favourite piece of music was the Ravel. The connection is made, and the audience now wonder whether Eric has the virus. If his body is infected, it is shown at the beginning of infection, as a body that could now waste away from opportunist infections.

Eric's naked body represents the future, yet it is an incident from his past that could have doomed his body. His nakedness offers a continuance to the men in the audience, a reflection of their own bodies. Of course, it can also be an erotic connection to the gay male member, watching a young man strip naked, taking that man temporarily out of the context of the play as the body becomes the focus for curiosity and interest. The use of the music connects the body of Eric to Reg, and the use of Eric's body connects him to the audience.

Like the male bodies in Chesley's works, Eric's naked body holds the past and indicates the future, contains both life and death, as all our bodies do. His body, however, is not signed with KS lesions, but signed with music, and also in contrast to Chesley's bodies, who are, even in the late stages of illness, shown as active, making choices, this body is *passive,* classically perfect. This passivity can sign the body with insecurities for fellow men viewing the nude, as Dutton has explained:

> Given the significance of facial and body hair as biological markers of masculinity, the male ideal might logically be the figure of a hirsute, bearded he-man; yet in fact the masculine images portrayed in Western media as ideal models are those of lithe smooth-bodied youths...For a man to be relaxed and inert and passive is a source of massive anxiety, for what then might enter his body? It means identification with the feminine, and that he is being worked UPON, rather than working. (Dutton 1995: 301).

Eric, the actor playing him physically smooth, youthful and lithe, stripping to a romantic piece of music, perfectly exemplifies Dutton's explanation of male nude passivity. Here, Eric's queer performance, the postures and poses, are female, passive. It is also a refrain, perhaps, of John's earlier queer performance as Dionysus in a jockstrap. Eric's unintentional revelation of his night with Reg to John (who understands the significance of this favourite piece of music), and therefore his revelation of possible HIV contraction, now signposts his body, in the third act, with a future of illness. Whilst viewing nudity in the context of an AIDS drama, the male viewer can reflect on his own body, his own sexuality, his own fragility, and, perhaps, his own health and responsibility for his sexual past/present/future. These are among the many responses aroused by Eric's queer/Camp/Passive/Erotic performance. Eric's youthful body is also the goal for the other men in the play, and is the focus not only for sexual yearning, but also for a yearning for youth, as many of the other characters approach middle age with trepidation and insecurity. The main criticism of *My Night With Reg,* was in its treatment (or non-treatment) of the subject of AIDS, the inability to confront the audience

with the reality of AIDS survival, and of gay sexuality. The portrayal of
gay life, with its insecurities and tart, bitchy one- liners, is accurate and
amusing, its characters well drawn. However, almost ten years after *The
Normal Heart,* and nearly fifteen years into the epidemic, the play has no
anger, no political message or edge. The characters are passive in the
reality of AIDS. Eric's body is shown in repose, perhaps already infected,
too late for him to change his status. However, what distinguishes *My
Night With Reg* is its queer Pause, when Eric's body leaves the chronology
of the play and is foregrounded.

The Queer Pause

Some clarification is needed here, of course, of my term. For me,
the Queer Pause is a moment, or sequence, when the narrative content of
the work is stripped of dialogue, and the discourse invites the audience to
view the stage world through Queer eyes. There are common constants in
the Queer Pause, a significant factor being the use of music, as I have
discussed in *My Night With Reg.* Male nudity, and textually the gay male
body, is another element, and the Pause often indicates a passing of time,
be it forward motion or a memory. Eric's Queer performance creates a
reflective sequence moving the action on from the second act, but also
raising the potential of a future with HIV for the character.

Other examples of the Queer Pause occur in Kushner's *Angels in
America Part Two: Perestroika,* when the naked Joe and Louis stand
before the audience, with music playing, before they get into bed with
each other, (Kushner, 1994: 14), and in John Roman Baker's *Easy,* (AIDS
Positive Underground 1993). Here the naked Frank rises from his death
bed and makes love to his partner Jim, stripping him naked. The song *Stay
With Me Baby* is played loudly throughout the enactment of gay male sex,
filling the auditorium, and the tenderness of the love making alters into a
struggle as Frank prevents Jim from getting into his "death" bed. The
Queer Pause, with its focus on the gay male body, encourages the viewer
to observe the drama through a Queer perspective, the music enabling a
Queer performance.

In plays that do not present 'ill' gay bodies as desirable, AIDS,
whilst being a constant presence, can appear as more abstract; yet in *My
Night With Reg* it is focused on Eric's nude body. The music Eric chooses,
and his rejection of prevailing homosexist attitudes such as an insistence
on promiscuity, his desire for monogamy, marks him out as 'queer' from
his gay peers. He expresses himself in a queer performance, which marks
his body with signs of HIV, which is then created as a site for memory, a

memorial, by the gay male viewer.

Jeffrey

Although humour had existed in earlier AIDS drama, the time perhaps was now right for plays that could be billed specifically as 'AIDS comedies' to make their appearance, and some gay commentators wondered why it had taken so long for them to appear. As in many aspects of any life, gay men have learnt to cope with the realities of the disease by adding layers of irony to the experience. These camp rituals and reactions are also captured in Paul Rudnick's American AIDS comedy, *Jeffrey*, (1993), where, following the AIDS-related death of chorus boy Darius, his colleagues from *Cats* pay tribute at his funeral with a rendition of *Memory*. In contrast to *My Night With Reg*, Rudnick's play places sex, and the need for gay male sex in the age of AIDS, at the centre of the comedy, reflecting Chesley's argument. In *Jeffrey*, safe, happy sex is a central goal, and the title character is shown constantly struggling to achieve the happiest sex with the least amount of worry. A montage of Jeffrey's safer sex promiscuity and its attendant problems, (condoms break, medical tests proving HIV negativity are required by his potential sexual partner, one encounter wraps himself in clingfilm, Jeffrey is in bed with a woman -until he wakes from that particular nightmare), lead him to renounce sex in favour of a lifestyle that he asserts will be less complicated without the interference of his gay hormones.

Of course, temptation moves in almost immediately. The moment Jeffrey decides to give up sex is, naturally, the time when he meets, and is powerfully attracted to, Steve, a muscular, handsome, confident gym buddy, who *just happens* to be HIV positive. Jeffrey's first encounter with this fit, healthy-looking gay man, is unencumbered by the knowledge of Steve's HIV status. Significantly, the play places two gay men at the centre of its tale, one of them living with being HIV positive, and, at the time, posed the almost unheard of *romantic* possibility of a successful 'mixed status' relationship where one partner has the virus, the other is HIV negative.

Although there is no nudity in *Jeffrey*, the male body remains highly significant, particularly in the character of Steve. One of Jeffrey's substitutes for sex is the gym, and it is here that he and Steve first meet, and are immediately attracted to each other. Steve's body therefore first presents itself as a superbly muscular chiselled example of masculinity, with a vest and pair of shorts appearing simply sprayed onto his body. His body and the situation they are in is used immediately for comic effect.

Steve 'spots' for Jeffrey on the weights, and as Jeffrey begins to struggle with the lifting, the dialogue from Steve, 'Push It, You Need It', 'Come to Papa', 'You're The Best', together with Jeffrey's groans and the disco music pumping in the gym, becomes a clever pastiche of a standard gay porn movie. Importantly, Steve, the HIV positive character, is confident, fit, does the chasing of Jeffrey, and is unafraid of commitment and his own emotions. Jeffrey is advised by his friends to fall in love and have a relationship, and once he gives in to this, Steve reveals his HIV status. That this does make a difference to Jeffrey not only exposes Jeffrey's vulnerability, but also Steve's. Issues of living with HIV are not glossed over in *Jeffrey*, they are central to the story and to the comedy.

However, as Sinfield has pointed out, there are more pressures, apart from the threat of Aids contagion, that Jeffrey lives under. The play raises 'disturbing questions about how HIV negative men are to handle the AIDS emergency.' (Sinfield, 2000: 100). The issue of living *without* HIV is not addressed in any way that supports Jeffrey's right to be negative, and to only want sex with negative men. The overarching optimism of the piece means that Jeffrey is under constant pressure from his friends to welcome a relationship with a HIV positive man. The agenda of the script is to place a more positive stance on relationships between those who are negative and those who are positive, and *Jeffrey* suffers from the genre it has to conform to, that of a romantic comedy. Yet it is still rare for the romance to be between gay men, and even rarer to be between a man who is HIV negative and a man who carries the virus. *Jeffrey* is important for, at the very least, committing itself to exploring this agenda, which is queer, within the expected happy resolutions of a romantic comedy.

Ron Athey

However, queer has, it seems to me, returned to the alternative, less mainstream, representations, particularly in performance art, where the body is the central narrative and symbolic component. In American performance artist Ron Athey's case, that body is queer *and* HIV positive. Athey was brought up by Pentecostalists, and was once a 'Bible- thumping Christian'. He remembers speaking in tongues and being part of his family's crusade to recruit new people and save their souls. At the age of fifteen, he began to question the extreme Christian thought he had been indoctrinated in throughout his childhood, and during his adult life began to dabble in S and M and an array of substance abuse, which eventually led to heroin addiction. He kicked the habit, and embraced performance art and alternative journalism as a vocation. The body has, for decades, been

central to the development and creation of performance art, and Athey
arises out of these explorations and traditions, part of a group of artists
who use their bodies and body fluids as art.

His works all employ aspects of S and M sexuality and ritual
including piercing, cutting and mutilation of the body, mummification,
flagellation, all under the auspices of tight-laced, rubber- clad clinical
'nurses'. This, needless to say, has caused controversy, particularly in the
United States. In March 1994, *4 Scenes From A Harsh Life* was being
presented at a Minneapolis nightclub sponsored by a local National
Endowment of the Arts centre. One act, *The Human Printing Press,*
involved Athey cutting the flesh of a fellow performer, then placing strips
of paper towel over the wounds and then hoisting the blood-soaked
tissues, via pulley, over the heads of part of the audience. One outraged
patron contacted local health authorities to complain (wrongly), that the
audience had been exposed to the HIV virus. Though no blood dripped
onto the audience, and although the performer cut was actually HIV
negative, these facts where lost in the ensuing outrage, fuelled strongly by
right-wing Senator and homophobe Jesse Helms. It was Athey's own
declared HIV positive status that led the audience member to claim that
the crowd had been spattered with HIV positive blood.

Athey's art draws viscerally on his life, with the intention, he
says, 'to overcome a bad memory, to portray it in art.' (Morris 1999: issue
4) His life has given him much material to channel his religion's
negativity about the body and his homosexuality and HIV positive status
into better use as a performance artist. In his Saint Sebastian act, he is
martyred with a literal crown of thorns that cause his blood to rain onto his
face and the floor while he is pierced with surgical steel arrows. Although
the accounts of HIV blood being hurled at the audience are untrue, people
often faint when the blood begins to flow, and he outlines some of the
rituals in his performances:

> One of the things I do mutilate on stage is my face, and people can't really
> disassociate themselves from the face. You can beat your body to death,
> but not your face. Most of what I do is puncture wounds, then mutilation
> within reason, so I'm not jeopardising my health. (Hays 1999)

Here is the most extreme representation and use of the body
within performance. The audience are actually presented with *real* HIV
positive blood, pouring out of Athey's body, and with the very real
ritualisation of body pain and masochism. His external body is clearly
signed and written with Athey's own personal history, using his body as
catharsis, as a way of revealing the secrets of their pasts and experiences

through his performance art. Foucault regarded SM as power games that were geared towards the aim of producing human (sexual) pleasure. For Foucault, SM is:

> ...the real creation of new possibilities of pleasure, which people had no idea about previously. The idea that SM is related to a deep violence, that SM practice is a way of liberating this violence, this aggression, is stupid. We know very well what all these people are doing is not aggressive, they are inventing new possibilities of pleasure with strange parts of their body-through the eroticism of the body. (Foucault 1976: 27-28)

Athey uses SM performance to explore his relationship with his own body, and AIDS affects that relationship further, he also has invented new possibilities of representation by using his very *real* HIV blood. He has written his own history onto his own body, he is heavily tattooed, 'Most of my tattoos are aesthetic, but definitely some of the ones on my face are a fuck-you statement.' (Hays 1999) He has emerged from his layers of oppression to now present his body complete with its own stigmata, which he has branded onto his body. He has reversed his shame and sense of disgrace into a strong statement of his sexuality and his HIV status, using masochism to portray the agony of the struggle. Athey uses his body to sign his stigmata. His work can be strongly identified as queer performance, distinguishing itself from gay performance, the Queerest of the Queer.

Works cited

Baker, Rob, *The Art Of AIDS,* New York: Continuum, 1994.
Bennett, Alan, *Talking Heads,* London: BBC Books, 1988.
Chesley, Robert, *Hard Plays Stiff Parts, (Night Sweat, Jerker, The Dog Plays),* San Francisco, Alamo Square Press, 1990.
Clum, John M., *Still Acting Gay,* New York: Columbia University Press, 2000.
Dutton, Kenneth R., *The Perfectible Body,* London: Cassell, 1995.
Elyot, Kevin, *My Night With Reg,* London: Nick Hern Books, 1994.
Esslin, Martin, *The Theatre of The Absurd,* London: Penguin, 1961.
Foucault, Michel, *The History of Sexuality,* London: Penguin, 1976.
Genet, Jean, *The Balcony,* London: Faber and Faber, 1958.
Hart, Kylo-Patrick, R, *The AIDS Movie,* New York: Haworth Press, 2000.
Hill, Kelly, 1 May 1999, letter to the author.
Horne, Peter and Reina Lewis, *Outlooks: Lesbian and Gay Sexualities and Visual Cultures,* London: Routledge, 1996.

Kelly, Louise, *Anti Body,* Unpublished. See Lucas, Ian, (1994), *Impertinent Decorum,* London: Cassell, 1994.

Kirby, Andy, *Compromised Immunity,* Unpublished. See Lucas, Ian, (1994), *Impertinent Decorum,* London, Cassell, 1994.

Kramer, Larry, *The Normal Heart,* London: Nick Hern Books, 1985.

Romn, David, *Acts of Intervention.* Bloomington and Indianapolis: Indiana University Press, 1998.

Rudnick, Paul, *Jeffrey,* New York: Plume, 1992.

Segal, Lynne, *Slow Motion: Changing Masculinities Changing Men,* London: Virago, 1990.

Silverman, Kaja, *Male Subjectivity at the Margins,* New York: Routledge, 1992.

Sinfield, Alan, *Out on Stage,* London: Yale University Press, 2000.

Thompson, Mark, *LeatherFolk,* Boston: Alyson Publications, 1991.

White, Edmund, *Genet,* New York: Vintage, 1993.

Websites

www.brightlightsfilm.com/24/athey.html Morris, G, (1999) *Hallelujah and Pass the Steak Knives! Cutting up with Ron Athey.* Accessed Dec 2006

www.montrealmirror.com Hays, M., (1999) *Ron Athey, America's Most Controversial Performance Artist...* Accessed Dec 2006

CHAPTER SEVEN

FEAR OF THE QUEER CITIZEN: FROM CANONISATION TO CURRICULUM IN THE PLAYS OF MARK RAVENHILL

SARAH JANE DICKENSON

Synopsis

Mark Ravenhill's plays resonate with a sense of danger invoked by homosexuality. The boy figure is omnipresent in his plays, and maybe it is through the metonymic quality of the boy figure that the perceived liberation, in making gay sex explicit, is counterbalanced by the continued vulnerability of those not conforming to the heterosexual norm. Or maybe the boy is a convenient theatrical motif, being drained for every last drop of his ability to encapsulate the perversities of the queer for the dominant ideology. In either scenario, the plays take resonance from the persistent sense of menace invoked by homosexuality; a theatrical presence distilling the dangerousness of the queer.

Micropolitics and macropolitics

Whilst Ravenhill's work has been recognised for its explicit staging of sex and violence, what is most chilling is that it forces the audience to confront more than physical threat. The longevity of a playwright's reputation relies on them tapping into more than just micropolitics. Ravenhill has continually attempted to tap into macropolitics, initially via canonised text, biography, or the historical event. As he has gained in confidence as a writer he has attempted to deal more overtly with the macropolitics of the present connecting with; terrorism, governmental policy and curriculum matters and he does so unequivocally when writing for the next generation. But his attempts have been uneven in their success. This is partly due to his recognition that he lives 'in our cool, knowing, weary world' where it is easier to 'write about the little victories, the little disappointment in our lives' (Ravenhill 2004: 1), instead of dealing with the global. But this duality in his writing can lead to an obscuring of his purpose.

Ravenhill doesn't give answers in his play but he feels a duty to highlight the problems; 'Can people change? Can the world change? Can art be part of this process? It's almost embarrassing to ask these questions as we muddle through the early 21st century in a haze of jolly irony and slow despair. But somehow we have to do it' (Ravenhill 2004: 2). However, sometimes his 'embarrassment' makes the plays top heavy on the side of the micro political, whilst the macro political relies heavily on the knowledge-base of the audience if they are to gain a full understanding of the wider politics of the plays. Ravenhill admits to writing with a sign above his desk 'The audience is smarter than you are' (Ravenhill 2003: 2). In real terms this means when considering *Handbag* they also need an understanding of past biographical and historical events and *Citizenship* demands an appreciation of current curriculum and political issues if they are to get the most from the plays.

Ravenhill's plays have always dealt with micropolitics, referred to as 'the finite local struggles championed by the French thinker Michel Foucault, who appears, thinly disguised as Alain, in (Ravenhill's play) *Faust Is Dead* (Buse 2005: 2). His plays examine the personal search for connectedness, love and family outside of conventional familial structures. There is always sharp social observation; moments of sentimentality, irony, and humour but ultimately his characters display an overriding dysfunctional compassion. This style is a reflection of the political preoccupations of the 1990's which as Sierz suggests 'come from the intense examination of private pain, rather than from scrawling on a large political canvas' (Sierz 2001: 241). But is would be a disservice to Ravenhill not to acknowledge that he attempts both.

Populism and cultural angst

Ravenhill has always managed to connect his work with what is current. From his appearance on the theatre scene in the 90's with *Shopping and Fucking*, with its oblique exploration of consumerism, to *Product* in 2005, the pitching of a love story entwined with the dark threat of terrorism, his work has always taken a controversial sideways swipe at what is currently obsessing the media. Even his work for young people *Totally Over You* and *Citizenship* deals with the pertinent, the cult of celebrity and the controversial citizenship curriculum in schools.

Ravenhill is skilled at playing the media, as Max Stafford-Clark points out 'Some are born to populism, some achieve populism and some have populism thrust upon them. I place Mark firmly in the first category' (Sierz 2001: 3). The fact that he and his plays do connect with the popular has sometimes led to his work being considered as lacking in substance. Dan Rabellato takes a different viewpoint stating 'The reason why some playwrights dislike him is that he was incredibly successful with his first play. When a debut runs for six months in the west end, people begin to ask 'is it really that good?'' (Sierz 2001: 2). But Ravenhill's plays resonate with more than just the zeitgeist and it is this that gives them their depth.

When *Shopping & Fucking* exploded onto the theatrical scene no critic labelled it a 'Gay Play', in part because it had been proceeded by a wave of gay plays including Jonathan Harvey's *Beautiful Thing* and Kevin Elyots *My Night With Reg*. *Shopping & Fucking's* main thematic focus is on a generation who is 'apolitical with no values except economic ones' (Rabellato in Ravenhill 2001: xiii). Whether they are gay or straight doesn't overtly figure, it just is. Ravenhill rejects the label of Gay Playwright or the label of anything:

'Does he see himself as a gay playwright? 'Not at all,' he says, thankful that he started writing at a time when audiences 'no longer expected a coming out speech or an AIDS related plot' Nor is he happy with the label 'Gay Man' which he argues has been appropriated by consumer culture What about queer? 'Well, the notion of queer is much more about being a radically different person, a sexual outlaw, but risks just being radical chic' The more ironic 'post-gay' makes him grin' (Sierz 2001:3).

I would contend that Ravenhill's resilience as a writer stems from his ability to tap into the persistent cultural anxiety connected to homosexuality; the fear of the queer. It is his continuing ability to disturb, highlight and play with this cultural fear which makes him durable as a writer. In order to identify this quality I will use as detailed examples Ravenhill's *Handbag* which borrows not simply from one of the most 'queer' plays in the canon but also from the playwright whose life has seeped into, or indeed produced, our queer reading of the text now, and the play *Citizenship* one of his plays for young people where he explores the tensions between governmental definitions of citizenship and personal, fluctuating, evolving sexuality. The queer resonance in both plays allows Ravenhill to explore both the micro and the macropolitics of the relationships. In addition it imbues his work with a durability which moves Ravenhill beyond ephemeral cultural fodder.

A playwright has to be either arrogant or naive to ignore the influence of the body of work that has gone before them. Some writers acknowledge it more publicly than others:

> 'Although most of us write alone, we do not write in isolation. We write with the knowledge –sometimes comforting, at other times terrifying – of tens of thousands of plays which have preceded ours, and the many more to follow' (Nagy in Edgar 2000: 123).

Ravenhill has always recognised the literary influences he has drawn on in his work. Sometimes the influences are purely historical as in *Mother Clap's Molly House*, which is set in an 18th century Molly House, a club where men could dress up as women, and act out their sexual fantasies. In Totally *Over You* a plot line is appropriated, in this case from Moliere's *Precieuses Ridicules* where young women who rebuff suitors lacking in courtly manners are tricked into falling for servants.
 But in his play *Handbag* Ravenhill attempts to express the present by connecting to an understanding of both historical, biographical events and previous canonised text.

Ravenhill's *Handbag*

Ravenhill's *Handbag* borrows not simply from one of the most 'queer' plays in the canon; *The Importance of Being Earnest,* but also from the playwright, Oscar Wilde, whose life has seeped into our queer reading of the text now. To appreciate the macropolitics Ravenhill is trying to articulate in *Handbag* it is imperative to gain a comprehensive understanding of the source material and its context. As a result it is then possible to perceive how *Handbag*, using a pre-existing cultural vocabulary, distils the persistently compelling dangerousness of the queer.
 Whilst the play stages explicit scenes, it is the resonance it borrows that gives it bite. Whilst Ravenhill accesses the lines, themes and imagery from the text – with varying degrees of success – this is not the dominant textual strategy. It is the use of the implicit which enables the text to leave a lasting impression. Spectatorship feeds off memory, prompting critics and reviewers to recall a multitude of resonances from past performances. Intertextual seepage often plays upon the spectator's consciousness in snatches and fragments. *Handbag* not only relies upon the construction of meta-characters but also upon the exploitation of the received iconography of Wilde which surrounds the source work (Dickenson & Iball 2002).
 The seepage between source text and biography becomes even more significant when approaching *Handbag,* because Ravenhill selects as

his source one of the queerest of all plays, yet one that makes precious little reference to homosexuality. This is the paradox that fascinates Alan Sinfield. Why, asks Sinfield, has *The Importance of Being Earnest* come to 'reek(s)... of queerness' (Sinfield 1994: vi)? It is his belief that our posthumous reading of the dissidence that gives Wilde's plays their edge, developed as a direct result of the public exposure of Wilde's sexual activity, brought about during his trial.

It is necessary to briefly unpick Wilde's situation and the impact of *The Importance of Being Earnest* to fully appreciate the influence of both on any reading of *Handbag*.

At the time of Wilde's conviction in 1895, many blamed him for his relationship with Lord Alfred Douglas, believing, as Queensbury did, that the older man had corrupted the younger. When Wilde took Queensbury to court the defence barrister emphasised that 'Queensbury had been animated from beginning to end "by one hope alone – of saving his son"' (Pearce 2001: 236). However, Pearce in his biography of Wilde puts a different perspective on the relationship. By 1891, Wilde was pushing his family further away to the margins of his life and surrounding himself with young male admirers. But he was still 'circumspect about his sexuality, in public at least' (Pearce 2001: 183). This behaviour is in marked contrast to Wilde during his relationship with Douglas. Pearce states;

'Douglas was promiscuous and introduced Wilde to the world of homosexual prostitution. From the autumn of 1892 onwards he encouraged Wilde to form casual relationships with young men who would prostitute themselves for a few pounds and a good dinner' (Pearce 2001: 204).

By 1893, Wilde's friends were beginning to notice the influence of Douglas on Wilde's behaviour in public.

'In August, Beerbohm observed Wilde, Douglas and Robbie Ross cavorting ostentatiously with vine leaves in their hair (...) "of course I would rather see Oscar free than sober, but still suddenly meeting him...I felt quite repelled"' (Pearce 2001: 215).

Wilde's relationship with Constance his wife had deteriorated to such an extent that by April 1893 she ended up taking his post to the Savoy hotel where Douglas and Wilde had a room. Constance 'besought him to come home but Wilde replied heartlessly that he'd been away so long that he'd forgotten the number of the house' (Pearce 2001: 215).

In Wilde's time, same sex passion 'was being presented as

essentially masculine' (Sinfield 1994: vii); the revelations made by the trials re-orientated the presentation towards a stereotypical assumption of homosexual effeminacy, rooted in Wilde's dandyism and aestheticism. This stereotype had established a firm hold on the collective consciousness by the middle of the twentieth century and it still continues to resonate. Thus, as Sinfield points out, 'Our interpretation is retroactive: in fact, Wilde and his writings look queer because our stereotypical notion of male homosexuality derives from Wilde and our ideas about him' (Sinfield 1994: vii).

> 'In their repercussions the Wilde trials belong more to the 20th century than the 19th. They not only helped impose a music hall view of homosexuality as the preserves of camping aesthetes and seedy sex workers, they also provided modern homosexuality with a date of birth, a charismatic martyr and some memorable legends'(Robb 2003: 36).

He goes on to say that homosexuality was only part of the story of the Wilde trials. Although Wilde's sexual habits were found to be scandalous to some, so too was his 'blatant disregard for class divisions that seemed to go with them....His ' associates, said the Solicitor-General, 'ought to have been his equals and not these illiterate boys whom you have heard in the witness box'.'(Robb 2003: p38). Furthermore Robb argues that Wilde's profession as an artist caused specific antipathy, which, according to Yeats, was a peculiarly British attitude.
'This hatred is not due to any action of the artist or eminent man; it is merely the expression of an individual hatred and envy, become collective because circumstances have made it so' (Robb 2003: 38). Ultimately Wilde was able to be damned because he was not English. It had been common cultural currency throughout Europe for some time to blame homosexuality on foreigners.
     'In 1810, when a flourishing club of 'mollies' was discovered in a London pub two newspapers blamed 'the evil' on the Napoleonic wars: Too many foreign servants and too many Englishmen exposed to foreign customs' (Robb 2003: 7). Ravenhill feeds directly off this fact in *Mother Clap's Molly House* an 'all singing, all dancing, all sodomising extravaganza', (Gardner 2002: 1) where he juxtapositions sex as a transaction and the role of the family in the context of capitalism. In this play we see Ravenhill begin, albeit tentatively, to place his work on a broader canvas.
     Regarding the Wilde trials, Robb is explicit in his opinion that to reduce their impact 'to a simple tale of 'martyrdom' (as both Wilde and Douglas later saw it).....is melodramatic....It promotes a highly localised

and pejorative view of homosexuality' (Robb 2003: 38). But Robb's perspective in his text is more concerned with law enforcement than social constructs. He rightly identifies that, for male homosexuals; 'As far as law enforcement is concerned it was in the 20th century that the Dark Ages began' (Robb 2003: 31). Robb appears to take comfort from the fact that although laws were in place for centuries prior to the twentieth, to restrict, outlaw and punitively punish homosexual acts they were only sporadically applied. This is of little comfort to any minority suffering from unfair legal prejudice. Historically it placed homosexuals at the mercy of patronage or whim. Patronage is a reoccurring theme in most of Ravenhill's plays and ties in directly to the fear of the queer, epitomised by the pre-man boy. The boy figure initially starts off seeking patronage but the patrons depicted are invariably self obsessed, resulting in the patronage being withheld or self serving. This drives the boy figure to claim ownership of his life, often with detrimental consequences for those around him. The essence of the boy links across texts and is a continual reoccurring theme in Ravenhill's drama; a theme directly referable to the Wilde trials.

In *Handbag* the boy figure is used as a metaphor for the complex identity politics of the nineties, the focus being the intense examination of private pain, (Sierz 2001: 241). But private pain was at the core of Wilde's work; his creative writing was constantly informed by the personal. He told Herbert Beerbohm Tree, who played the first Lord Illingworth in A Woman of No Importance that the character was 'certainly not natural, he is a figure of art, indeed, if you can bear the truth, he is myself' (Pearce 2001: 213). As Pearce states, 'Wilde's double life, the secret affair with Douglas, the clandestine liaisons with male prostitutes and the double-crossing of his wife on an almost daily basis, had enshrined the double entendre at the very core of his psyche' (Pearce 2001: 213). And yet Wilde insisted his creative writing was a way for him to get away from his problems. He wrote to the poet W.E.Henley that 'work never seems to me a reality but a way of getting rid of reality' (Pearce 2001: 224). The cathartic escapism he found in his work is evidenced in *The Importance of Being Earnest,* a text particularly and deliberately superficial. Pearce observes 'its lack of earnestness… (its) two-dimensional approach where the shallowness of the characters prevents either ascent to morality or descent to immorality' (Pearce 2001: 227). But, this quality is re-focused by our retroactive reading; a reading drenched in the stereotyping of queer identity that Sinfield believes originated in Wilde's biography. So, Wilde's notoriety makes even – or perhaps especially – the most shallow of his texts quiver with the dangerous energy of dissident sexuality.

The boy in *Handbag*

Handbag contains many of the themes that run through most of Ravenhill's plays; destructive paternalism, the abdication of responsibility, preening self obsession, the loss of collective and universal bonds, but Ravenhill takes the queer 'ambience' seeping from Wilde's biography as the supreme gift, and plays with the re-reading of *The Importance of Being Earnest* by writing a prequel that gives the frothy layers of misunderstanding a far bleaker frame. Handbag's 1890s scenes propose that there are disturbing reasons for the mislaying of Jack Worthing in the handbag on Victoria Station. Ravenhill juxtapositions this with scenes set in the 1990's which deliver explicit sex as sensationalist accompaniment to angst about parenting and the fear of commitment. The principle device employed by Ravenhill to bridge these two timeframes is the meeting of the characters Cardew and Phil, which is brutally apt given that *Handbag* resonates with Wilde's own dangerous fascination with attractive young men. Sinfield notes that, during the trials, the prosecution represented the boys 'either as corrupted by Wilde or as so corrupt already that no decent person would associate with them' (1994: 121). In *Handbag* Phil encapsulates the two positions of the boy; he is needy, childlike in his inability to look after himself and he is dangerous, manipulative and prone to violent behaviour. Both Cardew and Phil are predators, and, in this sense, they are each the other's victim. The main difference between them is that Cardew does care for and love his wards, but in a manner that is complex and socially deviant. He has a propensity to be drawn to lost boys; as a philanthropist and as a paedophile; whereas Phil comes to believe his own mantra, 'Be your own person' (Sc iii: 157) focusing completely on himself, with destructive consequences.

In the ambiguous hierarchies of the relationship between the boy (usually 'rough trade') and his 'steamer' (the customer), Sinfield finds the essence of the queer's dangerous circulations, its threat to the binarised organisation of the status quo. He notes that 'the queer is the leisure-class man and in so far as he commissions the lower-class boy he is superior, in the masculine position,' but, equally 'in so far as he is effeminate he is allowing himself to become inferior – in the feminine position' (Sinfield 1994: 122). This ambiguous hierarchy is evidenced in both the characters of David and Cardew in relation to Phil.

PHIL: He likes me to fuck him
DAVID: Oh come on
TOM: Really? He always said it hurt when I tried to do it.
DAVID: Please

TOM: Couldn't take it, could you, my love? Still I suppose when they're pre- pubescent (Sc viii: 190).

David had started off in the role of patron to Phil, but by allowing Phil to 'fuck' David and not his long term boyfriend Tom, Ravenhill is clearly defining the difference in the relationships. David labels Phil as 'a boy...I met a boy and he had no one and he needed looking after'. The label is reiterated in Tom's incredulous reply 'Boy? Destroyed everything now. For a boy. Some boy to fuck you and you destroyed everything' (Ravenhill 1998: 70). There are echoes of Ravenhill's earlier play *Shopping and Fucking* in his utilisation of the rent boy as a morally ambiguous central figure. Indeed, Sierz feels that in *Handbag* 'the image of the rent boy cutting himself, having anal sex and injecting heroin seems over familiar, almost mannered' (Sierz 2001: 142). In *Handbag*, it is Phil, the boy figure, who is the perpetrator of violence. The play confronts the tangled relationship between culture and sub-culture. The boy character Phil is the most 'straight' person in the play, but in real terms he is the most bent.

The baby and the boy

A motif that Ravenhill uses in *Handbag* and revisits in *Citizenship* is that of the baby. In both the baby is an emblem of family but highlights the distortion of social mores in the plays by the treatment meted out to it. In each, the violence enacted on the baby is perpetrated by the boy figure. In *Handbag,* Ravenhill uses the murder of the baby as a climax and outcome; which, although on a feeling level is theatrically shocking, on a reasoning level is not very sophisticated and - to Sierz's perception of 90s drama - refuses to provide answers, expressing instead a culture steeped in 'contradiction, half-truths and ambiguity' (Sierz 2001: 248). What the use of the baby does is underscore the fact that 'Ravenhill's work has a complex and difficult relationship with fathers' (Ravenhill 2001: xiii). Ravenhill sees parenthood as something earnt and learnt, not a biological given. This is best exemplified by the characters Tom and Mauretta when arguing over Tom's professed attachment to the baby.

MAURETTA: You wanked into a cup
TOM: It makes me Dad. I'm a father
MAURETTA: It makes you nothing... (Sc xiii: 217).

Phil is failed by potential father figures but he in turn fails twice in the paternal role. Through back-story we find out he let his drug dealer abuse his five year old daughter from a previous relationship, but when given the chance to partially redeem himself by looking after the baby he ends up torturing and killing it. Even when it is dead he doesn't stop; 'Just gonna be awkward? Just not gonna breathe, eh? Alright. Alright' (Sc xiv: 226). Ravenhill clearly depicts the complete lack of Phil's parental ability, but his eager wish to parent (Here, I'm good with him, I'll...(Sc xiv: 225)), combined with his callous torturing of the baby with lighted cigarettes, leaves us with a deep sense of unease, not easily dismissed. Once again Ravenhill doesn't provide answers, but by demonstrating such failings most explicitly in the boy figure he makes explicit the persistent sense of cultural disturbance both invoked by and surrounding homosexuality and the likelihood that simply by association it will provoke a violent response.

Citizenship

Citizenship, a play for young people, resonates with reoccurring thematic connections but it also demonstrates Ravenhill's urge to develop as a dramatist. *Handbag* is drenched in the past but in *Citizenship* Ravenhill is firmly looking to the future. He is again attempting to work on a broader political canvas which he endeavoured to do in 1999 with *Some Explicit Polaroids*. But whereas *Some Explicit Polaroids* clutched onto the past for some political security, as it was 'in part inspired by Earnst Toller's *Hoppla! Such is Life!*' (Ravenhill 2001: xix). *Citizenship* is boldly sourced in the political present. But it is the seepage from *Handbag* of the metonymic boy figure which disturbs the queer ambience of *Citizenship* providing its cultural bite.

There is still a pervading attitude in theatre made evident by Robert Hanks that 'there aren't many phrases that make a critics heart sink faster than 'youth theatre' (Hanks 2005: 1). This attitude is changing with more and more prominent writers, such as Edward Bond and Alan Aykbourne, writing for young people, and with 'First-division playwrights queue(ing) up to write for the annual Shell Connections Season, a yearly event. ..Commissioned by the National Theatre' (Gardner 2005: 1), then it is no wonder that Ravenhill has 'Always wanted to write a Connections play'. For him 'the chance to see your work performed by enthusiastic young casts all over the country is irresistible' (Ravenhill 2003: 1).

His first play for young people, *Totally Over You* connected to the literary past and was anything but contentious. So much so that one teacher from a school performing the play asked; 'My kids want to say 'fuck'…and there aren't any 'fucks' in the play. When we do the play can we, you know, add some 'fucks'?'(Ravenhill 2003: 1). But, in *Citizenship* Ravenhill allows his characters to be as dysfunctional as any in his previous plays and although the depictions of sex and violence are more implicit than explicit, rarely shown and cloaked in a gauze of humour, the sense of underlying threat, omnipresent in *Handbag,* is still there.

Citizenship and the curriculum

As with *Handbag,* Ravenhill is relying on the audience's pre-existing knowledge to gain a complete understanding of the macropolitics in his play *Citizenship*. This is a risk as it is likely that more people have a comprehensive understanding of Wilde and his work than do those who know about English educational curriculum matters. By naming the play *Citizenship*, Ravenhill is overtly relating the play to the Citizenship curriculum in English schools brought in by the Labour government of Tony Blair, a curriculum which should be a place for the discussion and understanding of difference, including homosexuality, but still suffers from shifting political pressure both at regional and national levels, leaving teachers implementing the curriculum with a sense of anxiety. For some the anxiety in underpinned by the experience of political edicts predating the Citizenship curriculum. In 1988 the Conservative government of Margaret Thatcher brought in to being

'Section 28 which prohibited local authorities from promoting homosexuality or teaching in state schools the acceptability of homosexuality as a 'pretended family relationship' (G.L.B.T.Q. 2005: 1).

Although the section was rescinded in 2003 by the Labour government, the effect it had was to make teachers at best reticent about discussing homosexuality in schools and at worst allowed to leave prejudice unshackled. This reticence on the subject of homosexuality still pervades as recognised by Mulligan in his writings on Ravenhill's *Citizenship*.

'It encourages teachers and students to talk about things that are not fully acknowledged, to make things a little more public, to deal with things that teachers and students know about but seldom talk about. In this sense *Citizenship* really does break new ground' (Mulligan in Ravenhill 2005: 266).

Globalisation and *Citizenship*

By relating to the Citizenship curriculum Ravenhill is connecting to wider political issues which he continually wrestles with in his plays. Many of Ravenhill's characters struggle with mini stories of their own creation to make sense of the world. As Robbie says in *Shopping and Fucking* 'I think we all need stories, we make up stories to get by' (Sc xiii, 67). But their determined obsessive spotlighting of their own micro stories means that they fail to connect to each other. Without connectedness there is no resistance to the omnipresent story of globalisation which is one of the biggest challenges to a cohesive society. In his previous plays Ravenhill allows the historical references and the irony imbued in his characters' behaviour, to obliquely augment the political perspective, but in *Citizenship* he connects directly to the current British political response to globalisation.

The Citizenship curriculum is connected to the Third Way political approach adopted by the labour government of Tony Blair. The Third Way when conceived was concerned with developing an alternative to what was perceived as the social fragmentation and social exclusion produced by eighteen years of Conservative Party Government with its focus on neo- liberal marketisation. It was also an alternative to previous Labour Party policies which concentrated on bureaucratic collectivism and corporatism of the social Democratic welfare state

'Third Way thinking is based on two interlocking premises. The first is that the state is relatively impotent in the sphere of economic dynamics in the era of globalization.... The second premise follows from the first. If the state cannot intervene directly in the economy, it must therefore focus on changing society, thus approaching the economic indirectly' (Cairns, Gardner & Lawton 2000: 95).

The Third Way percolated down the state structures and became an intrinsic part of the government's education policy. Subsequently the aims of Citizenship education were delineated in the Crick report as:

'To make secure and increase the knowledge, skills and values relevant to the nature and practices of participative democracy; also to enhance the awareness of rights and duties, and the sense of responsibilities needed for the development of pupils into active citizens; and in so doing to establish the value to individuals, schools and society of involvement in the local and wider community' (DfEE/QCA, 1998, Para 6.6, in Cairns, Gardner & Lawton 2000: 55).

There is much about activity, participation, informed choice making, critical understanding and social structure. Such matters are not the making of 'quiet citizens'. The Citizenship curriculum itself promotes, 'active learning' which encourages engagement outside the classroom and within the community. The nature of the Citizenship curriculum has been kept loose for a number of reasons and whilst this flexibility seems attractive, it also reflects the sense of lack of clear guidance in an education system now used to a prescriptive National curriculum. Consequently in too many schools Citizenship has been tackled defensively and unimaginatively.

It may well be that schools are not so much ill equipped to deal with the subject as uncomfortable with the suspicion that there is a hidden political agenda and that if they are too proactive they might find themselves outside the boundaries, particularly when governments change. The necessity for student involvement in citizenship issues within schools is pinpointed by Ravenhill in relation to his play:

> 'I think *Citizenship* will be challenging for many schools. If the play is put on in isolation then that might be difficult, but if there is a culture where students can discuss things and discuss the issues around the play it might help the school' (Ravenhill 2005: 265).

The labour government claims that schools are free to use whatever suits them to implement the Citizenship curriculum. It is difficult to know what a government would actually find acceptable as, as has been pointed out, this could be a recipe for political activism. Melanie Phillips in The Sunday Times when considering the proposals for Citizenship on the National curriculum observes;

> 'even more strikingly, it wants teachers to promote a particular form of democracy called active citizenship.... This is not so much political literacy as political activism. (The Sunday Times, 17 March, 1999, 17 in Cairns, Gardner & Lawton 2000: 82).

So here we have an interesting situation. Since the Conservative government of Margaret Thatcher schools have been used to a prescriptive National curriculum, subsequently when faced with a loosely constructed, flexible and interesting brief, there is a sense of unease (Dickenson & Kerridge 2004).

This unease is highlighted by Ravenhill in *Citizenship* through De Clerk The citizenship teacher, who is obsessed with the imminent school inspection: 'Nothing else matters but your coursework and the inspectors....there is nothing else in the whole wide world that matters apart from that' (Sc iii: 230). His role as conduit of the Citizenship curriculum is uncomfortable for him and he harshly deflects any discussion of the personal with Tom the main protagonist. Tom's persistence in pushing him for a response in relation to his confusing dream is ultimately rebuffed with broad school guidelines.

> DE CLERK: You know the school policy; we celebrate difference. You report Bullies. Everything's okay. You're okay.
> TOM: I don't feel okay.
> DE CLERK: Well - you should (Sc iii: 233).

The Shell Connections project in 2004 for which *Citizenship* was written involved over 241 schools or colleges. One copy of the anthology of the plays written for the project was placed in every secondary school in the country with the support of the Foyle Foundation. The plays were toured nationally culminating in a performance at the National Theatre in London. By such direct engagement with schools and by publishing the play text it, the project, in part, raises the status of plays for young people. This in turn helps disseminate the debates and contentions contained within the pages of the work. Most writers involved in the 2005 project have dealt with the micropolitics of the young people presenting a variety of sympathetic, dynamic, theatrically engaging perspectives. However, Ravenhill has targeted not just the young people but the educators for whom the understanding of the macropolitics involved would be acute.

The 'zig zagging' boy in *Citizenship*

Ravenhill is at his most engaging when creating characters and those in *Citizenship* are no exception. They demonstrate a similarity to most others in his plays, with a concentration on their own micro stories. There's a connection to *Faust is Dead* in that one of the characters self harms, there are echoes of *Some Explicit Polaroids* in the embracing of trite self help therapies, which obviously don't work, but what makes the characters different in *Citizenship* is the 'stark realism and acceptance by the young characters of things that adults either disapprove of or pretend do not happen' (Mulligan in Ravenhill 2005: 263). This provides the play with a perspective that sets it apart from the other text.
But once again it is the boy figure that agitates the queer ambience of *Citizenship* provoking cultural disturbance.

As in *Handbag* we have a pre-man boy, Tom, who moves quickly from being the prey to the predator. We find him at the beginning of a journey of discovery to explore his sexual orientation. It is not a straight path but 'a Zigzag path towards some idea of who you are' (Mulligan

2005: 263). He has a recurring dream, in which he is kissing an unseen person; but he can't tell if the person is a man or a woman. With initial, refreshing naivety Tom thinks that just by kissing people you can tell if they are 'the one' but it is obvious he thinks that he is gay, when his best friend Amy kisses him he says 'I didn't mean *you* to do that' (Sc I:219) . Similar to Phil in *Handbag,* initially, Tom is a victim. Succumbing to peer pressure to prove he is not gay he thumps his friend Gary and claims that he is having sex with his best friend Amy when he isn't. But quickly Tom becomes active rather than reactive. He tenaciously pursues his Citizenship teacher De Clerk attempting to seduce him with voracious determination. It is Tom's treatment of Amy which shows him at his most callous and self-seeking. 'It seems Amy is desperate for a role in Tom's life' (Mulligan in Ravenhill 2005: 263). But he uses her to discover whether if he is heterosexual. Throughout the play he professes a want to have adults direct him in his choices. When De Clerk walks through the wall and tells him to use protection when having sex Tom says 'It's telling me what to do. You should tell me more of that' (Sc vii: 252). But it is De Clerk's queer attention he seeks, not advice; as he immediately goes on to have sex with Amy without using protection, making her pregnant in the process.

The baby and the boy

As in *Handbag,* Ravenhill uses the motif of the baby to highlight the distortion of social mores by the boy figure. In *Citizenship* the baby is presented in three guises. Firstly, as a plastic doll used for life skills classes, then as a verbally eloquent essence of baby and finally as a real baby in a pram. Such theatrical contrivance provides a distance to the treatment meted out to it by Tom but it doesn't reduce the rippling disturbance his action produce. The characters' attitudes towards the plastic baby vary, from the obsessive to the indifferent, but it is Tom who is deliberately violent towards it. He deliberately drops the baby three times, each time becoming more brutal. When Amy goes to pick it up he tells her 'No-Leave it' (Sc vii: 248) and asks her to have sex. He too like Phil in *Handbag* has the chance to redeem himself as a father with the appearance of the real baby. He professes to want to baby-sit the child but this quickly changes to a desire for Amy the mother. When she rejects him he persists with the baby although by now it is clear that his interest is all about control.

TOM: I wanna see you again. I'm the Dad.
AMY: Gary looks after her – don't you?

GARY: Yeah.
TOM: Yeah – but still. (Sc ix: 261).

Resonant of *Handbag* Amy makes it clear that parenting is not a biological given. Unlike in *Handbag,* in *Citizenship* Ravenhill spares the baby, Amy won't let Tom pick it up so he doesn't have the opportunity to drop it, but his use of the motif, supported by his previous work leaves us with a reading which is unequivocal. *Citizenship* doesn't have the bleak emotional landscape of *Handbag* which has much to do with Ravenhill's awareness of his target audience. But he doesn't patronise by providing a happy ending. In a workshop for the play Max Stafford Clark identifies the pragmatism of the outcomes.

'An accurate assessment of Martin's and Tom's relationship?...Maybe two months....As for Gary and Amy's relationship? Perhaps a couple of years, no longer' (Ravenhill 2005: 273).

Such pragmatism encourages thematic reflection but the resonance of the fear of the queer not only in *Handbag* but in *Citizenship* overarches the thematic definitions of the plays sharpening the social impact of each which may not be explicit in a reasoning context but is implicit in a feeling context. As Edward Bond states:

'Imagination is needed to ask why. Imagination and not reason makes us human....the ability to reason does not make us rational. It is our imagination that reasons' (Nicholson 2003: 13).

Although each play's source material differs, each has a depth which can be mined for further understanding, but the disturbance from Ravenhill's work is due to the continuing manipulation of our imaginations. The essence of the boy figures is metonymic, encapsulating in their stage presence the way in which the effective manipulation of theatre form precipitates the collision of feeling and reason.
Ravenhill presents us with the continuing vulnerability of those not conforming to the heterosexual norm, but also in the same characters he encapsulates the persistent cultural sense of threat invoked by homosexuality, producing a theatrical presence which produces a metaphysical distillation of the dangerousness of the queer.
So why is Ravenhill criticised for being a writer who does not deal with big issues?
The problem for Ravenhill is that his ability to connect with the universal is often restrained by his recognition that he is only in part a responsible writer. 'Isn't there always something naughty, a part of us that wills chaos

and pits it against order?' (Ravenhill 2003: 3). This naughtiness in writing terms is attractive but leaves an impression that the significant is only ever touched upon.

When on a tour of Poland in support of *Some Explicit Polaroids* Ravenhill was asked a question by a Polish Professor. 'Mr Ravenhill, the great subject of your work is the metaphysics of evil. What can you tell us about that?' (Ravenhill 2003: 1). By his own admission his immediate response was one of naughtiness. 'The only words that came to mind were Gwendolen's from the importance of being earnest: 'Ah! That is clearly a metaphysical speculation, and like most metaphysical speculations has very little reference to the actual facts of real life, as we know it' (Ravenhill 2003: 2). Although this was not the answer he gave, he felt he didn't respond to the question effectively and came away feeling chastened. Ravenhill speculates as to whether he would be a better writer if he was to look beyond the sociological, the anthropological, the political and more overtly into the spiritual or metaphysical. But then states that it seems 'wrong to even think about the metaphysical at a time like this' (Ravenhill 2003: 2) and sees this collective guilt as the bind of the English playwright. This tension in his writing is still not resolved. But I would contend from the evidence contained in *Handbag* and *Citizenship,* that Ravenhill may yet write the truly metaphysical play.

Works cited

Cairns, Jo. Gardner, Roy. Lawton, Denis (eds), *The Education for Citizenship,* New York & London: Continuum, 2000.

Edgar, David, *State of Play: Playwrights on playwriting*, London: Faber & Faber, 2000.

Nicholson, Helen, Acting, Creativity and Social Justice: Edward Bond's The Children. *Research in Drama Education* Vol. 8, No. 1, pp 9-22, 2003.

Pearce, Joseph, *The Unmasking of Oscar Wilde*, London: Harper Collins, 2001.

Ravenhill, Mark, *Handbag,* London: Methuen, 1998.

—. *Mark Ravenhill Plays: 1,* London: Methuen, 2001.

—. *Citizenship* in *Shell Connections 2005: New Plays For Young People,* London: Faber & Faber, 2005.

Robb, Graham, *Strangers. Homosexual Love in The Nineteenth Century,* London: Picador, 2003.

Sierz, Aleks, *In-Yer-Face Theatre: British Drama Today*, London: Faber& Faber, 2001.

Sinfield, Alan, *The Wilde Century*, London: Cassell, 1994.

Unpublished papers

Dickenson, Sarah Jane & Iball, Helen. *Baggage, Choosing and Abusing the past: the Uses of Canonisation in Handbag & Weldon Rising.* 'In Yer Face Theatre British Drama in the 1990's Bristol. Sept 2002

Dickenson, Sarah Jane & Kerridge, Viv. *Shut Up, Sit Down, We're Going to Talk About Human Rights: Citizenship & 'The Landing' Project.* Drama as Social Intervention. The Fifth International Conference. Exeter, England. April 2005

Websites

http://www.contemporarywriters.com/authors/?p=auth258.Buse,   Peter, Mark Ravenhill. Contemporary Writers. Arts Council. Accessed 7 Nov 2005

http://www.guardian.co.uk/arts/features/story/0,11712,705390,00.html. Gardner, Lyn. (12 February 2002) Mother Clap's Molly House *Guardian Unlimited.* Accessed 20 Nov 2005.

http://www.guardian.co.uk/arts/features/story/0,,152373,00.html 20 Nov 2005. Gardner, Lyn, Shell Connections, *GuardianUnlimited.* Accessed 8 July 2005.

http://enjoyment.independent.co.uk/theatre/reviews/article298197.ece. Accessed 20 Nov 2005

Hanks, Robert, Shell Connections: Citizenship/Chatroom. National Theatre, Cottesloe, London, *The Independent.* Accessed 11 July 2005.

http://www.glbtq.com/social-sciences/clause_28.html.   GLBTQ: An Encyclopaedia of Gay, Lesbian, bisexual, Transgender & Queer Culture. Accessed 21 Nov 2005.

http://www.inyerface-theatre.com/archive8.html. Sierz, Alex. (2001) Profile of Mark Ravenhill. /Interview With Mark Ravenhill. Accessed 2 Aug 2005.

http://www.guardian.co.uk/arts/features/story/0,111710,919203,00.html, 8 Aug 2005. Ravenhill, Mark. A touch of Evil *GuardianUnlimited.* Accessed 22 March 2003.

http://www.guardian.co.uk/arts/features/story/0,4273,4712411,00.html. Ravenhill, Mark (15th July 2003) Freak Show *GuardianUnliited.* Accessed 20 Nov 2005.

http://www.guardian.co.uk/arts/features/story/0,,1239609,00.html. Ravenhill, Mark (16 June 2004) Life, Death and Estate Agents. *Guardian Unlimited.* Accessed 20 Nov 2005.

CHAPTER EIGHT

THE FLUIDITY OF BODIES, GENDER, IDENTITY AND STRUCTURE IN THE PLAYS OF SARAH KANE

SELINA BUSBY & STEPHEN FARRIER

Synopsis

The majority of Sarah Kane's work can be situated within a queer frame. We position Kane within this frame by constructing some queer readings of Blasted (1995), Cleansed (1998), Crave (1998) and 4.48 Psychosis (2000). In these readings we focus on the characters in the work (if any), bodies and their fluidity, as well as queer visions of gender as it is expressed in fluid identities. Also we look at how some forms of theatrical structure in her later work mark the text as open to queer reading. Crucially, these analyses are drawn with an eye on the cultural and historical context of both the work and of queer's rise in the UK of the 1990s.

*****

In this chapter, we start by focusing on a debate that critics and academics have about the problem of ideology in Kane's work. Commonly, in these discussions, there is a perception that the work lacks any particular ideological bent and that this is a problem for the notions of politics and change. Often this lack of ideology, and for some, a lack of political focus (Gottlieb 2003: 9), is related to Thatcher's children and the conservative government of the 1980s and 1990s. Critics and academics when writing about the relationship between the society of the 1990s and Kane's work, often rest on this idea of an ideological-less inheritance. Kane's work not only reflects the alienation of Thatcher's Children but equally, and in some cases more so, we argue, it echoes the 1990s queer movement in the UK. This movement refocused ideas about sexuality, ideology and subjectivity for a whole section of society and yet, generally, critics do not tend to comment on this influence. Rather, they tend to make statements about the alienation of youth and their relationship to commodity.

In order to have a debate about the relationship between queer and Kane's work we begin with a short discussion of queer's rise as an idea in the theatrical culture of the 1990s. Taking some of queer theory's key ideas we move on to see how queer Kane's work is, in order to fill the gap that most critics leave out when discussing her work. We start by linking responses to Kane's work with ideas about the fluidity of queer as an identity position. We then move on to look at some of Kane's plays to make more intimate connections between Kane's characters, settings and stage descriptions, and the definitions, sensations and concepts of queer.

Kane's work is often placed alongside other playwrights' work of the 1990s, forming a cluster of work variously called 'the Britpack' (Saunders 2002: 5), 'New Realism' (Gottlieb 2003: 5), 'Neo-Jacobeanism, New Brutalism, Theatre of Urban Ennui, In-Yer-Face' (Seirz 2004: 18), 'British Brutalism, [and/or] New European Drama' (Nikcevic 2005: 255). There is no consensus about Kane being part of a particular movement in theatre, nor her work fitting a particular form, indeed each of her plays are different in terms of form. Urban describes the difficulty of seeing the kinds of work that this group were producing, he says:

> ...the case for a movement is hard to make. An artistic movement needs a shared sense of purpose, a collective will, a manifesto, or at least a figure head with whom the artists align themselves. (Urban 2004: 354)

Although we could debate that a movement needs these aspects in order to be properly a movement, what we can see is that Kane's work emerged at a 'particular historical moment' (Urban 2004: 354). This historical moment was the 1990s, the same period in which queer became increasingly powerful on the street as a form of protest and in the academy as a subject area (Butler's key text for queers, Gender Trouble was published in 1990).

Queer when it first arrived in the UK in the 1990s, like the plays of Kane and her contemporaries, caused outrage in some quarters and support in others. Queer upset those who had invested in a lesbian and gay politics rooted in the traditions of gay liberation. Chris Woods in a short polemic published in 1995, the year of Kane's Blasted, says of queer:

> Queer is now a generic term for a generation of homosexual men and
> women who revel in opposition – to each other and to the wider society –
> who are unable to let go of the sense of specialness engendered by the
> conflict politics of the 1980s.   Part mock-punk (bring-down-the-gay-
> establishment anachronism), part anti-ideology free-fall, it is promoted by
> a post-1967 generation who see that year not as milestone but as millstone.
> A central conviction is that homosexual identity is self-constructed.
> Therefore, why not re-invent?   It sees the labels gay and lesbian as
> proscriptive, as having become as oppressive as heterosexuality in
> restrictiveness... (Woods 1995: 31)

The issue that Woods has with queer appears to be with the
particular kind of subjectivity (and perhaps identity) that seems rootless
and without an ideological drive.   However, queer as an identity is
purposefully anti ideological.   That is, Woods appears to be influenced in
his polemic by the efforts of the more ideological pre-1980s gay
movements, such as the Gay Liberation Front (GLF), which were often
rooted in Marxist ideals (see the GLF's manifestos in Walter 1980), but
that had failed because they could not manage difference. Walter suggests
the reason the GLF fell apart was because of the 'acute crisis of the gender
system' (Walter 1980: 40), and Weeks sees the GLF as 'the last major
product of the late 1960s euphoria' (Weeks 1977: 206).   Whatever the
reason, queer in the 1990s could be said to be responding to the failure of
liberation by taking the ideology out of identity.   As a consequence queer,
like Kane's work, was/is seen as politically difficult because of its lack of
a clear ideology at its base.

Other books written about gay life and the changing politics of
ontology were abound in the 1990s, all of which contributed to the rise of
queer in the 1990s.   Key in these volumes was an edited collection by
Mark Simpson entitled Anti-Gay (1996). This book examined, in a radical
sense, the relationship gayness as an identity has with economics, the
values of the market and the generation and circulation of the pink pound.
Simpson and his contributors wrote of a gayness that was conservative,
coercive and exclusive.   His work unpicked the emancipatory impulse of
gay liberation. Critically different than Simpson, Alan Sinfield's Gay and
After coins the phrase post-gay to take account of the subcultures of
gayness, and calls for 'a more intelligent and critical gay culture' (Sinfield
1998: 15).   These two volumes are emblematic of the UK (sub) cultural
discourses post the GLF.

The GLF trod the line between identity, sexuality and politics
through the self-affirmative joy of gayness.   Queer as an idea, in some
respects, rejects the gay project out of hand because of its refusal to
engage in a politics of identity that is as solidly rooted as the gay

utopianism of the GLF – although the GLF was, in its time, a radical alternative to that which had been before. It is within this milieu that the New Brutalist writers were drawing their own rootless disenchanted characters and writing plays that were driven 'by a total disillusion, often jauntily expressed, with social decay: specifically the breakdown of any binding moral code or common sense of decency' (Saunders 2002: 5).

Queer as an idea links very well to the way in which the New Brutalists draw their characters. Specifically, Kane's characters are difficult because they have a lack of an ideological framework that helps audiences know them, as Urban remarks of the New Brutalists' attitude to social concerns and issues of cruelty: 'what disturbs critics of "in-yer-face" theatre is that it does so without any moral framework or ideological certainty' (Urban 2004: 363). This rootlessness reflects exceptionally well the rootlessness of queer identity, an identity that resists foreclosure: 'Queer is by definition whatever is at odds with the normal, the legitimate, the dominant' [original emphasis] (Halperin 1995 in Sullivan 2003: 43). The fuel of this type of thinking and identity is that it refuses the normative, likewise the work of Kane, which refuses in a number of ways (especially compositionally) the normative of UK mainstream theatre. Cranny-Francis et al, likewise see queer as something that 'challenge[s] the mechanism of identity as a regulatory force' (Cranny-Francis 2003: 75). A result of this queer attitude is a focus on identity as a performative and that queer need not attach certain types of identity to certain types of ideologies or structures of representation. That is, queer as an identity is always in a state of becoming, it is never quite finished, as Sedgwick says, queer subjectivity is:

> ...the open mesh of possibilities, gaps, overlaps, dissonances and resonances, lapses and excesses of meaning, when the constituent elements of any one's sexuality aren't made (or can't be made) to signify monolithically [original emphasis]. (Sedgwick 1994: 8)

Again, here there is a striking resemblance when looking at Kane's work (especially the later works) with Sedgwick's description of queer subjectivity. That is Kane's work, like queer, is never finished (at least in terms of representation) because it too is not rooted to a particular ideological idea that gives the representation a frame though which an audience can make a direct relation to a politics in the outside world. As a result of this rootlessness Kane's work may appear to be indistinct in terms of intent and fuzzy in terms of the clarity of reading available to an audience.

As a consequence of queer coming to the UK scene during the

1990s, there was a focus on indistinct or fuzzy subjectivities that could be read as resisting the regulatory force of identity – queered people who existed in an oppositional space and expressed themselves in ways that did not root themselves to normative frameworks, see Beemyn & Eliason (1996), Foster, Siegal & Berry (1997). Kane's plays, and the characters within the plays, in this sense of queer are very queer indeed. That is, the plays do not fully represent a knowable world (especially her later works) but a world in which the root of an image, that which gives the image an efficacy by connecting it to a knowable outside world, can change quickly from one position to another. For instance in our readings of some of Kane's work below, we focus on the elements of text and the performance that may jump, jar or otherwise disorientate an audience. The result of this vacillation in Kane's work, its apparent rootlessness, can lead to consideration of it as problematic.

John Peter writing in the Sunday Times in 1995 says of Blasted that the 'problem is that her play is half-realistic, half-symbolic. She has a vision of life, and she illustrates it with characters who are either over-written or incomplete, both more and less than real people'. What Peter is intimating here is that the characters appear unfinished, or unknowable. It is almost as if he is describing a queer identity in the same way as Jagose comes to say 'queer marks a suspense of something fixed, coherent and natural...or...may be used to describe an open-ended constituency whose shared characteristic is not identity itself but an anti-normative positioning' (Jagose 1996: 98). Perhaps one of the reasons that Peter reads the characters as 'half-realistic, half-symbolic' is because the characters are not rooted, or framed, within a solid, fixed ideological frame.

In Blasted (first performed 1995), Kane's first major play, this shaking of an ideological frame can be seen by Kane's attention to switching form part-way through the play. In the play the first two scenes appear to be of one type of form (broadly realist) up until the explosion at the end of Scene Two at which point the solidity of that form is fractured and ripped apart. This blasting of the form is described by John Gross (1995) 'at first you worry about implausibilities. Then the whole question of plausibility ceases to arise, as the play loses its grip on any kind of reality and careers off'. Saunders (2002: 40-45) agrees that the moment of the explosion shifts the whole form, although he does not see this as a problem, which in turn makes the audience re-view the collapsed first half after the 'blinding light' (Saunders 2002: 39) of the explosion that implodes the hotel room. The result of such a dramatic shift from one half of the play to the other is deeply unsettling because it disconnects what appeared to be a form from its roots. The second half of the play becomes much more free-floating and not yet finished. Again this is very much like a queer sensation where there is a sense of unfinishedness to identity. Bearing in mind the queer milieu of the mid nineties and the play's rootlessness, Blasted is very queer, if indeed a play, or a form, can be said to have an identity. Because each of Kane's plays uses a different form there is also a sense that her body of work has a kind of undecidable identity hence the discussions by Sierz et al about where best to place her work in the contemporary field of UK theatre.

Kane's body of work not only shows the mutability of form, but also the mutability of the physical bodies of her characters. This mutability of bodies is most striking in Cleansed (first performed in 1998) when we look at the characters of Rod, Carl and Grace. The idea of rearranging body parts is most easily seen in the character of Grace who slowly, over the course of the play, assumes the physical form of her dead brother, Graham. The mutability of gender and sexuality that queer asserts is crystallised in an image a quarter of the way through the play when Grace's dead brother appears:

> Graham dances – a dance of love for Grace. Grace dances opposite him, copying his movements. Gradually, she takes on the masculinity of his movement, his facial expression. Finally, she no longer has to watch him – she mirrors him perfectly as they dance exactly in time. When she speaks, her voice is more like his. (Kane 2001: 119)

After this section there follows a sequence of dialogue where Grace copies everything that Graham says. What can be seen here is the moment when Grace realigns her physicality, in a performative sense, in order to acquire a form of masculinity – that of her brother. The acquisition of her brother's masculinity is a very beautiful and touching moment in the play. It is almost as if Grace has found a right way of being, indeed, Graham comments that she is more like him, than he is himself (119).

However, Grace's journey to her gender transformation is not without difficulty. Indeed, Grace breaks herself apart in order to acquire her brother's masculinity. When Grace dresses in her dead brother's clothes, she literally 'breaks down and wails uncontrollably' (113). This breakdown is so intense for Grace that she is physically restrained and medicated in order to calm her down. There is sense of a small journey for Grace's gender identity from scene three until the end of scene five. This journey takes an audience from when she breaks down and her gendered self falls apart, to where she acquires her masculinity. The point at which she appears to be more comfortable in her masculinity, is the

same point where she makes love with her dead brother (120). This taboo
is reflected in the tenor of queer theory as Sue Ellen Case sees it:

> ...Queer theory and practice are vampyric in that they consist of a
> perverse form of bloodletting, of the abject transgression of boundaries
> between the proper and the improper. (Sullivan 2003: 52)

Interestingly, Grace is in some sense sucking the life from her
brother through her transformation into him. However, Grace does not
stop at the acquisition of his clothes and his masculinity, she continues to
transform the boundaries of her body. That is, the character of Tinker
removes Grace's breasts and stitches male genitals onto her groin. At the
point at which Grace becomes transfused with Graham's identity and
morphology she is given his name, and in unison she and her brother say:
'felt it' (146). At this point Grace has transmogrified into her brother and
his character leaves the stage for good. After her brother leaves, Grace,
who 'now looks and sounds exactly like Graham', believes herself to be
'body perfect' (149). From the moment Grace says this, she is described
in the text as Grace/Graham.

In queer terms, what is interesting in this part of Grace's journey
is that there is a clear queering of modes of gender and of sex. What Kane
reveals in the character of Grace (as well as Carl & Rod, see below) is a
larger story about the constructedness of gender and sexual identity. Kane
shows that gender and sexual identity are mutable and related to
conditions of the performative. However, this representation of the human
in theatre can appear improper, it does not ring true with high-ranking
visions of what constitutes a proper subjectivity. Some of the critics
responded to this improper subjectivity by describing the characters as
'one-dimensional... and little more than shadows' (Spencer 1998), or that
they 'lack either social context or human depth' (Gross 1998) as well as
saying that the play has 'no sense of lived experience' (Gore-Langton
1998). These responses again, could be because the characters lack an
ideological frame and as such are not rooted and appear unfinished.
Grace/Graham, is drawn as if to be thankful and complete with her
unfinshedness, she not only thanks Tinker, but says she is 'safe on the
other side' (150) as if she has crossed some kind of boundary.

When we first meet Rod and Carl they are also on a boundary,
sitting 'on the college green just inside the perimeter fence of the
university' (109). At this boundary they are in a process of negotiating
how they express their love, this is focussed on the exchange of rings. Rod
and Carl's relationship is interesting for a queer reading, not only because
they are in a gay relationship, but also their discussion reflects some the

preoccupations of queer in the 1990s focused around assimilation, expressed in gay marriage and access to the military, and radicalism, articulated through groups like ACT UP, and Outrage! (see Edge 1995, Tatchell 1995, Tucker 1995, and Woods 1995). Rod and Carl are talking about commitment and the shape of their relationship. Carl and Rod exchange rings in a type of mock ritual. Carl, who is positioned as the romanticist of the couple, has pressed for this exchange of rings and Rod accepts the invitation to symbolise their relationship, but only on his own terms. In the exchange of rings Rod says:

> Listen. I'm saying this once.
> (He puts the ring on **Carl**'s finger.)
> I love you now.
> I am with you now.
> I'll do my best, moment to moment, not to betray
> you.
> Now.
> That's it. No more. Don't make me lie to you. (Kane 2001: 111)

This reflects the articulations that were going on in the mid 1990s about the status of homosexual relationships. During this period and up until the turn of the twenty-first century there were debates between assimilationists and liberationists about the status of gay relationships expressed in gay marriage. These debates, it could be said, end up being about the status of visibility. That is, assimilationists of the 1990s desired a gay marriage without a root and branch critique of the institution of marriage; they wanted a place at the table of the normal, to be visibly normal as part of the dominant, see Sullivan (1996). Liberationists, on the other hand, saw gay marriage as reinforcing particular social structures that oppressed difference (especially of gays) and that ended in the invisibility of gayness through its normalisation. That is, the debate says, if all gays become normal then they become invisible because they are like every other normal person, and gayness, which is built on not being normal (or built on embracing the position of radical) vanishes. As Woods, writing at the time says:

> Perhaps this was always the end-point of our desire for homosexual emancipation: being just like everyone else. Yet surely true liberation lies not in mimicking the past... (Woods 1995: 60)

The mimicking of the past that Woods mentions could be articulated by things like the tradition of marriage as an expression of a proper relationship. This desire for a proper relationship is centred on the

character of Carl. As Cleansed progresses, Rod and Carl are slowly erased
and silenced. The structure of Rod and Carl's story through the play
appears to be almost a manifestation of the liberationist debates in the
1990s: because Rod and Carl enter into a traditional-like relationship
(through the exchange of rings) they subsequently become de-voiced and
erased as gay men.

In Cleansed this erasure is expressed in a physical sense: Rod
falls from a great height (117) and has his throat cut and his body burnt
(142); Carl is beaten by an unseen group of men (116), has a pole inserted
into his anus (117), has is tongue cut off with a large pair of scissors (118),
has his hands cut off (and rats eat his hands) (129-130) his feet cut off
(136) and his genitals removed (145). Each of these tortures follows an
attempt by Carl to communicate. Tinker removes Carl's ability to
communicate, for instance, after having had his tongue removed, Carl
attempts to write. After he has finished writing, Tinker removes Carl's
hands. Carl later on attempts to show his love for Rod through a dance,
again when he is finished, Tinker removes Carl's feet. It appears at every
turn that after each conventional expression of romantic love Carl is
silenced and the bits of his body he uses to make his expressions of love
are erased (and in some cases consumed). Before the end of the play Rod
is murdered and removed even from Carl's sight. And finally, the most
conventional organ with which Carl can show his desire – his genitals –
are removed.

Of course, this is a specific reading of Carl's journey. To our
reading, the loss of his genitals is not only about a form of silencing that
can be mapped across a cultural debate at the time of Kane's writing. It is
important to the narrative to recognise that Carl's genitals are supplied to
Grace in order for her to assume the physical attributes she needs to
become Graham. Shortly after the point where Carl sees his genitals
missing he puts on Grace's clothes. Not only does this create a kind of
image symmetry (they both change) but also focuses on the mutability of
identity and the primary sex indicators of genitalia. It is almost as if Grace
has become Graham, thereby leaving a space for another Grace (in the
dyad of Grace and Graham) – and indeed at least one other Grace in the
form of the character of Robin has been present in the play. Carl, by the
end of the play has taken the position of Grace, if not been surgically
altered to become female at least through wearing her clothes. The final
image is fecund with hope, as the sun brightens the stage Carl and Grace
hold each other in an image of closure that functions not only as the end of
the play, but also has a sense that characters have reached a plateau in their
queer bodies and fluid identities.

Fluid identities as a marker of queer also appear in Kane's next play Crave (first performed in 1998). Although the identities do not function in the way they do in Cleansed. Cleansed has apparently rootless characters, yet nevertheless the characters are presented with a sense of a whole subjectivity, even if it is not easy to determine their motivations and those subjectivities also appear rootless. The structure of Cleansed is linear in the sense that there is a progression that is logical – once Carl has lost his tongue the audience do not see Carl with a tongue. That is, structurally the time narrative is sequential. However, the mutability of bodies as a sign of the queer that we see in Cleansed is extended to the structure of the characters C, M, B and A in Crave. Crave's queerness is most easily seen in the structure of the play, rather than in the mutability of the characters. Queer reading, like other kinds of reading, is not only confined to looking for the mutability of identities that show a different form of ontology (like Carl and Grace) it may also look for a novel mode of the performative especially when it relates to sexual identity. Connected to novel modes of the performative, queer reading also may rest on peculiar structures upon which identities are formed. The structure of play texts can be read as correlative with structures of identity, especially how these identity structures enable certain kinds of locution. For instance, Butler's view of gender identity is related to structures of regulatory regimes, which are regimes that allow certain kinds of subjectivities to be recognised as 'innate and stable' (Sullivan 2003: 82). As with regulatory regimes, the structure of play texts and performances enable certain kinds of subjectivities to be articulated. Crave's structure can be described in a similar way that Sedgwick described queer above. To reiterate, she focuses on an 'open mesh of possibilities, gaps, overlaps, dissonances and resonances, lapses and excesses of meaning… [which do not, or cannot] signify monolithically (Sedgwick 1994: 8). In the way that Crave's structure coheres to Sedgwick's vision of queer, we can intimately relate structure and queerness.

The structure of Crave appears very fluid in the sense that the audience receive a flow of fragmented stories and memories. What the fluid structure of the play enables is, yet again, a kind of rootlessness. This rootlessness is manifest in the way the structure intercuts various stories in such a way that no overarching narrative emerges. By lacking the appearance of cohesion brought by overarching narratives, Crave progresses more in terms of montage, bricolage, and collage than linear narrative expressed through a character's actions or a description of the setting. That is, the fluid nature of the structure in a queer sense disenables the characters to be knowable in the sense that they occupy stable identity positions.

Sometimes Crave shows characters whose stories are not only intertwined, but are articulated by more than one character:

> B   Something clicked.
> M   But I would never say that we were ever in love.
> B   Found her
> A   Loved her
> C   Lost her
> M   End.
> *A Silence*
> C   Something has lifted,
> A   Outside the city,
> B   Before the shit started,
> A   Above the city,
> C   Another dream,
> M   I crossed a river that runs in shadow, (Kane 2001: 196)

Here, before the pause, the story of 'her' seems to fit together as if it were one person speaking ('Found her/Loved her/Lost her'). Equally, after the pause there is a sense of a story about the city that is articulated by all four voices. This sharing of speaking positions by CMBA makes it very difficult for a reading to see the characters as fixed or finished, in the sense that a character can occupy a solid identity location.

However, at times the characters are separated in their speech and stories. For instance, the long monologue on love that A speaks (169) relates, it appears, to a specific speaking position. That is, it belongs to the character of A. Similarly, watching a production of Crave can seem to fix an identity position simply through casting. Rebellato, when speaking to Kane asks about the identities of the characters in Crave, she says:

> To me A was always an older man. M was always an older woman. B was always a younger man and C was always a young woman. (Rebellato in Saunders 2002: 104)

However, Kane didn't see this way of casting the play as proscriptive, rather she says:

> M was simply Mother, B was Boy and C was Child, but I didn't want to write those things down because then I thought they'd get fixed in those things for ever and nothing would ever change. (Rebellato in Saunders 2002: 104)

In a sense Kane is speaking of the possibility of characters not

being fixed at particular identity positions. This idea of positioning an
identity in such a way that it only ever articulates unfinishedness,
resonates with a queer position as we have described it above. This
connection between the characters in Crave and queer ideas is only one
such connection. Another connection could be made when we think of
queer as always is a state of becoming. This state of becoming could be
articulated as a focus on the potential for mutability. Kane's comments
above also connect with the potential of the characters through their
mutability when presented in different productions. So, it could be said
that M need never be represented as 'Mother'. Indeed any representation
in performance need not resonate with any fixed position.

However, we are keen to point out that not all people writing
about Kane would agree with the idea that the characters in Crave present
an opportunity for fluidity and a resistance to a fixed identity position. For
instance, Saunders says of the characters in Crave:

> The characters stand for specific archetypes... Kane's 'voices' are also
> gender specific, both in the writing itself and subsequently through the
> performance of each actor embodying an individual character [original
> emphasis]. (2002: 104-105)

Saunders is responding here to Kane's comments about the
fixedness of the characters in Crave. Consequently, his focus is on an
effort to piece together fragments of narrative in the play in a puzzle-like
fashion in order to articulate the characters' identity positions, as well as
performers who might play those characters. Our queer reading, with its
focus on the unfinishedness of identity, does not accord with Saunders'
way of thinking about the play. From a queer perspective, the categories
of gender are always in a state of flux and the categories of man, woman,
child, mother, and boy etc. are never ontologically finished.

Equally, Sierz (2001), like Saunders, does not acknowledge this
queer fluidity in Crave. Rather Sierz expresses the need for 'four different
reading strategies to fully uncover its meanings' (118). Sierz describes
these four strategies as: a rationalist approach, an English Literature
approach, a bibliographical critique and experience of the performance
itself (118-9). What Sierz says here is that there are competing ways of
coming to an understanding of Crave, but he seems reluctant to
acknowledge that there is a plethora of other reading positions, themselves
related to the identity position of the reader. The possibilities of multiple
reading positions that could express manifold identity positions are
germane to the queerness of Crave as we are reading it here. However,

Crave as play can elicit a sensation that there are hidden meanings that if uncovered, all will be revealed. It could be said that this is the function of the play, this is what the play does; it educes a sense of craving for answers to the nebulous meanings it provokes. Kane's next play 4.48 Psychosis (2000) is a much more queer play in the sense that it does away with the temptations to work it out by removing the potential for fixed identity positions.

In 4.48 there is less potential for fixed identity positions to be expressed in its performance. This reflects the fluidity of queer (non) identity positions. The play does not have a cast list, for instance, indicating that the play could be performed by any number of bodies. Equally, the writing itself does not appear to bring about fixed identity positions in terms of a character that a performer might play. In this sense it offers a peculiar challenge to theatre makers to find methods of producing the play that adhere to its fluidity without fixing identity positions. This challenge to theatre makers is not only presented within the play's hazy meanings, but also how the words are presented on the page:

I don't imagine
 (clearly)
that a single soul
 could
 would
 should
 or will

and if they did
I don't think
 (clearly)
that another soul
and a soul like mine
 could
 would
 should
 or will   (Kane 2001: 222)

It is perhaps this fluidity on the page as well as in performance that brings critics to say 'it's [4.48] too splintered to be pieced together with any confidence' (Cavendish 2000). The play and its performance force particular kinds of interaction between the reader and the text (by text here we mean both the written text and the performance text). This interaction is characterised by an acknowledgement that the play is in a state of fluidity and that the speaking voices do not come from any particular position of fixity in the sense that they emanate from a finished identity position: there are no well-rounded characters, in fact, there are no characters. In Kane's other plays (as we have discussed them) characters appear queerly rootless, in 4.48 this rootlessness is extended to the play as a whole. By removing traditional formal qualities such as characters, setting, dramatis personae and stage descriptions, Kane eradicates primary sign systems upon which a production process (and a reading of the performance) might initially fall. Kane deracinates these central foundations thereby creating the sense of rootlessness of the play as a whole. In production at the Royal Court in 2001, this rootlessness was reflected in the set and the way that the performers used the stage space.

Most striking about this performance was a giant mirror sloping at forty-five degrees from upstage to the top of the proscenium arch. The effect of this mirror was to reflect what was happening on stage. Effectively the audience could see both the performers and the performers' reflection simultaneously. This doubling of the performers via the mirror served the sense of the unfixedness of the speaker. That is, an audience could see two bodies for each performer (the performer and his/her reflection). Each time a performer spoke, the audience could see two bodies from different angles with a singular voice (a performer and her/his refection). In some sense the production enabled voices to come from multiple places simultaneously, which brings into question the fixity of the voice and the identity positions that might produce that voice. This seems very queer to us because there is, in the same way that Jagose describes queer, 'a fundamental indeterminacy... always ambiguous, always relational' (1996: 96) aspect to the experience of the performance. An excellent example from the performance of this indeterminacy and rootlessness came from a particular image when the performers lay on the floor and appeared to be floating in the mirror: like human shaped helium balloons or a human version of Warhol's Silver Clouds (1966).

There are other aspects of the text that resonate with the idea of queer, especially in terms of the way that queer is resistant to the normalising impulses of foreclosed identities. Towards the middle of the play is a section where Kane describes drug treatments and their side effects. This quite lengthy section describes drugs that might be used in a psychiatric setting. There is an implication in the text that these drugs are used to help a person maintain a functional relationship with the world. The list of drugs starts after a specific diagnosis of 'pathological grief' (223) and it seems reasonable to read the list of drugs as attempted treatments for this state of grief. What the treatments seem to be aiming towards is a singularity of voice as this singularity of voice is an index of functionality.

Right from the beginning of the play, the voice describes itself as plural, as a hermaphrodite who uses the word 'hermself' (205). Pluralities of voice do not seem to fit the medical model that is described in the list of drugs. If we focus on the word 'pathological' we can see that it breaks into patho, meaning disease, and logical, meaning rational. The voice then seems to be suffering from grief or loss of rationality because the voice's logic is diseased. The treatment might seek to bring the voice back to a logic that is functional – that is, to normalise the voice. It appears reasonable to read the anger of the voice in this section, 'Mood: Fucking Angry. Affect: Very angry' (224), as an expression of its resistance to the normalising impulses of psychiatric drugs. Resistance from the voice is very important when we note that it tells us just before diagnosis that it is 'drowning in a sea of logic / this monstrous state of palsy' (223). The state of palsy, where musculature ceases to function, seems to be brought about because the voice is drowning in a sea of logic – a logic that does not seem to be able to express the plurality of the voice because of logic's normalising impulse, which pushes the voice towards a position of singularity.

The rejection of the singular voice in 4.48 is so powerful as to inflect itself in any reading of the play and its performance. In response to the work Billington comes to say: 'But does the play, which takes us inside Kane's head, have any general application?' (Billington 2000). This question, in terms of our discussion here, can be seen, once again to be a response to the apparent lack of ideological frame on to which audiences might cling. 4.48 has no 'general application' because its multiple voices speak simultaneously to multiple listeners. In this sea of voices an audience member might not hear all of them – and it is this polyphony that is very queer as it resists application in the sense that application fixes the voice to a usefulness expressed in a knowable identity. This fundamental unknowability of 4.48 not only makes it a queer play, to our reading, but also keeps the play enigmatic and attractive to future audiences and readers. To fix the voice by explaining it, is to root it to a position that the form and the content resist. That is, queer resists the normative and likewise the voice in 4.48 resists the theatrical normative desire to fix a vision.

Wrapping up Kane

Kane's work can be seen as queer through its rootlessness and apparent disconnection with a wider politics, also the fluidity of gender in Kane's plays resonates with the mode of queer as a person who is indistinct especially in terms of a gendered identity. However, as the word queer in common parlance has increasingly become a synonym for gay, some of the radical aspects of queer become subsumed into the mainstream use of gay as a word. This is, perhaps, why the work of Kane is not usually associated with queer. However, we feel that there is an intimate relationship with her work, as well as the potential of her work, and the potentials of a queer in the 1990s (in addition to in its current incarnations). Yet, there is still relatively little discussion of her work that focuses on the queerness of the plays. This may be because Kane's work is primarily seen as relating to theatrical culture rather than to the movements focussed on gender and sexuality. That said, some of the 1990s milieu of playwrights named as New Brutalists, were very interested in the shape of gender and sexuality (not least of all Kane's friend Mark Ravenhill and others from the New Brutalists such as Jez Butterworth, Anthony Neilson and Philip Ridley).

If there is a general acceptance amongst critics, academics and intellectuals that plays reflect the culture in which they are performed and written, there is a sense that queer as an idea and a way of reading text and performance developed alongside Kane's work in the 1990s. We are keen to make this link not because we wish to coerce a queer reading from the texts and their performances, but that the texts themselves seem to contain images and structures that in themselves seem very queer. Hence, we have omitted one of Kane's works for the theatre. We have not presented a queer reading of Phaedra's Love (first performed 1996), as this appears to be a play that is less open to a queer reading. The play does contain some references to homosexual activity; however, having gay characters is not always a mark of the plausibility of a queer reading. What shows the play to be less open to a queer reading is that the characters are presented as somewhat more rooted. As such, these roots of the characters are less fluid in the sense that they proffer an opportunity for a display of mutable bodies or mutable subjectivities. Characters in Phaedra's Love are more finished than they are in her other works for theatre.

Kane's works for the theatre can be difficult (technically as well as their content) and it is this difficulty that is appealing to queer readers. The anti-normative positioning of queer fits quite snugly in opposition to the responses to her work. By the time 4.48 was first performed critics had a better sense of Kane's work, however, consistently they appear to feel uncomfortable with the fluidity of the plays. It could be said that at the base of critics' readings of her work lies a desire to hegemonise the plays' fluidity and push them towards a more solid state where we might know what these plays are about. Now that Kane is dead, her diffuse body of work remains as nebulous as it ever was. Dead authors often become canonised in various ways and their work sorted, labelled and described. Kane's constant reworking of form between plays and the rootlessness of her characters may go some way to resisting even this wish to hegemonise her work into the theatrical canon. It is perhaps the resistive nature of the work that marks it most fundamentally as queer.

Works cited

Beemyn, Brett & Eliason, Mickey (eds), *Queer Studies: A Lesbian, Gay, Bisexual, and Transgender Anthology.* New York: New York University Press, 1996.

Bond, Edward, *Saved*, London: Methuen, 1966.

Butler, Judith, *Gender Trouble*, London: Routledge, 1990.

Cranny-Francis, Anne, Waring, Wendy, Stavropoulos, Pam, & Kirkby, Joan, *Gender Studies, Terms and Debates*, London: Palgrave.

Edge, Simon (1995), *With Friends Like These: Marxism and Gay Politics*, London: Continuum, 2003.

Foster, Thomas, Siegel, Carol & Berry, Ellen E. (eds), *The Gay '90s Disciplinary and Interdisciplinary Formations in Queer Studies*, New York: New York University Press, 1997.

Gottlieb, Vera, 'Theatre Today – the New Realism' Contemporary Theatre Review, Vol.13, No.1, 2003.

Jagose, Annamarie, *Queer Theory: An Introduction*, New York: New York University Press, 1996.

Kane, Sarah, *Sarah Kane: Complete Plays*, London: Methuen, 2001.

Nikcevic, Sanja, 'British Brutalism, the New European Drama, and the Role of the Director' New Theatre Quarterly, Vol. XXI, Part 3, 2005.

Sellar, Tom, 'Truth And Dare: Sarah Kane's Blasted' Theater, Vol. 27, No.1, 1998.

Saunders, Graham, 'Out Vile Jelly: Sarah Kane's Blasted and Shakespeare's King Lear' New Theatre Quarterly, Vol. 20, No. 1, February 2004.

—. 'Just A Word On A Page And There Is The Drama, Sarah Kane's Theatrical Legacy' Contemporary Theatre Review, Vol. 13, No. 1, 2003.

—. *Love Me or Kill Me, Sarah Kane and the Theatre of Extremes*, Manchester: Manchester University Press, 2002.

Sedgewick, Eve, *Tendencies*, London: Routledge, 1994.

Sierz, Alex, 'Still In-Yer-Face? Towards a Critique and a Summation'
Theatre Quarterly, Vol. XX, Part 1, 2004.
—. *In-Yer-Face Theatre British Drama Today*, London: Faber and Faber,
2001.
Simpson, Mark (ed), *Anti-Gay*, London: Continuum, 1996.
Sinfield, Alan, *Gay and After*, London: Serpent's Tail, 1998.
Sullivan, Andrew, *Virtually Normal, An Argument About Homosexuality*,
London: Picador, 1996.
Sullivan, Nikki, *A Critical Introduction to Queer Theory*, Edinburgh:
Edinburgh University Press, 2003.
Tatchell, Peter, *We Don't Want To March Straight! Masculinity, Queers
and the Military*, London: Continuum, 1995.
Tucker, Scott, *Fighting Words, An Open Letter to Queers and Radicals*,
London: Continuum, 1995.
Urban, Ken, 'Towards a Theory of Cruel Britannia: Coolness, Cruelty, and
the Nineties' New Theatre Quarterly, Vol. XX, Part 4, 2004.
—. 'An Ethics of Catastrophe, The Theatre of Sarah Kane' PAJ, No. 69,
2001.
Walter, Aubrey (ed), *Come Together – The Years of Gay Liberation 1970
– 73*, London: Gay Men's Press, 1980.
Weeks, Jeffery, *Coming Out, Homosexual Politics in Britain, From The
Nineteenth Century to the Present*, London: Quartet, 1977.
Woods, Chris, *State of The Queer Nation*, London: Cassell, 1995.

Newspaper reviews

Billington, Michael , The Guardian, 30 June 2000.
Cavendish, Dominic, The Independent, 15 August 1998.
Gore-Langton, Robert, The Express, 10 May 1998.
Gross, John, Sunday Telegraph, 10 May 1998.
—. Sunday Telegraph, 22 January 1995.
Peter, John, Sunday Times, 29 January 1995.
Spencer, Charles, Daily Telegraph, 7 May 1998.

CHAPTER NINE

TRANSGENDERED MASCULINITIES IN PERFORMANCE: SUBCULTURAL NARRATIVES LAID BARE

CATHERINE MCNAMARA

Synopsis

This chapter looks at three performance events staged in British venues between 1999 and 2005 and explores the significance of the constitutive potential of performing transgendered masculinities. Consideration of the cross-dressing, male impersonation and female-to-male cross-gender living within performance history, and the debates around biological, and constructivist perspectives on (trans)gender contribute to a discussion of subcultural and marginal representations and reception of trans bodies on stage.

*****

The transsexual performer has a trump card to play... the disrobing of the transsexual excelled the usual sartorial markers of gender as a performance enhancement... the transsexual, by taking the irreversible step, has somehow put gender identity in question in a more decisive way than cross-dressing possibly can. (Senelick, 2000:495)

In the final chapter of *The Changing Room: Sex, Drag and Theatre*, Laurence Senelick establishes a relationship between transformation manifested through costume as a device in performance, and bodily change undertaken by a transsexual or transgendered performer. The implication attached to this binary is that naked transsexuals will 'upstage' any other performative semiotic device in terms of exploring gender, and that the trump card of a hormonally and/ or surgically altered body beats plain cross-dressing and impersonation. This chapter takes three particular examples of performance practice from three London venues and looks at the ways transgendered bodies have been variously presented, constructed and displayed within live performance. Each of the performers identifies themselves as other than 'woman' in one sense or another, and sometimes several. Each of the three works, while being created and performed by a person or people of what might be described as indeterminate or trans gender, invites discussion of the issues of representation and perception of trans, and of those who have chosen to perform themselves in the public sphere of the theatre. The performances themselves are instances of discourse. These performers are Jennifer Miller, self-titled 'Lady with a Beard' (Hoxton Hall, 1999) and Joey Hateley, self-identified transgendered female (Oval House Theatre, 2004), as well as the female-to-male (FTM) trans performers of a piece staged as part of *A Night of Tall Women and Short Men* (The Pleasure Unit, 2005).

I use the term 'transgender' here, in the sense that it has become an umbrella term for those within a political and social community who choose to identify with it, 'because they cross-dress some of the time, because they cross-gender live much of the time, because they undergo gender reassignment, or just because their gender identity or gender role is not conventional' (Whittle, 2000:16). The performers within this discussion are various in their relationship to transgendered subjectivity. Looking to performance history in Britain for a context, as well as to the contemporary references, cross-dressing, cross-gender living, transsexuality and alternative gendered subjectivities contribute to this particular notion of trans.

In her 1994 essay 'F2M: The Making of Female Masculinity', Judith Halberstam asked 'why, in this age of gender transitivity, when many queers and feminists have agreed that gender is a social construct, is transsexuality a widespread phenomenon?' (Halberstam, 1998:146). This matter of agreement surrounding the idea of gender as a social construct is one that troubles me, and one that I seek to trouble through an exploration of performance and representation of female-to-male masculine identities in contemporary theatre practice. Post-structuralist and queer theories of gender assert that a body becomes sexed through a performative 'becoming'. In *Bodies that Matter: On the Discursive Limits of "Sex"*, Judith Butler argues that the body (which of course includes the brain, endocrines, hormones and genitals – the 'matter' of the body) is not sexed prior to being in the world – that it is not a 'static condition' (Butler, 1993:2). The world, or culture, generates the sexed, gendered body, as there is no existence without cultural inscription. There is movement however, within trans lives and Trans Studies which is turning away from this notion of the constructed being and bringing the biological back in to the debate. Evolutionary biologist Joan Roughgarden points out that:

> Too many sociologists don't accept transgendered people at their word, perhaps because doing so would admit that there is some truth to the biological account. Instead, these sociologists cling to the belief that vestidas and other transsexuals have 'chosen' to live as a different sex... Transgendered people don't choose their sex, or gender, any more or less than nontransgendered people do. (2004: 384)

Wrong body/ right body distinctions remain common within trans theory and trans narratives and contribute to this debate on biological determinism, essentialism and gender binaries as social constructs. In *Post-War British Drama: Looking Back in Gender*, Michelene Wandor asks questions about the nature of sexed identities and gendered social roles, and ways of being in the worlds of each decade of the twentieth century, and more specifically, the 'imperative of gender' as a framework within which to critique the theatre of the post-war, post-censorship era. She asks 'what is it to be a 'man'? What is it to be a 'woman'? Who is asking the questions, and how does their perspective (male or female) affect the play and its dilemmas?' (Wandor, 2001:37). It has been suggested that theatre in this new century is in crisis and that:

> Identity politics has splintered artists to such a degree that a certain kind of voicelessness has begun to subsume the role an artist can play in society. It is as if the claiming of identity that was so much a part of the 1980s and early 1990s has left artists exhausted of the further possibilities that its claiming can bring. (Svich in Delgado and Svich, 2002:16)

The politicisation of the domestic in feminist theatre of the late 1970s and 1980s and the increasingly provocative style of work in theatres in the 1990s, look perhaps to be shifting once more. It has been suggested that the confrontational, brutally sexualised portrayals of gender within late 1990s British theatre, specifically in the work of writers such as Ravenhill, Kane and Neilson etc., are over. Aleks Sierz asserts that 'by 2000, there were signs that the heady days of outrage were numbered... that the tide was turning and that an era of confrontation had come to an end' (2001:249). I am interested in these cultural shifts and in the ways they relate to female masculinity and more specifically, FTM and transgendered identities and how their manifestations are reflected or rejected as we move further into the second millennium.

Cross-dressing, or transvestite theatre, has flourished during historical periods when attitudes to sexuality and the position of women have been challenged – during the Restoration, through the nineteenth century when the industrial revolution altered the face of urban and family life, and in certain respects in today's theatre. (Wandor, 1986:25)

Twenty years on from Wandor's tentative assertion that transvestism was having a revival, I suggest that attitudes to gender and identity and specifically the position of female bodies/ born transgendered individuals is more conspicuous in the 2000s than has historically been the case. As New Gender Politics and the discipline of Trans Studies develops, we might look back on the new millennium as a point when discourse around cross-dressing proliferated and issues of female masculinity and transgendering in performance flourished. While this discussion concerns transgendered performers on the contemporary stage, acknowledging the point in history when women formally entered the performance space in 1660, and the roles they played, including male impersonation is a significant step in tracing the emergence, appearance and recognition of transgendered representations in British theatre.

After the Renaissance tradition of casting boys and young men in female roles, the Restoration period's long delayed recognition and encouragement of women performing on stage under Charles II came about after an eighteen year gap in theatre production during Interregnum. Public and royal support for the professionalising of female performers was strong and a 'shift in attitude can be linked to a wider change in how relationships between the sexes were defined' (Howe, 1992:21). Male impersonation was the part of several actresses' repertoire, as well as playing male roles, such as Sarah Bernhardt's Zanetto in Copée's *Le Passant* in 1869 and later, Hamlet in 1899. Bessie Bonehill and Vesta Tilley are acknowledged as successful male impersonators, though 'Tilley was the one male impersonator of the period to be mythologized and endlessly replicated: her icon all but obliterates her competition, and her well-turned-out striplings are stamped out of the mould well into the 1930s' (Senelick, 2000:336).

Just as feminist historians have embarked upon a project to reclaim women's position and presence in the world, so might Trans Studies investigate the possibilities of re-visioning and reclaiming some of the narratives as told. In re-reading the lives, actions and work of individuals described as women, and as lesbians in an effort to interrogate 'assumptions based on gynocentrism or androcentrism, using biological deterministic arguments, and subsuming relationships under the rubric of lesbianism' (Cromwell in More and Whittle, 1999:58) we might consider

Charles Hindle, the 1860s British-born music-hall performer and male impersonator (called Annie at an early stage in his career). Senelick discusses Hindle as being a lesbian. He talks about the male impersonating becoming more 'veristic' from the point of separation from 'Annie's' husband of a few months: 'her physique thickened, her voice deepened, and she took to shaving regularly, so that the down on her upper lip bloomed into a moustache and her chin sprouted the stubble of a beard' (2000:329). Where verism specifically pertains to strict realism or naturalism in art and literature, this choice of vocabulary, and Senelick's choice of personal pronoun in reference to Charles Hindle might mislead. Where Hindle lived full-time as a man, he surely conducts himself not with verisimilitude, with the appearance of truth or realness, but with veritas. Accounts of history suggest that Hindle's life choices, which he affected in the everyday, were not a masquerade. Regardless of what the content of his stage performance was, his maleness was an actuality.

Gender Dysphoria though, or acute unhappiness or hopelessness relating to one's gendered self, emerged in the 1970s as the medical profession's 'preferred term' (King in Ekins and King, 1996:96) to collectively describe people who identified as having a variety of difficulties surrounding gender identification. A sense of living within an uninhabitable body is not necessarily or solely the domain of transsexual people, nor is it not confined to certain sets of individuals or to one gendered identity in particular. However, if we consider identity as being the 'essential self' or 'a set of characteristics that somebody recognises as belonging uniquely to himself or herself and constituting his or her individual personality for life' (Bloomsbury English Dictionary (2nd ed.), 2004), gender and biological sex are two of the primary characteristics of human existence and within the context of the performers discussed here, identity is gendered and is sexed.

The diverse and complex historical and contemporary debates surrounding gender offer perspectives and positions from which to view this notion of the uninhabitable body. Kessler and McKenna acknowledged that 'gender may be too pervasive and permanent to be considered a role and may be better thought of as a status or identity' (1978:19) Shiach analysed the concept of 'gender' and its emergence as a category of cultural analysis, acknowledging 'the longstanding complexity of the semantic field associated with this term' (1994:27). The tensions that are key to the debate around and the histories of gender clearly shift as a result of social change and indeed, according to whose history we are hearing. The gender identity paradigm emerged and developed through the work of medical practitioners and researchers such as John Money, Anke

Ehrhardt and Robert Stoller in the 1950s and 1960s (Hausman, 1995:73-4). Robert Stoller's conception of pluralistic, rather than unitary identity led to the notion that gender was one aspect of a person, though 'the integration of the personality as a whole was largely focused on the sense of being a male or a female' (Connell, 2002:88).

Feminist theory and feminist literary criticism sought (and still seeks) to change both individual and institutional awareness concerning the cultural and social role of the gender 'woman' (Showalter, 1986), though not always, and perhaps, rarely in connection with female bodied people who identify as 'not woman'. Janice Raymond (1980) and Catherine Millot (1990) and Sheila Jeffreys (2003) are key commentators from a feminist academic position and contribute a notable antagonism where discussion of gender begins to include transgender identities. Raymond considers transsexuality to be a behavioural desire and argues that transsexuals never become men or women, but remain the man or woman of their birth sex, remain 'constructed' men or women, thus undermining the very existence of the experiences of the transsexual. This insistent undermining is clear in each writer's use of personal pronouns, where trans men are discussed as 'she' and 'her'. FTM transsexualism is declared as an 'emergency for lesbian politics' (Jeffreys, 2003:122) in that it is viewed as a method 'being used to get rid of lesbians' (*ibid*). Trans theorist critiques of this work are vehement: 'Janice Raymond's book is an example of hatred and exclusion. An academic intellectual, she has been infested by another aspect of the patriarchal she professes to attack' (Riddell in Ekins and King, 1996:186).

This is something of the landscape within which I locate the documentation and discussion of particular female-bodies/ born transgendered bodies on the contemporary British stage. We might look to examples of controversial cross-casting such as Fiona Shaw in male role as Richard II at the Royal National Theatre in 1995, where director Deborah Warner realises her perspective of Richard as gender ambiguous, in that she bestows upon him a sense that he imagines himself to be above such earthly things as notions of man and woman – 'a creature beyond gender' (Shaw in Goodman and de Gay, 1998:xxiii). Alternatively, we might analyse transgendered representations offered by characters such as Grace in Sarah Kane's *Cleansed* (Royal Court Theatre, 1998; Arcola Theatre, 2005). Here there are parallels with *Twelfth Night's* use of the motif of disguise where 'in *Cleansed* this use of disguise is not done for theatrical or comic effect. Grace adopts the clothing and mannerisms of her brother in an attempt to actually become her brother... demands to be seen as such by others: "I look like him. Say you thought I was a man"

(3:114) (Saunders, 2002:95). To return to the three specific instances of
trans as observed on British stages in very recent years offered for
discussion, I begin with a woman with a beard.

'Is that a man or a woman?'

'I live in a very liminal place,' Ms. Miller says. '"Liminal" means an 'in-
between place,'" she explains. 'It means "in a doorway, a dawn or a
dusk." It's a lovely place. In the theatre, it's when the lights go out. And
before the performance begins.' (Smith, 1995)

Jennifer Miller is a performance artist. Her sideshow act *Zenobia:
The Amazing Lady with the Beard*, focuses specifically on the idea of the
freak or the exhibiting of human oddities. She subverts the nineteenth
century notion of the Bearded Lady as passive victim, epitome of
femininity and model of Victorian domesticity. The production played at
Hoxton Hall in East London in 1999, a small alternative venue described
as a Victorian Music Hall theatre space. The audience numbered
approximately 40 and though the staging was proscenium arch, a relatively
intimate relationship between the solo performer and the spectators was
created as a result of the size of the space. The interplay between the
spectator and the performer (whether on or off stage) in Miller's case
fluctuates and seems to be something that Miller courts. In interview she is
noted as saying '"My daily life is a mundane thing. The beard rarely exists
except when I talk about it." Ms. Miller turned. "I'm seeing this as a
performance project," she says, "talking to you"' (Smith, 1995). She
performs herself as flirtatious in interview or during face to camera
sections of film[1] or as direct and open with children as she prepares for a
performance in a park. Miller's portrayal of Jennifer Miller changes
according to interactions with people around her to a heightened extent.

Miller has described her performance work as political and as
feminist. She has performed this act as part of Dick Zigun's Coney Island
Sideshows by the Seashore, and as the founder of Circus Amok, a political
community theatre company, she performs in their productions, which tour
city parks and outdoor venues in New York. Circus Amok devise
entertainment that explores contemporary controversies relevant to the
lives of New Yorkers such as police brutality, jaywalking laws, budget

---

[1] Miller is the subject of filmmakers' work in pieces such as *Juggling Gender* (dir.
Tami Gold, 1992) and *Un Cirque de New York* (dir. Fréderique Pressman, 2002).

cuts and anti-immigrant proposition 187[2]. Their form could be said to be queer in as much as it synthesises elements of traditional circus with aspects of parody, camp and cross-dressing. Expressions of gender identity are not the focus of Circus Amok's shows, however, Miller's beard is a constant source of fascination for many of the spectators: '"Is that a man or a woman?" a woman in the audience whispers. "She's a woman with the beard glued on," a boy sitting next to the woman says' (Smith, 1995). It is often children who will ask most openly if Miller is a woman or man and with them, she is direct, telling them that she is a woman with a beard and it's there because it grows there. While in one sense she insists that she is many things other than and as well as a woman with facial hair, this one detail, in its unusualness, pervades her life and work. She has said that she does not mind this continual questioning but also added 'it's hard for me to keep having fresh thinking about it' (Carr, 1998). Her facial hair has been a part of her body since she was in her early 20s. She is not sure what made it grow and with a few exceptions in the last 20 years, has not felt the need to remove it. She states "I don't think of it as a problem, so I'm not looking for a cause... But if I didn't keep my beard it would be a statement of hopelessness. Keeping secrets requires energy that's debilitating, especially when it's out of shame or fear " (Smith, 1995).

Miller's appearance can be interpreted as the performative queering of norms of gender, while reactions to her reveal the force of normalisation that pulls us towards conventional understandings of bodies and identities. Smith asks, if Miller sees her beard as normal, why perform as a freak in circuses and sideshows. She replies '"it's a strong, feminist piece of theatre. Ten times a day, I address in the strongest, most forthright terms feminist issues of appearance and dress. I use the platform of the sideshow to defreakify"' (Smith, 1995). In Foucauldian terms, Miller is an embodiment of resistance. Making reference to an extract of her performance during this interview with Smith, she says

> The world is full of women with beards...or at least they have the potential to have a beard . . . instead of spending the time, and the money, on the waxing, and the shaving, and the electrolysis and the plucking. We all know someone who plucks. Pluck, pluck, pluck, as if these women were chickens! (Smith, 1995)

---

[2] Proposition 187 (1994) is anti-immigrant and aimed to deny health and education services for illegal immigrants and encouraged state employees to report undocumented aliens to the authorities. The proposition was approved by voters but overturned by state courts.

Miller's refusal to 'mutilate' her own body by shaving or undergoing electrolysis leads to her possession of one of society's most visible indicators of maleness. This fact is cause enough for the spectators present within daily life and at performances by Jennifer Miller, to react and furthermore, to feel they have a right to voice their opinions about this one aspect of her appearance: 'Treated like a man, she becomes manlike. It is not her beard but rather people's reaction to its mark that has altered her gender…their gaze is her gender mirror. Like their gaze, her gender is both multifaceted and culturally specific; thus it disrupts unified concepts of gender' (Straayer in Duberman, 1997:152-3). Jennifer Miller's gender indeterminacy is visual and bodily in that it is her beard that disrupts a reading of her. Others construct her and perceive illusion while she seeks to sustain the actuality of her body.

Autobiography with an A:Gender

Joey Hateley's solo performance piece *A:Gender*, directed by Natalie Wilson, explores the binary gender system from a masculine female perspective and uses mixed form, multiple characters and film. The production played for 12 nights at Oval House Theatre's Theatre Upstairs, a fringe venue with an auditorium which seats approximately 60. I am referencing the performance at Oval House Theatre on 1st April 2004. Hateley seeks to refute gender and identity categorisation within the performance and does this in discussion and interview, claiming to be a 'gender terrorist'. When asked to describer her own gender, she says 'I identify as a transgendered female…I'm proud to be a woman' (www.gaydarradio.com). In conversation after one performance, she spoke about her audience and expressed pleasure at the idea of men coming to see the show after presuming she was a gay boy from looking at promotional material. Reviews of the production emerged primarily and interestingly, from lesbian websites though nowhere does the publicity claim *A:Gender* as 'lesbian theatre'. London lesbian guide *GingerBeer.com*'s Roz Rural decides that 'the script is well written and accessible and has the power to appeal to a diverse audience. It works on a grassroots level to lure in newcomers to gender issues but contains enough theory to tickle the attention of the hardened gender menace, without it feeling spoon-fed…[it] boldly challenges assumptions made within exclusive gender binaries and creates an alternative arena: a beautiful, tender and peaceful place'. *Dykesdiary.com* describes the work as 'bold', 'striking' and 'a searing, heartfelt piece of performance'.

The deviant bathroom user

The production's form uses a montage of characters and scenes, some one-off vignettes and some that were part of a sequence or thread, recurring throughout. One example of how the distinct episodes served to explore the various perspectives on gender, draw on what was a principle character or protagonist who provided a through-line. A voiceover introduces the audience to the main character as 'our deviant bathroom user', who enters the female public toilets. With four toilet scenes, this thread is woven throughout the performance. The voice adds comment within each, assessing the 'performance' of the character in terms of how effectively she managed the situations she encounters. The voice is American-accented; the vocabulary and tone suggest analysis similar to that of a behavioural psychologist, or perhaps a documentary narrator, evaluating what they see for the benefit of the viewer. In the first encounter, we see the character check under each cubicle, looking for the feet of other bathroom users. The cubicles, the toilet and the sinks are implied through mime rather than real, and a sense of relief that the character is alone and therefore likely to avoid any difficult interactions is clear. Hateley's physicality here is strong and bold. As she moves across the stage, around the public bathroom, she is self-assured. Costumed in jeans, heavy work boots and a dark, loose t-shirt, the mannerisms and short, cropped hair all combine to offer a clear, unambiguous representation of a masculine woman. While in the cubicle, she hears someone enter the bathroom, so braces herself for a potential problem as she leaves. She is met with the voice of a woman saying 'er…this is the lady's toilet, young man'. The voice is that of a caricatured middle class woman. While washing her hands, the main character says 'Yes. I did know that. But did you know the middle class toilets are situated down the corridor and up your own arse?' The laughter that this evoked would seem to stem from recognition of the scenario, and pleasure at the blunt response one wishes one could give in such a confrontational, awkward social interaction.

In the second toilet scene, a security guard who tries to intervene after another bathroom user has complained about the 'man' in this women-only space confronts the main character. The guard is confused when he hears the character speak from inside the cubicle. With no visual signifiers of gender, he hears a 'female' voice and comedy is used again as the character articulates her irritation. The character is hassled by a young woman next, who begins with 'Oi You! Get out of the women's toilets' but then tries to engage in conversation. She asks what type of woman the protagonist goes for, and then invites her to party. Hateley's physicality indicates that the woman moves into the character's personal space and begins to flirt and again, laughter is the response as the audience recognise the situation. Later still, a more aggressive encounter involves a woman represented with a deeper voice and Northern accent asking 'what are you doin' in 'ere? Are you a tranny or a queer? Trannies are the biggest fuck ups that ever walked this earth'. The main character is physically pushed hard enough for her to stumble and she tries to counter the abusive comments with a remark about the woman's own masculinity, saying 'you're more of a man than I could ever be' before turning and running from the bathroom to the woman shouting 'you little fucker!' By this point, the repeated joke about gender ambiguity in public bathrooms is familiar, so the implicit notion that the threat of violence can quickly become actual is made explicit through the use of language. 'Taboo words such as "fuck" or "cunt", work because we give them a magical power, which makes them more than simple signs... the swearword aims to compact more than one hatred, becoming a verbal act of aggression, a slap in the mouth (Sierz, 2001:8).

Hateley's autobiographically inspired devised work uses personal history to construct the narrative. Kate Bornstein has declared that 'the best of the as-yet untold tales of the queer underground still belong to the FTMs' (http://www.geocities.com) and similar work is being devised and staged in the United States. *B4T (Before Testosterone)* is a solo piece, written and performed by Imani Henry, and directed by Diane Beckett (Highways Performance Space, 2006). *B4T* is a multi-media theatre piece that explores race, sexuality and gender expression through the lives of three Black, masculine, female-bodied people. *Next Magazine's* listings describe David Harrison's production *FTM* as a 'one-man drama [which] explores his transsexual journey from female to male based on his own personal experiences' (2003:39). The piece, seen at the Pyramid Theatre, New York, (14 December 2003) focussed on self-image and perception of self, interpersonal relationships with friends, lovers and family and the impact of gender re-assignment on everyday life. It employed the convention of monologue and multiple roles. Harrison says of the form:

> I wanted to do my own thing and didn't want to follow someone else's style...I didn't write it *[FTM]* to be a conventional play. The form of it is actually an expression of the content if that makes any sense. Form and content are interlinked (personal conversation with the author).

The main vehicle for the exploration of the theme of transition from childhood to adulthood as a transgendered person was the relationship between the protagonist and his mother. Harrison alternated between portrayals of both characters throughout, and within the narrative, a parallel was established whereby Timothy, a trans man, was taking testosterone as part of the process of transitioning and his mother was receiving testosterone as part of her cancer treatment. The two positions and attitudes to the radical step of altering one's hormonal state were juxtaposed to generate new insights into both experiences. This narrative provides a cohesive framework for the exploration of the facets of life as a transgendered person where a situation contains and surrounds the actions of the central character. Halberstam suggests that 'the transgender man expresses his desire for a manhood that will on some level always elude him' (2005:52). Jay Prosser's affirmative stance suggests that transsexuals become real through authorship: 'narrative *composes* the self. Conforming the life into narrative coheres both "lives" on either side of transition into an identity plot. This is not simply to remark autobiography as healing...but autobiography as constitutive' (Prosser, 1998: 120).

Subcultural phenomena: Transfabulous - *A Night of Tall Women and Short Men*

The third example of transgendered bodies on stage traces a cultural phenomenon back to its source in order to 'restore a different kind of prestige to the subculture and honour its creativity in the process' (Halberstam, 2005:127). I am extending Halberstam's critique of a contemporary film here to focus on a subcultural reclamation of one appropriation of marginal masculinity. She critiques *The Full Monty* (dir. Peter Catteneo, 1997), calling it an English Abject Masculinity film, built around the surprising vulnerabilities of the English male body and psyche (2005:127). She talks about the affiliation between the dominant and the marginal, identifying a relationship between the subcultural performance genre of Drag Kings and this film's focus on alternative masculinities and acknowledges Hebdige's notion of subcultures as marginalised cultures, which get quickly absorbed by capitalism and then robbed of their oppositional power. Halberstam asserts that some subcultures do not necessarily fade away as soon as they have been 'mined and plundered for material' (ibid).

This is the story of *A Night of Tall Women and Short Men* (2 July 2005), and specifically my story of the event, which will not, of course, be shared by all. The Pleasure Unit, Bethnal Green, London is a small, intimate nightclub which hosts monthly nights such as *Unskinny Bop*, attended by a queer bunch of people, and was the venue for an event organised by Jason Barker and Serge Nicholson of *Transfabulous*. This particular event included an act billed as the *FTM Full Monty*. Jason, Serge and a third trans man, Jay imagined the act as the main dance/ strip sequence from the film, with themselves as performers. Jason and Serge fully anticipated being able to back out, as word spread and other people volunteered to participate, however, they were joined by only one other person (Hamish) and the troupe was established as the four of them. Rehearsals took place. A sequence was choreographed and the strip routine practiced. Discussions about costume led to an array of construction worker apparel with hard hats and fully equipped tool belts.

The night came and punters gathered, heading to the bar and filling the space. Prior to the act, myself and another female companion were asked to move to the front in order to cheer and scream as the strip began, in case the audience reaction was lacking in enthusiasm. The four performers left to get changed and prepare themselves (out in the street) while we manoeuvred to the front. There seemed to be a hitch over by the door, causing a delay but then the music was cut and Jason announced the act. Versions of the story of what had gone on outside include neighbouring residents complaining of seeing flashers and Police asking the four men what they were doing, changing their clothes in the street. Jason simply told the crowd that the act had to be done quickly before someone from the council arrived to stop it, but that the act was about to happen. The four men made their way through the crowd and took the stage. Four fully costumed construction workers assumed their stances as Joe Cocker's 'You Can Leave Your Hat On' began. Each of the performers worked the crowd with their part in the sequence so innuendos were played out as Jay pulled a big screwdriver from his carpenter's belt and looked at it with an anxious expression, then pulled out a very small screwdriver and had a look of recognition on his face. The stripping began. Ben, a fellow-spectator, talks about the act of stripping in this context as being brave. These men are not professional strippers and there is an undoubted risk inherent in being naked in public. The performers were exposing themselves literally and those selves might be considered to be lacking, in a mainstream context. Here though, in a subcultural space, the vulnerable position of being naked was also a powerful position:

> In that moment, they weren't just themselves. They were all of us, and we were all of them. As I was watching the strip, which is a sexual performance, and this *was* a sexual thing, I was also thinking, where's my body in relation to this? There was something self-reflexive going on. I was having a really good look at four naked people, their movements, the dancing and the ways they were using their bodies but because we were all

inside the moment, it wasn't exploitative. It was kind of innocent (Ben, in personal conversation with the author)

The politics of stripping are altered here, where transgendered men are the objects of a pluralistic audience constituted of multiple gendered and sexed identities. Viewed in relation to women as object, or women's objectification of professional performers in acts such as *The Chippendales*, or women looking at their own men (husbands, fathers, brothers, friends etc.) as in *The Full Monty*, the cultural specificity of the *FTM Full Monty* as a sub-cultural phenomenon means that the voyeurs here are a queer bunch. The gaze is queered.   Hard hats were used strategically to build suspense, with a clear tease-moment where the four men turned away from the audience and raised their hats above their heads. Fully naked, we got a good view of their behinds to tantalise but as they turned back, the hats were replaced. The final crescendo was the 'money-shot', with four naked trans men displaying their bodies, inviting our eyes to look, enjoy, compare, appreciate, judge, envy, wonder.

> Our FTM *Full Monty* was nearly stopped after a warning to the club from Tower Hamlets Council. Oops, I forgot all about strip licenses! I kept pleading "but we're FTMs!" as if that was a defence. It worked though. We won a reprieve and so, at midnight, four transmen stood on the stage dressed in construction worker gear ready to do the world's first FTM Full Monty. All I remember is that the crowd went absolutely wild. It was like Beatlemania! There was a wall of noise, friends said later that they'd screamed themselves hoarse. When we stood in a line and lifted our strategically placed builder's helmets so revealing our four tranny bodies, naked in front of everyone, it was as if we were rock stars. We felt like the kings of the world! (Jason Barker, www.transfabulous.co.uk)

Alberstam's analysis of the final shot in the film suggests that it 'refuses to make the visibility of the phallus into the totality of maleness; the finale of the strip show is filmed from the back of the stage, and a freeze-frame captures the six naked men from behind and the crowd of screaming women full on. The *full* monty, then, is this shot that includes the female voyeur looking and the male body on display' (2005:141) Here, we did get the *full* monty, in terms of full frontal nudity (if that's what the phrase alludes to) but again, and in a different way, the visibility of the phallus is not the totality of maleness.

This performance and the context within which it took place is constitutive. The performers, in reciting inter-textual gestures, signs, choreographed steps and specific images that 'are drawn from a shared cultural reservoir that comes from before and exceeds the performer'

(Sullivan, 2003:90) further constitute the multiple subjects present in the space – themselves and those spectating. Lucas, another fellow-spectator who is FTM, describes looking at the aesthetic of each performer's chest. He talks about seeing what might be possible for himself and his own body, seeing what he wants for himself when he undergoes his own top-surgery. We might say there is a 'fast-track' constitution going on here, where the literal exposure of the flesh, of four different transgendered bodies are juxtaposed on stage, seen by an audience which is constituted by the trans community, creates an intensity whereby many individuals are engaged in the constitutive moment.

Visibility constructs the subject, 'so go ahead: look!'

We will always wear a scarlet T that marks us for treatment as a pretender, as other, as not normal, as trans. But wearing that T proudly – owning the label and carrying it with dignity – can twist that paradigm and free us from our subordinate prison. By using our own bodies and experience as references for our standards, rather than the bodies and experience of non-transsexuals (and non-transgendered people), we can grant our own legitimacy. (Green in More and Whittle, 1999:123)

The performers discussed here use theatre and performance as a strategy to twist the paradigm that Jamison Green alludes to here as one that has the power to render bodies illegible as shame and fear collude to instil a desire for disappearance. One goal of transsexualism could be said to be 'passing' as someone that you feel yourself to be (though at the same time, deemed by others *not* to be). This way of thinking, or this act in and of itself would seem to suggest a transgendered person might seek invisibility, where an individual's aim might be, in Sandy Stones' words, 'to erase h/erself, to fade into the 'normal' population as soon as possible' (1991:11). Performers invite readings of their bodies by positioning themselves in the public sphere of the stage. This notion does not necessarily sit well with the reality that transsexuality may be about achieving a desired state of being which will result in a kind of disappearance. Jay Prosser offers this perspective:

While sex reassignment surgery brings with it the chance of incorporation as a man or a woman, an unremarkability (a passing as real that should not be undervalued), becoming fully unremarkable requires the transsexual to renounce the remarkable history of transition – the very means to this unremarkability (1998:130)

In his paper 'Impossible People: Seeing the Trans Person',

Stephen Whittle suggests that while invisibility has widespread negative connotations, visibility as a result of publicising oneself as trans is not often wholly positive (2004). However, he continues, suggesting that it is exactly this 'being seen' and being read, as well as the viewer's acts of seeing and reading, that enable trans people to 'come into existence'. Laura Mulvey's notion of the active male gaze and passive female gaze becomes interesting in this context in that my witnessing of *Zenobia: The Amazing Lady with the Beard, A:Gender* and *the FTM Full Monty* generated a practice of seeing and reading where the male/female binary is complicated and we have 'trans body as image, biological woman as bearer of the look'. There were of course transsexual women, biological men, transsexual men, people of various transgendered identities and sexualities – a long list of alternatives to the original 'bearer of the look' (Mulvey in Goodman and de Gay 1998:274) at work in the performance and reception of the various transgendered identities on stage. Sullivan references Merleau-Ponty in considering the notion that the body-subject 'is constituted by mimesis and transitivism: by identification with and against others, and by the imitation of gestures, actions, and so on... the other is the medium through which the body-subject achieves an awareness of itself as self' (2003:93). Phelan's notion of 'non-ascriptive' community asserts that identity is about group identification rather than primordial essence. She conceptualises community as process, saying 'in the process of community, personalities are created. Persons do not simply 'join' communities; they become microcosms of their communities, and their communities change with their entrance' (1984:87). Cohen suggests that the reality of community lies in its members' perception of the vitality of its culture: 'people construct community symbolically, making it a resource and repository of meaning, and a referent of their identity' (Cohen 1985:118). The production of self is ineluctably connected to the subcultural contexts described in this chapter, where the doing of one's own body in the company of others enables those present to further become.

Sandy Stone suggests that a posttranssexual manifesto, or revised, specifically transgendered position will require individuals to 'take responsibility for all of their history, to begin to rearticulate their lives...as a political action begun by reappropriating difference and reclaiming the power of the refigured and reinscribed body' (Stone, 1991:13). Trans performance work still gets left out of conversations. Engaging with trans art, trans artists and trans viewers of trans art, brings very specific readings into the public domain. It is not necessarily the making of the work that necessarily makes it trans, but reading the work from a trans perspective. The work discussed here is variously trans through the biography of the artist, the context in which it is produced, the mode of aesthetic presentation and the spectatorship, readership and the deconstruction of the image using a trans gaze.

Works Cited

Bloomsbury English Dictionary (2nd ed), London: Bloomsbury, 2004.

Butler, Judith, *Bodies that Matter: on the Discursive Limits of 'Sex'*, New York: Routledge, 1993.

—. (1999) *Undoing Gender*, New York: Routledge, 1999.

Cohen, A. P., *The Symbolic Construction of Community*, London: Tavistock, 1985.

Connell, R. W., *Gender,* Cambridge: Polity, 2002.

Cranny-Francis, Anne et al, *Gender Studies: Terms and Debates*, Hampshire: Palgrave Macmillan, 2003.

Cromwell, Jason, 'Passing Women and Female-bodies Men: (Re)claiming FTM History' in More, Kate and Whittle, Stephen (eds), *Reclaiming Genders: Transsexual Grammars at the fin de siècle*, London: Cassell, 1999.

Ferris, Lesley, *Acting Women: Images of Women in Theatre,* Hampshire: Macmillan, 1990.

Foucault, Michel, *The History of Sexuality Volume I: The Will to Knowledge*, London: Penguin, 1998.

Green, Jamison, 'Look! No, Don't! The Visibility Dilemma for Transsexual Men' in More, Kate and Whittle, Stephen (eds), *Reclaiming Genders: Transsexual Grammars at the fin de siècle*, London: Cassell, 1999.

Halberstam, Judith, *Female Masculinity*, Durham: Duke University Press, 1998.

Halberstam, Judith 'Jack' and Volcano, Del LaGrace, *The Drag King Book*, London: Serpent's Tail, 1999.

Halberstam, Judith, *In a Queer Time and Place: Transgender Bodies, Subcultural Lives,* New York: New York University Press, 2005.

Hausman, Bernice, *Changing Sex: Transsexualism, Technology, and the Idea of Gender*, Durham: Duke University Press, 1995.

Howe, Elizabeth, *The First English Actresses: Women and Drama 1660-1700,* Cambridge: Cambridge University Press, 1992.

Jeffreys, Sheila, *Unpacking Queer Politics*, Cambridge: Polity Press, 2003.

Kessler, Suzanne J and McKenna, Wendy, *Gender: An*

Ethnomethodological Approach, Chicago: Chicago University Press, 1978.

King, Dave, 'Gender Blending: Medical Perspectives and Technology' in Ekins, Richard and King, Dave (eds), *Blending Genders: Social Aspects of Cross-dressing and Sex-Changing*, London: Routledge, 1996.

Millot, Catherine, *Horsexe: Essay on Transsexuality*, New York: Autonomedia, 1990.

Mulvey, Laura, 'Visual Pleasure and Narrative Cinema' in Goodman, Lizbeth and de Gay, Jane *The Routledge Reader in Gender and Performance*, London: Routledge, 1975.

Phelan, Shane, *Getting Specific: Postmodern Lesbian Politics*, Minneapolis: University of Minnesota Press, 1994.

Prosser, Jay, *Second Skins: the body narratives of transsexuality*, New York: Columbia University Press, 1998.

Raymond, Janice, *The Transsexual Empire*, London: The Women's Press, 1980.

Riddell, Carol, 'Divided Sisterhood: A critical review of Janice Raymond's *The Transsexual Empire*' in Ekins, Richard and King, Dave (eds), *Blending Genders: Social Aspects of Cross-dressing and Sex-Changing*, London: Routledge, 1996.

Roughgarden, Joan, *Evolution's Rainbow: Diversity, Gender and Sexuality in Nature and People*, University of California Press, 2004.

Saunders, Graham, *'Love Me or Kill Me': Sarah Kane and the theatre of extremes*, Manchester: Manchester University Press, 2002.

Senelick, Laurence, *The Changing Room: Sex, Drag and Theatre*, London: Routledge, 2000.

Shiach, Morag, ''Gender' and Cultural Analysis' in *Paragraph* 17, 1, ed. Cath Sharrock, Edinburgh: Edinburgh University Press, 1994.

Showalter, Elaine (ed), *The New Feminist Criticism: Essays on women, literature and theory*, London: Virago, 1986.

Sierz, Aleks, *In-Yer-Face Theatre*, London: Faber and Faber, 2001.

Straayer, Chris, 'Transgender Mirrors: Queering Sexual Difference' in Duberman, Martin (ed), *Queer Representations: Reading Lives, Reading Cultures*, New York: New York University Press, 1997.

Sullivan, Nikki, *A Critical Introduction to Queer Theory*, Edinburgh: Edinburgh University Press, 2003.

Svich, Caridad, in Delgado, Maria M. and Svich, Caridad (eds), *Theatre in crisis? Performance manifestos for a new century*, Manchester: Manchester University Press, 2002.

Wandor, Michelene, *Carry On, Understudies: Theatre & Sexual Politics*, London: Routledge & Kegan Paul, 1986.

—. *Post-War British Drama: Looking Back in Gender*, London: Routledge, 2001.

Whittle, Stephen, *The Transgender Debate: The Crisis Surrounding Gender Identities*, South Street: Reading, 2000.

—. 'Impossible People: Seeing the Trans Person' paper given at Art Becomes You: Parody, Pastiche and the Politics of Art: Materiality in a Post-Material World, Birmingham Institute of Art and Design, 2004.

Reviews

Carr, C (14 July 1998), 'Circus Minimus: Miller Wows 'Em in the Nabes!', *The Village Voice*, http://www.villagevoice.com/news/9828,carr,438,4.html.

Listings (12 December 2003), *Next Magazine*, Issue 11.23.

Smith, Dinitia (9 June 1995), 'Step Right Up! See the Bearded Person!', *New York Times' Weekend Section*, http://www.circusamok.org/press

Performances/ Films

Cattaneo, Peter dir. (1997), *The Full Monty*, UK

Gold, Tami dir. (1992), *Juggling Gender*, USA

Harrison, David (2003), *FTM*, Pyramid Theatre, New York

Hateley, Joey (2004), *A:Gender*, Oval House Theatre, London

Henry, Imani (2006), *B4T (Before Testosterone)*, Highways Performance Space, Los Angeles

Miller, Jennifer (1999), *Zenobia: The Amazing Lady with the Beard*, Hoxton Hall, London

Pressman, Fréderique dir. (2002), *Un Cirque de New York*, France

Transfabulous, (2005), *A Night of Tall Women and Short Men: the FTM Full Monty*, The Pleasure Unit, London

Personal Conversations

Gooch, Benjamin (30 December 2005), personal conversation with Catherine McNamara

Harrison, David (3 February 2004), personal conversation with Catherine McNamara

McKenna, Lucas (21 August 2005), personal conversation with Catherine McNamara

Websites

www.transfabulous.co.uk Accessed 2005

www.dykesdiary.com Accessed 2005

www.gingerbeer.com Accessed 2005

www.gaydarradio.com Accessed 2005

www.geocities.com/imani_henry Accessed 2005

Smith, M. K. (2001) 'Community' in *the encyclopedia of informal education*, on *http://www.infed.org/community/community.htm*.2001.

Stone, (Sandy) Roseanne Allucquere (1991), The Empire Strikes Back: A Posttranssexual Manifesto on *www.sandystone.com/ empire-strikes-back*, 1991.

CHAPTER TEN

THE DIALECTICS OF DESIRE: *AUNT MARY* AND TRANSGENDERED REPRESENTATIONS[3]

DIMPLE GODIWALA

Synopsis

This chapter seeks to analyse the roles of the three transgendered characters of Pam Gems' play Aunt Mary. Sinfield and other western metropolitan theorists' 1990s discovery via Other (mainly Eastern) cultures that there are 'radically different ways in which [gay] people can conceive their subjectivity and focus their desire' is an issue pre-figured by Pam Gems in Aunt Mary by nearly a decade. Written as far back as 1982, the drama anticipates much of the gay, transgender and transvestism theorizing of the 90s and the present day. Gems is on the pulse of cultural iconology by having written this piece so early and what is interesting is that the characters escape easy definitions and tidy categorizations. This is a performance of the identity of drag and queer framed by a play: the shifting and fluid space in which the identities of the players locate themselves is a study in the psychology of transgendering, transvestism, and transsexualism.

*****

---

[3] This chapter was first published as an article in 'Gender Queeries', *Gender Forum* No. 8. It was subsequently published as part of my monograph *Queer Mythologies: The Original Stageplays of Pam Gems*, Bristol & Portland, Oregon: Intellect, 2006.

'[T]o take sex out of transvestism is like taking music out of opera'
—H. Benjamin, *The Transsexual Phenomenon*

'It is not the reader's 'person' that is necessary to me, it is this site: the possibility of a dialectics of desire, of an *unpredictability* of bliss: the bets are not placed, there can still be a game'
—Roland Barthes, *The Pleasure of the Text*

A dramatist as prolific and talented as Pam Gems ought not to need an introduction. Her plays have been celebrated feminist additions to English drama in the Long Twentieth Century[4]. In *Breaking the Bounds: British Feminist Dramatists Writing in the Mainstream since c. 1980* (Godiwala 2003), I introduced the work of Pam Gems. Unlike the other feminist dramatists who were the concern of my previous work, Gems is cannily on the pulse of the cultural moment and she proves it time and again in her work. It was once said of Marina Warner that she was able to spot cultural pre-occupations before they became part of the cultural zeitgeist. Gems' dramaturgy pre-figures many such cultural moments, now reified by prolific academic theorizing on the subject.

Aunt Mary, first produced in 1982, anticipates by more than a decade the prolific output of queer theorizing in the Anglophone world. The triad seems to be an appropriate answer to the destructive potential of the nuclear family as theorized by Deleuze in the 1970s: 'Oedipus is the figurehead of imperialism, 'colonization pursued by other means, it is the interior colony, and we shall see that even at home … it is our intimate colonial education.' […] Oedipus is everywhere' (Deleuze xx).

Gems' white mythologies are *herstories* but also histories:

Metaphysics - the white mythology which reassembles and reflects the culture of the West: the *white man* takes his own mythology, Indo-European mythology, his own *logos*, that is, the *mythos* of his idiom, for the universal form of that he must still wish to call Reason. *Which does not go uncontested.* (Derrida 213)

Contesting the *logos* and *mythos* of male reason, Gems creates characters, both women and men who debunk the stereotypes of western culture. Significantly, she also challenges the domination of *white man* as she brings in the Other. Not only is Woman cast as the Other, Freud's dark

---

[4] The Long Twentieth Century extends the twentieth century into the present day, continuing the influences of the late twentieth century in terms of ideas, style and form. See my book, *Breaking the Bounds: British Feminist Dramatists Writing in the Mainstream since c. 1980* for the multiple transgressions wrought by feminist dramatists on patriarchally inherited forms and styles.

continent of otherness, but Other cultures, eastern and western are brought into play with characters from 'home.' White man too is rendered in all the shades of his beingness: straight, gay, transgendered, bisexual.

To say that *Aunt Mary* is a play about three gay people would be misleading. The transgendered identities and triadic domestic arrangements of this 1982 drama challenge the notions of traditionally gendered space and the nuclear family. Pam Gems is on the pulse of the gender theorizing of the 90s well before it happened: she pre-empts the transgendered spaces of gay and queer theory in the early 80s when fledgling lesbian theory had not given way to queer and gay theorizing quite yet. Gender here is set against a heterogeneous social background to give us 'Aunt' Mary, a middle-aged gay man, Muriel, a bisexual middle-aged woman and Cyst, an aging transvestite male, who star in this three pronged drama about love, sexual relationships and privacy. When Alison who works for a media mogul wants to take the eminently saleable lives of this threesome into the glare of the public eye of television, they refuse to give up the privacy of their provincial lives. Indeed, the subtitle of the play is *Scenes from Provincial Life*, making the metadramatic statement of performing exactly what Alison the media person wants: putting the three transgendered people into the frame of the stage and bringing into confrontation the difference from the normative in contemporary Britain. This is a performance of the identity of drag and queer framed by a play: the shifting and fluid space in which the identities of the players locate themselves is a study in the psychology of transgendering, transvestitism, and transsexualism, which perform versions of a variously gay identity space.

The play avoids the easy exclusions that the new identity positions place on people named gay, bisexual, lesbian, and transvestite/transsexual (TV/TSS) As Alan Sinfield theorizes, the notion of the subject as defined by these, albeit fairly new, cultural terms, is a constraint. He notes that these terms may prove a hindrance to activists and analysts rather than an aid (Sinfield 150). Although the term 'transgender' is currently used to encompass the subjective identities of all TVs and TSS, Jay Prosser explains that 'transgender' was used initially to denote a stronger commitment to living as a woman than 'transvestite' or 'cross-dresser,' and without the implications of sexuality in 'transsexual' (Sinfield 163).

Cyst, Mary, and Muriel defy definitions of constraint through this play by occupying different positions within exclusivity and difference. Although certain behaviours sound conventional in the play such as cross-dressing (Cyst enters from within, wearing a half-made dress. Mary follows, tape measure round neck. Sc. iv), so-called 'effeminate behaviour' in the literary space of their café and a manufactured masculinity (Mary with a cigar and in trousers) tempers gay behaviour to be socially acceptable in the triad of wo/men.

Alan Sinfield and other western metropolitan theorists' 1990s discovery via Other (mainly Eastern) cultures that there are 'radically different ways in which [gay] people can conceive their subjectivity and focus their desire' (Sinfield 164) is an issue anticipated by Pam Gems in *Aunt Mary* by nearly a decade.

Transvestism (TV) and transsexualism (TSS) were traditionally diagnostic terms for categories of mental disorders (Docter viii and Chapter 2). More recently, in 'self theory' where the self is a hypothetical construct, the concepts of identity, gender identity, and cross-gender identity are conceptualized by Richard F. Docter as 'subsystems of the self.' Docter et al hypothesize that the self has a capacity to 'share control, and even [...] be 'overthrown' by subordinate units of the self' (vii). One approach to transvestism is the *intrapsychic / psychodynamic* model. According to R. F. Docter, the best of psychoanalytic models of transvestism 'describe this as a disorder of the self stemming from major difficulties in early object relations. Women's clothing are said to be symbolic ties with the mother and to serve as transitional objects providing security and anxiety reduction.' Docter opines that 'this theory seems more in harmony with the developmental behaviour of a transvestite than the earlier 'phallic woman' model that drew mainly on castration anxiety and the oedipal complex as explanatory theses.' The *developmental/learning* model 'attempts to explain transvestism and transsexualism based on the principles of learning and the process of socialization. The idea is that these behaviours are acquired through classical conditioning, operant conditioning, and modeling and imitation, just as are so many other behaviours.' Since the different models explaining TV and TSS conflict with each other, Docter devises four thematic constructs in order to view these behaviours conceptually. He seems to ignore the *biological* or medical model entirely and favours developmental psychology. The four constructs are: *sexual arousal* and sexual excitement at cross-dressing; the *pleasure* associated with cross-dressing in the sense of its mood-altering power; *sexual scripts* which guide complex behaviour; and *cross-gender identity* which is switched on and off by the act of cross dressing (Docter 1-3).

There seem to be two main explanations for transvestism: one is that it is a means for achieving sexual pleasure and arousal; the second is that transvestism is part of a personality struggle stemming from trauma and conflict. Docter aims to go beyond these two theories to question 'how

identity and gender identity are formed, how arousal and pleasure are
generated, how sexual scripts are learned and rehearsed, and how intense
envy and fear of women may contribute to becoming a transvestite'
(Docter 6).

It does seem that even contemporary analysts see transgendered
behaviour as abnormal or problem behaviour though their terminology is
couched in a more progressive and acceptable language of analysis. The
formation of gender and sexual identity, the generation of pleasure and the
playing out of sexual scripts are not peculiar to transgendered people, and
these can be as differently and variously constructed and enacted as there
are gender and sexual identities. In the play we see the three transgendered
wo/men play out these various sexual scripts. The female impersonator in
Aunt Mary is 'Cyst.' Her favourite impersonation is the character of
Blanche DuBois, a favourite of the cross-dressing community, perhaps
because in *A Streetcar Named Desire* she symbolises the dichotomy
between inner and outer self, the core of self and the façade of self,
lending the cross-dresser the 'magic' of Blanche's outward coy femininity
masking the 'realism' of the impersonating male self. Here we see the self
has a capacity to share control, and even be 'overthrown' by subordinate
units of the self: transsexualism.

> I don't want realism. [...] I'll tell you what I want. Magic! Yes, yes, magic!
> I try to give that to people. I misrepresent things to them. I don't tell the
> truth. I tell what ought to be truth. And if that is sinful, then let me be
> damned for it! - *Don't turn the light on!* (Blanche in Williams 204).

Cyst hates the real light of day as does Blanche, perfectly in
character and also quite apt psychologically as she is an agoraphobe who
never leaves the environs of the house and the garden. Cyst enjoys
women's clothing which serves as a transitional object providing security
and anxiety reduction. Cyst is the impersonating wench.

The wench as played by male impersonators on the stage is traced
by Laurence Senelick to the burlesque of *La Dame aux camélias* (or
Camille as it is known in the US) which has Sam and Julius re-creating
Dumas' tragedy. Senelick also traces the interweaving of the psychology
of race relations with the sexual desire, 'particularly in such manifestations
as dominance and submission, exoticism and the attraction of opposites.'
He traces the later genre where 'men frankly portrayed lovely white
women' to Charles du Val, a mid-Victorian performer. However, the
extravagant   wardrobes,   close   male   partnership   and   prolonged
bachelorhood, as deeply suspect as they are to the modern theatre
historian, did not plunge the performers into disrepute: 'no breath of

homosexual scandal touched [the] unmarried female impersonators of the minstrel stage. They were actors, and that explained everything' (Senelick 248-50).

Richard Howard in a preface to Barthes' *The Pleasure of the Text* deconstructs English amorous discourse as 'coarse or clinical.' '[B]y tradition our words for our pleasures, even for the most intimate parts of our bodies where we may take those pleasures, come awkwardly [if] they come at all. So that if we wish to speak of the kind of pleasure we take - the supreme pleasure, say, associated with sexuality at its most abrupt and ruthless pitch [bisexual, gay, TV/TSS] - we lack. [...] [W]e lack *jouissance* and *jouir*.' Howard reminds us that Sterne [*The Life and Opinions of Tristram Shandy* 1759-1767] said, 'they order this matter so much better in France' (Howard in Barthes v-vi).

Interestingly, or perhaps predictably, today's amorous discourse in England is constituted by the new gay, queer and trans-gender studies writings and performance. Sex and sexuality, repressed in the heterosexual closet, come out in an abundant *jouir* as well as possess a *jouissance* beyond the 'phallus' (the system) in the matrix of these performative and analytic discourses.

Cyst can also be seen as trans-gendered, which Sinfield recognizes as a *gender* identity rather than a sub-category of sexual identity. Kenneth Marlowe defines two kinds of homosexuals: the 'effeminate' and the 'masculine.' '[I]t is paternal rejection of the 'sissy' that makes the boy homosexual: sexuality is consequent upon gender attributes' (Marlowe 12-13; Sinfield 157) Sinfield traces the historical fact that the notion of trans-gendered identity has always existed: 'the kind of gay man whose effeminacy was tantamount to trans-gender [was always] visible.' Recognizing Quentin Crisp as trans-gendered, he is defined thus by his very words: the kind of persons who 'must, with every breath they draw, with every step they take, demonstrate that they are feminine' The kind of person who is continually 'propositioned, harassed and beaten by total strangers. Employers and the army reject him on sight' (Crisp 21; Sinfield 157).

Cyst may also be played as a hermaphrodite or by a transsexual actor as in Kate Bornstein's 1988 enaction of Herculine Barbin, Michel Foucault's case study. Barbin's interstitial position between the sexes is voiced by Bornstein the transsexual actor who identifies with 'hir':

[T]he journey I want to portray is, did [Barbin] really have to be a he or a she? Was he really some other gender that was trying to survive? And that's the way I feel myself... I certainly don't feel I'm a man, and many times I question whether I'm a woman. I laugh at a world that permits me to be only one or the other. (Ferris 4-5)

Barbin's memoirs were written as a study of what Michel Foucault saw
as the essentialist position of the '*true* sex.'

> Do we *truly* need a *true* sex? With a persistence that borders on
> stubbornness, modern Western societies have answered in the affirmative.
> They have obstinately brought into play this question of a 'true' sex in an
> order of things where one might have imagined that all that counted was
> the reality of the body and the intensity of its pleasures. (Foucault vii)

Foucault brings into question the persistence of the Western
practice of perceiving the sexes as a duality. '[I]t was a very long time
before the postulate that a hermaphrodite must have a sex - a single, true
sex - was formulated.' Sexuality for Foucault was always constructed
within matrices of power as Butler reminds us (97). In the play we have
Cyst as an indefinable space in the text, the gay cross-dressed actor or
indeed a transsexual actor who responds to Aunt Mary's masculinity but
also provides a female/feminine power of 'hir' own. They function in a
two-pronged matrix of power relations as they finally include Muriel into
a triadic domesticity which is, in a subversion of the Deleuzean oedipal-
nuclear triad, a benign power relation. In a metadramatic twist we see the
characters of Cyst and Mary 'perform' for us, as they reject in a final
gesture the beckoning materialist temptation of media celebrity and
exposure. They are not, in the play, public impersonators but privately, a
gay couple leading a 'provincial life.' As in *Franz into April* their life
unfolds in a theatrical space, as the theatre doubles as a private
(confessional) and public (performative) space which contains the flows of
their desires. An understanding of Gilles Deleuze and Félix Guattari's
theory in *Anti-Oedipus: Capitalism and Schizophrenia* sheds light on the
central gestus of this play. The triadic arrangement which closes the play
is a line of flight from heteronormative institutions of repression; it is also
a flight from gay sexual constraints by the acceptance of bi-sexuality,
deemed 'natural' by some essentialist theorists such as Hélène Cixous.
The triadic union of male impersonator-as-woman, a gay man and a
woman in a legitimized marriage is the triadic answer to Deleuze's critique
of the nuclear family (and capitalism) as source of all repression as well as
a solution to the repressed feminine of the male-male bonding of
conventional gay sexuality. It is the realization of 'freedom in difference
and through differentiation, the principle of permanent revolution made
possible in the universal history inaugurated by capitalism' (Holland 121).
The rejection of society's bad organizations, capitalism and the nuclear
family is achieved by this Deleuzean triad by rejecting media exposure

and entering into a bonding which defeats both, the nuclear family as well as homosexuality's rigid sexual apartheid. The media seeking to undermine the stability and force of free-form desire is rejected as they achieve their status as the Deleuzean schizos emerging at the end-of-history as the principle of freedom in permanent revolution. As Holland points out, schizophrenia [Deleuze's schizo] is not merely the principle of permanent revolution: it is also the process of revolution itself. It is the *modus operandi* of subject groups, subjugated groups (here, the triad of Mary, Cyst and Muriel), whose very existence and form of operation subvert the dominant mode of organization (in Gems' play it is the nuclear family, gay binary coupling and capitalism, as there is a consensus to reject materialistic public exposure in the media). As Holland puts it, 'the chances for realizing permanent revolution [...] stem from neither individual lines-of-flight nor the operation of subject groups occurring in isolation, but from the intersection and assemblage of individuals and groups into a critical mass whose combined effect it would be to lift the mortgage of the infinite debt and finally liquidate capital and the barriers it poses to freedom and enjoyment' (Holland 123).

Aunt Mary then is a performance of this permanent revolution acted out in a private provincial space occupied by three people who form a beneficent triad which replaces or supplants the Deleuzean Oedipal triad. We have here the Barthesian '*unpredictability* of bliss: the bets are not placed, there can still be a game.' The refusal to play the game (of media exposure and capitalistic exploitation) and the risk of the game of triadic arrangement (a line-of-flight) puts Gems on the pulse of cultural iconology here as her dramaturgy predates the prolific theorizing on gay, bisexual and transgendered bodies in the 90s.

This article was first read as a paper at the July 2004 Manchester University Conference 'Queer Politics and Cultural Production' which was dedicated to the work of Alan Sinfield.

Works Cited

Alderson, David, and Anderson, Linda. Eds. *Territories of Desire in Queer Culture: Reconfiguring contemporary boundaries*. Manchester: Manchester University Press, 2000.

Barthes, Roland. *The Pleasure of the Text* [*Le Plaisir du texte*, 1973]. Trans. Richard Miller, Farrar, Straus and Giroux. London: Cape, 1975.

Benjamin, H. *The Transsexual Phenomenon*. New York: Julian Press, 1966.

Butler, Judith. *Gender Trouble. Feminism and the Subversion of Identity*. New York, London: Routledge, 1990.

Crisp, Quentin. *The Naked Civil Servant*. New York: Plume, 1977.

Deleuze, Gilles and Guattari, Félix. *Anti-Oedipus. Capitalism and Schizophrenia* Vol. I. [1972]. Trans. Robert Hurley, Mark Seem and Helen R. Lane. London: Athlone Press, 1984.

Derrida, Jacques. 'White Mythology' (1971). *Margins of Philosophy*. Trans. Alan Bass. Chicago: Chicago University Press, 1982.

Docter, Richard F. *Transvestites and Transsexuals. Toward a Theory of Cross-Gender Behaviour*. London: Plenum Press, 1988.

Ferris, Lesley. Ed. *Crossing the Stage: Controversies on Cross Dressing*. London and New York: Routledge, 1993.

Foucault, Michel. *Herculine Barbin. Being the Recently Discovered Memoirs of a Nineteenth-Century French Hermaphrodite* [*Herculine Barbin, dite Alexina B.*, Gallimard 1978]. Trans. Richard McDougall, London: The Harvester Press, 1980.

Gems, Pam. *Aunt Mary. Scenes from Provincial Life. Plays by Women*. Ed. Michelene Wandor. London: Methuen, 1983.

Godiwala, Dimple. *Breaking the Bounds: British Feminist Dramatists Writing in the Mainstream since c. 1980*. University of Oxford: 2001; New York: Peter Lang, 2003.

Holland, Eugene W. *Deleuze and Guattari's* Anti-Oedipus. *Introduction to Schizoanalysis*. London and New York: Routledge, 1999.

Howard, Richard. 'A Note on the Text.' *The Pleasure of the Text* [*Le Plaisir du texte*, 1973] by Roland Barthes. Trans. Richard Miller, Farrar, Straus and Giroux. London: Cape, 1975.

Marlowe, Kenneth. *The Male Homosexual*. Los Angeles: Medco, 1968.

Medhurst, Andy, and Sally R. Munt. Eds. *Lesbian and Gay Studies. A Critical Introduction*. London: Cassell, 1997.

Senelick, Laurence. *The Changing Room. Sex, Drag and Theatre*. London, New York: Routledge, 2000.

Sinfield, Alan. 'Transgender and les/bi/gay identities.' *Territories of Desire in Queer Culture. Reconfiguring Contemporary Boundaries*. (eds) David Alderson and Linda Anderson. Manchester: Manchester University Press, 2000.

Williams, Tennessee. *Penguin Plays: Sweet Bird of Youth/A Streetcar Named Desire/The Glass Menagerie*. Harmondsworth: Penguin Books, 1959.

CHAPTER ELEVEN

NOTES ON CHERYL MOCH'S
CINDERELLA, THE REAL TRUE STORY

DIMPLE GODIWALA

Synopsis

Cheryl Moch's fairytale has inspired many lesbian dramatists, including Sarah Daniels. The lesbian fairytale is the prototype of both, alternative pantomime and serious mainstream play. Comic reversals in terms of gender, race and sexuality are a recurrent pattern of this type of play.

*****

The mythmaking which is Cinderella re-told was Cheryl Moch and Holly Gewandter's wish-fulfilment play which drew enthusiastic lesbian audiences in Britain and the USA. The personal struggle to come out led to the enactment of an archetype: 'archetypes run deep, fairy-tales are the myths of the contemporary nursery: in childhood it was Cinderella, not Persephone, who loomed large.' (Moch in Davis 1989: 147). As Moch puts it, 'The emergence [...] of lesbian plays can be traced to the emergence of lesbian, feminist and gay-controlled spaces and theatre groups as well as to the playwrights.' The unfolding of gay and lesbian dreams is most clear in this fairytale wish-fulfilment play which epitomizes much early lesbian theatre.

The matriarchal working out of the myth is apparent in the Grandmother Clock which takes the place of the fairy godmother and effectively replaces the traditional grandfather clock. The central lesbian-feminist gest is worked out with Cinderella in princely drag at the ball, the Princess leading the dance symbolic of her higher status to the cleaning girl. The figure of an abusive stepfather provides the counterfoil to a wise King who is father to the Princess and has the ability (after the stereotypical parental objections to homosexuality) to change the laws of the kingdom which is the twist which provides for lesbian wish-fulfilment. In the afterword, Moch reveals that most parents, even if accepting of children's homosexuality, maintain a distance from the gay lives of the offspring and much hostility is engendered. Although the play does have the two girls go into exile the wise father upon realising the societal censure they face accepts Cinderella into the palace and changes the laws of the kingdom.

This early lesbian piece charts out the themes which have informed much lesbian drama, especially the societal reasons for women constructed to choose lesbian lives and these are voiced by both, the Princess as well as Cinderella.

> PRINCESS: [...] another Ball to find a man for the Princess. Another collection of the rude, the crude, the ill mannered, ill conceived... [...] Tonight my father, King Philip the Bold, flings wide the Palace doors and through them will come every last eligible man in the Kingdom, to gawk and to grab at the Princess. (Moch in Davis: 114-115)
> CINDERELLA: Grandmother, Stepfather has started to look at me funny. Yesterday, he sat right here, his eyes followed me around the room and he said, 'Well, I can see that at last you're favouring your mother!' And then he laughed a mean, cruel laugh. Oh, why is laughter sometimes the sweetest sound and sometimes the cruellest? And then, as I tried to get away, he grabbed me! (116)

While the Princess is tired of the stereotypically crude grovelling and fondling of wannabe suitors, Cinderella turns away from men in response to the abusive and unwanted attentions of the stepfather and the crudity of the step-brothers.

The wish-fulfilment of the story lies not only in the acceptance of the wise King, but also in the wisdom and advice provided by the Grandmother: 'Haven't I taught you, 'what limits people is their mind'? Tonight Cinderella, you're a man! [...] If a mouse can be a coachman and a pumpkin a carriage, you can be a man.' Her advice to Cinderella is also a lesbian wish-fulfilment device and stratagem. She advises her that 'there's nothing' to acting like a man: 'Just move like you're not only entitled to your own space, but like you're thinking of taking everyone else's. Walk like you're pushing, really pushing, to get somewhere. And talk the same way.' (116-117)

The gender constructedness of being male and the societal constructions which formulate the sexual choices of homosexuals come to the fore in this play which has the ingredients of the ideal fantasies of western women: the Prince (who is now princess), the Palace, wise parental models who understand and accept children's wishes, and the story in which all ends well and everyone lives happily ever after.

The fantasy play is stereotypical of homosexual coming-out drama which skilfully avoids the real-life indecisions, failed relationships, prejudices of the parents, the church and society just as heterosexual fairytales end with ideal marriages. The finding of the ideal mate is the end of all western fairytale, rather than the beginning of real life stories which may not end well. Just as no western fairytale ever charted the ups and downs of normal marriages, so do the lesbian fantasies cater to all round imagined happiness which continues forever in a bid to escape the harsh realities of modern life.

Works cited

Cheryl Moch, *Cinderella, The Real True Story* in *Lesbian Plays: Two*, ed. Jill Davis, London: Methuen, 1989.

CHAPTER TWELVE

THROUGH THE LOOKING GLASS WITH SARAH DANIELS[5]

DIMPLE GODIWALA

Synopsis

'Breaking the Bounds' charted melodrama as the ideal genre re-worked to suit the lesbian condition. Daniels re-fashions melodrama to write 'Ripen Our Darkness', 'Neaptide' and 'The Madness of Esme and Shaz'. Seen from the context of the groups and performers invisible to the audiences and critics of the British mainstream, groups like Split Britches and The Gay Sweatshop, Daniels' texts are 'assimilationist' texts. Looking in at her texts from these western radical-lesbian margins which parade their biographies and sexualit/ies, pleasures and partners on stage and within their performance texts, and for whom 'the most transgressive act at this historical moment would be representing [sadomasochistic and other kinds of pornographic performance] to excess, in dominant and marginalized reception communities', Sarah Daniels is the 'conservative' British mainstream dramatist who speaks of lesbian as a trope for bonding, likened to motherhood or sisterhood.

*****

In *Byrthrite* and *Morning Glory* Daniels' characters occupy what Adrienne Rich called the 'lesbian continuum' which included 'a range

---

[5] I am grateful to Peter Lang for granting permission to reproduce some of the material from *Breaking the Bounds: British Feminist Dramatists Writing in the Mainstream since c. 1980*. Oxford: University of Oxford 2001; New York & Oxford: Peter Lang 2003.

[...] of woman-identified experience [which includes] the sharing of a rich inner life, the bonding against male tyranny, the giving and receiving of practical and political support (Rich in Zimmerman 1986: 205). Lillian Faderman defines lesbian as 'a relationship in which [...] women's strongest emotions and affections are directed toward each other. Sexual contact may be [...] entirely absent.' (Faderman in Zimmerman 1986: 206).

Whereas in *Byrthrite* the women bond against male tyranny (see below), the three old-age pensioners of *Morning Glory* unite to fight against teenage rebels who burgle houses and violently attack pensioners. Brett, Luke and Mel are the rowdy young gang of hoodlums who attack Rose and leave her unconscious. Discovered by her friend Grace who is accompanied by Adele, the three fighters of the French Resistance arm themselves for revenge on the hoodlums.

Drinking vodka out of teacups, the trio of women gird themselves to spy on the young ruffians as Adele, dressed as a nun, smokes out the Nazi knife which was stolen from Rose's wardrobe. They lure the teen criminals to Rose's house as they spray them with mace, procured on a day trip to France. All six of them are discovered by the police as they torture each other. The play ends with the pensioners and the teenage hoodlums doing community service.

Not surprisingly, a critic as radical in her views on lesbian representation as Jill Dolan would not even take Daniels seriously enough to consider writing about her. However, it is with her words which in turn evoke bell hooks', that I introduce my analysis of Daniels as *a radical writer of the British mainstream:*

> Saying "I am lesbian" has been validated in cultural feminist discourse as speech that breaks the silence of lesbian existence under heterosexual hegemony.

Undoubtedly too politically correct for the radical lesbian margins of Anglo-America, Daniels undeniably 'comes out' in her writing albeit metaphorically. The first woman to announce 'I am a lesbian' to the stages of the British mainstream she is lambasted by the (mainly male, overwhelmingly hetero-normative) critics, thereby taking her position centrestage as *the* radical lesbian writer of the 1980s, still conservative, *mainstream* stages of Britain. It is interesting that Elaine Aston struggles to establish that Daniels is *not* a mainstream writer because she has been performed 'on "alternative", studio stages rather than in mainstream playhouses [thus] in the "margins" of mainstream theatre.' She compares her to Churchill and Wertenbaker (whose plays have also largely played at

studio venues similar to the venues Daniels has played at, apart from the
fact that they are all Royal Court writers) (Aston 1995: 393,394). From
1972 to 1995 (the date of Aston's article) the 'most mainstream' theatre
(to use Aston's nomenclature) to produce any Churchill play was the
RSC's Barbican Pit where the - here comes patriarchy's invisible
structural rule in operation - *all-male* version of Foucault's *Discipline and
Punish, a play which had no gender content* to upset the system even
unconsciously - *Softcops* was performed. All other plays by Churchill till
the date of Aston's article were at venues such as The Dartington College
of Arts (*Cloud Nine*) and Almeida Theatre (*Fen*), apart from The Royal
Court which often staged the plays of all three writers. Wertenbaker has
been performed at the RSC because she (even when indicting patriarchy)
speaks in patriarchal high-language or the acceptable guise of classical
Greek tragedy. *The Thebans* was performed in 1991 and *The Love of the
Nightingale* played in 1988. The latter is a re-writing of the Greek myth of
Philomel and Procne, told in the lost play of Sophocles, *Tereus*. Although
Wertenbaker's play is an indictment of patriarchy, past and contemporary,
the skilful re-working of a classical myth makes its case to the RSC.
Arguably, Daniels is then the 'most successful' playwright as her
(undoubtedly lesbian) *Neaptide* was performed at The Cottesloe in 1986,
at a time when the young writer's career had barely begun, whereas
Churchill had to wait three and a half decades to be performed at the same
venue. Wertenbaker is a fine dramatist, but not strictly feminist, and
therefore oughtn't be compared to Daniels at all. Churchill's case, though,
makes a nonsense of Aston's observation that Churchill was more
successful *because* her plays moved to 'more mainstream' stages. They
didn't. That Churchill is, indeed, more successful, in spite of the venues
Aston defines as non-mainstream, speaks for these venues being just that.
They are where mainstream audiences *do* go. These are the mainstream's
adjacent stages which form the supplement to places like the Cottesloe.

Daniels' drama gives the audiences, used to hetero-normative
texts, an opportunity to step through the looking glass into a world which
exists on the fringes of androcentricity. However, her dramatic mode
contains a reappraisal of issues which are important to women, to
feminism, to gay rights, and ultimately, to the thinking person.

> I'm not interested in feeding into prejudices or writing something that
> could have been done in mainstream entertainment. If there was no
> prejudice, no violence against women by men, I probably wouldn't be a
> writer. (Daniels in Goodman 1993: 130).

Daniels' plays are a fierce attack on and an exposure of

patriarchal society as prejudiced and biased with its hetero-normative ideology which is inscribed on its very structure. She also gives us women like Jennifer (*Masterpieces*) and Tara (*Ripen Our Darkness*) who collude with men, consciously and unconsciously, to perpetuate the patriarchal order and its practices. Women in the traditional roles of heterosexual-patriarchy are exposed as trapped and guilty in play after play, as traditionally patterned relationships prove ineffectual and usually to the disadvantage of the woman as they inhibit her self-development as an individual and warp her sense of self. Daniels' lesbianism is not posited as an 'alternative' or 'the solution' to the problems of women. She uses *lesbian* as a *principle* and a *strategy* to break the boundaries of the hetero-normative traditions of British drama, to shatter or penetrate the strait/straight-lacing of our minds and bodies, by giving us a metaphor for women's need for solidarity through mutual support. She uses *lesbian* as a trope of reassurance which says there *are* alternative ways to live.

Lesbian becomes a trope for the powerless and invisible persons of society, like the deaf Dawn of *Beside Herself* who never bodily enters the discourse of the play as St. Dymphna's can't accept a person who is unable to hear (a fire alarm). Daniels unearths prejudices about gay and the mentally ill in *Beside Herself*, and also the guilt and secrecy that the abused often live with by uncovering the horror of incestual rape, as in the later *The Madness of Esme and Shaz*. Baring male minds in a pro-censorship indictment of pornography, she reveals the pervasive misrepresentation of women in the sign systems of western culture (*Masterpieces*) as *lesbian* becomes a sign of woman's awareness of the invisible oppressive text of patriarchy (See Godiwala 2001, 2003). *Ripen Our Darkness* and *Neaptide* lay open the hollowness and exploitative nature of traditional heterosexual relationships, as a concrete and united sisterhood is posited as the ideal utopian answer. Idealistic, wish-fulfilment endings serve as a compromise for harsher realities in several plays. It is Daniels unique stance, which emerges from her personal and political lesbian subjectivity (which is inevitably silenced or marginalized) which makes the content of her drama seem so radical in the mainstream context. This is a brave and daring 'coming out' as she simultaneously 'outs' other silenced, marginalized and oppressed subjects by being inclusive under the sign *lesbian*. This underlying concern for the silenced invisibles and the ability to give them a voice in the middle-class mainstream, sets her apart from what by way of difference appears as Churchill's ambiguity and wavering in the face of social issues. Daniels does not hesitate in showing the way to solutions, offering hope mingled with a refreshing ability to infuse the most hopeless situations with

laughter. It is in the offering of solutions that Daniels texts differ from
Churchill. They are also, by this very quality, transmuted into a complex
and utterly contemporary rendition of melodrama. Despite a rich seam of
interesting radical and feminist lesbian theatre on the fringe, Sarah Daniels
is the only lesbian-feminist to have been performed in the mainstream and
its adjacent/ supplementary stages through the 80s and 90s, carrying away,
as she did, two awards for most promising playwright as well as the
George Devine Award. Daniels proves herself a strongly socialist
dramatist, mercilessly exposing the hypocrisies which lie at the core of
British society, in texts which are a series of radical political, even
didactic, statements, yet maintain a strong appeal to the mainstream
audiences. In this lies her success in mainstream theatre.

The harsh, oft quoted reviews attracted by her texts betray not
what the critics actually say, but rather, their pressing though unconscious
impulse to function (as critics) in ways which would maintain the hetero-
normatively ordered systems and its underlying structures. To maintain the
regularity of discourse patriarchy deploys the subjects constituted within
the system to support its regime of hetero-normativity. Their attitudes and
utterances are always already inscribed and thus dictated by the invisible
patriarchal impulse *which works against the feminist intervention* to
suppress and repress any evidence of transgression, to silence the radical
voice, to ostracize into oblivion any instance of disruption to the order of
things (See Godiwala 2001, 2003; 2006). I cite here examples of what the
critics said about *Masterpieces* (see critique in Godiwala 2001, 2003)
which is a watershed in feminist theatre. 'Confused the 'match with the
bonfire'; 'it can't all be due to dirty books' (Barber 1983); a 'crime of
overstatement'; a 'rabid feminist play'; 'hysterical style and content'
(Tinker 1983); a 'sweeping statement'; an 'irritating play' (McFerran
1983); and, the 'respectable broadsheet' critic, Robert Cushman of *The
Observer*, dismissing the play in one short paragraph ('the argument [...] is
circular and not worth much'), proceeds to dedicate the next paragraph to
the three female actors and a description of their legs (1983).

a. The Feminist-Lesbian appropriation of a genre: Melodrama

'The worst thing a play can be is embarrassing. Being
unintentionally melodramatic is equally high in the "cringe" awards', says
Daniels in her preface to *Plays: One*. John Burgess concurs, describing
Daniels' first playscript as 'hover[ing] on the edge of melodrama.' Both
misunderstand melodrama to mean that which, in the colloquial sense, is

'as intellectually implausible as it is emotionally convincing'; that which, through a 'monopathy of triumph' so overwhelming brings an audience close to tears; in other words, melodrama has a tendency to be perceived as sentimental and embarrassing (Heilman 1968: 79).

I am seeking to establish that melodrama - accurately defined, and reworked to suit contemporary issues - as a dramatic form (transformed) is singularly suited to lesbian dramaturgy. As Griffiths and Woddis have pointed out, traditional drama based on conflict and difference is considered unsuitable to a single-gender experience, which leads to a need to interrogate kinds of forms which would be emergent from a dramatic focus on similarity (Griffiths and Woddis 1988). R.B.Heilman argues that while the tragic protagonist is essentially 'divided' by 'a basic inner conflict', melodramatic protagonists are essentially 'whole' (Heilman 1968: 79). In melodrama, the protagonist remains undivided as s/he has only external pressures to fight against, as e.g., the Duchess of Malfi or the Trojan Women, in the absence of *hamartia* or *hubris*, seek self-preservation as opposed to the tragic protagonist (*e.g.*, Lear)'s progression towards self-knowledge. The Duchess and the Trojan Women are innocent victims of defeat from external forces. Melodrama, unlike tragedy, is concerned with the restructuring of relations with other people or events or things, rather than the universe at large. Smith isolates triumph, despair and protest as the basic emotions of melodrama: 'the art of working each to its highest pitch occasions the *catharsis* of the form. In melodrama we win [*The Madness of Esme and Shaz*] or we lose [*Ripen Our Darkness*: 'Dear David, your dinner and my head are in the oven'], unlike tragedy where we lose in the winning [*Macbeth*] or win in the losing [*Antony and Cleopatra*].' (Smith 1973: 7-10).

William Sharp identifies three genres of drama: tragedy, comedy and melodrama. Recognising that the tragic hero rises above society, and the comic hero sinks below it, he categorizes melodrama as that genre which 'focuses on the nobility of a hero who would change society...either...he [sic] is willing to change or ...society realizes it must change'. It is because of this possibility that 'melodrama is the form used for those plays that push for social change or reform' (in Redmond 1992: 270-271).

Daniels' protagonists (women, lesbians, the oppressed and invisible) are, by the very nature of their conflict, pitted against external adversity (in the various forms of men, social prejudices, and patriarchal structural rules which serve to normalize and regularize the constitutive subjects of the system). The resolutions are usually extreme solutions designed to produce an overwhelmingly 'monopathic' catharsis. As Smith points out, this may seem naïve, trivial and second rate when compared with the rich complexities and broader moral dimensions of tragedy, but nevertheless, 'in terms of real life one often takes a side and accepts its credo: a football match, like an election campaign, must be lost or won. Melodrama is *the dramatic form which expresses the reality of the human condition as is most usually experienced by us*' (Sharp in Redmond 1992: 10-11 my emphasis). Similarly, the lesbian condition and the woman condition as exposed in the plays of women dramatists, is most often fighting against external oppression from the patriarchal/hetero-sexual and normative system which is the perpetrator, and therefore a form most suited to these issues is the one chosen almost inadvertently by Daniels: Melodrama.

Smith further points out that between the mighty opposites of Right and Wrong there can be no compromise; the drama has to end in Triumph or Defeat. Either serves to rally new supporters to The Cause, and both provide a satisfying, simplified *catharsis*. Victory can be enjoyed only by blocking our sympathy for those defeated (as in the defeat of the social-welfare and criminal-justice systems by the love and commitment of a family tie, however newly forged, in *The Madness of Esme and Shaz*); while defeat arouses righteous anger at undeserved injustice (as, *e.g.,* in *Ripen Our Darkness*). The pattern of social protest can be framed exceptionally well by melodrama, and a common strategy to pinpoint a contemporary evil is to set up a blameless protagonist as a victim of the system, who is then subjected to such inhuman persecution that the empathizing audience explodes with indignation and demands an immediate repeal of laws which perpetrate such cruelties. However, such drama is effective only to the already converted, or indeed, the amenable, and effective protest takes account of the complexities which prevent a too facile and shrill denunciation of, in this case, the extant system ruled by an inflexible hetero-normative ideology (cf. Smith 1973: 72-77). To be sure, this latter is a structural principle which substrates the extant society, and as such, it is not immediately apparent that this is what is at stake in this lesbian rendition of melodrama. However, this makes the traditional melodramatic form appeal to unconscious levels (of prejudice), divesting the drama of its monopathic tone and rendering it more complex than traditional forms of melodrama can usually be.

Daniels' art also makes the usually blameless victims of the system more complex than merely uni-dimensional beings, lending the melodramas a more tragic air than is commonly achieved by this genre. A further complexity is achieved by making some of the villains victims as well: Jennifer (*Masterpieces*) and Jim (*The Devil's Gateway*) are victims *and* perpetrators of unjust systems, albeit unconscious ones. Another victim is Shaz (*Esme and Shaz*), whose crime is of an extreme nature, and requires a great deal of courage (from both, the characters as well as the audience) to come to terms with, whilst Evelyn (*Beside Herself*) is a distant and aloof character who may alienate some from too close an empathy. Not all of Daniels' plays can be categorized as melodramas, but most partake of some of the best characteristics of the genre. This, combined with uncharacteristically complex, even tragic, protagonists, and an ability to infuse some of the most painful and despairing situations with well placed wit, Daniels manages to rework traditional, male, forms of drama, eliciting empathy, sympathy and pity with the genius of humour. Thus the traditional site of melodrama is restructured to create a new form suited to lesbian-feminist issues, the form of Radical and Complex Melodramas of Triumph.

This restructuring of morphology (a kind of 'morphing') can also be regarded as a *citation* via Judith Butler, but, perhaps closer to my interpretation, as a strategy of camp. In *The Politics and Poetics of Camp*, Moe Meyer attempts to re-define and reclaim the discourse of Camp from what she calls the always already assimilating mainstream. Speaking of the need to account for the *decentred power* of gay and lesbian subjects, Meyer accedes that it is a power 'that is able to resist, oppose and subvert'. Daniels manages to do this well within the dominant discourse of the mainstream, and her strategy - the reappropriation of a traditional genre, melodrama - can be seen as 'camp' if approached through Meyer. She defines 'camp' as 'the strategies and tactics of queer parody' wherein 'parody is an intertextual manipulation of multiple conventions, an extended repetition with critical difference that has a hermeneutic function with both cultural and even ideological implications'. Thus queer parody is derivative, a kind of dressing in drag. Just as drag entails a dependence on an already existing text in order to fulfil itself, the strategies of camp, especially parody, depend upon and feed off the dominant discourse. In my opinion, whether or not the strategy is used consciously, this dependence stems from a certain internalizing of the dominant ideology.

The dominant ideology would substrate the dominant discourse, which has been reified over a period of time, the ideology being internalized by the minds and bodies which are the constitutive subjects of the discourse. Since the function of ideology is normalizing and regulatory, all subjects are imbricated within the grip of its power, and it is therefore impossible to locate oneself *outside* of it. If my explanation is interpreted with dramatic discourse in mind, we realize that every English/

British dramatist writing in this moment is writing in the shadow of a long and honourable lineage of discourse which has been valorized within dramatic critical discourse since its heydey in the Renaissance. Breaking away with a centuries old tradition is difficult enough. Having no models to emulate is perhaps hardest of all. We learn from the earliest moments through emulation - thus Butler's theory of gender formation as 'performance' or 'drag'. In the breaking away there is almost always a citation, a reappropriation, a reformulation, as the old dominant discourse feeds into and helps formulate the new, which will in turn serve as an early model for, in this case, camp dramatic discourse. Within the new discourse the persistence of the old serves in part to valorize the former but always in *sanctioning its own erasure.* Thus, writing with the conventions of a traditional drama, whether it is a lesbian reworking of melodrama as found in Daniels or, indeed, a feminist indictment of a valorized patriarchal discourse (Greek drama) in Timberlake Wertenbaker's pieces such as *The Love of a Nightingale,* a breaking with the old necessitates a quotation. The erasure (of the old) comes from the deconstructive nature of the strategy itself: *the old is cited in order to destruct the dominant cultural and ideological formations and reconstruct new alternative ways of seeing* (See Meyer 1994). When Alice steps through the looking-glass things appear to be the same, but she soon finds out about the deceptive nature of the surface of things.

As Meyer puts it, 'without the process of parody, the marginalized agent has no access to representation, the apparatus of which is controlled by the dominant order. Camp, as specifically queer parody, becomes then, the only process by which the queer is able to enter representation and to produce social visibility.' This intervention into dominant discourse is double-edged: although the vehicle is transgressive and disruptive, it 'simultaneously invokes the spectre of dominant ideology in its practice, appearing, in many instances, to actually reinforce the dominant order.' (Meyer 1994).

Ripen Our Darkness; Neaptide; The Madness of Esme and *Shaz*: Feminist-Melodramas of Triumph

i. *Ripen Our Darkness*

Mary's defeat in *Ripen Our Darkness* has begun before the play opens. The attitudes of her husband and son are stereotypical, conventional male attitudes to the wife/ mother whose life is one of domestic servitude: a 'life [which is] at best monotonous, and at worst unbearably painful' (The Deity in Scene xiii). To Mary, her life is 'a half finished jigsaw while everybody else seems to have completed their pictures' (Scene i). Mary metonymically evokes the subtextual metaphor for the neglected Virgin as wife of the Anglican Churchwarden David. Father and son represent the male oppression of woman through the centuries as the woman's defeat (suicide) is transformed into omniscient transcendence as she arrives in a matriarchal heaven where she is greeted by a female trinity. A melodrama of defeat which uses stock characters (oppressed and oppressors) is combined with a subversion of other stock characters (the trinity) to reverse a (real) defeat into a triumph of almost comic wish-fulfilment. The reversal, using the principles of essentialist and separatist feminism, posits the drama successfully in the realm of radical feminist theatre seen for the first time on the mainstream stages of Britain. Radical by its context, it is interesting that Daniels' drama made it to the viewership of middle-class mainstream audiences as early as 1981, debunking, as it does, heterosexual and normative lifestyles. Using popular belief in the everafter as an agent of the transformation, the resolution is one of comic and sentimental triumph which, by the nature of being the converse of the traditional belief in an everafter with God made-in-the-image-of-the -patriarch, mocks the tenets of David's religion whilst it makes for a rather comic spirited feminist triumph. This achieves an effective purgation in this contemporary feminist reworking of traditional dramatic patterns.

Parallel to Mary's despair runs the story of Rene's victimized existence. Although Rene defends her violent, foul-mouthed husband (Alf) to others, when left on her own she betrays herself as trapped:

> Dear Mary Grant, I have a husband who drinks all my money away. I have two jobs to try to give him enough so he doesn't feel the need to slap me and my daughter around, but I usually fail. I have to lie in piss-soaked sheets, as my husband wets the bed every night. My daughter's severely handicapped baby has just died [...] I have dreams of doing myself in. Please don't reply as my husband rips up my mail regardless. (Scene iii)

Rene's triumph is pseudo-realistic. Again, through the use of a stock situation - here, the convenient demise of the oppressor-husband - Daniels provides for Rene's release.

By projecting Tara solely through the dramatic device of a voice-over, Daniels distances her as a potential site for (heterosexual-female audience) identification or (heterosexual-male audience) desire, using her brief speech as material for an authorial final word on heterosexual unions. If the two traditional, domestic, heterosexual women are revealed as leading unfulfilling lives, the third (Tara) is condemned as exploitative of her heterosexual marriage:

> Between you and I, Marsh has begged me to divorce him. Why should I? I don't want to live in some pokey little flat where some social worker might try and certify me for being batty. No thanks. I like being posh. Don't listen to this live without men rot. The way forward is to use them and have some fun. (Scene v)

Daniels in this first play projects lesbian relationships as ideal in a world of failed and failing heterosexual blunders. Mary's daughter (Anna) lives in lesbian union with Rene's daughter (Julie): a life ideally free from conflict. Mary, although resigned to the fact that she is 'the only mother-in-law... with three sons and four daughters-in-law', appreciates, though somewhat wryly, that Anna and Julie 'can both make lunch' (scene vii). Mary, constituted as a normalized and normalizing subject of heteronormative ideology, cannot accept her daughter's lesbian life which prevents much emotional closeness between the two.

Ripen Our Darkness, as Daniels first play, sets the pattern for most of the rest of her dramatic work. Debunking heterosexuality by revealing it as emotionally unfulfilling and disempowering for women, or (interestingly, from a lesbian dramatist) as economically parasitical on the man, Daniels projects single-sex unions as a viable alternative in this piece. Lesbianism is the central Brechtian *gest* at the gamut of her work: it serves as a trope for sisterhood, female bonding and emotional union, all of which are denied in heterosexual relationships. In her later plays, the mother-daughter relationship supercedes lesbian attachment, as *e.g.,* in *Masterpieces* where the only significant moments of female bonding are where Jennifer, Rowena and Yvonne share a sunny afternoon, picnicking (scene xiii) and recalling childhood memories. Similarly *The Madness* has Esme and Shaz forge and duplicate a mother-daughter bond rather than a lesbian bonding.

As a melodrama of triumph *Ripen Our Darkness* is a skilful reworking of cliched contemporary situations and characters into a fairly complex and sentimental melodrama in a lesbian-feminist mode. By the use of realism, Daniels lulls her audience into heterosexual assumptions which are then cleverly subverted. By presenting lesbian union as the dominant ideological ideal within the text of the play, heterosexist cultural *mores* are challenged as the patriarchal perceptual screens from behind which mainstream audiences are used to viewing, are dismantled and an alternative, interrogatory, viewership is proposed. This visible manifestation of an alternative ideology on the mainstream stage (and the

Royal Court is undeniably mainstream and establishment even as it encourages new writing) is at once provocative and political, setting the agenda for her later more mature work where *lesbian* almost ceases to be about relationships or practice, but diffuses into a metaphor for broadly feminist concerns.

ii. *Neaptide*

There is a [neap]tide in the affairs of [wo]men...

In *Neaptide* Daniels dramatizes the metaphor of lesbians coming out in one bold sweep, illuminating by the same token the prejudices of the heterosexual majority. *Neaptide* at its most fundamental level is about 'the performance [of] the "act" of coming out' (Goodman 1993: 114-119). In this act, both private/ personal and public/ political fuse in performance. This is the lesbian dramatist's act of refusal: a political refusal in its rebellion against the norm of heterosexuality, and a personal one in promoting new forms of subjectivity through the public mode of performance on the mainstream stages. The necessity to provide a platform for lesbian subjectivity is a pressing political and personal need which Daniels' drama courageously aims to fulfil, making her texts perform the awkward and public act of coming out which has become central to lesbian theatre on the fringe. Inadvertently echoing Foucault, Goodman points out 'the need to reclaim and name self', the lesbian private-become-public self, in the face of a resistant heterosexual world order. The simultaneous double-bind the lesbian experiences as she is individualized as a woman and totalized within a heterosexual system of normativity affects her politically and personally. The act of coming out is a re-claiming of self, the grasping and endorsing of a new form of subjectivity which rejects and refuses the bind imposed by the world and its constitutive stages. As Goodman points out, 'many lesbians do not 'come out' but lead private lives very different from their public ones'. The act is a highly personal one, even when 'ritualized into the most public of performances' (Goodman 1993: 114-119). Indeed, for most lesbian women it is truistic that their choice of same-sex partner does not necessarily indicate a different life style, *i.e.*, leading a private lesbian life may not impinge on other areas of one's life. Many lesbians do not come out, and Daniels dramaturgy vocalizes the silence of a silent lesbian majority by stressing the political need to do so and challenge the multitude of heterosexist prejudices.

Thus, Claire and Bea Grimble's act of coming out is painful but necessary in its implications. Simultaneously Daniels cuts through the plethora of heterosexist and normative prejudices with characteristic wit. Circumscribing the play is the Greek myth of mother-daughter bonding and patriarchal enslavement and authority, while dominating the centre lie the modern 'myths' or falsehoods about lesbian sexuality, behaviour and lifestyles. As long as myths about the latter exist the former (ideal) will always be a struggle for lesbian mothers who are denied control in parenting and the custody of their children (Claire) through mis-representation and lack of understanding.

Val's opening is semi-choral in initiating the Greek origins of what pervades the play as subverted myth. A pun on the doctor's name (Herr/ Hare March) subliminally evokes patriarchal persecutionin the dramatic text, a metaphor of possibility which runs through Daniels work. The heterosexual Val's insanity and her refusal to reenter the 'normal world' posits her as a Persephone relegated to Hades - or an Alice lost through the looking glass:

> Here I sit, mad as a hatter with nothing to do but either become madder and madder or else recover enough of my sanity to be allowed back to the world that drove me mad. (*Neaptide*, I, i)

Claire and Poppy through their reading of (Phyllis Chesler's version of) the Demeter myth symbolise the mother-daughter bonding which is central to this story. In the repudiation off heterosexist and normative fairytales ('I certainly like this better than Cinderella or Sleeping Beauty') with their stereotypical hetero-utopian and-they-lived-happily-ever-after endings, and in the turning to a Greek myth which dwells on sister/mother/daughter hood, Claire is educating Poppy differently. The repudiated fairytales serve to frame the structure of Daniels tale *Neaptide* presaging the alternative ending.

The scenes set in the staff-room reveal the prevalent prejudices encountered by gay men and women. Discussing the Peter O'Toole *Macbeth*, Annette's internalized heterosexist-prejudicial response is:

> ...it brought a whole new perspective to the characters of the three witches, you know, a hint of, er, female intimacy... between them... which gave a real tinge of reality to their evilness. (I, iv)

The use of theatrical space which swings from public (the school) to public/private heterosexual (the staff room) to private-lesbian (Claire and Grimble's homes) contrasts in turn heterosexist attitudes and how they impinge upon and hegemonically disrupt private lesbian lives. The audience is cleverly manipulated to view normalized attitudes as prejudicial revealing the deconstructive potential of Daniels texts as they attempt to reformulate and displace the dominant ideology of the mainstream audiences. The heterosexual spaces of the play reveal the many misconceptions about lesbians: that they always dress in male attire and are not 'attractive' nor biologically natural.

The irony is that both the headmistress and the deputy lead private lesbian existences, and, by a stretch of coincidence, the two lesbian schoolgirls discover Beatrice Grimble's secret.

> TERRI: (gets up and surveys the bookcase). Boring. Boring. Boring.
> DIANE: (finds a small framed photograph behind a plant). Hey, look at this, an old photo of Bea with her arm around a woman.
> TERRI: (looking at the photo). They all did that then. Gawd, look at those shoes.
> DIANE: She's still got them by the sound of it. (She opens the desk drawer and tentatively rummages around its contents).
> TERRI: (alarmed) Don't do that.
> DIANE: She poked her nose into our lives.
> TERRI: We shoved our lives under her nose, you mean.
> DIANE: (pulls out a card). Look, an anniversary card.
> TERRI: Blimey. Maybe she was married then.
> Both of them look at it.
> TERRI} DIANE}(exclaim in unison). All my love, Florrie.
> They look at each other.
> TERRI} DIANE} Miss Grimble's one.
> (II, iv)

Grimble's sudden reversal of public attitude toward lesbianism after a lifetime in the closet signals her act of coming out, while Joyce's solution to her daughter Claire's dilemma signals an acceptance (which was denied by Mary to her daughter in *Ripen Our Darkness*), and provides the drama with a (lesbian) wish-fulfilment closure, where the father, having been granted custody, is left knocking on the door of an empty flat, while mother and daughter leave the country with grandmother's help.

It would be too facile to read the endings of Daniels plays as patterned after traditional patriarchal forms ending in closure. Daniels' closures encode a subversive strategy as they spell new beginnings for the minoritized. However, these texts are located in the context of the mainstream, and since the majority of mainstream audiences and critics view the performance through private heterosexist screens, an audience sympathy for Claire is crucial and cleverly constructed. Daniels' strategy of melodramatic reversals of triumph for the marginalized is essential to her texts which function as alternative fairytales within the conventions of

realism. Embedded within the traditional dramatic form are the seeds of its
destruction as normalizing and /or regulating discourse. The conventional
dramatic framework also lulls the audiences into a false complicity with a
seemingly hetero-normative order which is then revealed as prejudiced
and limiting. Those lulled into a complicity of empathy with Grimble and
Claire would finally find themselves caught up with the lesbian Other side.

The closure is idealistic: hopefully there will no longer be a need
for 'the closet' and the future seems ready for a new and equally credible
ideology. In her attempt to portray that they (also) could live happily-ever-
after, Daniels mixes wit with optimism and laughter. In seeking an ideal
place for her characters who are constituted within frameworks of
prejudice, triumphant idealized reversals seem to be a necessary ending,
allowing impossible situations to be infused with a measure of hope
making her dramas the fantasies of Lesbos in an age where alternative
sexuality has yet to be legitimised.

iii. *The Madness of Esme and Shaz*

Every [wo]man's life is a fairytale written by God's fingers.
—Hans Christian Andersen

The Madness of Esme and Shaz [...] [i]s not about issues, only people.
—Daniels, Theatre Programme for the 1994 Royal Court production

Representing the dominant ideology once again loaded with
subversive dice, in *Madness*, Daniels celebrates the role of the family as
an important stabilizing factor in the often confusing and alienating
modern societal structures. By the emotional bonding of a distant aunt
with a long-time institutionalized niece - the only survivors of a separated
family - in a sentimental melodrama of triumph over material values and
state apparatuses, Daniels sketches a meritorious piece which offers hope
with characteristic humour. The stereotypical psychiatrist lampooned in
Ripen Our Darkness and again in *Masterpieces*, here proves symptomatic
of the entire psychiatric welfare system, over which the strong emotional
bond of family ties gains ascendancy.

Esme and Sharon could not be further apart as individual
personalities: the one, devout, religious and ever conscious of her duty to
society and her neighbours; the other, a foul-tongued young woman whose
only knowledge of the outside world comes from television, having been
institutionalized for almost her entire life. Esme's first act of taking
Sharon in care is one guided by duty and a 'sign' from the Lord.

Shaz forms a relationship with Pat in a bid for love and affection,

but, like Mary, Esme cannot come to terms with Sharon's lesbian
relationship, and for the first half of the play her attitude is one of stoical
(in)tolerance. Shaz needs demonstrations of love which Esme cannot find
in herself to provide, unused as she is to emotional attachments. Although
both Pat and Esme accept the fact that Shaz had been institutionalized, the
former is horrified to hear the reason is because she murdered her father's
baby. If she had killed the abuser she would have been 'a heroine in
[Pat's] book'; to Pat's radical-separatist-essentialist thinking it would have
been excusable, even, if Shaz had murdered the little *boy*, but killing the
baby girl was 'killing the wrong person'. Shaz, who in her years at
Broadmoor has reached a kind of self-knowledge, cannot comprehend
Pat's short-sightedness: 'There is no right person, there is no fucking right
person' (scene vii). Surprisingly, it is Esme who empathizes and connects:

> ESME: My father, your grandfather was a -. As a Christian I don't have
> the words to describe him. He was one of those men. When... when we
> were children, your father and I, he wouldn't leave us alone. You know to
> what I'm referring?
> SHAZ: Yeah?
> ESME: And I suspect, I expect that my brother repeated the same pattern
> of behaviour when you were a child.
> SHAZ: (looks down)
> ESME: That's the difference between men and women. They can't seem
> to help themselves. Or rather they do help themselves. We don't -
> SHAZ: No, no. We only destroy ourselves instead.   (Scene viii)

Although this description of gender difference with regard to
child abuse is separatist and actually subscribes quite conveniently to
dominant ideological beliefs, it foregrounds the reason for Shaz's action of
killing her father's baby: she 'saves' the baby from almost certain sexual
abuse by suffocating her to death. In destroying her father's girl-child,
Sharon destroys her self, and continues to do so daily, slashing her arms in
symbolic self-destruction.

Esme's inability to offer love instead of duty is distressing for
Shaz, and, when she is taken back into the psychiatric care unit after her
assault on a police officer, she refuses to see her aunt. However, Esme,
with uncharacteristic aggressiveness born of concern for her niece, pushes
her way into the unit:

> ESME: ... Don't worry we'll soon get you out of here.
> SHAZ: I love you.
> ESME: (Takes a step back)
> SHAZ: I don't mean like that. I don't mean nothing sexual or nothing. I

mean -
ESME: I don't think I've ever loved anybody.
SHAZ: Yes, yes you have.
ESME: No.
SHAZ: Jesus. What about Jesus?
[...]
ESME: Oh Jesus.
SHAZ: Me?
ESME: You? I don't know.
SHAZ: You took me to live with you, you must have seen something good
in me?
ESME: No, that was because of a sign from God. (Laughs)
SHAZ: Then you cared for me.
ESME: Duty, duty, duty.
SHAZ: And now you've come all the way down here and you must have
kicked up a hell of a row for her to let you see me in seclusion.
ESME: Actually, one could argue that I did it for me. (Scene xiii)

Esme's refusal or reluctance to face her true feelings for Shaz are
indicative of her repressed emotional existence and also of a wider societal
disorder which a repudiation of love represents. Shaz's persistence in
drawing her out is a dramatist's attempt to demonstrate what is required:
an acknowledgement that love exists and must be vocalized and
demonstrated within familial contexts. Esme's tentative acknowledgement
of her (maternal) love is also a 'coming out', and reveals Daniels' broad
use of 'lesbian' as a metaphor. Esme 'comes out' as she sees a reflection
of her self in Shaz - they are, incredible as it may seem, mirror images of
each other:

SHAZ: I don't want to go. [i.e., leave the psychiatric institution]
ESME: Are you demented?
SHAZ: And I don't want to see you again unless it's only because you
love me.
(Pause)
ESME: If love is longing for the half of ourselves we have lost, then
alright. (ibid.)

Both Esme and Shaz progress toward a deeper self-knowledge,
and Esme's final courage to venture into the unknown for the sake of her
niece is her way of breaking the bounds, demonstrating in the process a
deep insight into the necessity of and the ability to break with a lifetime of
habit (constructed attitudes) when required. For Esme, Shaz symbolizes
not merely her lost family, but also daring youth, both of which inspire a
necessary forgiving and healing with the past. Shaz brings into Esme's life

a desire to live and enjoy life to the fullest, in spite of having been a victim of abuse and after a lifetime of cautious guardedness in forming emotional attachments. In scene xiv aunt and niece almost exchange personalities as Esme, having discovered a hidden well of adventure-seeking bravado, drives recklessly, scaring the usually brazen Shaz:

SHAZ:... Brake!
ESME: (Braking) Now which peddle [sic] is that? Just kidding.
SHAZ: (reclines her seat and shuts her eyes)
ESME: What are you doing?
SHAZ: Praying.

When Shaz realizes that Esme has sold her flat to take her away to live on a faraway island, that she will never have to be taken into psychiatric care again, that she is loved, forgiven and understood, she understands that Esme's declaration of love has exceeded all her expectations. Again, the metaphor 'lesbian' frames the text, as they journey to Mytilene, which is the birthplace of the poetess Sappho and a port of the islands of Lesbos. This is where they are ready to heal and be whole again, having left the society and context which fostered their festering wounds:

ESME: ...will you wear a tee shirt or something with short sleeves?
SHAZ: I can't. I can't.
ESME: Yes, you can.
SHAZ: No.
ESME: Why?
SHAZ: I don't want to.
ESME: Lots of people think battle scars are something to be proud of.
SHAZ: But I ain't done nothing to be proud of.
ESME: I'm proud of you.
SHAZ: Are yer?
ESME: Yes.
SHAZ: But they are so ugly.
ESME: (Starts to roll up one of Shaz's shirt sleeves) How will they ever heal otherwise.
SHAZ: (Starts to roll up the other one) Come on then let's go mad.
(The end)

The lesbian metaphors that frame the text - 'coming out' of Broadmoor (the closet), 'coming out' to an acknowledgement of love (relationships), the journey to Lesbos - are the seeds which spell destruction within the traditional vehicles of realism and the stress on familial bonds. Daniels strategy defines lesbianism far beyond Dolan's narrow endorsement of the public representation of the gay sexual act. Same sex bonding - indeed, any human bonding - goes far beyond sex and sexuality. How subversive is the endorsement of public representation of sexual intercourse when society is a sustained by a network of other, possibly more important, kinds of intercourse? Theorists like Dolan, when they privilege the performance of sexuality over other kinds of performance fall into the trap of patriarchal reversal and take the stage into the realm of pornographic representation. Dolan duplicates patriarchy, Daniels deconstructs it. Pornography in representation would only bring in a voyeuristic audience and reinforce ideas of gay and lesbian relationships as sexually deviant. Same-sex bonding, like other-sex bonding has a sexual side to it, but by foregrounding sexuality to an extent where pornographic representation is valorized reinforces stereotypical attitudes and ways of seeing (reception) whereas Daniels strategies serve to displace and reconstruct the ideology in operation.

In *Madness*, the lesbian metaphor is one of sisterhood and family ties, constructed to mean commitment, love and responsibility combined with the daring required in the 'performance of coming out' (Goodman 1993: 117-120). Many lesbian dramatists of the 70s and early 80s wrote coming out messages in their plays and Daniels extends this message to make it all embracing and positive thereby valorizing it in the context of the mainstream.

Daniels' plays are able to break the bounds which separate the mainstream from the alternative or fringe because they are framed within the bounds of patriarchal discourse, much as Timberlake Wertenbaker's indictments of western patriarchies are framed within the respectable guise of Greek drama. These texts achieve the task of reconstructing conventional ways of seeing in those reception communities which are most resistant to change - the mainstream which is substrated by commercialism (capitalism) the means to which lie in the age old strategies of patriarchy. Although it remains of vital importance to preach to the converted in order to support and further the practice of the alternative stage, it is perhaps more difficult to *preach to convert* as one risks being booed off the stage collectively (Miller and Román 1995). Daniels' strategic potential then is ultimately more subversive as it skilfully manages to elicit audience sympathy for characters who are subsequently revealed as constituted within alternative ideologies. Underlying this strategy is her genius of humour which surfaces in the most despairing situations. In *Madness* she posits the most unlikely characters in the realm of audience sympathy. She reworks and re-visions the 'old maid' and gives us a foul tongued yobbish young murderer. Both are victims of patriarchal hegemony and caught up in the cruel workings of state apparatuses which are resisted and overcome through bonding. The resultant self-knowledge, freedom and happiness (gayness?) makes for a complex revisionist melodrama - an old genre 'dragged' through the looking-glass and firmly posited in Lesbos.

Daniels demonstrates that it isn't merely gay and lesbian lives that need airing as she 'drags' out a range of issues from the British closet. The melodramas present a diverse range of characters - caricatures even - re-visioned into a contemporary feminist melodramatic mode. These are issues seldom seen on the mainstream stages, and these texts represent a dramatist's 'coming out' with a verve and ferocity of intent in order to demolish the performance of hegemony on the British stage.

b. The rites of/ the rights of birth: *Byrthrite*

> ...why are the senior IVF doctors all men? Do they want to control women's bodies and play games with their eggs? [...] One of the more controversial techniques Craft uses... is selective reduction... where a multiple pregnancy is reduced to two by injecting the excess fetal sacs with lethal potassium cyanide.
> —Life, The Observer Magazine, 4 June 1995

> Parson: Don't be foolish, women don't make history. (II, ii)

Daniels' *Byrthrite* is a radical lesbian-separatist attempt at re-vision and re-presentation of what is undeniably manmade history. The retrieval of the figure of the stereotyped witch linked with a radical representment of the history of current trends in what a leading (female) IVF practitioner terms 'gynaecological plumbing', takes us back in time to trace the beginnings of 'control over women's reproductive processes [which] began to change hands from women to men'(Hamner's foreword in Daniels 1991).

Byrthrite was damned by theatre critics (both men and women) for being 'historically unrealistic' (Mary Harron), 'a lecture' (Mark Lawson), 'ghastly', 'forced' (Michael Billington). These reactions betray the 80s and 90s social climate for lesbians as society continues to use a heterosexist perceptual screen: if we assume 'heterosexuality to be the only natural form of sexual and emotional expression' we are guilty of 'heterosexism', '*the* perceptual screen provided by our [patriarchal] cultural conditioning' (Zimmerman in Showalter 1986: 201). Re-writing history from the perspective of women is essential to the feminist and lesbian mind. Re-presenting women involves re-presenting the past, and

the historical neglect of women's role is echoed in much critical thought in
the 1980s (See Beer in Belsey and Moore 1989). Gillian Beer emphasizes
'the re-presentment of past history and literature to justify the present',
echoing Virginia Woolf who, in *A Room of One's Own*, spoke of the 'lack
of facts' about past woman: 'History scarcely mentions her'. Speaking of
the possibility of 'a supplement to history', 'calling it, of course, by some
inconspicuous name so that women might figure there without
impropriety', Woolf presaged the feminist writing of 'herstory'. A re-
ordering of the past might be crucial to understanding the present, but it is
also important to posit this retrieval in the *fictions* of the present. If a
fictive re-present-ment of the past becomes necessary to provide the
neglected genderized Other with a sense of causal history, it becomes
imperative to the lesbian in the complete absence of their history. Thus the
lesbian critical tradition has been one of 'peering into shadows, into the
spaces between words, into what has been unspoken and barely imagined'
because past lesbian writers have had to resort to 'coded and obscure
language and internal censorship' for fear of censure. Zimmerman speaks
of the lack of role models for lesbians and Daniels' creation of lesbians in
the seventeenth century reflects the lesbian critics search for 'the mythic
presence of lesbians in fiction'(Zimmerman in Showalter 1986: 212).

Daniels creates a mythos which interlinks the persecution of
single, old and /or helpless women with a radical overview of the history
of reproductive technology, creating a legitimate, if fictive, herstory in
which lesbianism is natural for women. Daniels delineates a group of
women who are peripheral to a persecutionist patriarchy. At the core of the
company is Grace: a re-working of the stereotype of the witch figure, here
re-presented as an educated and wise old woman who is also a competent
herbalist. Grace demonstrates her wisdom in diverse ways: the young
Rose, who, demonstrating a hatred for her developing body which attracts
the unwanted sexual attentions from the farmer, requests a potion to
'rather wilt than grow', is gently rebuked - 'The farmer is the problem not
your body.' (I, vi) In the creation of Grace Daniels provides lesbians the
figure of an alternative archetype: a gentle matriarch reworked from the
domineering models of witches handed down by androcentric historians
and mythmakers. Grace is a strong dependable woman who believes in the
cohesion of the sisterhood they have formed: this is indicated by her
sadness at their fragmentation (I, viii). The separation of the diverse group
as each woman's dream takes her where she desires, serves as a metaphor
for the individuality and plurality of womankind. Grace's education
received from her father 'when [he] saw he wasn't to have no sons' (Rose,
I, v) makes her position precarious in the cultural conditions of her time.

By locating the old and wise matriarch's words within contemporary lesbian-feminist discourse, Daniels effectively creates a feminist mythology:

> JANE: How can it be women of our time are stronger than ever before and yet persecuted worse at the same time?
> GRACE: When those who are accumbred kick back, the oppressor kicks harder.
> JANE: But they pick on frail, defenceless old women...
> GRACE: First there is your reason, is easy. Second, some have power, such as they see it in health and advice over women's bodies, particularly in childbearing. And they want power over that. [...] New inventions and persecutions step together, in time.
> (I, iii)

> GRACE: Our sex with its single power to give birth, pose a threat to men's power over whole order of villages, towns, counties and countries. That control depends on women cur-tailing to men's ideals of how they should behave.
> ROSE: So, if it is fact you want from me, happen there was women enough to cause trouble against each other.
> Grace: Because not only are men set against the woman named wicked, but also the women and children whose livelihood depends upon the approval of the men.
> (II, viii)

In a reversal of the then unformulated theory of phallic envy, Jane, the soldier, anachronistically discourses on creation-envy - the feminist reversal, womb-envy:

> JANE: So then, and I've been thinking of this, maybe is compensation for their inabilities. Alarmed that they cannot give life they do find glory in death... 'tis envy of birth...(II, i)

That patriarchy was seen as a repressive and regulatory structure by women of the seventeenth century cannot be disputed on the basis that recorded history reveals no such readings. The androcentric recording of history and the subsequent silencing of women's voices is dramatized in Part II, ii as the parson chronicles 'plain statement of fact':

> PARSON: (reads as though delivering a sermon) 'The war has rid us of many evils not least of the evil embodied in some of the female sex who were weighed in the balance and found wanting. Suitably dealt with through rigorous court procedures and brought to justice either swum or hung.'

HELEN: (curtly) You've repeated the word 'evil' twice.
PARSON: (casually) 'Tis part of women's nature since life began with
Eve.

Although the parts for men are few (played by a single actor) and
rendered necessarily restrictive, they represent the reified spectre of
patriarchy as tyrannical in its influence over every aspect of the women's
lives. The fictions that surround the androcentric concept of witchcraft
(that witches 'fly'; the idea of 'carnal copulation with Satan' - Part I,
scene iii), and the terrorist 'pricking out' of 'witches' demonstrate this, as
did Churchill's *Vinegar Tom* (1976) which seems to have served as a
model for this radical text. Daniels continues Churchill's mythological
theme of the male fear of control over their (male) sexuality: Jane jokes
about this almost as if she might have heard the Jack of *Vinegar Tom*
(scene xii) complain that he had 'heard how witches sometimes get a
whole boxful and they move and stir by themselves like living creatures
and the witch feeds them oats and hay':

> Jane: (to Mary and Rose) They are of firm belief that women collect male
> organs and keep them in bird's nests where they move about by
> themselves and eat corn and oats. (I, iii)

The arrival of Jane in the group composed of diverse women - the
young Rose, the old Grace, married Helen - transforms female
affectionality into lesbian togetherness. Lesbian critical discourse, which
in its early stages sought to be integrated with feminist discourses, is
varied in its definition of the lesbian body. Lillian Faderman defines
'lesbian' as

> a relationship in which two women's strongest emotions and affections are
> directed toward each other. Sexual contact may be [...] entirely absent. By
> preference the two women spend most of their time together and share
> most aspects of their lives with each other (Faderman in Zimmerman.
> Showalter 1986: 206).

Whereas Adrienne Rich sought to establish the idea of a 'lesbian
continuum' which would include

> 'a range - through each woman's life and throughout history - of woman-
> identified experience; not simply the fact that a woman has had or
> consciously desired genital experience with another woman [... the lesbian
> continuum includes] the sharing of a rich inner life, the bonding against
> male tyranny, the giving and receiving of practical and political
> support...'(Zimmerman in Showalter 1986: 205).

The group might be seen in Rich's sense as a lesbian category, as each occupies a position on 'the lesbian continuum' and pledges a lasting oath of sisterhood. Faderman's definition of lesbian (which is subsumed by Rich's continuum) would map the relationship shared by Rose and Jane. By cross-dressing they break the bounds of their time; in transgressing they search for equality and discover the futility of the (male) violence of war (Rose, II, iii) but men's attire gives them a power, 'a wonderful freedom to go charging about where I want' (Rose, II, iv) they would not otherwise had access to, as women. Rose's guise enables her to rescue Grace and the deaf Ursula from gaol, but she later regrets her absence from the village in 'Rosie's song' (II, iv):

...what they have got is a soldier to fight
And one woman less to defend her birthright.

The freedom to pass as a man is a curse -
No woman would choose that for her life -

Helen's search for equality leads her to reject everything the Parson stands for to become a preacher herself: a legitimate Quaker. Women's search for power where they had known only servitude is traced historically: 'woman shall laugh till she cries at the very notion of being pinned down to man' (Helen, ibid.) as twentieth century parallels, echoed by the contemporary songs, reverberate to the metaphors encoded in these seventeenth century women.

The central mythos of *Byrthrite* is the history of the origins of reproductive technology re-viewed from the lesbian perspective and forecast to the end of the road: the creation of wombs in men and/ or total extra-corporeal gestation. The fear is that once men secure total control over the birth process, the survival of women will depend upon what has proved a centuries-old patriarchy. With the 80s and 90s controversy over lesbian-mothers this surfaces as a lesbian fear of being kept on the fringes. With international examples of state control over women's bodies the control of reproductive processes by an outside agency translates into a very real fear for women *as well as men.*

Byrthrite's mythology is a lesbian feminist one. Faced with an irrecoverable past, recourse to an imaginary history becomes essential to the lesbian feminist dramatist who creates a mythical text in order to provide women with role models and archetypes posited historically. The dialogue in Part II, viii is a form of dramatic meta-discourse. Rose's playtext is a metaphor for the greater text of Daniels' playtext. Both are 'stories' 'to entertain' and Daniels' attempt to re-present the lives of seventeenth century women is not an attempt at historical realism but, rather, a need to *contemporize* lesbian history and establish continuity with an unrecorded past unheeded by androcentric history. As Rose puts it: 'Is not s'posed to be a list of facts and dates. There must be other women interested in recording exact history. I cannot do all. Is a story I've written, out of my imagination, to entertain. Not a bible.'

The burying of the playtext symbolizes the buried gifts of women through the ages. As Adrienne Rich puts it:

> ...we all know women whose gifts are buried or aborted. Our struggles can have meaning and our privileges - however precarious under patriarchy - can be justified only if they can help to change the lives of women whose gifts - and whose very being - continue to be thwarted and silenced.

Daniels well placed wit might alleviate a heterosexist discomfort in the radical presentation of controversial issues in this re-visioning of history essential to her alternative perspective. In the gamut of her work she manages to elicit laughter in the most critical or pensive situations making for a cathartic effect, and here it cuts through the didacticism, making the issue-based play entertaining. That *Byrthrite* was performed in a mainstream venue at all is surprising because it typifies gay fringe plays addressing a selective audience. The radical feminist-Brechtian distancing created by the provocative songs should help to get past the patriarchal perceptual screens in mainstream audiences, but the severally bad reviews the play received are indicative of the pervasiveness of normative rationality. Men and women are not accustomed to men being elided or kept on the fringes of (even) a play. The effect of this patriarchal expectation extends to women in the audience who are culturally conditioned to accept that women might be on the fringes or even entirely absent from 'great' contemporary drama. In spite of the overwhelmingly bad press it received, *Byrthrite* remains a play with depth and intensity as it tells the slanted truth about women's right to the rites of birth and takes mainstream audiences through the looking-glass and beyond.

In terms of content, Daniels' texts are radical in their placement on the centre(s)stage, and it's not surprising that in the end she proved a force too radical for the mainstream and was boo-ed off the stage to write television drama. However, she did have the opportunity to stage her confrontation with straight society with its manifold prejudices lurking behind their patriarchal heterosexist perceptual screens bringing such drama out of 'the ghetto'. This served to create an awareness of issues which are usually elided. Daniels broke the bounds of heterosexist society by bringing her texts into the arena of confrontation: the mainstream stages of Britain thereby rupturing forever the heterosexual matrix within which these stages are constituted.

Works cited

Aston, Elaine, 'Daniels in the Lion's Den: Sarah Daniels and the British Backlash', *Theatre Journal*, Vol.47, No.3, Oct. 1995.

Barthes, Roland, 'Sade II: The Helmet' in *Sade, Fourier, Loyola*, [1971], trans. Richard Miller, Hill and Wang, 1976.

Beer, Gillian, 'Representing Women: Re-presenting the Past', in *The Feminist Reader: Essays in Gender and the Politics of Literary Criticism*, ed., Catherine Belsey and Jane Moore, Macmillan, 1989.

Case, Sue-Ellen, (ed) *Performing Feminisms: Feminist Critical Theory and Theatre*, Johns Hopkins University Press, 1990.

Case, Sue-Ellen, 'Towards a Butch/Femme Aesthetic' in Lynda Hart, (ed.) *Making a Spectacle: Feminist Essays on Contemporary Women's Theatre*, University of Michigan Press.

Cixous, Hélène, 'The Laugh of the Medusa', in *Literature in the Modern World*, (ed) Dennis Walder, Oxford University Press, 1991.

Daniels, Sarah, *Daniels—Plays One*. Methuen, 1991.

—. *Daniels—Plays Two*. Methuen, 1994.

—. *Morning Glory*. Faber and Faber, 2001.

Deleuze, Gilles and Félix Guattari, *Kafka: Toward a Minor Literature* [1975], trans. Dana Polan, University of Minnesota Press, 1986.

Dolan, Jill, *Presence and Desire*. University of Michigan Press, 1993.

Dolan, '"Lesbian" Subjectivity in Realism: Dragging at the Margins of Structure and Ideology' in Sue-Ellen Case, (ed.) *Performing Feminisms: Feminist Critical Theory and Theatre*, Johns Hopkins University Press, 1990.

Fanon, Frantz, *Black Skin, White Masks*, Pluto Press Limited, 1986.

Godiwala, Dimple, *Breaking the Bounds: British Feminist Dramatists Writing within the Mainstream since c. 1980,* Oxford University, 2001; New York & Oxford: Peter Lang 2003.

—. 'The performativity of the dramatic text: domestic colonialism and Caryl Churchill's *Cloud Nine*', Studies in Theatre and Performance, Vol. 24.1, 2004.

---. 'The Patriarchal Impulse' *Interactions* Vol 15.1, Ege University Press, Istanbul, Spring 2006.

Goodman, Lizbeth, *Contemporary Feminist Theatres: To Each Her Own*, Routledge, 1993.

Griffiths, Trevor R. and Carole Woddis, *Bloomsbury Theatre Guide*,

Bloomsbury, 1988.

Hart, Lynda and Peggy Phelan (eds) *Acting Out: Feminist Performances*, ed., University of Michigan Press, 1993.

Hart, Lynda, (ed) *Making a Spectacle: Feminist Essays on Contemporary Women's Theatre*, University of Michigan Press, 1989.

Heilman, R.B., *Tragedy and Melodrama: Versions of Experience*, University of Washington Press, 1968.

Hutcheon, Linda, *A Theory of Parody: The Teachings of Twentieth-Century Art Forms*, Methuen, 1985.

Meyer, Moe, 'Reclaiming the Discourse of Camp' in *The Politics and Poetics of Camp*, Routledge, 1994.

Miller, Tim and David Román, 'Preaching to the Converted', *Theatre Journal*, Vol.47, No.2, May 1995.

Redmond, James, (ed) *Themes in Drama 14: Melodrama*, Cambridge University Press, 1992.

Reinelt, Janelle G., and Joseph R. Roach (eds) *Critical Theory and Performance*, University of Michigan Press, 1992.

Rich, Adrienne, 'When We Dead Awaken: Writing as Re-Vision' in *On Lies, Secrets and Silence*, Virago, 1980.

Sharp, William, 'The Structure of Melodrama', in James Redmond, (ed) *Themes in Drama 14: Melodrama*, Cambridge University Press, 1992.

Smith, James L., *Melodrama*, Methuen, 1973.

Zimmerman, Bonnie, 'What has never been: an overview of lesbian feminist literary criticism' in *New Feminist Criticism*, ed. Elaine Showalter, London: Virago, 1986.

Newspaper reviews

'Life, The Observer Magazine', 4 June 1995. Dr. Jill Lockwood, to Maureen Freely and Dr. Cecilia Pyper in an article on in-vitro fertilization (IVF).

John Barber, *Daily Telegraph*, 11 October 1983.

Michael Billington, *The Guardian, 1983.*

Robert Cushman, *The Observer*, 1983.

Jack Tinker, *Daily Mail*, 11 October 1983.

Ann McFerran, *Time Out*, 11 October 1983.

Nicholas De Jongh, *The Guardian*, 10 January 1994

Milton Shulman, *The Standard,* 1983.

All theatre reviews are from *Theatre Record*, which is organized according to the year and title of the plays.

CHAPTER THIRTEEN

SOAP, SEXUAL IDENTITY, AND MIDLIFE CRISIS – LESBIAN DRAMA BETWEEN ESSENTIALISM AND GENDER TROUBLE

KATHLEEN STARCK

Synopsis

This chapter explores the ways lesbianism was presented on the stages of the mid- to end 1980s. The examples of Debbie Klein's Coming Soon, Catherine Kilcoyne's Julie and Sandra Freeman's Supporting Roles are placed within the framework of lesbian identity politics, critical writing, theatre practice and the social/legal developments of that time. The plays illustrate an advancement beyond a monolithic definition of lesbianism. However, they do not question the category 'gender'.

*****

The 1980s saw the publication of the first two anthologies of British lesbian drama by theatre manager, photo-journalist, Arts Council drama panellist and lecturer Jill Davis. In her introduction to the first volume, published in 1987, she points out that it was put together from a position which claims homosexuality to be a political matter (Davis 1987: 7)

> It [her position] proposes that human sexuality is shaped by, and can be understood by reference to, the specific political and ideological system within which an individual is brought up. This is a view which rejects a purely biological, or purely psychological, explanation of sexuality. (Davis 1987: 7)

This, of course, is in line with more recent writings in gender studies. There is an understanding that not only gender is a social construction, but also the body and its sexuality are constituted by social forces. There is no prediscursive body, we always perceive it through structures which are there before we 'arrive on the scene', as Judith Butler puts it (1997: 409). Butler, in agreement with Simone de Beauvoir, sees the body as a historical situation, since it is an embodying of possibilities determined by historical convention (Butler 1997: 405). Moreover, it has been suggested that sexuality, even the sexual act itself, is historical and a social construct. Social construction theorists such as Carol S. Vance claim that it does not carry with it a universal social meaning. Instead, '[...] physically identical sexual acts may have varying social significance and subjective meaning, depending on how they are defined and understood in different cultures and historical periods' (Vance 1995: 42).

In accordance with these constructionist ideas, Davis claims that the liberation of homosexuals could be achieved in a first step through the recognition of their oppression and then by challenging stereotypical images by providing new ones. Within this context, it is particularly the theatre which Davis sees fulfilling the function of a political weapon in that it can demonstrate ideas to a wider audience (Davis 1987: 7). However, she continues to explain, only very few radical/feminist plays had been in print at the time of the publishing of *Lesbian Plays*, which, in turn, provided motivation for Davis to publish her anthologies. She further emphasises that her 'selection of plays [...] has been made to reflect a diversity of perspectives on lesbian issues, not to represent a particular political or cultural view' (Davis 1987: 11). With this statement Davis has already articulated the ,agenda, of many lesbian plays from the 1980s on, as I will demonstrate below.

However, during the nineteen seventies and early nineteen eighties the situation was rather different. There prevailed a 'homogenized vision of lesbian feminism that appealed primarily to gender identification – and specifically to the "woman-identified woman" as the main basis for political action' (Roof 1998:32). Rose Collis describes the 'mood' of the time as follows:

> For lesbians as a theatre audience, there was a need for work that affirmed lesbian politics, lifestyles and relationships. For a time, it seemed that if a woman performer said 'I'm a lesbian' within her first speech she was virtually assured of a standing ovation. (Collis 1993: 79)

This need to identify with and at the same time to be constituted as a subject by lesbian art is explained by Tamsin Wilton for the lesbian reader:

> For the baby dyke, whether she be 14 years old and emerging from childhood or 40 and emerging from marriage, what confronts her is her own invisibility. She is also undoubtedly aware that to be a lesbian is dangerous, so it is something she must hide. This combination of invisibility and danger means that lesbian books often provide not only the first non-homophobic context within which a lesbian reader may begin to understand her existence but also the first lesbian 'community'. Additionally, the process of 'reading lesbian' constructs the lesbian reader *as* lesbian. (Wilton 1995: 121, original emphasis)

I would like to extend this statement to include the theatre. It is particularly the aspect of the 'lesbian community' which suggests this move. According to Sandra Freeman, the audience of plays such as *Any Woman Can* would be predominantly lesbian and thus develop and/or maintain a special relationship with the performers. The theatre could be experienced as a 'safe space'.

> It was reassuring to actors and spectators alike to realize that they were part of a larger community than they had imagined. There was an assumption that coming to see a play about lesbian concerns, written by a lesbian, performed by lesbians, was to make a statement of solidarity, which, in some instances, was tantamount to 'coming out'. The actors came out to the audience, the audience came out to the actors. Needless to say the nature of the performance is particular under such circumstances, when the performers have the confidence that spectators will recognize references to their own personal experience, will hear the characters making statements on their behalf, statements which they may not yet have dared to make. (Freeman 1997: 166)

Although the relationship between audience and performers remained rather special in places such as the Oval House (for which Freeman attests an enthusiastic and supportive sisterhood (1979: 79)) and the Drill Hall, which became established venues for developing and producing lesbian plays, confidence had grown enough by the mid nineteen eighties to move beyond ·coming-out· plays. The existence and recognition of lesbian subject positions started to be taken for granted. In the theatre as in the critical writing of the late 1980s and early 1990s the 'primary strategies [...] [were the] deconstruction of the lesbian as a unified, essentialist, ontological being and reconstruction as metaphor and/or subject position [...]' (Zimmermann 1992: 3).
From this 'secure' position playwrights now ventured to explore what Davis describes as a wide range of lesbian voices. Thus, in her

introduction to *Lesbian Plays: Two*, she repeats and extends her call for diversity from the first volume:

> [...] lesbian theatre, lesbian culture needs to hear as wide a range of lesbian voices and experiences as possible. It would be absurd, given the long silence imposed on lesbians by the heterosexual world, if we imposed our own form of censorship, screening out from public utterance all but one agreed definition of the lesbian experience. (Davis 1989: x)

In line with this, the three plays I analyse in this chapter, all of them published in *Lesbian Plays: Two*, provide very different portrayals of lesbian lives. They were first performed in the mid/end 1980s, a time when lesbian theatre had moved beyond ·mere· coming-out plays, such as Jill Posener's *Any Woman Can* (1975). However, it had not yet arrived at what Elaine Aston describes as the younger generation advocating queer politics, who

> looked to more flexible views on identity, ways of crossing a range of identities, rather than occupying just one. In terms of lesbian politics this involved a shift from the desire to claim a lesbian identity to a questioning (or queering) of identity that involved the interrogation of the category 'lesbian' itself. [...] [Q]ueer politics emerged in the 1990s seemingly as a 'corrective' to lesbian identity politics, and ideas of gender-bending performativity (à la Butler) challenged the ontological claim *to be lesbian*. (Aston 2003: 98-99, original emphasis)

One of the examples which Aston gives are the plays by Phyllis Nagy who 'tends to contest gay and feminist orthodoxies in the interest of stirring up gender trouble. Her theatre is less about claiming an identity than exploring the possibilities that arise when identity gets displaced' (Aston 2003: 100-101).

In contrast with this, I claim and in the following will proceed to demonstrate that Debbie Klein's high-camp soap opera *Coming Soon*, Catherine Kilcoyne's *Julie* a ·finding out· play (as opposed to ·coming out· (Freeman 1997: 31)), and Sandra Freeman's *Supporting Roles*, which focuses on the subject of age, are to be located somewhere between the two poles of 1970s ·lesbian essentialism· and the 1990s risk of 'anything goes' (Aston 2003: 99) provided by the queering of identities.

Debbie Klein: *Coming Soon*

Debbie Klein is probably best known for being a member of the comedy duo Parker and Klein, which she founded together with Karen

Parker in 1985. Their duo had grown out of the lesbian theatre group Hard Corps, founded in 1982 and disbanded in 1985. According to Sandra Freeman, 'Parker and Klein wanted to continue to provide lesbians with a good night out' (Freeman 1997: 78). Thus, it is not surprising that Klein's play *Coming Soon* was performed with almost the original Hard Corps team. Like many other lesbian theatre groups, though, due to lack of funding, Parker and Klein were only able to survive for a few years.

   Coming Soon was written as a celebration for Gay Pride 1986 and directed specifically at 'a welcoming audience [...] [of] lesbians who felt they deserved good entertainment and who were fed up of being worthy [...] [as well as] for anyone else who wanted a good night out' (*Coming Soon*, 33). Klein specifically points out that *Coming Soon* is not a ·lesbian issues· play and that its only 'political' message is, 'Lesbians are glamorous, sexy, and sophisticated, and we know how to make fun of ourselves. Aren't you just a little envious that you're not one too?' (*Coming Soon*, 33). Moreover, she wanted to reclaim the trivial and 'to crack, once and for all, the myth that only gay men can be camp' (*Coming Soon*, 33). Thus, the play is usually described as a high-camp soap opera, or, as in its subtitle 'A Sapphic Sudsaga'. Jill Davis characterises it as follows:

> Nice, 'normal', right-on lesbians fall in lust with butch swimming-pool attendants and nuns in full habit, watched over by a photograph of a partly clad Joan Collins. Not at first sight a common lesbian experience. But fancying women is, and Debbie Klein's work, which she describes as 'putting the sex back into sexual politics', is very popular with lesbian audiences. Her comedy [...] succeeds because it breaks taboos and speaks the unmentionable. It offers a night off from the double pressure lesbians are under, the pressure of refuting the negative images we've been brought up with, and the pressure of trying to live up to the new positive images we have ourselves created. In Debbie Klein's work we can laugh at the contradictions we deny in real life. (Davis 1989: ix)

   Klein states that *Coming Soon* was inspired by 1980s TV soap operas such as *Dynasty* which starred the fabulous Joan Collins. This was an American prime time television soap, aired from 1981 to 1989. 'The show epitomized an era of glamour and decadence and was the talk of the nation. Even former president Gerald Ford guest-starred as himself on 21 December 1983' (www.en.wikipedia.org/wiki/Dynasty: television).
   As a consequence, Klein's plot centres around sex and sexual attraction and is presented

> through supremely over the top, and therefore subversive, stereotypes, such as a psychosexual counsellor, her swinish twin sister and a lesbian sex-object body builder. [...] This was lesbian theatre at its boldest,

funniest and sexiest. (Collis 1993: 82)

In her author's notes Klein, in fact, writes that *Coming Soon* should not be staged in a naturalistic way. On the contrary, her instructions read '[t]he more stylized and outrageous the better' and that the play should 'be performed as rampantly as theatre and self-censorship will allow' (*Coming Soon*, 33).

Thus, it is with a nod to *Dynasty* that the set for the play was bright pink and 'presided over by a photograph of Joan Collins in her underwear, lit by a glowing pink triangle' (*Coming Soon*, 33). Further reminiscent of the successful TV soap are the theme tunes which were given to the individual characters and were used to emphasise dramatic moments in the plot (*Coming Soon*, 33). The plot itself with its many twists and turns - such as the secretly changed wording of a newspaper advertisement for a roommate, the reappearance of a long-lost daughter and a supposedly dead lover, and the breaking up, reunion and subsequent repeated breaking up of relationships - likewise mirrors soap opera plots. At the same time, though, the frequent entrances and exits of the characters, mistaken identities, a sudden death and an unexpected inheritance as well as the complete, rather unmotivated, transformation of a character from 'quiet little mouse' (*Coming Soon*, II, iv) into a self-confident, out and proud lesbian clearly add elements of the comedy or even farce.

I would like to suggest that one of the characters might in fact be modelled on *Dynasty's* Alexis Carrington/Colby, played by Joan Collins. In the TV soap, it is particularly this character who causes 'bad blood' when time and again she tries to interfere with her ex-husband's second marriage. In addition to her attempts to ruin her former husband, she relentlessly tries to undermine his current wife which in a handful of episodes even results in 'catfights'. This character finds her equivalent in the *Coming Soon* character of Jade, the evil twin sister. Not only is she described as 'Kay's identical twin, but [...] dressed very differently, à la Joan Collins' (*Coming Soon*, I, v). It is also made clear from her very first line, 'Poor little Ginny. Still the emotional incompetent?' (I, v), that she is the play's villain. As the driving force of one of the sub-plots, she unscrupulously wants to evacuate Kay and her flatmate from their house, which she is planning to repossess as the result of a failed business transaction. This villain does not even attempt to conceal her intentions when she unmistakably states:

> Kay cut me out of Mummy's will just as she cut me out of her heart. Goody-goody Kay, always the little favourite. Well she's not going to see

a penny of it, do you hear? I want to see my prissy sister in the gutter. [...] you [addressing Ginny] can tell my sweet sister that she has a week to get out of here and to find somewhere new while she can still earn a salary. I'm going to turn this place into a clinic. You see, altruism does run in the family. [...] Plastic surgery. The world needs more beautiful women. Don't you agree? (I, v)

Readers/spectators familiar with *Dynasty* will find it quite easy to imagine the character of Alexis making such a pronouncement. In contrast to the soap, however, in *Coming Soon* the evil twin is punished. In the fashion of a *deus ex machina* Kay and Ginny's neighbour, Miss T., re-enters the plot with the news that the married man with whom her errant mother was having an affair is, in fact, Jade's husband. Since he has suddenly died, leaving his fortune, including the house in question, to Miss T.'s mother, likewise deceased, everything now belongs to Miss T. In an act of neighbourly love she gives the house to Kay and thus saves her from evacuation. This plot development is also one of the examples of comic and farcical elements in the play.

Following this comical twist, though, Jade once more displays soap opera qualities with her last statement of the play: 'All right, you win, but don·t think you·ve heard the last of me. I'm a survivor, and I'll find a way to pay you back for this, all of you. One day I'll have my revenge and it will be lethal!' (II, iv). As a consequence, *Coming Soon* could easily be merely one episode in a long-running soap which ends in the manner of the 'infamous [*Dynasty*] cliffhanger storylines' (www.en.wikipedia.org/wiki/Dynasty_(television)).

At this point, I would like to take up once more the idea of a 'special' audience. This certainly holds true for the performances of *Coming Soon* at the Oval House where handkerchiefs (squares of pink toilet paper) were distributed to the spectators before the performance (*Coming Soon*, 33) which then

> would be used by the audience in a flamboyant symbolic way, a pretence of sympathy, just as the boos and hisses greeting a pantomime villain [...] are a conventional symbol of our condemnation of wickedness. The message is not 'friends are more faithful than lovers'. If there is a message at all, it is rather 'we have appropriated this form of entertainment and given it a meaning for us. We too can have our soaps.' (Freeman 1997: 80)

Furthermore, there would be an additional layer added to the play's ·meaning· or 'reading' through the audience's familiarity with the comedy duo Parker and Klein, who now appeared in the roles of the two main characters.

> By the time *Coming Soon* was produced, Karen Parker and Debby Klein
> were a well-known double act in lesbian venues. The Oval audience would
> therefore recognize them not simply as characters but as themselves, in the
> roles of Ginny and Kay. The fact that they are alone together, raising their
> glasses to friendship at the end of the play, would therefore have another
> layer of meaning for their 'fans'. (Freeman 1997: 82)

What had been achieved earlier for the form of cabaret and stand-
up comedy by groups such as Monstrous Regiment with their *Floorshow*
in 1977 (Wandor 1986: 71), was now being done for the heterosexual form
of the soap opera. As in the cabaret and stand-up of women's theatre
groups, in *Coming Soon* Klein takes a well-known form and changes its
content, thus standing on its head. Freeman puts this as follows: *'Coming
Soon* takes a heterosexual dramatic form, the soap opera, the descendant of
nineteenth century melodrama, and turns it into a highly camp lesbian
version in which every emotion is clearly false' (Freeman 1997: 80).
This appropriation is rendered even more intriguing in the light of Sally R.
Munt's remark on the relationship between homosexuality and
heterosexual iconography:

> Our relationship with heterosexuality is paradoxical and vexed. We have
> adopted heterosexual iconography, but we reproduce it in masquerade, as
> a knowing copy, thus as an analogy which cannot simply return to a
> reidealized, retrenched original. (Munt 1998: 11)

The crucial phrase here is 'knowing copy', as it assumes a
'knowing audience' who would recognize und understand the reproduction
of heterosexual iconography in masquerade. This 'knowing audience',
though, is not only assumed by the performers of *Coming Soon*, but at the
same time comes into existence through their performance. The
construction of such an 'ideal audience' is, according to Jill Dolan,
achieved through the performance apparatus (curtain, lights etc.), which
subsumes the spectators· individuality under an assumption of
commonality (Dolan 2003: 288).

> The spectators become the audience whom the performer addresses [...] as
> a singular mass. The performance apparatus that directs the performers'
> address, however, works to constitute that amorphous, anonymous mass as
> a particular subject position. The lighting, setting, costumes, blocking, text
> – all the material aspects of theatre – are manipulated so that the
> performance's meanings are intelligible to a particular spectator,
> constructed in a particular way by the terms of its address. (Dolan 2003:
> 288)

Traditionally, Dolan continues, this ideal spectator would have been white, male and heterosexual within a North American context (Dolan 2003: 288), an observation which likewise holds true for the British theatre. For performances of *Coming Soon*, however, a very different kind of audience was constructed – a predominantly lesbian one. So Klein uses the very performance apparatus which 'normally' produces heterosexual soap opera and in subsequence constitutes a heterosexual audience and creates something very different, lesbian soap opera for a lesbian audience. Thus, I suggest, *Coming Soon* is not so much concerned with investigating or justifying the lesbian subject position. Rather, this subject position is taken as a given and serves as a frame to which a specific dramatic form is appropriated in order to make it suitable for providing a predominantly lesbian audience with 'a good night out'. In addition, appropriating popular heterosexual forms can also

counteract the absence of lesbians from much of heteropopular culture [...], [it] undercuts the notion that heteropatriarchy 'owns' these popular forms, inscribes lesbians into popular culture and subverts some of the ideological conservatism inherent in formulaic texts by asserting the existence of lesbians and by thus questioning the stereotypes which govern much mainstream popular culture. (Griffin 1993: 3)

Catherine Kilcoyne: *Julie*

Catherine Kilcoyne's play *Julie* was one of two women's plays chosen for rehearsed public readings at the Drill Hall during the Gay Sweatshop Times Ten Festival in 1985 (Freeman 1997: 29). Later that year it received full production at the Oval House.

This one-woman piece, a series of monologues which, according to Kilcoyne, can be moved around in any order (*Julie*, 36), tells the story of a woman discovering, doubting and trying to come to terms with her sexual identity. Although Julie does have sex with men, this increasingly feels 'wrong' to her while at the same time it is addictive. On the other hand, she cannot imagine expressing her love for women in a physical way: 'I am a lesbian, but I can't have sex with another woman' (*Julie*, Section v). Writing the character of Julie, Kilcoyne was inspired by a scene from Posener's *Any Woman Can*:

As the play was written specifically for Gay Sweatshop x 10 Festival, I chose as my starting point a few lines from the first Gay Sweatshop women's play, *Any Woman Can* by Jill Posener, by way of a tribute to that first important step. Those lines focused on the fear and joy of first expressing your love for another woman in a physical way. I wanted to write a piece that was accessible to as many women as possible, that included heterosexual and bisexual women as well as lesbians. (*Julie*, 46)

In Posener's play there is likewise a character named Ginny who pleads with another character, called Julie, to explain why she won't make love:

GINNY: Explain to me.
JULIE: You know why. I'm not a lesbian, you know I'm not, it's unfair to you to make demands.
GINNY: You love me, don't you? You've just said you love me.
JULIE: Yes I love you, but I can't touch you. I do love you but I can't.
GINNY: Are you ever going to be able to?
JULIE: I'm not sure. Perhaps not. I don't know. (*Any Woman Can*, 19)

In both plays, Julie feels that sex with men comes to her more 'easily'. Thus, in *Any Woman Can*, Julie explains to Ginny: 'If you were a man everything would be all right, I can see I'll go back to men. [...] It wouldn't be the same, but it's the only way I seem to know. [...] At least it's familiar' (19). In *Julie*, this scene is re-enacted by Julie, playing both roles, her own and Ginny's. Although the scene is slightly changed, some lines are identical: 'If you were a man everything would be all right. [...] I can see I'll go back to men. [...] It's the only way I seem to know' (Section v). However, Kilcoyne places Julie's *quest* for a sexual identity at the centre of her play, whereas in *Any Woman Can* the focus is on Ginny and the *result* of her quest: 'coming out'.

Julie's motivation for 'wrong sex' with men in Kilcoyne's play is seen by Freeman in the relief that it gives her 'from the isolation which she is afraid of if she "crosses over" once and for all' (Freeman 1997: 30). I agree with Freeman, yet would like to point to another aspect which determines Julie's actions, i.e. the dichotomy of shame and pride. According to Sally Munt, it resembles the loci of inside/outside or closet versus society.

Coming out into the Modern Lesbian and Gay Movement we have celebrated a rubric of pride. Outside, in this context, meant claiming a place in society. Inside carried the connotations of the closet, as a prison of shame. The lesbian inside/outside structure is characterized by this *affect* – the binary opposition of shame/pride. [...] For lesbians, shame sediments specifically in the swamp of female sexuality. It is interminably difficult for women to resist experiencing some shame about our bodies, particularly around our genitals and sexual behaviours. (Munt 1998: 4-5, original emphasis)

Unable to escape her 'prison of shame', Julie's apparently weak, powerless and fragmentary subject position is constituted by the 'heterosexist gaze' (Munt 1998: 6). She monitors her actions through 'heterosexual eyes'.

> The heterosexist gaze has a doubling effect – to include at the same time as it casts out. It is an act of appropriation, owning, and non-consensual classification replete with voyeurism. The heterosexist gaze is intended to mark us: the glance is a strike. The heterosexist gaze is a profoundly exposing stigmatization, and as an act of shaming its effect is to paralyse. (Munt 1998: 6)

It is this feeling of paralysis which Julie experiences in her attempt to 'come out' to her friends. Although she intends to 'tell them', she ends up 'checking out tasty men':

> And tonight? My friends. In that place I couldn't tell them the most significant thing about me. [...] Saturday night? We're going to Annabelle's. Jackie's meeting this guy. We're going to check him out. See if he's got any tasty friends... [sic] Say no. I picked what I was going to wear. I felt odd about it. The chameleon changed its colours. I was going to tell them. My friends. In that place, with those men, the reason we were there. Who we were and who we'd once been. I felt isolated. I wanted to tell them but it didn't fit in that context. The club, the heat, the now. I couldn't tell them, so I joined them. (Section vi)

The stigmatization and voyeurism of the shaming heterosexist gaze are most blatantly demonstrated in a scene where Julie is provoked into 'proving' her lesbianism to her heterosexual flatmates. She has sex with one of the women while the other one is watching. Thus, Julie does not only literally permit the heterosexist gaze (being watched by a heterosexual woman), but she adapts that gaze herself: 'Moved through it. The motions. Not seeing. Not feeling. *Like I was standing watching as well'* (Section iv, my emphasis). The shaming becomes most effective when Julie's partner climaxes and then asks, 'Eh – Is that it? Is that all?' (Section iv). Julie is shamed into denying her sexual identity. 'I hated all women after that. All of them. I didn't trust any of them, not an inch. I'd look in the mirror, hating myself' (Section iv).

Before, at the end of the play, Julie undergoes a transformation, triggered by the relationship with her lesbian friend Jane, the audience sees her removing her ·going out· make-up. As she does this, she comments on each individual part of her face as promising heterosexual sex and her made-up face as a 'fantasy' and the 'man's woman' (Section vi). Only after wiping out the 'man·s woman' is she able to inhabit her 'true' identity. This crucial fact is highlighted by the stage direction which immediately follows: 'A significant change in manner. Like a great weight has been lifted off her shoulders' (Section vi).

Finally, in the last scene, Julie's 'true self' emerges after she states, 'I want myself back' (Section ix) and then proceeds to take off all her clothes in front of a big mirror. This is emphasised by her naming and touching parts of her body – she repossesses her body and thus her sexuality. 'Meeting yourself for the first time. [...] Moving into your own body. Coming body to body with your own sex. Confronting yourself. [...] She [Jane] gave my body back to me. I've got it back. It's mine' (Section ix). Moreover, Julie, at last, is able to admit her sexual desire for Jane.

Although this scene is not a 'public' coming out, it is Julie's breaking free from her 'prison of shame'. As Munt argues, the issues of shame and pride are linked to visibility and non-visibility (Munt 1998: 10). Julie emerges into visibility on three different levels: first, she is literally able to watch herself in the mirror and take pleasure from that watching, second, she becomes visible to herself sensually by touching herself and, finally, she is able to recognise, to 'see', her sexual identity. Consequently, by reclaiming her body and her sexual identity she emerges into the realm of pride: 'They were robbing my pride. My self-respect. My body. [...] This belongs to me. This is my body. [...] *It feels so good.* I am a woman who loves another woman. I am nothing but a lover' (Section ix, my emphasis).

The play ends with her saying, 'My body does not belong in male hands any more. The man's woman meets the woman's woman' (Section ix). Yet, in contrast to Ginny in *Any Woman Can*, it is not clear whether Julie will remain a 'woman's woman'. Whereas Ginny opens and closes the play assuring the audience that she is a 'screaming lesbian' (*Any Woman Can*, 15; 23), the spectators of *Julie* witness confusion if not bewilderment for most of the play. It is also for this reason that the original title *Crossing Over* (from heterosexuality to lesbianism) was changed. Freeman claims that 'the journey might be made again in reverse' (Freeman 1997: 29). She writes on the difference between Posener and Kilcoyne's plays:

Any Woman Can in 1975 had marked the first lesbian ·coming out· in British theatre. Ten years later it inspired a play concerned with 'finding out'. Ginny [in *Any Woman Can*] was never in doubt about her lesbian inclinations; Julie [in *Julie*] who has been much more thoroughly socialized by the heterosexual world [...] is forever vacillating between cock and cunt. (Freeman 1997: 31)

Thus, the subject position portrayed in *Any Woman Can*, although written ten years *earlier* than *Julie*, is one which should chronologically *follow* that of Kilcoyne's play – 'finding out' would be expected to precede 'coming out'. My explanation for this apparent contradiction is that it was only possible ten years after *Any Woman Can* to write a lesbian character who is uncertain of her sexual identity. In 1975 it was still felt that in order to provide positive role models for an emergent lesbian community, these had to be presented as reassuringly confident and constant in their self definition.

Sandra Freeman: *Supporting Roles*

Sandra Freeman's *Supporting Roles*, first performed in 1988, was commissioned for Kate Crutchley's theatre company Character Ladies (founded in 1986) when Crutchley was programmer at the Oval House. The Oval had been known as devoted to new work, yet under Crutchley, due to her background in feminist, gay and lesbian theatre, offered even wider opportunities for women (Freeman 1997: 124). Also in 1988 Freeman cooperated once more with the Oval and Crutchley. She wrote the stage version of *Ladies of the Vale*, which had originally been planned as a film on the subject of the Ladies of Llangollen, 'famous for their romantic friendship at the end of the eighteenth and beginning of the nineteenth centuries' (Freeman 1997: 128). As in *Supporting Roles*, Crutchley played one of the lead roles.

It is also this close cooperation which helped to shape *Supporting Roles*. When Freeman wrote the play she returned to a subject she had addressed in an earlier play called *Sharing*. Although this had male characters at its centre, one of its most prominent subjects was 'the fulfilment of the protective, "parental" impulse towards young people that gays and lesbians experience' (Freeman 1997: 126). In *Supporting Roles*, this aspect of lesbian life is taken up through the character of Jo. She had lived with a single mother and had fulfilled the role of a parent. When the relationship failed, Jo lost both, her lover and 'her' child. All of this takes place before the opening of *Supporting Roles* and a 'crisis' is brought about when, after years, the 'child' returns. Freeman writes that she showed this particular scene, the reunion between Jo and 'her' child, to Crutchley:

> I showed the reunion scene, which I felt was by far the best moment, to Kate, who, with the judgement of long experience, suggested that it was entirely wrong, too heavy. She was right. I scrapped it and the play took a different and much better turn, becoming lighter, developing into farce. (Freeman 1997: 126)

The main issues in *Supporting Roles* are the physical and, more importantly, emotional changes the characters experience while going through their menopause. According to Davis, it portrays what could be seen as the most common lesbian situation, a long-term domestic relationship. Yet, in contrast to *Julie*, the focus is not on sexual identity, but on age, menopause and mid-life crisis (Davis 1989: x). The audience is presented with older lesbians' point of view with the main characters being in their fifties. Their long-term ·domesticity· is introduced as a subject from the very beginning. Thus, the play opens with Suzie, who, without warning, is in the process of leaving her partner Lyn, discussing her cooking:

> LYN: You can't just go.
> SUZIE: I am, I'm sorry.
> […]
> SUZIE: I thought you'd still be asleep. It's still early.
> LYN: I woke up with terrible indigestion.
> SUZIE: I'm sorry.
> LYN: It wasn't your fault I had indigestion.
> SUZIE: I suppose it was. I suppose that casserole was a bit heavy. I should
> have known it would upset you. I ought to have skinned the tomatoes, but
> I didn't. And I used the last bit of the biocarbonate of soda in the chocolate
> cake. (I, i)

Their domesticity is almost rendered absurd in act two. Here, Lyn is finally able to talk to Suzie, who refuses any contact, if only because she manages to grab the telephone from Jo:

> Suzie! Oh Suzie, darling where are you? (*Pause.*) Yes, but (*Pause.*) I did!
> Suzie I … [sic] (Pause.) I don't care about that! Where? (Pause. She
> replaces the receiver slowly.) She hung up. (*Pause.*) All she said was – did
> I take the washing out, would I turn the iron off, and the cleaner ticket for
> my jacket was under the clock in the bedroom! (II, iv)

The impression of a harmonious long-term relationship is intensified in the following conversation between Suzie and her friend Jo:

> JO: Last time I came round you seemed very harmonious. Of course, you
> can't always tell.
> SUZIE: We are. Very. Why shouldn't we be? There's nothing to disagree
> over, is there? We sorted our differences out a long time ago. Or we
> learned to live with them. We don't have problems with money, the
> mortgage is nearly paid, we respect each other's work, each other's
> privacy. We've had more room since we had the loft converted. We're very

harmonious. Very. (I, ii)

In spite of this harmony, Suzie feels 'utterly miserable' and 'a pain in the neck to [her]self' (I, ii). Suzie's emotional turmoil is paralleled by her friend Jo's decision to change her life and give up her job and by her physical inconveniences. These are addressed when Suzie is seeking 'asylum' at Jo's and learns that her friend is 'fine, almost. The odd aching in the joints now and then. And I've started to have migraines' (I, ii). Later Jo explains the interconnectedness between the physical and emotional changes that she experiences:

> I've no idea what I'm going to do yet [about a new job]. I'm not going to decide in a hurry. What is definite is that this choice is going to be the big change. Things are happening to my body. I'm losing my strength. I'm feeling weak, sometimes ill. I'm not ill, I know that, but I'm not quite the same as I was. I want to take account of that. I want to confront middle age before it can get me unawares. (I, iii)

Moreover, she suggests the same interrelation of age and life-changing decisions for Lyn and Suzie:

> LYN: You see it must be a breakdown, it's not reasonable.
> JO: Could be her age.
> LYN: What!
> JO: (*slowly*): I said, it could be her age.
> LYN: She's my age. More or less.
> JO: Yes.
> LYN: I'm not behaving in that irrational fashion.
> JO: Some people might think you were. Wanting to go off on a wild-goose chase [trying to find Suzie] the length of the British Isles. A bit over the top, I would say.
> LYN: What do you mean?
> JO: Come on Lyn, you know what I mean.
> LYN: This is all simply a middle-age crisis?
> JO: Not simply. It's not simple. (I, iv)

Similarly, Lyn makes a reference to her age herself when she mentions that she will need her glasses for reading Suzie's farewell letter (I, i). The subject of 'old age' is established with Jo's friend Rick, a character in her seventies, who is introduced reminiscing about her dead lover (I, ii). The somewhat climactic point is reached when Suzie states, 'I don't want to be old' (II, iii). Finally, it is made unmistakably clear by Jo's adopted daughter Anna that in *Supporting Roles* not lesbianism but age is the issue at stake: 'I'm not making judgements about you [Jo and her

current lover] being gay. That's stupid. I've told you, as far as I know, I
could by myself. *It' only the other, the age* [there is an age difference of
about twenty years]' (III, i).

In addition to middle-age and its effects on the characters' lives,
Freeman clearly focuses on long-term relationships. Lyn and Suzie own a
house together and have lived with each other for sixteen years, Jo cannot
forget her life with ex-partner Angela and 'their' daughter (this is
emphasised when Anna, the daughter, returns in act one scene three) and
Rick had lived with her lover for thirty years before she died.

Davis, in fact, calls it a 'brave play' (Davis 1989: x) since
Freeman lay herself wide open to criticism from radical feminists who
'charged' her for showing traditional heterosexual 'couplism'. The author
cites one particular example where a reviewer described *Supporting Roles*
as 'politically incorrect, distasteful even, and was reported to have said that
she wouldn't allow her girlfriend to see it' (Freeman 1989: 91).
Interestingly, Freeman expresses sympathy for this point of view:

> Personally I thought such comments were only to be expected from
> someone twenty years my junior. Lesbianism is not here offered as a
> radical alternative to established society, it is shown functioning
> comfortably within that society. The characters are not consciously
> rebelling, they are simply trying to get on with their lives. (Freeman 1989:
> 91)

Her 'justification' for writing 'politically unsound' characters is
that, at least in this play, she wanted to write about something she is
familiar with from personal experience.

> It is quite true that Supporting Roles does not emphasize lesbian difference
> – I don't think. I have to admit that I do not know from personal
> experience how heterosexual 'couples' work, because I have never been
> part of one. But I am part of a long-term lesbian couple and I want to write
> about *that*, whether it is considered politically correct or not! (Freeman
> 1997: 127, original emphasis)

Within the context of my analysis, it is particularly Freeman's
remark regarding the age difference between herself and one of her most
vehement critics which points to the difficult location of *Supporting Roles*
on the continuum between lesbian essentialism at one pole and the
questioning of the very term ·lesbian· in queer theory at the other. Not only
did the 1980s produce a general move away from 1970s essentialism, but
at the same time this might have happened on a personal level. With
Freeman being twenty years her critic's senior, she had clearly moved
beyond questions of 'political correctness' and the demonstration of bold

lesbian pride. With her play she shows that lesbianism is not a fixed identity, but that the lesbian self, like any other, undergoes changes throughout an individual's life. Moreover, lesbianism is not a monolith. By emphasising her personal experience as the basis for the issues in *Supporting Roles*, Freeman illustrates that there are a myriad of lesbian identities, which do not necessarily correspond with a preconceived idea of 'political correctness'.

However, the criticism which the play provoked betrays a discrepancy between developments in lesbian theory and some lived experiences. It seems that some parts of the 'lesbian community' were not yet 'ready' for diversity. I suggest that this is due to a common strategy in minority politics. In order to achieve political aims, a 'strategic homogeneity' is assumed. Thus, the critical reactions to *Supporting Roles* might have been in the light of political developments such as the notorious Section 28 of the Local Government Bill, introduced in 1988, which

[...] prohibits Local Authorities from the 'promotion' of homosexuality whether by publishing material for that purpose, by teaching in schools 'the acceptability of homosexuality as a pretended family relationship', or by giving 'financial assistance to any person' for either of these purposes. (Davis 1989: xi)

According to Davis, this act attacks not so much private lives but 'the rights of homosexuals in public and as members of the community' (Davis 1989: xi). Therefore, bearing in mind the political importance of the public image of homosexuals as a group, it is not surprising that *Supporting Roles* should have produced concern about political correctness. Thus, any attempt at critically assessing Freeman's play will be somewhat caught between political necessity and the right for individual freedom.

Jill Dolan writes about the relationship between feminist theatre and its audience:

The process of reception and the entire hermeneutical endeavour will – and should – be different for different spectators. The meaning derived from any one performance will vary endlessly. For a feminist theatre to dictate a proper meaning is as ideologically and politically suspect as any of the mystifications implicitly condoned by the dominant culture's theatre. (Dolan 2003: 293)

I would like to argue with Dolan that the same should hold true for lesbian theatre. Identity politics notwithstanding, there should be no dictation of meaning. At any rate, in addition to the production process of a play, the audience is always also an active producer of meaning and there is no author's or individual spectator's monopoly on the 'message' of a text.

In conclusion, *Coming Soon*, *Julie* and *Supporting Roles* illustrate how lesbianism changed in its self-definition, how its perception in critical writing started to be modified/diversified and also how its public image took first steps towards social recognition during the 1980s. Whereas the 1970s monolith of the lesbian was deconstructed, it was not yet replaced with a general questioning of the category 'lesbian' and the 1990s notion of gender performativity.

In *Coming Soon* and *Supporting Roles*, the issue of lesbian identity is hardly addressed. Instead, the characters take their subject positions for granted. Although the characters are 'out and proud', they do neither feel the need to demonstrate this pride, nor do they attempt to explain their sexual identity. It is 'simply' part of their selves and in *Supporting Roles* even takes the back seat to the issue of age. In spite of the farcical elements in the plots of both plays, lesbianism is presented as something ordinary, which, in turn, produces 'normality' for the audience.

The case is slightly different for *Julie*. Here, sexual identity is the central subject of the play. Moreover, the shame of 'coming out' is addressed and shown to cause deep personal conflict. At the same time, though, Kilcoyne's work points to a shift in lesbian identity politics. It allows for disorientation and uncertainty with regard to sexual orientation. Lesbianism is shown as a fractured and unstable identity.

The diversification of 'the lesbian' is likewise what lends a political aspect to *Supporting Roles*. Freeman insists on the importance of the lived experiences of individual lesbians and thereby claims a space for lesbian heterogeneity. Finally, despite the fact that its main message is 'having fun', *Coming Soon* contributes to a 'normalisation' of lesbianism by celebrating its 'fun side' on the one hand and appropriating a heterosexual dramatic form to do so on the other. Thus, like *Julie* and *Supporting Roles*, Klein's play, too, corresponds with Davis' view of homosexuality as a political matter.

Works cited

Aston, Elaine, *An Introduction to Feminist Theatre*, London: Routledge, 1995.
—. *Feminist Views on the English Stage. Women Playwrights 1990-2000*, Cambridge: CUP, 2003.

Butler, Judith, "Performative Acts and Gender Constitution. An Essay in Phenomenology and Feminist Theory," in Katie Conboy et al. (eds), *Writing on the Body. Female Embodiment and Feminist Theory*. N.Y.: Columbia UP, 1997.

Collis, Rose, "Sister George is Dead," in Trevor R. Griffiths and Margaret Llewellyn-Jones (eds.), *British and Irish Women Dramatists Since 1958*, Buckingham: OUP, 1993.

Davis, Jill (ed), *Lesbian Plays*, London: Methuen, 1987.

—."Introduction," in Jill Davis (ed.), *Lesbian Plays: Two*, London: Methuen, vi-x, 1989.

Dolan, Jill, "The Discourse of Feminisms: The Spectator and Representation," in Lizbeth Goodman & Jane de Gay (eds.), *The Routledge Reader in Gender and Performance*, London: Routledge, 2003.

Freeman, Sandra, *Supporting Roles*, in Jill Davis (ed.), *Lesbian Plays: Two,* London: Methuen, 1989.

Freeman, Sandra, *Putting your Daughters on the Stage. Lesbian Theatre from the 1970s to the 1990s,* London and Washington: Cassell, 1997.

Griffin, Gabriele (ed), *Outwrite. Lesbianism and Popular Culture*, London: Pluto, 1993.

Kilcoyne, Catherine, *Julie.* in Jill Davis (ed), *Lesbian Plays: Two,* London: Methuen, 1989.

Klein, Debbie, *Coming Soon*, in Jill Davis (ed), *Lesbian Plays: Two*, London: Methuen, 1989.

Munt, Sally R. (ed), *Butch/Femme. Inside Lesbian Gender*, London: Cassell, 1998.

Posener, Jill, *Any Woman Can*, in Jill Davis (ed), *Lesbian Plays*, London: Methuen, 1987.

Roof, Judith, "1970s Lesbian Feminism Meets 1990s Butch-Femme," in Sally R. Munt (ed), *Butch/Femme. Inside Lesbian Gender*, London: Cassell, 1998.

Vance, Carol S., "Social Construction Theory and Sexuality," in Maurice Berger, Brian Wallis & Simon Watson (eds), *Constructing Masculinity*, N.Y. & London: Routledge, 1995.

Wandor, Michelene, *Carry On, Understudies: Theatre and Sexual Politics,* London: Routledge, 1986.

Wilton, Tamsin, *Lesbian Studies. Setting an Agenda,* London: Routledge, 1995.

Zimmerman, Bonnie, "Lesbians Like This And That. Some Notes on Lesbian Criticism for the Nineties," in Sally Munt (ed.), *New Lesbian Criticism. Literary and Cultural Readings,* N.Y.: Harvester

Wheatsheaf, 1992.

Websites

Dynasty. http://www.en.wikipedia.org/wiki/Dynasty_(television),
    Accessed 16 January 2006.

CHAPTER FOURTEEN

WE SINFUL DYKES[6]: LESBIAN SEXUALITY IN VALERIE MASON-JOHN'S *SIN DYKES*

ASHLEY TELLIS

Synopsis

Valerie Mason-John's work has moved away from her Black lesbian concerns which made her something of a pioneer in the early 1990s, and branched into diverse genres such as fictionalized childhood memoir, children's plays, race plays and self-help books! Her central intervention in lesbian theatre in Britain has been, and remains, her incendiary and extremely successful play *Sin Dykes*. In this paper, I argue that, in *Sin Dykes*, Mason-John goes to the heart of intractable problems in the articulation of race and desire and the conjunction of the two. Framing them within the context of S/M sexual practices, Mason-John opens up the faultlines in British society, whether gay or straight. While she struggles between politically correct US identity-speak and more complex accounts of subjectivity, the theatricality of S/M sexuality perhaps redeems the play from its own often simple-minded dichotomies.

*****

Valerie Mason-John's, aka Queenie's, writing career has moved

---

[6] I borrow this title from Pakistani feminist poet Kishwar Naheed's poem 'We Sinful Women' which Rukhshana Ahmad takes as her title for her anthology of Pakistani women poets *We Sinful Women: Contemporary Urdu Feminist Poetry* (London: The Women's Press, 1991). Kishwar's poem inverts the sin attached to women by sarcastically taking on the label sinful even as she makes clear that all the sin is committed by men. Mason-John does something similar with the Black lesbian.

across different cultural spaces and modes of address over a fairly short
span of time. Between her early work that came out of the feminist
movement and the Black lesbian movement of the 80s and early 1990s in
Britain[7] and her recent performances and publications, which include a
novel/memoir,[8] plays on race,[9] plays for children[10] and a self-help book
(!)[11], there is a gulf that makes it difficult to believe that these disparate
bodies of work are by the same writer.

The most obvious change lies in the gradual erasure of the
thematisation of same-sex politics in the writing. In terms of her plays, *Sin
Dykes* remains really the only play that deals with lesbianism, and it is
lesbianism and not queerness which is the subject and context of the play.
The term 'queer' is not applicable to the play or to any of the writings in
her collection *Brown Girl in the Ring*, so the term lesbian will be used
throughout this essay.

In this essay, then, lesbian politics and lesbian desire will be the focus
and only one play by Mason-John, *Sin Dykes*, will be looked at closely,
perhaps her most powerful and probing work. Lesbian politics, of course,
is constitutively linked to racial politics in her work as a Black British
playwright and the productive frictions of this conjunction make it the
explicit theme of the play. Mason-John's mediation of race across her
oeuvre lacks any kind of structural subtlety. Whether in the rather random
monologue of *Brown Girl in the Ring* as England's Black queen or the
differential treatment the white-skinned son (as opposed to the black-
skinned son) gets from the police in *You Get Me*, a play about a white
woman, married to Black man with these two sons, the racial politics is
driven home to the audience in ways that leave little to the reader/viewer's
imagination and can often damage the impact of the play.

However, in *Sin Dykes*, the spectre and practice of interracial lesbian
desire complicate any straightforward account of racial politics. Though
the play is both written and located in the late 1990s, the burdens of a

---

[7] See, for example, Valerie Mason-John, *Lesbians Talking: Making Black Waves*
(with Ann Khambatta) London: Scarlet Press, 1993) and Valerie Mason-John (ed.)
Talking Black: Lesbians of African and Asian Descent Speak Out (London:
Cassell, 1994)

[8] Valerie Mason-John, *Borrowed Body* (London: Serpent's Tail, 2005)

[9] Valerie Mason-John, *You Get Me* (Unpublished)

[10] Valerie Mason-John, *The Adventures of Snow Black and Rose Red and The Totz*
(Unpublished). Of course, none of these plays can be placed into compartments
based on these themes as many of the themes overlap.

[11] Valerie Mason-John, *Detox Your Heart* (Birmingham: Windhorse Publications,
2006)

Black and feminist politics of the 70s and 80s haunt the characters and are
sought to be overcome. Yet the play does not settle for a facile post-race
same-sex politics nor is desire or fantasy ever located outside the complex
of race. As such, then, it is a play that confronts the most difficult
questions about race and desire without flinching from the implications it
may have for cherished conceptions of racial and sexual politics.
Ultimately, it offers a lesbian politics that in its specificity and materiality,
a specificity and materiality worked out in strictly theatrical (bodily)
terms, seeks to overcome the booby traps of a simplistic racial or sexual
politics through the corporeality of sexual desire.

Sin Dykes has six main characters, three black (Trudy, Kat and Clio)
and three white (Gill, Trace and BD), all located in the lesbian club and
bar scene of late 90s London. The main sexual complex in which all the
characters are implicated is sado-masochism (henceforth S/M) and its
potentially explosive combination with race. Given the histories of slavery
and colonialism, not to mention contemporary racism, sexual desire that
explicitly plays out roles of submission and domination is one that dare
not speak its name. Lesbianism is articulated without fear, indeed the
entire world of the play seems exclusively and comfortably lesbian – this
is the heart of the subculture in urban Britain – but the intertwining of the
lesbian with the racial, especially in the language of desire, is what
struggles to find a voice.

This voice is located in one character around whom the play revolves,
the ingénue and novice Trudy, for whom the play both stages its questions
and their answers. The play's cultural references and racially identitarian
language is distinctly US American; Britain never developed its own
language for dealing with race preferring to pretend it did not need one or
that racism did not exist. The lesbian language also borrows from the
United States. The play, after all, unfolds in the late 90s and Britain is well
into the Americanization of its gay subculture. This makes for a very
curious British theatrical space. The British – both black and white – are
able to talk only because of this foreign language of racial and sexual
politics, even if in Cockney and patois accents.[12]

The resultant dialogue is the contrasting of two blocks of dramatic
writing: fluid, conversational British and heavy-handed US identity talk.
The artificiality of this contrast may make for contrived reading but frames
the difficulty of articulating interracial lesbian S/M well in dramatic terms.
Indeed, the play trots out clichés both in terms of character (BD is a South

---

[12] In the play, for example, the characters refer to themselves as Zamis which
comes from Audre Lorde's influential autobiography *Zami: A New Spelling Of My
Name A Biomythography* (New York: Crossing Press, 1982).

African butch dyke who is a closet S/M queen and loves to be beaten up as payback for her ancestors' sins against black folk in South Africa) and complex (Kat is forever sermonizing Trudy on what a perilous mistake sleeping with white women is, though it is discovered that she herself sleeps with white women on the sly) but somehow it still works because it lays intractable questions open for examination. Indeed, its success as a box office sellout can be attributed less to the fact that S/M offers sensationalist value and more to the airing of questions that both black and white Britons would rather not talk about.

Indeed, the play proceeds almost chronologically from one under-discussed issue to another: S/M, interracial relationships, interracial relationships seen as race betrayal, power politics in interracial relationships, racial memory, Black feminism, S/M vs. sexual abuse. Each of these constitutes a dramatic moment in the play and each moment is saved from prosaic artifice by the continuing dramatic enactment of desiring bodies colliding, often against the words being spoken by characters. Mason-John uses physical theatre and mime at various strategic points to transform the scene from polemics to the dynamic pull of desire almost against the subject's will. It is precisely these moments that work dramatically as opposed to those where an issue is theoretically laid out for discussion by the dramatic personae.

Two moments in the play where an almost methodically theoretical working out of a problem is pitted against dramatic action that tells a different story are particularly important and it is on these two moments that the play hinges. The first is when Trudy comes to discuss her interest in exploring S/M and be initiated with her ex-girlfriend the white Gill; the second is when Trudy and Clio, her new black girlfriend are getting together at the end of the play. In the first scene, Gill is astonished at Trudy's new-found interest because it was Trudy's refusal to partake of any S/M that appeared to be the reason the relationship ended and Trudy tries to explain that the real reason is the racial difference and what that makes of the S/M experience that made it impossible for Trudy. The references to slavery and Black ancestors being whipped by white owners make the whole exchange heavy-handed and somewhat simplistic. An account of sexual violence that Trudy faced at the hands of policewoman (BD is an ex-cop who left her job in a sense because of Trudy) is thrown in for good measure as is the scene that reveals BD, the butch South African, as a closet S/M queen. There is a clear privileging of Black politics here as when Trudy talks about race interfering in her relationship with Gill, the tone, despite the contrived dialogue is serious:

TRUDY: How could I let you tie me up? How could I let you whip me? How could I? Those same whips were used to keep my ancestors at work on the plantations. My mother's and father's backs peeling raw, blood oozing, a tree trunk of slashes that can never be the same. I am the scar, my thoughts are still in pain.[13]

However, when Gill 'broke down crying. Blabbering how sorry she was that things in South Africa hadn't seem to have changed' and asked Trudy 'to whip her as much as my ancestors had been beaten by her people' stage directions show 'Trudy and Gill crack up laughing' (WSD 73). In either case, the way in which the issue is talked about does not work dramatically or otherwise. It lies rather flat and takes on the aspect of the contrived. The real moment, however, is when the race politics is not foregrounded but submerged in the desiring impulse, when bodies, black or white, give up and unto each other and Mason-John's instructions read:

Note: The following part of this scene, up to and including the dildo sequence uses physical theatre and mime, and should last between 10-15 minutes *(WSD 74)*.

During the dildo sequence, it is only when one body has surrendered to the other in trust that the moment begins:

GILL grabs TRUDY and puts her hands over her eyes.
GILL: Trust me. Close your eyes, relax and count up to a hundred.
(Straps a waist-and-leg harness and dildo onto Trudy, over her trousers. Spins her around gently.) You can open your eyes now.
TRUDY nervously opens her eyes, looks straight ahead in fear, GILL pushes her towards the mirror.
GILL: Go on look into the mirror.
TRUDY faces front stage, into imaginary mirror, and looks petrified. She looks down at the dildo very slowly and freezes. This and the rest of the dildo sequence is acted out in mime technique.
GILL: Go on, move your hips a bit. Get comfortable, familiar. Get in touch with its power. Let the energy pulsate through your body (WSD 75-76).

Further down in the scene:

TRUDY looks down and diligently puts the condom on. As she rolls the

---

[13] Sin Dykes is published in Valerie Mason-John's mixed-genre collection Brown Girl in the Ring (London: Get a Grip Publishers, 1999) 70. Henceforth references to the play will be within the essay and marked as WSD.

condom down the dildo, she slowly becomes turned on. Engrossed with
putting the condom on, her hips begin to gyrate. GILL snuggles up behind
her and grabs her hands.
TRUDY: How do I look?
GILL: Dare I say?
TRUDY: Oh go on. I trust your opinion.
GILL: Horny.
They burst out laughing. As they calm down they begin to gently move,
falling into rhythm. They both appear to be turned on in a subtle manner.
GILL begins to grope at TRUDY who responds, just as they are about to
kiss.
Sound of door bell ringing frantically (WSD 76).

The sadomasochistic scene is not one in which, because the socio-
historical is submerged, it ceases to exist. It provides the fuel for desire
and is part of what constitutes the sexual fantasy. Pat Califia writes:

> The key word to understand S/M is fantasy. The roles, dialogue, fetish
> costumes, and sexual activity are part of a drama or ritual. The participants
> are enhancing their sexual pleasure, not damaging or imprisoning one
> another. A sado-masochist is well aware that a role adopted during a
> scene is not appropriate during other interactions and that a fantasy role is
> not the sum total of her being… The S/M subculture is a theatre in which
> sexual dramas can be acted out (Califia 1981: 31).

This seems like too antiseptic a conception of S/M, relying too
heavily as Elizabeth Cowie notes, on 'knowledge and intention' (Cowie
1990: 153). Mason-John appears to endorse this free will and choice-based
understanding of sexual desire when she a) makes the real scene safe
because it is between two black women b) foregrounds the comfortability
and trust of the sadomasochistic scene. The latter is especially the case in
the ultimate scene where S/M is reduced to almost childish, giggly play
with handkerchiefs. Indeed, in the run-up to the final scene, Trudy and
Clio have an explicit conversation about the politics of S/M:

> TRUDY: You, BD and your slave, it gives me the creeps, but part of you
> excites me. I've never felt so charged before.
> CLIO Can you name it? What are you feeling?
> TRUDY: All I know is that the same thing which turns me on, is the same
> thing which scares me. You push my boundaries, press my buttons, and I
> just hate feeling out of control.
> CLIO: But you will always be in control if we talk about sex first. Talk
> about what we will do and what we won't. That is the exciting thing about
> sex, talking, exploring fantasies. Acting out what we feel comfortable with
> (WSD 88).

At this point, Trudy says 'Black girls don't do your type of sex' which leads Clio to snort incredulously and blame Black women for teaching this to other black women. This is the sequel to the earlier attack on feminism. Sexual heat is what is important, Clio asserts, not race or size. It is in this Dionysian state of sexual desire that the play ends. Indeed, what redeems both scenes theatrically is the incorporation of a bodily, corporeal language through which desire is enunciated and speaks its own language. This is especially true of the last scene which gives the lie to a tepid, domesticated S/M as the scene and the play draw to a close:

CLIO: Come on, let's play a little. Ead fucking gives me chronic migraine.
TRUDY: No, I hate those bondage games. You and BD...Yuck.
CLIO: Ow about some magic? *(She takes a bow and pulls out a hanky from under her collar. She entrances* TRUDY *seductively with the hankies during the following.)*
TRUDY: You're always playing with hankies, what does that mean?
CLIO: I'm appy to take either role tonight. *(Clenches her left hand into a fist and stuffs the hanky down it. She blows into her first like a conjurer and beckons* TRUDY *to do the same.)* It's your treat, you pull. *(*TRUDY *begins pulling from the first and a white hanky appears.)* Um, a girl who knows what she wants, you'll do both of us, will yer? *(*TRUDY *giggles, and pulls again, a mauve one appears.)* Um, naval fetish.
TRUDY begins to pull quickly and several coloured hankies appear. CLIO grabs the string of hankies tight. She waves the last colour – yellow – at Trudy and laughs.
TRUDY: My favourite colour.
CLIO: What, water sports?
TRUDY: I love anything to do with water. *(Spins into* CLIO*'s arms, bound by the hankies.)*
CLIO: Not this type, surely? Even I can't cope with yellow ankies babe.
TRUDY: You're frightening me. *(Pulls away, and the hankies fall to the floor.)*
CLIO: So name your game. What's your fantasy? Lighten up.
This rest of the scene is acted in physical theatre style.
TRUDY smiles. She does a cart-wheel.
CLIO: Oh no, none of that fancy stuff.
TRUDY continues to act physical., farcically, egging CLIO on. She stands upright all of a sudden and pushes her chest out. She starts beating on her chest.
TRUDY: *(Tarzan call)* Me Tarzan.
CLIO: *(with surprise)* Me Jane, be-ave.
TRUDY: Why not?
They act out a short Tarzan-Jane skit. CLIO breaks the fun.
CLIO: I'm Samson and you're Delilah.
They act a short Samson and Delilah skit. TRUDY breaks the fun.

TRUDY: I'm Romeo and you're Juliet.
CLIO: Slowly and wise, they stumble who run fast.
TRUDY: Thumbelina, all the better to fuck you with.
CLIO: *(gasps)*. I'm Sleeping Beauty
TRUDY: King Kong *(Walks in a King Kong style toward his Sleeping Beauty.)*
CLIO: *(screams)* Take me, take me, take me, I'm Alice in Wonderland. *(Moves in slow motion, showing her delight at seeing* TRUDY, *exuding sexuality. She gently takes her hand, hair, and reacts with delight.* TRUDY *begins to feel awkward from the attention.)*
TRUDY: I'm Tom
CLIO: I'm Jerry
They take turns to act out Tom and Jerry. They play with the whip, sexualizing, using it as their tail, snatching the whip off each other. CLIO is excited and gets carried away as Tom. TRUDY becomes excited too as Jerry, she stands up on two legs and roars like a lion. CLIO picks up the whip and acts as a ring leader. They act out this scene. TRUDY grabs hold of the whip and begins to crack it. She becomes intoxicated by its power. They pull the whip from each other, cracking the floor with it. CLIO remains sexual in her whipping style, while TRUDY becomes excited, dangerous, out of control, unsafe, going beyond boundaries. She begins to crack the whip at CLIO and becomes more and more excited and carried away.
CLIO: Stop!
Instant blackout (WSD 88-90).

The fluidity with which roles change undercuts the persistence of the active/passive complex in fantasy; the roles make free with cultural icons. However, the scene really gains momentum around the phallic whip. The key change is that Trudy is the one who is 'out of control', 'intoxicated', and 'carried away'. It is as if Trudy has connected finally with her own desire. This surfeit of desire comes once the repression caused by the racial complex is overcome, when she 'lightens up'. Mason-John's anarchic conception of sexual desire, as some how beyond ideology, produces a blackout which the lesbian spectator can only be unsettled by.

In psychoanalysis, fantasy is clearly always already public even if it disavows the public in articulating itself as personal. However, this simple 'lightening up' of the racial and social complex into an untainted domain of sexual desire is what makes Mason-John's dramatic *mise-en-scene*, her staging of desire, ultimately unconvincing both as Black and as lesbian. It is only the excess of the questions that swirl in the mind of the spectator in that final moment of sexual excitement that allow the possibilities of radical sexual desire to liberate themselves in the space of the blackout, for the spectator.

Works cited

Ahmad, Rukshana, *We Sinful Women: Contemporary Urdu Feminist Poetry*, London: The Women's Press, 1991.
Califia, Pat, "Feminism and Sadomasochism," *Heresies* Vol 3, No. 4, 1981.
Cowie, Elizabeth, "Fantasia" *The Woman in Question m/f,* eds. Parveen Adams and Elizabeth Cowie, Cambridge: Massachusetts: MIT Press, 1990.
Lorde, Audre, *Zami: A New Spelling Of My Name A Biomythography,* New York: Crossing Press, 1982.
Mason-John, Valerie (with Ann Khambatta), *Lesbians Talking: Making Black Waves*, London: Scarlet Press, 1993.
—. *Talking Black: Lesbians of African and Asian Descent Speak Out*, London: Cassell, 1994.
—. *Brown Girl in the Ring*, London: Get a Grip Publishers, 1999
—. *Borrowed Body,* London: Serpent's Tail, 2005.
—. *Detox Your Heart,* Birmingham: Windhorse Publications, 2006.
—. *You Get Me,* Unpublished.
—. *The Adventures of Snow Black and Rose Red,* Unpublished.
—. *The Totz,* Unpublished.

Thanks to Valerie Mason-John for sharing with us her unpublished play manuscripts.

CHAPTER FIFTEEN

IMPERMANENCE AND DISPLACEMENT IN
WELDON RISING, THE STRIP AND *NEVER LAND*
BY PHYLLIS NAGY

KATHY MCKEAN

Synopsis

'We're so close to the edge, we can't even see it coming'

In *Weldon Rising* (Nagy 1998a), *The Strip* (Nagy 1998a), and *Never Land* (Nagy 1998b), impermanence and displacement become metaphors for the inability of societies and individuals to adjust to the fluidity of the identities they must encompass. Nagy examines questions of metaphysics, asking what is due to humankind from individuals, and whether social and political connections increase that responsibility. Phyllis Nagy's exploration of gay and lesbian identities in *Weldon Rising* reveals how divisions heighten when otherness forces increased political awareness and accountability. In *The Strip*, ignorance of where one stands in relation to individual, international and historical identities dooms one to darkness and repetition. *Never Land* shows Henri Joubert constantly striving to be consigned an identity other than that naturally prescribed for him. Henri is a Frenchman 'passing' as English and his inflexibility on matters of identity reflect the problems of binaries in sexuality and the refusal to embrace anything other than what we are, or pretend to be. The intransigence on matters of identity found in the plays' characters reveals the consequences of isolation, and need for imagination, in the search for authenticity in life and in self.

*****

If I were to name my recurring themes they would be identity, in terms of the politics of identity, social and economic and racial, and the way in

which a lack of identity in any of these areas leads to disaster. (Nagy
1999a: 11)

> Just now everybody wants to talk about identity. As a keyword in
> contemporary politics it has taken on so many different connotations that
> sometimes it is obvious that people are not even talking about the same
> thing. One thing at least is clear – identity only becomes an issue when it
> is in crisis, when something assumed to be fixed, coherent and stable is
> displaced by the experience of doubt and uncertainty. From this angle, the
> eagerness to talk about identity is symptomatic of the postmodern
> predicament of contemporary politics. (Mercer 1990: 43)

Phyllis Nagy's exploration of identities reflects her own fluidity of
movement between Britain and the United States. Following an exchange
between New York Dramatists and the Royal Court, Nagy moved to
London in the nineties, where many of her plays subsequently premiered.
Her work for the stage includes *Weldon Rising* (1992), *Butterfly Kiss*
(1994), *Trip's Cinch* (1994), *The Scarlet Letter* (1995), *Disappeared*
(1995), *The Strip* (1995), *Never Land* (1998) and *The Talented Mr Ripley*
(1999). She is a playwright, screenwriter and director whose move to Los
Angeles in 2005 coincided with the release of her first feature film, *Mrs
Harris*, which premiered at the Toronto Film Festival. Whilst living in
London, Nagy observed: "people are very afraid of losing literal identity.
Me, I've never had that fear because I've always lived elsewhere from
where I come from, and I've always been interested in living elsewhere
and losing identity to a certain extent, and then replacing it with another
identity, or not. I'll always be American. And yet I'm not American,
anymore. And that's the fluidity of identity."(Nagy 1999a: 29)

Weldon Rising

JAYE: What are you doing?
TILLY: Melting. Moulting. Something. (43)

Natty cannot tell anyone who he is in terms of his sexual identity,
so he is defenceless when attacked on those grounds. The Boy kills Jimmy
in an act of violence precipitated by Natty's self-hatred and fear. In
Weldon Rising, the weather takes over when the characters refuse to
acknowledge their social and moral obligations. Jaye and Tilly, a lesbian
couple who share the neighbourhood with transvestite hooker Marcel,
observe the event. They all make active choices not to help out of a sense
of self-preservation, just as Natty chooses to run. Jimmy returns to life,
providing the others with repeated chances to act differently, to be brave as

he is. The impermanence the killing accentuates for the survivors provides the opportunity for them to alter action and identity. The failure to be truthful about oneself results in a destructive displacement with repercussions beyond the individual.

Weldon Rising takes place in the West Village of New York City in the early nineties, a stronghold for the gay occupants representing a self-displacement of imagined community and safety. The shadowy, non-naturalistic landscape establishes a world where anything from beer to violence can materialise from thin air. The impermanence of this sanctuary forces the characters to rethink their position within the immediate environment and towards those who share it. The Boy accentuates the other characters' sense of impermanence by his ability to command the neighbourhood and displace its inhabitants. Natty literalises his homelessness by taking to the streets with all of his possessions in the wake of Jimmy's murder. Tilly's residual fear from the paralysis she experienced witnessing the killing manifests itself in a dread of leaving her apartment. The divisions between and within individuals undermine the idea of a community existing because of proximity of social or sexual identification. The instability reflects the social and moral collapse represented by and resulting from Jimmy's death, accentuating a lack of conviction in the characters themselves.

The characters erect boundaries for themselves and each other, which restrict physical and emotional movement and displace the idea of home. Jaye and Tilly choose to displace themselves within an enclave of men, but find behind the aspirational associations an impermanent assortment of residents including a middle class couple, a homophobic killer and a transvestite whore. The Boy claims the neighbourhood as his own through actions and words that parallel Marcel's resentment of any invasion of 'his' space. The Boy's decisive erosion of his place and presence in the world and Natty's move into his territory undermine Marcel's identity. The characters proceed to domesticate the outside world that has been the site of such terror for them. Jaye and Tilly break down social boundaries when they take to the streets with Natty, combining the domestic with the decadent by stealing to share. The characters establish a cautious community evident in the moment when Natty collapses and Marcel calls on the girls to help him. Since the characters' world is impermanent, actions become important in establishing a kind of home in each other.

The characters express a desire to travel as a means of escape, which they only achieve by facing the truth about themselves and changing it. Jimmy and Natty never travel anywhere and suffer attack in their home environment, undermining the notion that it is safe to stay still. Tilly and Jaye try to shield themselves by staying indoors but have to embrace risk to experience life. Marcel as a reflection of his environment moves from lying face down in garbage to flying in a consuming light. Within an environment of instability, the notion that things will be different elsewhere predicates the desire for escape. Natty articulates the idea of being someone or something different in a different place, seeing possibilities in postcards. Jimmy gives him another opportunity to be brave in a different time that he again runs from, forcing him to see the lie of his imagining. Natty removes the postcards from the mirror, simultaneously tearing up his fantasies and confronting the true image they obstructed:

> NATTY: (*a great realization*) Something's busting up. I'm... imploding. A fluorescent bulb I am a bulb a light a sickness an arrested development an ember the world in my pocket and and and I WANT HIM BACK I WANT A CHANCE TO NOT DIE IN THIS HEAT I WANT I WANT –
> (42)

Natty sees the light he has been hiding in himself, surrounded by the low-wattage darkness in which he works. The characters' internal and external homophobia renders them invisible and subsequently impermanent in terms of what their sexual identity means for themselves and others. Jaye describes how she always hears the word "pouf" when it is spoken, so in the moment it is uttered by the Boy she is interpellated into his system of meaning. At the beginning of the play, Natty's moral and political impermanence finds expression in his physical diminishment. Marcel wants to choose his own definition and objects to Jaye's assignment of a male pronoun he has already applied to himself. He resents his place within a frame of reference he aspires to operate outside, yet ultimately finds he cannot. Marcel's identity depends largely on a readability that alienates him from self and society, yet visibility displaces him. When the Boy's invasion forces Marcel to see himself as he appears to others he tries to make himself invisible. The characters' inability to reconcile the divisions within themselves accentuates the divisions within any community that may exist.

Marcel's displacement is a post-modern impermanence: what he reflects in others and projects of his self do not correlate (Nagy 1997: 25). By speaking in the third person, Marcel articulates the Lacanian gap between spoken and speaking subject and emphasizes the lack of unity in poststructuralist subjectivity. His speech comprises a fractured assortment of references from popular culture and, in striving to be something other than he is, he negates himself. Marcel's profession is timeless and his worldliness gives him otherworldliness, which at times provides voice and insight into social truths. He is the centre of his world but he is at the centre of the broader world too, its perpetrator and its product. Marcel is the reflection of his environment and he predicts the future for the unseen world of the play. His exit thus parallels both his wider and immediate situations: he explodes in the heat of society's expiration and the light emanating from the other survivors illuminates him. Marcel displaces himself to find salvation and in travelling away from the world he represents, he affects a dual freedom.

Terms of sickness describe the idea of hiding aspects of identity; denial becomes a disease. Tilly, Natty, Jaye and Marcel all lie to protect themselves from the displacement and impermanence that are the paradoxical consequence of lying. To shield himself from life, Natty lies, which renders him vulnerable because he cannot say who he is. His lies displace Natty and it is subsequently easy for the Boy to supplant him, with repercussions for the wider environment. There is a simultaneous outing and closeting in the "Nobody knows" (34) syndrome with sexual politics formulating in response to the sexual identity assigned. Jimmy refuses to allow Natty the lie of his invisibility or the Boy's request for his own. In a play where love, self, and even death are impermanent, the importance of individual action and accountability increases. The murder compels the characters to face the truth about themselves and their actions by exposing the fabric of deceit:

> JIMMY: Hold me close and tell me who you are. Take me places and show me that we will be legion, marching in rows as far as the eye can see and we are all telling each other who we are. Over and over. (24)

Natty's union with Jaye and Tilly gives him the courage to leave which brings Jimmy back. The challenge presented by the Boy is that he looks at the other characters and in their refusal to let him see them they position themselves as victims. Marcel, Tilly and Jaye avert their eyes literally and symbolically, and even in the police station, Natty cannot look at the Boy to identify him. Jimmy alone holds the Boy's gaze in terms of objectifying him and denying his power both in life and in death. Jimmy appears poppered-up and dancing to the music of the past, evoking the optimism of a pre-AIDS era. When Tilly and Natty are ready to embrace life with Jimmy's courage, the disco music returns as a soundtrack to which they are reborn. The physical connections establish a permanence that takes place when the characters choose not to implode but to fight.

The Boy exists in the context of the play because of a self-imposed impermanence in the shame that exists in all of the survivors. Tilly and Jaye are defensive when interviewed by the police, identifying with homophobic victimisation and actively defining their relationship in an effort to legitimatise themselves. Lesbian identity is something they challenge – Tilly is uncomfortable with her prettiness and Jaye with her stereotypical viewing habits. Their physical relationship charts the political progression from passivity to active participation in the play. The couple go from not touching in public and negotiating sex in private, to a celebratory scene of union, expressing courage and love. Tilly and Natty exchange clothes in the street, shorn of possessions and shedding the shame of their former selves. They make themselves and their identity enduring by being brave and open about who they are.

In a world where community is lacking, communion exists when individuals acknowledge their responsibility to each other. Tilly and Jaye watch Jimmy's murder and do nothing to intervene, their fear for themselves replacing action. Their response is representative of a society that is not unable but unwilling to help, separating themselves from violence by attributing it to men. They initially watch Natty's demise through the same window, eating popcorn and drinking beer, before making the active choice to help rather than ignore him. The women are not naturally nurturing and there is a fear inherent in adopting a caring role towards men when it is not reciprocal. Nagy thus rejects the stereotypes of gender and of gendered behaviour in the interchange between men and women. *Weldon Rising* features characters that in a sense go through a process of politicisation, forced to confront the reality of their humanity. Whilst acknowledging the spectrum of identities within individuals and communities, Nagy suggests that if one is part of a minority then responsibility within and to that group is greater, because the need is greater also.

The disintegrating world of *Weldon Rising* demonstrates that courage and responsibility become moral imperatives when fear and apathy result in destruction. The action takes place against the backdrop of a mass exodus, accentuating the fear paralysing those who remain:

NATTY: I'm shivering. Sick. I'm paying for something.
JAYE: Bullshit. We never pay for anything. Be quiet. (42)

In this play, the characters do pay: they feel guilt so they make a change and take responsibility for what happens around them. Tilly and Jaye introduce themselves as liars but, disgusted by their meanness, find truth in each other. The scenes of sacrifice, resurrection and stigmata have obvious religious connotations, as does Natty's denial of Jimmy. Jimmy is able to return because he does not obey the limits imposed on him, or on his love for Natty. The actions of the characters have repercussions for other lives and other worlds.

The characters' displacement of their responsibility onto one another has a catastrophic effect on the environment, accelerating an actual global crisis. The sense of a wider dystopia manifests itself through climate change, accelerating violence, and societal breakdown, with the terrible heat carrying theological echoes of apocalypse, judgement, and hell. The weather is a manifestation of emotional extremities in a city where nothing is safe and everyone is criminal and victim concurrently. The population of an unseen world who, faced with environmental disaster, take to their cars, mirrors the denial of culpability that concerns the characters:

> TILLY: You ought to see it out there. It's wild. Not a soul in the streets. Supermarkets deserted. Restaurants abandoned. But the cars. Wow. More cars than I've seen packed together like... like butane lighters waiting to explode. (28)

The radio goes to static, cars combust, planes explode, buses melt, lights extinguish, bridges collapse and rivers dry. The weather takes over when people relinquish responsibility for their lives and the future of their fellow man. The car headlights seen throughout the play illustrate the impossibility and impracticality of an isolated existence.

The action of *Weldon Rising* parallels the plight of American civil rights movements through the charting and analysis of dissent. It considers the unity and divisions that permeate any group brought together by political alienation. Nagy explores the tension in the gay community in the aftermath of the AIDS crisis that necessitated and defined it. The image of blood pouring from Tilly's wounds acquires a heightened potency when viewed in this context. The only way to live is with a sense of moral responsibility beyond the self-preservation that motivates city-dwellers. The characters begin the play displaced from each other - Tilly and Jaye aspire to gay male privilege and Marcel resents the dykes' presence. Ultimately, they must acknowledge their differences so they can set them aside to save Natty and thus save themselves. Jimmy and Natty cut through the map at the end of the play and by leaving the world, they change it.

The Strip

CALVIN: Arlington, Virginia. President Kennedy's buried here. Would you like to see his grave?

AVA: Fuck off.

CALVIN: Respect history and it will respect you.

AVA: You're unbelievable. It's like you drop a coin in your mouth and some stupid saying comes out your ass. (202-3)

     The impermanence and displacement of *The Strip*'s characters lead them through literal and lateral journeys of discovery. The characters ostensibly divide into two national groups, but neither passports nor accents are reliable factors of determination. The action unfolds in one location representative of the palimpsestic present in place: in front of the Sphinx and pyramid reproducing the Luxor Hotel in Las Vegas on stage. These are the only pieces of set the play requires, with location directly and indirectly referenced by the characters as the narrative unfolds. There is thus an individual and collective exploration of the need to transcend lack of imagination in and through the action. *The Strip*'s structure parallels the play's progression through time, image, metaphor and emotion as layers add to the initial themes presented (Nagy 2005). The setting and structure reinforce the ideas of interconnection and fate examined from the opening tableau when everyone hears the phantom jackpot payout. The idea of palimpsestic spaces is present in the construction of character also, as individuals try to evade or erase the past. Ava, an American, borrows a map from an English stranger to try to navigate across America, frequently finding that cartography cannot contain where she is or where she wants to be. This provides a metaphor for America and other hybrid societies in which conventional systems of categorisation have failed to contain or describe individuals and communities, as well as the characters' failed expeditions. The characters all travel but never really move anywhere, their journey to recognition of this being the significant one.

     The impermanence, or fluidity, of aspects of identity is apparent in the play when characters attempt and sometimes affect the alteration of cultural, gender, and sexual signifiers with costume changes. By adopting stereotypes of English language and dress (indicating the preoccupation with class in identity perceptions), Loretta – a foreign fugitive – becomes Lady Marquette whose son will grow up to "be an Earl or something" (212). Otto and Calvin are the English abroad, one with an American passport and the other an American accent. Otto has dual nationality and a dual identity producing an impermanent sensibility. In being both, he is neither:

OTTO: Sometimes I'm one, sometimes the other. There is no harm in it.

And it's really none of your concern. (236)

Ernesto Laclau has described the modern world as a place with a plurality of centres rather than a clear core resulting in a 'dislocation' of individual identity (Laclau 1990: 40). In a world of cultural displacement, characters often define themselves in terms of what they are not. The presence of white supremacists serves as a reminder of the racist attitudes that continue to structure the way in which people view one another. Individuals refuse to embrace the 'other' even if the 'other' is themselves: Loretta, a Virginian, denying her Southern origin. The impermanence of national identity suggests a move towards a global identity yet economic dominance dictates the Anglo-American perimeters of internationalism also present in the 'new globalization' described by Stuart Hall.

Ava Coo's performance as a female impersonator simultaneously constructs and deconstructs notions of gender, as does Otto's recognition of her disguise. Failing to conform to conventional femininity in appearance or vocation, Ava identifies "that one way of getting on in the world is to become a drag queen" (Nagy 1995: 45). Ava fails to convince as Madonna, yet succeeds in impersonating her mother as both women swig regularly from bottles of liquor. Abandoned by Lester when she gave birth to a girl, Tina Coo attempts another level of female impersonation by creating an imaginary relationship with her husband, Mr. Marshall. Nagy juxtaposes the lack of nurturing in the females of the play with the maternal "coo" in these women's shared name. Suzy, like Jaye and Tilly in *Weldon Rising*, offers unpractised comfort when Tom breaks down, reluctantly patting his back. Through the macho posturing of Martin and Lester the play also critiques the performance of masculinity. The destruction inherent in prescribed gender roles is apparent when various pairings reproduce associated behaviours through the course of the play.

The fluidity of sexual identity is evident in the experimentation that takes place within and between the characters of *The Strip*. The opening tableau featuring Suzy's casual masturbation explodes conventions of female sexuality and establishes a liberality of attitude for the character. Suzy identifies as straight but falls in love with Kate, her lesbian stalker, who also pursues Ava with Suzy's ex-boyfriend Calvin. Lester's misreading of - and identification with - the codes of Martin's all-male bar exposes the machismo and misogyny inherent in the homoerotic environment. Lester's misreading of the gay bar, accentuating the traces of different cultural meanings in its signifiers, is one example of Homi Bhabha's 'Third Space' in a play where the hybridity of place and identity is continually referenced (Bhabha 1994). Martin kisses Lester and blames him for the subsequent physical deterioration that is really a manifestation of the prejudice he fosters within himself:

> MARTIN: Listen to me you animal. I come from a place that's full of
> light. A light that you have tried to obliterate through the ravages of scorn
> and ignorance. Look at me closely, Lester LOOK. [...] Do you see my
> defences, Lester? I have built an impenetrable core of darkness to replace
> all that lost bright light and believe me, it's wonderful to have you here
> like this, up-close and at my mercy. (230)

Martin and Lester forge identities based on their resistance to the
difference the other represents, ultimately finding those exclusions at their
core. Sexual impermanence works as a metaphor for how open the
characters are to change, responsibility, and courage in their lives and
loves.

Las Vegas is a modern temple of irresponsibility characterised by
a mantra placing action outside time and conscience: *what happens in
Vegas stays in Vegas*. In the world of *The Strip*, where everything is
connected, everyone is responsible – and at times held accountable – for
their acts of cowardice and courage. When Martin confronts Lester about
his homophobia, he exposes the lie of Lester's claim to have "DONE
NOTHING" (230). Lester presses a button and people die yet the
fingerprints found at the crime scene do not belong to him since he has
changed his name and assumed another identity. The defining moment of
his life becomes one he is in one sense displaced from though neither this
nor his ignorance absolve him. The characters ignore the impact of their
actions on one another and have to see themselves as they are before they
can accept responsibility.

Las Vegas is a symbol of existence, a time and place of
reproduction where chance and risk are material terms. The faced of the
Luxor represents a double displacement symbolising both ancient
civilization and postmodern kitsch, capturing a hybridity further layered by
the theatrical environment itself. The sphinx and pyramid acquire an
impermanent significance when their origin is ignored in a world where
symbols of love are counterfeit. The pawnshop that Otto owns and
employs Tom then Lester to run is testament to the hollow and temporary
nature of modern aspiration. Loretta believes in her belief, the talking
clock and in fame as an end in itself, just as a passport is a symbol of
glamour for Ava. Calvin understands the significance of history but
abandons this interest at the altar of a big jackpot win. The gambling
metaphor that aurally echoes throughout the action renders the distinction
between winning and losing in life problematic (Nagy 1999b: 132). Otto
demonstrates the impermanence of the characters' material motivation by

splitting the pyramid – and history – apart to reveal the triviality of their aspirations. Vegas is a place where the past is copied but unexamined is empty, a vessel the characters invest with meaning for want of truth.

The action takes place when coincidence is commonplace and the lead up to the eclipse heightens everything. Everyone wants someone to take care of them and they allow Otto to dictate the course of their lives because it provides a sense of purpose. When Otto loses Loretta at the end of the first act and releases a cry of sorrow, the responses of the other characters sever but simultaneously reinforce human and spiritual connections. The individuals collectively look up in search of answers to questions they have yet to understand the need to formulate. Religious iconography permeates image and language, though the characters displace its meaning with faith in horoscopes, telepathy, Ouija boards, Oprah and Amish "voodoo hoodoo crap" (202). Circumstances challenge convictions as Suzy's predictions become accurate, revealing that one customer's future is that he has none. The Courts of Justice are closed and deserted, and trains shake the ground underfoot as Tom and Loretta wander around in the circles dictated by a world in which safety and justice are "mutually whaddyacallit whatever" (237). *The Strip* considers characters living without faith or feeling, and the fear that is both motivation and repercussion.

The Strip considers the nature of love and loss in a world where Otto's flowers can extinguish the eternal flame but fail to light a fire in Loretta's heart. Obsessive love is everywhere: Kate stalks Ava and Suzy, and the latter reciprocates; Calvin stalks Ava; Tom and Lester fall in masochistic thrall to Martin. Otto is a god-like figure who wants his love returned so when his heart is broken his world – the play's world – temporarily falls apart. Love and the loss of love can displace the self, but love itself is impermanent in its tangible and intangible forms:

> OTTO: [I]f one has left behind the object of one's desire, if the love one harbours is no longer in sight, one doesn't really know if the love is destroyed. (256)

Kate and Suzy reject and fall in love with one another without meeting, before chance or destiny unites them. The question of how and when love exists finds an answer only in the moment asked.

The scenes of *The Strip* begin and end in overlap, representing another level of connection in a play of spherical motion. The disparate individuals and locations connect literally in their stage unity and laterally through the play's narrative. Ava auditions for her mother's boss for a job at the hotel where Tina works; travelling towards the family she is anxious to escape. Accompanying her on her journey are Calvin and Kate, who is obsessed with Calvin's ex Suzy who lives with his brother Martin who travels to Vegas with Ava's father, whom Kate is trying to find. The fractured nature of Ava's existence permeates her personal and professional life though she finds new talent and romance by following a seemingly pre-destined path. Tina cannot recognise her own nor her daughter's voice yet they communicate on a disconnected telephone symbolic of their fractured yet unavoidable bond.

Tina has a curiosity about the metaphysics of existence and tells the most lies because she recognises the most truth, including her abandonment by husband and daughter. Tina acknowledges the destructive pattern of Ava's lack of interest in her own history that parallels one of the wider concerns of the play:

> AVA: God forgive me and I don't know why I love you Ma. I love you and I don't know where I'm going next and I don't give a shit about some drunk daddy I never met and I sure as fuck don't know how you know where I am but I wish you would just send me some money and call it a day. (219)

Just as ties to the past occupy the present, Tina and Ava cannot sever the link they share, though they rarely listen to each other. When Tina drops the Dictaphone into which she speaks to Ava into a bucket of water, her daughter starts to drown. Ava must acknowledge the connection with her mother and with history if she is to survive in the present.

On one level, the play follows a teleological path of final cause and purpose in which Otto Mink is the prime mover. Martin produces beer from thin air, Otto a contract, and a mobile phone from Baby Ray's discarded Ku Klux Klan robe. Globalism has been described as a teleological doctrine of historical inevitability advancing the tenets of US capitalism through mass production, communication and consumption (Ferguson 1992: 87) evident in Otto's "I've got what you want" pitch (263). Destiny may be predetermined but the characters make active choices to follow certain paths, their fate decided by the responsibility that they assume which begins with willingness to question:

> TINA: [W]ell, there may be a reason for everything, but I can't figure out a reason for anything. I think that's why we have philosophers, to figure out those reasons. But I have noticed that most philosophers tend to be French or German, and not American [...] So if we don't get philosophers here, I wonder if that means we're doomed never to think of the right answers for why stuff happens. (245)

The individual choices the characters make can and do disrupt the cyclical movement of persons and events.

The permanent presence of the sphinx and pyramid onstage references the fact that the characters are at all times living in and with history. The propositions of time and place become confused by and for the characters who repeat the cycles they ignore:

> TOM: Suzy. We went someplace, didn't we?
> SUZY: We went back. Or forwards. I'm not sure. (262)

This connection between 'where' and 'when' echoes the way the passing of time was marked prior to modernity's realignment of the way space, place and time were defined (Giddens 1990). The pairs that emerge from the blackout are mixed up but all connected to one another in some way. During the blackout, the music that begins to play is 'Go West', referencing the frontier mentality of the early American settlers whose reproduction village Calvin and Ava visit on their road trip (262). Both the settlement with its replica Native Americans blistering in the sun and the sentiment of the song indicate the colonial legacy of the movement that turned 'space' into 'place'. The first image to appear is of a mother and a child, again indicating the cyclical course of history. Though Tina is not the mother of Baby Ray, she accepts the burden of him, unaware she holds her daughter's half-brother. Tina's earlier monologue intersects with Ava and Calvin's dialogue about the significance of history, and makes the connection between personal and political legacies. When Otto splits history apart, he exposes the fragile constructs that replace attempts to acknowledge and understand it, but also opens up the possibility for a new beginning.

Baby Ray's cry at the end of *The Strip* is a demand for difference and an awakening that all the characters hear. Cycles structure the play – of images, relationships, journeys, responsibilities, and of opportunities. The crying is a call for change that in itself embodies a change for a group who at the play's opening heard the bells of a casino win. The cry is an act of rebellion against the values the characters represent, and their subsequent displacement. It is a reminder of the positive possibilities of globalism if used as a term "for values which treat global issues as a matter of personal and collective responsibility" (Albrow 1994: 4). The characters displace themselves within their own lives by displacing themselves from history through deliberate ignorance. Baby Ray's rage at once parallels and undermines Ava's performance of frustration on stage from miming 'Rescue Me' to screaming "MY GENERATION" (260). The first utterance from the mute baby broke Tom's pattern of behaviour with

Martin, when he finds the courage to leave him. The possibilities that Tina offers Baby Ray are those that he rejects and he thus provides an alternative to the cycle the others may otherwise propagate.

Never Land

> HENRI: [...] I refuse to leave the dock and I conjure an act of monumental will to banish expel expunge the depressive stench of my father the fisherman's trade and I the unmoved fool instead exchange the stench of one trade for the other and am I any the sweeter any the wiser I am. Not. I am. Sorry. To disappoint you. Henri. We are. Sorry. To miscalculate. Our. Your. Position. On the docks. And so what else to do what else to move towards but the natural course of events? (67)

A lack of authenticity of self leads to an impermanence of identity which results in a refusal of the Other. In *Never Land*, Henri's actions constitute a peculiar embrace of the other to the extent that he obliterates the self, exchanging the stench of Frenchness for Englishness to the exclusion of a national identity that is not an absolute. Henri's extreme position and his neurotic refusal of his own past reflect the identity crisis of many individuals. *Never Land* explores how a lack of fluidity of national identity leads to destruction, as do problems of sexual identity in *Weldon Rising* and *The Strip*. Henri speaks perfect English with an RP accent that displaces him from his French origin and identity. Anne's relationship with Henri displaces her from other ideas of happiness when her loyalty proves as strong as his love for her. The play takes place on a number of levels, with the characters' interior lives creating an otherworldly existence in parallel to the story. Working within 'well-made-play' conventions, Nagy experiments with ideas around the impermanent nature of time. Each of the three acts unfolds from the perspective of a different member of the Joubert family, undermining notions of a single shared experience. Nagy continues her exploration of the spectrum between isolation and community through the pathos of living in a familial community striving for a group identity whilst experiencing life as an individual. Henri renders the Jouberts' existence impermanent in his quest for an English identity that can never be realised.

Henri's England exists only as an expression of everything his idea of France is not: an other for his otherness. He is haunted throughout by a fear of the "menace" (42), resisting and 'othering' difference in his attempts to establish an integrity of identity, before coming to the inevitable recognition of the Other as part of the self. In associating everything negative with France, Henri negates himself, throwing away his language and his identity in pursing his obsession:

> HENRI: English is the language of love.
> ANNE: FRENCH IS THE LANGUAGE OF LOVE YOU ASS.
> HENRI: IT IS NOT.
> ANNE: IT IS FUCKING SO.
> HENRI: IT'S NOT IT'S NOT IT... IS... NOT... ANYTHING.
> NOTHING. FRENCH IS NOTHING NOTHING.
> *A very awkward silence.* HENRI *slumps down onto the floor and sits in
> the midst of a pile of trash.* (39)

The play opens with Elisabeth performing a cleansing ritual to the strains of a Purcell anthem. She assigns French place names to different parts of her body and scrubs herself, simultaneously locating and displacing these aspects of her identity. Anne has no desire to leave France – nor for much of anything anymore – but having forgotten her native language she recognises England as an alternative to the limbo of their current life. She makes suits for Henri in an English style, her uncertainty of this distinction accentuating the mutability and performativity of how to ascribe national identity. Judith Butler's Foucauldian exploration of gender performance may here be applied to nationality. Like the drag of Marcel in *Weldon Rising* and Ava Coo in *The Strip*, Henri's performance of national identity appropriates a stereotypical English identity in *"a kind of imitation for which there is no original".* (Butler 1991:21)

The "imagined community" (Anderson 1983) that is England to Henri is a place without accents or diversity and in this respect matches the England the Caton-Smiths create for and around themselves. They lack imagination, avoiding the French in France and the English in England and letting class distinctions dictate their communication with everyone, including each other. At no point do we hear the Caton-Smiths speak French, indicative of the "perceived cultural value" in their attitude towards the language (Godiwala 2007). Anne exposes the casual racism characterising middle-class prejudice and fear when she goads Heather into attacking the French. The ease with which Heather slips into offering clichéd theories of foreignness echoes Michael's more virulent language of hate. Michael's arrival prompts further revelations as the characters immediately go on the defensive in their racist assumption that he is a criminal because he is black. Elisabeth herself plays on this cliché in her dichotomous casting of Michael as her possible salvation, an angel of death or delivery. The *Fawlty Towers* sketch performed within the play accentuates the reliance on national stereotypes in contemporary humour in a comedy where failures of communication have consequences other than laughter.

Michael and Elisabeth find eroticism in one another's difference, each requesting the other speak in a language symbolic of an identity that displaces them. In his speech about his homeland, Michael repeats the word "me", simultaneously declaring his right to and the impossibility of autonomy for a black man in America (33). The abbreviation Elisabeth makes of his name is synonymous with American mainstream culture, just as the Jouberts' names reference another doomed English family. There is a displacement in language evident in the French lesson where Michael discovers not just French but English when Elisabeth interrogates his word choices. Elisabeth, a native French speaker, appeals for help from Michael in the language of English textbook French role-play. Anne adopts the language of social convention when she meets Mickey, and he responds by dropping his broken bottle and attitude to return the courtesy. Elisabeth describes the Caton-Smiths as arseholes and Heather later drops to her knees to release a meaningless flow culminating in a repetition of "oursouls" (44). The instability of language accentuates a fluidity of meaning through the uncertainty inherent and available in words.

A displacement occurs in the Caton-Smiths refusal to accept responsibility for their treatment of Henri, present in Henri's discussion with Albert about destiny and will. Heather and Nicholas reveal a lack of imagination and subsequently compassion in their dismissal of the Jouberts' acts of courage and determination. Henri conspires with Albert to turn wine into tea, a game that Heather rejects with her disruptive intrusion into the male domain. Nicholas displaces his responsibility by sending Heather to dismiss Henri, and she blames their accountant, Albert, and a French employment system she doesn't understand. Nicholas admits his culpability when Anne enables him to empathise with Henri, in part through his shared desire for her beauty. She renders him vulnerable by leading him through a variety of charades until Nick breaks down in recognition of the despair in his own existence. In asking the Caton-Smiths to imagine other lives with them, the Jouberts provoke an acknowledgement of the casual destruction they have effected on the family's lives.

In *Never Land*, relationships based on manipulation prove fragile and honesty the anchor that holds the heart. Michael and Elisabeth establish inconstancy between them in the lies they tell each other, and subsequently in the possibility for love. Michael refuses Elisabeth's claim to an existence separate to the change the intrusion of other people induces. Elisabeth's chance for escape through a relationship with Michael is impossible in a world where - literally or metaphorically – she cannot connect with him. Michael proves to be a mistake rather than a possibility since he lacks the kindness of her parents to which Elisabeth aspires. There is kindness also in Albert's relationship with Henri, endeavouring to protect his friend from the "disease" he perceives in him (63). Heather and Nick's relationship is another built on impermanence since they individually and collectively perform identities seeking the other's approval. An absolute understanding and acceptance of each other's virtues and flaws is finally the foundation of the Jouberts' relationship.

When Elisabeth instructs Henri to imagine that they three alone exist in the world there are a number of levels on which this is a statement of truth. The action occurs in the Jouberts' home – which, in terms of the set, also encompasses the perfume factory in act two – and it is from each other they fail to escape. The Jouberts are trapped in a cage of their own creation and there are good and bad aspects to their ties of loyalty and love. Henri looks always to outside factors when the protection necessary is from the menace inside himself and his family. There is nothing sentimental in Nagy's presentation of a failing marriage and frustrated offspring and the family thwart their own and conventional expectations. Anne drinks but holds the family together and her treatment of Henri and Elisabeth is both brutal and protective. The Joubert family represents an alternative kind of belonging rooted in people rather than place.

The displacement that love embodies is a transcendent entity that can transform an act of despair into one of optimism. Anne and Henri both describe their failed attempts to escape one another to avoid inevitable destruction. It is the bond that prevents them leaving that ultimately provides their escape, not from but through each other:

> ANNE: [I]t's a funny thing, this inability of mine to forget a simple act of kindness. [...] In that instant I know Henri is the only man who will hoist the burden of me upon his shoulders and run with me all the way to the end. And that is worth... my fidelity. My complicity. In each of his endeavours. Isn't it? (100-1)

Anne recognises Henri as the killer in her nightmare so she denies him his desire for her until their first and final shared kiss in the play. *Never Land* concludes in a moment of perfect communion between them, Anne providing Henri with the courage not to waver from their united purpose.

The three-act structure becomes a temporal form involving time and space travel in a manner reflective of the interior lives of the characters. Elisabeth's displacement is characterised by her longing for a holy vision that captures a place outside the time that ages and wearies her.

Since act one is told from her perspective, time stops for the other characters at the moments it stops symbolically for Elisabeth. At the critical instants when she may find possible redemption or destruction time freezes as Elisabeth searches for her vision and her release. She can displace herself from time without freezing it also, as when Michael brutally rejects her and she retreats into herself. The act ends with her playing funeral music for the queen she no longer expects to see, letting loose a scream whose meaning resonates with the despair of Baby Ray. The second act belongs to Henri and he too freezes time, though Anne in the third act does not, her dreams forming a temporal loop of inevitability and knowledge. In another sense, Anne freezes time in the final scene in her (re)creation of a moment of happiness and possibility for herself and her husband. The handling of time in *Never Land* heightens the various levels of reality on which the action takes place.

Anne and Elisabeth reconcile themselves to their fate and in so doing choose it, pursuing death as the only progression available to them. In the moment this happens, they commune with each other to the exclusion of Michael as in a sense they are already beyond the world of which he remains a part. When they are ready for Henri's return, the women summon him:

> ANNE: Hold tight. Hold steady, Elisabeth. It's time.
> EILISABETH: I am. Steady. I am. Tight.
> ANNE: Oh my my my – what exquisite motion. What clarity it brings.
> ELISABETH: I am. I am. IamIamIAMIAMI. AM.
> *And suddenly,* HENRI *enters. He's so soaked he looks as if he's not been out of water since birth. A silence, as he considers them and they him.*
> ANNE: We have no food, my love, and there's no hint of any to come. But we are moving. Listen. Listen to the waves. (94)

Elisabeth rejects Henri's protestations and leads him outside with her, wrapping his fingers around the barrel of the gun. Anne comforts Henri as they dance with the gun between them before compelling him to seize the opportunity to fire at her.

Elisabeth envisages the Jouberts' end at the beginning of the play and language and action evoke the idea of destiny throughout. The Caton-Smiths enter with an open umbrella dripping rain into the Jouberts' home and sabotaging Henri's dreams of a perfect meeting. Elisabeth suggests Mickey shoot her parents and their guests and, with Anne, later unsettles him with talk of omens. Henri's wilful blindness to the nature of the "menace" becomes literal when sight – and the Caton-Smiths – fails him.

Elisabeth reconciles Henri to the inevitability of their fate and consoles
him with the thought that this is the only escape she desires. Finally, it is
less important where the family are at the point when they are facing death
than their ability to travel. In her final scene with Henri, Elisabeth
envisages the circumstances in which others will find their bodies,
establishing another future from which time will displace them, and
another world that gives credence to the otherworldly.

   The otherworldly development that occurs alongside the
sequential action of the play introduces the idea of metaphorical time and
place. There is displacement in the characters' worlds of visions,
nightmares and dreams that achieves transcendence before the Jouberts
embrace it through death. The killings are therefore not murders nor
suicides but the only way in which the characters can move forward in
terms of meaningful existence. The family's situation is metaphorically
realised in set and setting, the family home on an isolated hill that is
disintegrating. Elisabeth's scream precipitates the rainfall that grows
heavier and more erosive until the beginning of the final scene of the play.
The flood imagery first evoked by Michael carries with it ideas of
punishment and forgiveness, and of new births and new nations also
present in the family's sacrifice. Like Natty in *Weldon Rising*, the Jouberts
do not necessarily travel to a divine place, but do move somewhere, their
legacy allowing the possibility of progression in the world they leave
behind (Nagy 1994).

   Never Land explores the need for and the difficulties of the
sacrifice of individual national identity to facilitate a broader European or
global identity:

> What *Never Land* was about for me was the impossibility but the great
> necessity for the European community. We need to have it in order for us
> to move onto something else, to a better identity. (Nagy 1999a: 29)

   This chimes with Stuart Hall's description of cultural identity as
a position of 'becoming'. The Jouberts' sacrifice is for and of one another
but also for a world as it could or should exist. Henri's view of national
identity is at once narrow and imaginative, yet in its literal confines
impossible to sustain. His existence captures the irreconcilability of a
fluidity of identity with an uncertainty of identity when only the former
can survive. *Never Land* opens with an attempt to purge a literal
understanding of identity and ends with a scene that displaces it.

Conclusion

Phyllis makes us go to a place emotionally that is deeply uncomfortable. If you're brave enough to go there the reward is extraordinary. If you are an emotional or moral coward, being asked to go there is an act of assault. (Kenyon 2006)

The acts of transcendence that occur within the plays dislocate the audience by offering them an ephemeral experience with which they may – or may not - choose to engage. The problems inherent in a limited or literal understanding of one's own or others' identities lead to destruction; the acknowledgement of division within local and global communities is as important as recognition of the divisions within oneself. Notions of impermanence become political concepts in Nagy's plays, since what is not fixed can change (Greig 1999: 66). The characters evolve from a narrow understanding of identity to embrace the responsibilities such enlightenment bestows. Phyllis Nagy reworks and appropriates the religious language and resonance of visions, light and darkness and life after death to explore the crisis of identity in the modern age. The last word of *Never Land* is 'opportunity', of *The Strip*, 'possibilities'; Natty Weldon instructs Jimmy, 'Lift me', rising to meet his lover risen from the dead. The apocalyptic resonances in the endings of these plays reflect the disintegration of the present and offer an alternative way to begin.

Works cited

Albrow, Martin, *Globalization: Myths and Realities: Inaugural Lecture*, London: Roehampton Institute, 1994.

Anderson, Benedict, *Imagined Communities: Reflections on the Origin and Spread of Nationalism,* London: Verso, 1983.

Aston, Elaine, *Feminist views on the English stage: Women playwrights, 1990-2000,* Cambridge: Cambridge University Press, 2003.

Baum, Rob, 'Oedipus' Body & the Riddle of the Sphinx', *Journal of Dramatic Theory and Criticism*, **21** (1), 2006. pp. 45-56.

Bhabha, Homi, 'The Third Space: Interview with Homi Bhabha', in Jonathan Rutherford, (ed) *Identity: Community, Culture, Difference*, London: Lawrence & Wishart, 1990, pp. 207-221.

—. *Location of Culture*. London: Routledge, 1994.

Butler, Judith, *Gender Trouble: Feminism and the subversion of identity,* London: Routledge, 1989.

—. 'Imitation and Gender Insubordination', in Diana Fuss (ed) *inside / out: Lesbian Theories, Gay Theories,* New York: Routledge, 1991, pp.

13-31. 1993.
—. *Bodies that Matter*, London: Routledge, 1991.
Coveney, Michael, 'Introduction', in Phyllis Nagy, *Plays: One*, London: Methuen, 1998. pp. xi- xvi.
Edgar, Andrew and Peter Sedgwick, (eds),. *Key Concepts in Cultural Theory*, London: Routledge, 1999.
Edgar, David, (ed), *State of Play: Playwrights on Playwriting*, London: Faber and Faber, 1999.
Ferguson, Marjorie, 'The Mythology about Globalization', *European Journal of Communication*, **7** (1), 1992. pp. 69-93.
Fuss, Diana, 'Inside / Out', In *inside / out: Lesbian Theories, Gay Theories*,. New York: Routledge, 1991. pp. 1-10.
Freeman, Sandra, *Putting Your Daughters on the Stage: Lesbian Theatre from the 1970s to the 1990*, London: Cassell, 1997.
Giddens, Anthony, *The Consequences of Modernity*, Cambridge: Polity Press, 1990.
Godiwala, Dimple, 'Postcolonial Desire: Mimicry, Hegemony, Hybridity', in Joel Kuortti and Jopi Nyman, (eds) *Reconstructing Hybridity: Post-Colonial Studies in Transition*. New York & Amsterdam: Rodopi, 2007.
Greig, David, 'Plays on Politics', in David Edgar, (ed) *State of Play: Playwrights on Playwriting*, London: Faber and Faber, 1999. pp. 66-9.
Hall, Stuart, 'Cultural Identity and Diaspora', in Jonathan Rutherford, (ed) *Identity: Community, Culture, Difference*, London: Lawrence & Wishart, 1990. pp. 222-37.
—. 'The local and the global: globalization and ethnicity', in Anthony D. King, (ed) *Culture Globalization and the World System: Contemporary Conditions for the Representation of Identity*. London: Macmillan, 1991, pp. 19-40.
Laclau, Ernesto, *New Reflections on the Revolution of Our Time*, London: Verso, 1990.
Mercer, Kobena, 'Welcome to the Jungle: Identity and Diversity in Postmodern Politics', in Jonathan Rutherford, (ed) *Identity: Community, Culture, Difference*, London: Lawrence & Wishart, 1990. pp. 43-71.
Nagy, Phyllis, 'Afterword' to *Weldon Rising*, in Annie Casteldine, (ed) *Plays by Women: Ten*. London: Methuen, 1994. pp. 144-5.
—. Playing with fire. Interview with Carole Woodis, *Diva*. February, 1995. pp. 44-5.
—. 'Phyllis Nagy', in Heidi Stephenson and Natasha Langridge, (eds), *Rage and Reason: Women Playwrights on Playwriting*, London:

Methuen Drama, 1997. pp. 19-28.

—.*Plays: One.* London: Methuen, 1998a.

—.*Never Land.* London: Methuen, 1998b.

—. 'An Expatriate Voice', *Plays*, **14** (5), 1999a..

—. 'Hold Your Nerve: Notes for a Young Playwright', in David Edgar, (ed) *State of Play.* London: Faber and Faber, 1999.

Nagy, Phyllis and Mel Kenyon, 1995. 'Provocations: Season of lad tidings', in Rutherford, Jonathan, (ed) *Identity: Community, Culture, Difference.* London: Lawrence & Wishart, 1990.

Weedon, Chris, *Identity and Culture: Narratives of Difference and Belonging.* Berkshire: Open University Press, 2004.

Werbner, Pnina and Tariq Modood, (eds), *Debating Cultural Hybridity: Multi-Cultural Identities and the Politics of Anti-Racism.* London: Zed Books, 1997.

Kathryn Woodward, (ed), *Identity and Difference.* London: Sage Publications, 1997.

Interviews

Kenyon, Mel, Interview with the author. 7 Dec 2006.

Nagy, Phyllis, Interview with the author. 13 Aug 2005.

Newspaper reviews

'Mel Kenyon and Phyllis Nagy attack the misogyny of male culture', *The Guardian.* 4 Dec 2000.

SECTION II:

QUEER TELEVISION

CHAPTER SIXTEEN

NON-HETEROSEXUAL CHARACTERS IN POST-WAR TELEVISION DRAMA: FROM COVERT IDENTITY AND STEREOTYPING, TOWARDS REFLEXIVITY AND SOCIAL CHANGE[14]

CHRISTOPHER PULLEN

Synopsis

This chapter explores the emergence of non-heterosexual characters within television drama, with a focus on gay male and lesbian representations - as there have been few bisexual and transgender roles. Tracing an historical emergence, this chapter explores the impact of defining moments in broadcast television, in conjunction with the agency of openly gay producers and writers. The political context of gay identity is prioritised here, as relevant to both audience identification and character production. This becomes a contentious issue in exploring the potential of mainstream broadcasters who employ the commodity of minority identity. Here transgressive agents are working within television production, against dominant ideas.

Introduction

Jack Babuscio (1976) records the insight of a thirty-eight year old man called Claude who consulted literature 'in the hope of finding some acceptable sense of self-as-homosexual' (p. 6):

---

[14] I would like to indicate that the archival work of Keith Howes (1993) and David Wyatt (2005) has been very helpful in the construction of this essay.

> The heterosexual inhabited a golden world from which I was forever
> excluded. I felt very much like an alien. It's rather like the title of that
> book, *Invisible Man*. That's how I felt, like an invisible man. (Babuscio
> 1988: 6)

Like the search for the homosexual self in literature, the quest to
find desirable representations of non-heterosexuals[15] in post war television
drama is a story of practical invisibility and active denial. Where such
'reflective' images are produced, they fail to connect to meaningful social
lives. From the emergence of covert and discontented characters in the
early post war period to the late 1960s, through to the appearance of
stereotypical types in the 1970s, to the progression of social types in the
1980s, and the spectacular event of *Queer as Folk* in the late 1990s, the
narrative of non-heterosexual characters in TV drama reveals invisibility,
stereotypical compression, political attempts at progressing identity forms,
and (notably) a lack of accommodation.

Despite resistance to the expression of gay identity, an
advancement to some degree has occurred. Evidence of this may be seen
in *When I'm 64* (BBC2 2005) written by Tony Grounds. This tells the
story of a retired bachelor school teacher, who (by chance) meets a
widowed taxi driver of a similar age, and they fall in love (despite the
disapproval of the driver's family). Here we are presented with the idea
that not only can older gay (or bisexual) men fall in love, but that such
love may possess tenderness and respect. This inverts stereotypical ideas
of gay male sexuality, usually placed at the periphery, and connected with
undesirable sexual acts, and explores the intimacy of same sex desire -
making it equivalent to heterosexual romance.

This essay explores a progression which might lead to the advent
of texts like *When I'm 64*. This involves the agency of inspiring
individuals, some well known such as Quentin Crisp, Russell T. Davies
and Sarah Waters, other less celebrated such as Tony Grounds and Johnny
Capps, and numerous scriptwriters and producers who remain nameless
yet have made important contributions. This essay largely tells the story
of these influential people, who have produced 'pro-gay' discourse within
television, and have engendered change. It also contextualises advances in
representational norms associated with homosexuals (and the larger arena
of non-heterosexual identity) within the following themes:

---

[15] The term 'non-heterosexual' has been employed to cover the diversity of sexual
identity. To examine the social potential of homosexual and transsexual lives see
the work of Weston (1997), Weeks et al (2000), and Kaeser and Gillespie (1999).

- The significance of early covert and discontented identity
- The defining, and spectacular moments in drama
- The progression of social types in soap opera
- The ambivalence of stereotypes in situation comedy
- Issues of quality in period adaptation

This essay progresses a discussion within these themes, but it does not necessarily reveal a distinct advancement. The thematic observations are traced within a history of television drama which documents both opportunities for change, and strategies of containment.
The narrative of non-heterosexuals in drama is not a gathering mass in coalescence (revealing change): rather it is the trajectory of fragmented components working in isolation (offering ideas of change). This centres on the significance of 'individual agents' who potentially offer 'self reflexive' (Giddens 1991) visions of homosexual identity: producers work in isolation and represent their personal ideas within their characters (Pullen 2005a, 2005b, 2006). However before we commence this journey, it is important to foreground the context of the 1939-45 world war in relation to changes in gender identity, and explore strategies used in the media to represent the homosexual.

Post war gender issues, continuing covert identity

The post war period offered the potential of reinventing gender identity. This was certainly true of the recontextualisation of women's roles within the war period. This may be seen in the significance of women involved in masculine roles (such as manufacturing munitions), and those active in the services themselves: this offered new scope for progressing the female role (see Kingsly Kent 1999). Similarly the war period brought together gay men who found not only companionship between themselves, but also some were afforded a strengthened sense of identity (see Berube 1990). Often gay men expressed their identity in the army, and among peers they found a sense of community. However after the war whilst the female role was (to a degree) recast, the role of the homosexual as 'outsider' remained largely unchanged. After the war, dominant society continued to label homosexuality as deviant, despite this period revealing the emergence of gay communities (in America).[16] Not

---

[16] This was largely stimulated by gay men and women finding a sense of identity within the war effort. This contributed to the construction of same sex

surprisingly post-war television continued to adopt representational strategies already established in film and theatre, which persistently rejected the potential of homosexual social lives.

Whilst film and theatre have different histories, and have been connected to varying theoretical insights (such as the connection of film to psychoanalysis, and the connection of drama to performativity), their influence informed expectation within television. Therefore Vito Russo's (1987) observation of polarised gay identities (such as the 'sissy' and 'dyke') in early Hollywood cinema, and John M Clum's (1992) exploration of the impact of stereotypical traits on gay identity within theatre, may be viewed as influential to expectations in television.

This provenance is not only connected to Hollywood's influence on gay character types (seen in Vito Russo's evaluation), but also to conditions in British theatre which contributed to the concealment of gay identity.   Restrictions in theatre executed by the Lord Chamberlain between 1737 and 1968, engendered the character of the homosexual to be practically invisible, often covert and essentially contorted. Through the necessity of playwrights having to avoid open depictions of homosexuality, the character types that were produced became recognised as outsiders, and veiled apparitions.

In this way whilst audiences were not provided with representations of homosexual social types, they were provided with evidence of covert homosexual types which became fixed to specific performative traits.   John M Clum (2000) points out that in order to replicate the homosexual identity, without verbal affirmation or physical juxtaposition, a repertoire of male homosexual stereotypes may be used. These include:

Effeminacy (mincing, limp wrists, lisping, flamboyant dress)

Sensitivity (moodiness, a devotion to his mother, a tendency to show emotions in an un-manly way)

Artistic talent or sensibility [an emblematic sign reinforcing the idea that gay men belong to distanced artistic worlds, rather than normative productive social worlds)]

---

communities in areas like San Francisco, where former servicemen (and women) set up new homes together (Berube, 1990).

Misogyny [this contextualised the perceived failure of gay men to
outgrow their bond with maternal figures, and become sexually
interested in females][17]

Pederasty (… this became the stereotypical formula for
homosexual relationships, with its connotations of arrested
development and pernicious influence) …

Isolation (the homosexual's fate, if he or she remained alive at
the final curtain) (Clum 200:77)

Through engagement with these traits or devices, playwrights
would construct a 'covert homosexual character' type, disconnected from
any idea of an 'open social homosexual' form. Consequently, through
presenting the homosexual character as a covert identity only visible by
reading the signs, a wholly un-natural spectre emerged, distanced from
realism. The homosexual character became a marginalized entity unable
to integrate or engage with realistic contexts. Evidence of this may be
seen in numerous plays where the homosexual character must die or is
punished, in service of returning the narrative to a normal world at the
closure of a text (see Clum 2000).

Therefore before the emergence of post war television, the
conditions were set which reinforced the rejection of a meaningful
homosexual social identity. Television continued traditions set in film and
theatre which dramatized and compressed homosexual character traits,
rendering these as marginal, and often disturbing.

Early TV and binary stereotypification

The suggestion and denial of gay social identity is an inherent
theme of early post war television leading up to the legalisation of male
homosexual activity in 1967. As John M Clum (2000) tells us 'by both
suggesting and denying the existence of homosexuals, the plays of this
period dramatise and maintain the closet' (71). This is particularly
apparent in plays which were adapted for television broadcast, which
continued to contextualise gay identity as covert, dangerous and 'other'.
Evidence of this may be seen in the numerous productions of *Rope* (Peter
Hamilton 1929), 'a psychological thriller about two Oxford graduates who
murder a fellow student' (Vahimagi 1996: 34), which possessed a

---

[17] This might be related to Freud's (1901) discussions on the 'Oedipus complex',
signalling a failure to achieve full psychological development.

subliminal reading of homosexual desire and satisfaction in the act of murder. Whilst Alfred Hitchcock's film version (1948) is more well known, and perhaps more readily discussed in homoerotic terms (Howes, 1993: 694), the television adaptations are noteworthy for their consistent presentation and reconfiguration of a veiled gay identity connected to murderous intent. Although the debut of the play on television was in 1939, there had been a number of adaptations after the war, broadcast in 1947, 1950, 1953 and 1957.[18] These appearances were emblematic of playwrights' continued 'concealment' of gay identity within television. At the same time this contextualised the 'covert' gay man as outcast, villain and monster.

The situation comedy *Hancock's Half Hour* (1954-59) also became emblematic of covert gay identity (albeit more humorously), in the tension provided with Tony Hancock sharing a dwelling with various males. Howes (1993) notes that the character of William Kerr was described (by Hancock) within the script as 'my best friend', 'spinster of this parish', 'my Filipino houseboy' and (for tax purposes) 'dependent relative' (334). In this way a homosexual tension was alluded to, fuelled not only by the iconic status of Tony Hancock as a tragi-comic unfulfilled character (not unlike that of the depiction of homosexuals at the time), but also in the comic schematics, including the depiction of two single adult males sharing a bedroom.

The motif of the early years of 'covert' male homosexual identity in television drama consequently oscillated between the depiction of extreme mental disturbance which would render the character dangerous, and the inference that gay males were benign: they could be comic, yet they were unfulfilled and peripheral. In this way the characterisation of gay males involved a locus trapped between 'binary stereotypes' (Hall 1997). This equated to depicting the gay male between the 'villain' and the 'sissy', with no room for progression. Should the gay male audience member fail to identify with one of the binary stereotypes by responding against it, and attempt to disprove this through behaviour modification, he ultimately conforms to the other: behave less like a sissy, and you become more villainous; behave less villainously, and you become more like a sissy.

---

[18] Noteworthy in these early versions is the participation of Dirk Bogarde (1947) and Peter Wingarde (1950), who would become known as gay iconic actors (Bogarde for his appearance in the film *Victim* – discussed later, and Wingarde as the sexually ambiguous character of Jason King in the television crime series of the same name which originated in *Department S*).

As the potential of gay life began to be explored from the late 1950s when the Wolfenden report was published, an increasing interest in gay sexuality developed. This advanced in the late 1960s when male homosexuality was decriminalised in England and Wales.[19] Increasingly at this time strategies of binary stereotypification would be employed in representing homosexuality. This would translate to defining binary oppositions polarising the homosexual between the idea of 'active, over masculinised and predatory', and of 'passive, effeminate and subjective'. Character representations began on the one hand to over articulate the idea of the homosexual as predator - someone who would be sexually dangerous, and on the other the idea of the homosexual as passive - someone who would possess sexual desire, but would lack agency. Consequently as the 1960s advanced, interest in representing a sexualised homosexual emerged, involving an increasing bias towards binary stereotypification. This would also remain an inherent quality within the defining moments of non-heterosexuals on television.

Defining moments: acceptance over equality

I would argue that the defining moments in television representation of non heterosexual characters commenced shortly after the legalisation of male homosexual acts with the broadcast of *Victim* (Basil Deardon, 1961) in 1968.[20] Later *The Naked Civil Servant* (ITV 1975) became an important defining text which revealed a new confidence in gay identity. The advent of AIDS stimulated a media advertising campaign (between 1986-8) which not only shocked British audiences, but also stimulated television dramas such as *Sweet as You Are* (BBC2 1988) (and soap operas) to deal with the issue, and more recently the broadcast of *Queer as Folk* (Channel 4 1999) became a media event which significantly influenced the emergence of new character types. These four events may be seen as the landmark moments on British television which influenced

---

[19] In 1967 sex was made legal between 'two men over 21 'in private', (i.e. no one else in the same house), if neither of them was in the Armed Forces or the Merchant Navy. Significantly this applied only to England and Wales.' (see Edwards 1994).

[20] *Victim* [was] transmitted on 'Rediffusion' 31.5.68 at 10.30 p.m. [and] 'Thames' 24.4.74 at 10.30 p.m.. (BFI 2001; ITC 2001). Rediffusion and Thames were regional commercial television broadcasting companies, who consecutively transmitted programming to the London area in the United Kingdom. The 1968 transmission is likely to be the first in the United Kingdom.

and altered strategies of representation surrounding homosexuals.[21]

Television began to explore the characterisation of male homosexuals in the 1960s, with the appearance of homosexual social actors in factual TV (in documentary and news reporting), and the plays of Joe Orton. However this continued the emphasis on homosexuality as peripheral, discontented and over sexualised. The release of the film *Victim* in 1961 marked a shift away from this, contributing to discourse about the impact of law on homosexual social lives (and the issue of blackmail). This presented a new type of understanding where non-heterosexuals were depicted as 'independent agents' (Pullen 2005, 2006). Rather than being seen as subjective objects, they began to represent themselves. Although *Victim* focused its narrative on blackmail, it became an important text for gay audiences (Bourne 1996: 155), as it offered a potential reflective version of a gay community (or at least networks of gay men). Also it potentially contributed to public opinion which may have resulted in the eventual change in law. The broadcast of *Victim* on television after the legalisation of male homosexuality not only translated recognition of a new era in the potential offered by television, but also its transmission to 'domestic audiences' signalled a new acceptance of the discussion of homosexual 'social and political' lives within family homes. This was partly engendered by the participation of the highly acclaimed actor Dirk Bogarde in the leading role, who actively supported the project, yet remained a closeted gay man. Furthermore *Victim's* narrative drive supported the idea of changing the law, and is particularly evident in the film when the more respectable characters (such as the police detective) advocate this need.

However, whilst the broadcast of *Victim* is emblematic of change, its textual bias still focuses on binary stereotypes. *Victim* is largely constructed around the idea of victim and villain, both of which are connected to gay identity. This is demonstrated when some homosexuals are depicted as victims of blackmail, while others are cast as perpetrators of blackmail and extortion. Therefore *Victim* still engages in dominant norms of subjectivity as to the construction of homosexual identity, but it also offers progressive discourse.

The Naked Civil Servant (1975) was based on the autobiography of Quentin Crisp, a flamboyant, openly gay author and social commentator. The drama focused on his life in London between the 1920s and the 1970s. This involved scenarios where Crisp would go out in

---

[21] Other important textual moments are discussed later as influential, but these possess less cultural/social significance.

public dressed in an effeminate manner, potentially transgressing dominant gender norms. Also his sexual engagements (before he became celibate, in later life) often focused on encounters with married men and army service men, suggesting a confrontation and effacement between stereotypical ideas of masculine and effeminate identities.

We may consider that Quentin Crisp as an intelligent effeminate male through such engagements, involved himself in breaking down norms. As Alan Sinfield notes 'The 'effeminate', leisured literary intellectual [who] sought relationships either personal or (equally provocatively) impersonal – with masculinity and the working class [undermines] the affiliations and barriers' (1989: 66) within sexual and class paradigms. Furthermore, in crossing class and sexual divides Quentin Crisp benefited from his supporting network of friends (both gay and straight). This is particularly evident in the sequence where Crisp is in court charged with soliciting, where numerous 'upstanding', and seemingly 'normal' members of 'respectable' society make testaments in support of him. *The Naked Civil Servant* brought gay and straight identities together, revealing the personal story and humanity of Quentin Crisp.

The transmission was highly impactful as it was broadcast by Thames television through the ITV network, reaching large audiences in the United Kingdom. Also responses from audiences suggested that homosexual identity could form an acceptable part of television entertainment. As Howes notes 'according to a survey commissioned by the Independent Broadcasting Authority, only 18 out of the 475 viewers [who] switched off [did so] because of [unsuitable] content ... [a]nd 85 per cent said that the production was 'not shocking', [while] few felt that Crisp's story 'encouraged' homosexuality' (1993: 535). Furthermore, not only did the character of Quentin Crisp become esteemed as an insightful, likeable and humorous contemporary social philosopher, but also it established the idea of the gay male as a political agent within drama, resisting subjugation. Evidence of this is provocatively seen in the closing sequence of the drama, where Crisp sweeps aside a gang of aggressive male youths who are demanding money (on the threat of telling a policeman that Crisp had sexually interfered with a young boy) with the statement "you cannot touch me now, I am one of the stately *homos* of England". The irony of this proclamation is that Quentin Crisp did indeed become a loveable old character who contextualised British culture. Furthermore, his appraisal by audiences was not that dissimilar to the way in which the British public felt a fond affection for old historic buildings which reflected the past (like a *stately homo*), yet still contextualised the distance between the classes, and sexes.

Consequently whilst the *Naked Civil Servant* may be considered as the foundation stone which in many ways stimulated interest in non-heterosexual characters (particularly within the arena of 'autobiographical' drama), it at the same time continued to re-inforce 'distance'. In this way the character of Crisp was viewed as a likeable 'other', rather than a new citizen. He was valued for cultural commentary, not social participation. This continuing distance of homosexual identity in drama maintained the idea that gay people were disassociated from the normal family. This became further impacted after the advent of AIDS, and responses to this within the British media.

In 1986 the British government responded to the threat of AIDS by commissioning a national poster and leaflet campaign addressed at educating (and warning) the population. This led into a series of national television adverts in 1987. The 'poster and leaflet campaign [commenced] with the slogan [of] "Don't Aid AIDS". This [later] changed [when the adverts were broadcast] into the theme of "Don't die of ignorance"' (Avert, 2005a). The British public had been aware for some time of the issue of AIDS, but this had mostly been connected to the spread of the syndrome among gay men in America. The leaflet, poster and advert campaign was designed to warn people that the threat had spread beyond minority groups, and now was within the mainstream. This is evident in the iconography of the television advertising campaign which used an iceberg about to make impact, possibly suggesting the threat had come adrift from 'elsewhere', and that there were unseen horrors below the surface. Similarly an advert featuring a volcano erupting and a man carving the word AIDS onto a tombstone (Avert 2005b), potentially connoted homosexual male identity with the inevitability of natural disaster and the spectre of death. The advertising campaign highlighted the threat to the general public, and signalled the likely culpable groups. This is particularly evident in the voice-over of the tombstone advert, where we are told:

> There is now a danger that has become a threat to us all. It is a deadly
> disease and there is no known cure. ...*So far it's been confined to small
> groups, but it's spreading.* So protect yourself, and read this leaflet when it
> arrives. If you ignore AIDS, it could be the death of you. So don't die of
> ignorance (my italics). (Avert 2005b)

This set an agenda where in British drama it was necessary to address potential 'ignorance'.

The first dramas inspired by this period possessed a didactic, yet moralistic quality.   This is particularly evident in *Intimate Contact* (Central Television 1987), where we are presented with 'the ostracism of a small boy who contracted AIDS via [a blood] transfusion, and [the casting of Daniel Massey who plays] a successful [married] businessman who contracts [the syndrome] via unprotected sex' (Johnh 2005).[22] In this way a threat to the idea of normal heterosexual family is posed with the presentation of danger to children, and the reckless sexual exploits of a bisexual married man.

This danger posed to normal life is vividly portrayed in *Sweet as You Are* (BBC2 1988), starring Liam Neeson, and Miranda Richardson. Neeson plays a bisexual university lecturer who contracts the HIV syndrome whilst having a brief affair with one of his male students. Richardson plays an innocent wife, who on discovering the threat endures three days of intense emotional reflection and contemplation whilst waiting for the results of an HIV test. Whilst the wife is represented as caring for the young male protagonist who brought the threat of AIDS to her marriage (the student, now rejected by the husband), and is saved from the threat of AIDS (the test is negative), it is suggested that the husband succumbs, and contracts AIDS. This is presented in the closing stages of the drama where we see the young couple looking into the mirror (the void) together, and the camera gradually focuses on a red mark on Neeson's face, likely to be a Karposi's Sarcoma (a well known disease connected to AIDS). Consequently *Sweet as You Are* contextualises the threat of AIDS to family, at the same time signalling the danger of gay male sexual behaviour. Whilst at this time soap operas would also deal with the issue of AIDS (most notably *Eastenders* - see below), this period stimulated a number of 'cautionary tales' in drama. It also reflected alleged public emotional concern, and governmental legislative aims in the act of Clause 28, which prohibited the open discussion of homosexuality within schools.[23] This directly challenged the suitability of gay identity within television. Gay men were not seen as welcome, or efficient members of a working dominant society: they were cast as a threat. Also it was estimated that any gay community would lack powerful members. This would begin to change with the advent of *Queer as Folk*.

Russell T. Davies' *Queer as Folk* (Channel 4 1999) changed the way gay people could be represented on television. Whilst there had been ground-breaking filmic texts (just prior to this), such as the adaptation of

---

[22] Daniel Massey had appeared in the seminal text *The Roads to Freedom* in 1970, discussed later.
[23] Clause 28 became Section 28 of the Local Government Act on May 24th 1988 (Lucas, 1998: 5).

Jonathan Harvey's *Beautiful Thing* (1996) which represented youthful gay romance in an accepting and understanding community, televisual representations of non-heterosexuals on television still retained a covert, marginal and peripheral quality. *Queer as Folk* offered a sensational vision of gay identity, which located the non-heterosexual characters as central storytellers, and heroes. Whilst its impact may be remembered for its story of under-age sex, and exotic homosexual exploits, seen particularly in the depiction of lead character Stuart engaging in anal sex with 15 year old Nathan, the text also constructed a sense of an empowered gay community. Set in the gay area of Manchester (around Canal Street), it offered up a hedonistic vision of gay males unashamedly indulging in promiscuous sex, at the same time revealing gay men and lesbians as highly successful in their careers, and involved in family making (Stuart fathered a child with a lesbian friend). This impetus for gay identity, suggesting a move towards the potential of social and commercial commodity, transgressed representational norms which had previously assigned non-heterosexual identity to the periphery. Through the publicity afforded the series, it became a discursive springboard which would involve non-heterosexuals both criticising, and praising the series. Whilst many viewed the drama as over sensational, and stereotypical in connecting gay male sexuality with promiscuity, numerous commentators considered the series as progressive. This equated to a dichotomy in opinion concerning *Queer as Folk*, between desire for the representation of real gay citizens (who would seem 'everyday'), and a desire for more provocative gay representations which would stimulate debate, however contentious they may be.

This balance between the potential of presenting citizenship ideals (rejecting stereotypes), and the potency of drama (which may engage in stereotypes productively) is a central issue. Jane Arthurs (2004) argues that the 'equality and provision of sexual minorities should acknowledge what drama does best: being a space for psychological complexity and pleasurable fantasy that goes far beyond the demand for citizenship rights in an 'oppositional public sphere' (p. 127). In this way Arthurs considers *Queer as Folk* as a site of psychological inquiry, which expresses a debate exploring the complexity and ambivalence of representational signs, which is useful. However, as Sally Munt (2000) notes, *Queer as Folk's* address to the issue of shame is contentious. Whilst the series does indeed provide a discursive foundation of a potential new world order rejecting the 'shame' of gay sex, it at the same time focuses on shame as a locus of attention. If we consider Michel Foucault's (1976) model of power in this context, and the potency of power resistance (that this is complex and involves a matrix of distribution and reaction), whilst indeed *Queer as Folk* does attempt to deal with shame, in doing so it re-energises the emblematic theme of shame. In other words whilst *Queer as Folk* attempts to move beyond shame, as it becomes a textual character it persists, and propels this as a central theme - which continually needs to be addressed.

Therefore my reading of *Queer as Folk* is ambivalent. I would argue it that it indeed represented a watershed offering a new world order, which stimulated the production of further creative texts which experimented with non-heterosexual identity. Evidence of this may be seen in the productions of *Metrosexuality* (Channel 4 2001), a fantasy drama which offers a social world where non-heterosexuals are the majority; *Tinsel Town* (BBC 2, 2000) an evocative text set in Scotland which, whilst focused on club culture and recreational drug taking, did represent the complexity of gay teen desire in the depiction of a young man who had a 'forbidden' relationship with an older (police)man, and *Attachments* (BBC2, 2000), a drama focusing on young people working within a web based company, which depicted a young lesbian as shameless and provocative. Similarly it is possible to argue that the dynamics of *Queer as Folk* have directly led producers to construct a variety of gay characters within more mainstream serial dramas such as *Bad Girls* (ITV 1999) which was set in a female prison; *Teachers* (Channel 4 2001) which focused on teachers in a secondary school; *Footballers' Wives* (ITV 2004) which presented a voyeuristic focus on the lives of footballers and their spouses, and *Shameless* (Channel 4 2004) which involved the representation of family and community within a socially deprived neighbourhood.

However, despite this stimulation of potential it is possible to argue that *Queer as Folk* has inhibited the integrated representation of gay people with 'equality'. In this way through its focus on commodity, sensualisation, and shamelessness, it has set an agenda where non-heterosexuals remain outsiders. Whilst a proliferation of texts that followed *Queer as Folk* readily included, and prioritised gay identity as a new staple role (such as those discussed above), many did so focusing on 'acceptance', whilst denying 'equality'. This becomes particularly evident in examining Russell T. Davies' *Bob and Rose* (ITV 2002).

Commissioned by ITV, and broadcast on primetime television, *Bob and Rose* reached large audiences. However, whilst it offers the signature of Russell T. Davies in its focus on gay identity, the story involves an address towards dominant heterosexual ideas: that gay men can change their nature. The story involves a gay man who has been on the 'scene' for many years. After a chance meeting with a woman, and despite everything (including peer pressure to remain exclusively gay) the gay man falls in love with her and they share an active sexual life. Whilst the story is attributed to the personal experience of Russell T. Davies, in that he had met a gay man who was rejected by his peers after falling in love with a woman, its ready acceptance by ITV as a story suitable for primetime transmission reveals a bias towards accepting the idea of gay identity as a commodity 'other', rather than treating it with parity to heterosexual norms. This suggests that whilst *Queer as Folk* changed the representational landscape, its impact within contemporary drama still involved a focus on addressing acceptance over equality.

Soap operas and sit-coms have similarly addressed acceptance, and resisted equality. However, through their consistency in scheduling (by keeping gay identity in the picture) and in textual form (through adhering to recognisable mainstream formats) to a degree they have offered more enabling visions of gay identity within more substantial everyday social arenas.

Everyday social identity and stereotyping in soap and sit-com

Soap operas as a genre of television drama have been used as vehicles for the contemporary depiction of gay men and women (Pullen, 2000). Similarly, situation comedies have focused on gay characters with recurring frequency. Both genres play a pivotal role in the depiction of society on television, where social norms (and departures from this) are contextualised. Whilst soap operas are considered as presenting 'everydayness and [they provide a] sense of co-presence with the audience',[24] and sit-coms contextualise everyday worlds, but focus more squarely on stereotypical forms, both provide social frames of reference which reinforce the periphery of the norm. In this way, both soap and sit-com express the rules of normalcy, and play out these ideas through continually stretching and compressing group membership ideals. The frequent casting of non-heterosexual characters in these genres raises questions, and often provides answers -- who belongs, or who does not. In order to discuss this further I will examine soap opera, then contextualise sit-com.

It's difficult to establish the exact point of the first appearance of

---

[24] A phrase borrowed from John Ellis (2000), originally used concerning the nature of contemporary broadcast television.

a non-heterosexual character in British television soap opera, as from the 1970s various homosexual types started to appear in soap-like texts. Soap-like serial dramas such as *Angels* (BBC, 1976-82), *Rock Follies* (ITV 1976-77) and *The Crezz* (ITV 1976) might be considered as early points of reference towards this. *Angels* (a hospital drama) had two gay male nurse characters who became lovers (Howes 1993: 29), *Rock Follies* (a pop music drama) depicted a gay male character who also had a lover (Howes, 1993: 690), and *The Crezz* (a comedy drama) represented a gay couple who lived openly within a middle class community. Whilst *The Crezz* depicted a polarisation between gay male types in the couple (one camp and one masculine), as the representation of two males living together within an 'accepting' community, this must be considered as a central precursor to the representation of gay men in soaps. Consequently these early appearance may have encouraged the dynamic landmark appearance of non-heterosexuals in the soaps *Brookside* (1982) and *Eastenders* (1985-present).

   Brookside (Channel 4 1982-2003) became the first British soap opera to portray a gay character, but also from the outset it attempted to represent the difficulties experienced by young gay teens attempting to find identity and fit in with family. In this way its depiction of male teenager Gordon Collins, 'who for some time lived at his [parent's] home with his lover' (Howes 1993: 86), became a highly progressive text, potentially addressing Channel Four's foundational public service remit to be innovative, and represent diversity in society (see Harvey 2000). Later *Brookside* would include two gay themed storylines in its 2001 season.[25] However its depiction of a young lesbian (Beth Jordache) in the early 1990s is worthy of discussion here. This event marked a watershed in mainstream television drama, as prior to this, lesbians had only rarely been seen in single dramas, and were cast as outsiders.

   The lesbian representation in *Brookside* became a point of contention with the actress who played the role. Perhaps indicative of the attitudes of the time, Anna Friel tried to distance herself from the character she played:

> It was pretty daunting, going into work in the morning knowing that I'd got to kiss another girl. Looking back, I don't know how I did it. I suppose it's part of the job. (Tibballs 1995:99)

   Whilst the soap opera appeared to promote gay identity, the

---

[25] In 2001, *Brookside* developed two gay themed storylines simultaneously; one featuring a lesbian, Shelly, and another a gay man, Lance.

actors involved were not necessarily supportive of the political causes.

Sensitivity towards distancing heterosexual actors and audiences from the representations they encountered could also be seen in later representations in soap opera. This is particularly evident in *Coronation Street* (1960-present) with the introduction of a transsexual (male to female) character called Hayley Patterson (in 1998), who would be played by a heterosexual female (Julie Hesmondhalgh). Whilst Hayley became an audience favourite, later storylines in *Coronation Street* failed to integrate homosexual identity within normative family life. This is particularly evident in the representation of gay male Todd (in 2004), where he is depicted as breaking up the family unit and is held culpable, by his girlfriend and her family, for the death of his new born child, suggesting that his homosexuality and infidelity are directly connected to the death (see Pullen cited in Martin 2004). Whilst the character of the young and handsome Todd had seemed promising and this marked a shift in *Coronation Street's* reticence to deal with homosexuality (Todd was the first openly gay character), this maligned representation was not only unwelcome to gay audiences (Martin 2004) but also it revealed that *Coronation Street* was out of step with audience expectations. Series like *Brookside* and *Eastenders* had been far more progressive from the outset.

Eastenders cast openly gay actor Michael Cashman to play its debut gay role (Cashman later went on to become a member of the European parliament). Whilst Cashman's character (Colin) became stereotypically concerned about the HIV syndrome, it is significant that he never succumbed to it: rather, the popular 'straight' character Mark Fowler was ultimately found to be HIV positive. This would be particularly provocative, as Mark Fowler remained a central character in Eastenders for many years (until 2004), thereby continually distancing gay identity from AIDS. Whilst later there were numerous gay and lesbian characters in *Eastenders*, the appearance of openly gay Michael Cashman in the character of Colin was the most provocative. Evidence of this may be seen in the popular press with the response to the first gay male kiss in soap opera in 1987. *The Sun* (a tabloid national newspaper) responded to this with the headline 'Eastbenders'. Like Anna Friel's response to playing a lesbian, this signalled discontent with the idea of representing sexualised non-heterosexuals on television. Whilst soap operas were experimenting with gay identity in the 1980s and 1990s, it would not be until after the millennium (and after the impact of *Queer as Folk*) that such representations would become more commonplace, and more readily accepted.

Such contemporary agency may be found in the representation of

a gay male couple (Tom and Bradley) who had care of a young teenager in
the soap opera *Crossroads* (Carlton 2001),[26] and the appearance of a
sexualised gay male teenager (Alex) who would be represented as equal to
his peers in the teen soap *As If* (Channel 4 2001). Both texts juxtapose gay
and straight social values, and prioritise the experience of gay men.

In *Crossroads*, Tom and Bradley are represented as guardians of
a young teen who lives with them, after the death of a relative. Their
storyline concerns evaluating their suitability as parents. It is significant
that in one episode, Jake (a straight man of dubious sexual fidelity) makes
positive comments on the suitability of the gay couple, telling his son
"Tom and Bradley love each other very much".[27] This juxtaposition of
'flawed, unstable straight relationship' (Jake cheats on his wife,
continuously) with 'successful, stable gay relationship' (Tom and Bradley
are depicted as loving partners) makes serious commentary on the
suitability of gay men as partners and parents. Significantly, it was
broadcast at 'lunchtime' and 'teatime', and therefore was deemed suitable
material for family viewing.

As If (produced by Johnny Capps, and others, discussed below)
concerns itself with the lives of six teenage Londoners who together form
a close knit unit of friendship, and includes within this a gay character
called Alex. The essence of its style of delivery is confessional. In each
separate episode, we hear the personal perspective of an individual
character, delivered directly to the camera. The suggestion is that through
confessional and therapeutic discourse (White 1992), problems or issues
can be raised which may or may not be resolved for the character but
which are presented to the viewer in a manner that re-inforces their
significance.

It is through this emphasis on the representation of the 'inner-
self' with which the character of Alex is depicted as a contemporary of his
friends, and represented as an equal to his peers. Evidence of this can be
seen throughout the series, where Alex is represented as content with his
sexuality, and he experiences emotions associated with 'normal'
heterosexual romance -- long term partnership goals, rather than

---

[26] Originally produced by ATV, Crossroads was transmitted in the United
Kingdom from 1964-1988. After 4,510 episodes (Vahimaghi, T., *British
Television* - Oxford University Press, 1996) the series was cancelled in 1988 to be
later resumed by Carlton TV in 2001.
[27] Episode of *Crossroads*, (Carlton TV) April 2001. Interestingly the Crossroads
website tells us of Tom and Bradley 'The heart throb and café owner Tom and
Bradley are Kings Oak's Elton John and David Furnish' (Carlton, 2001)
referencing a real celebrity gay couple.

'peripheral' homosexual engagement - stereotypically associated with sexual promiscuity. This is particularly evident in the first series, where the scriptwriters prioritise the romantic relationship of Alex with Dan, over other potential heterosexual couplings.   Alex tells us (direct to camera) concerning his feeling for Dan:

ALEX: I think I'm in love.

ALEX: My mates know I'm gay and its like that's Al sorted. And then they go on how tough it is being straight.

ALEX: I'll have you! (gesture of a kiss thrown out with both hands to himself).

The presentation of this inner confidence, and the express representation of success in finding a suitable partner, prioritises the homosexual over the heterosexual (similarly its transmission on Sunday mornings sets an agenda for the mainstream acceptance of homosexual discourse).[28]   While such favourable juxtaposition is less easy to find in sit-com, it is notable that gay identity has been a consistent motif within the genre since the 1970s.

Are You Being Served? (BBC1 1976-83) undoubtedly set an agenda for the representation of gay character types, if not an openly gay character.   Consequently the casting of John Inman in the role of the effeminate Mr Humphries (as a shop assistant selling men's clothing in a department store), set a landmark of representation which signalled a man who was very definitely homosexual, but failed to announce this. Consequently the audience read the signs of his homosexuality, through recognition of stereotypical performative traits (effeminacy and camp behaviour), but it was an unspoken truth. The immense success of *Are You Being Served* contextualised the audience's content in recognising stereotypes surrounding gay men, and potentially signalled a preference to withhold a sexualised form. Within sit-com this engendered effeminacy and camp to become the signs of normalised homosexual behaviour, and connoted the hiding of sexual agency.

---

[28] The first series of *As If* originally commenced broadcast on 22nd January 2001 on E4 (Channel 4's digital channel). It was then broadcast on Channel 4, between March 7th and May 31st 2001. The original transmission format on Channel 4 was two half-hour episodes on Wednesday/Thursday which were then repeated on the following Sunday morning. As the series became established, this changed to one episode (Thursday) repeated on Sunday.

Whilst later sit-coms would continue to experiment with gay identity, these representations still remained anchored in stereotypical forms. Whilst *Agony* (ITV 1979-81) depicted an openly gay couple, a 'bald black lesbian mother, and a would-be transsexual' (Howes 1993: 15), and it was created by an American gay activist (Len Richmond) and successful agony aunt (Anna Raeburn) (suggesting political agency), it still reflected dominant ideas about gay stereotypes. Similarly, more eccentric situation comedies focused on gay identity. Evidence of this may be seen in *'Allo 'Allo* (BBC 1 1982; 1984-1992) a parody of the war time French resistance which included an unfulfilled German gay soldier called Lieutenant Gruber; *Brass* (1982) a partial parody of the period classic *Brideshead Revisited* (discussed later) which focused on a foppish eccentric gay male (Morris Hardacre), and *Mapp and Lucia* (Channel 4 1985-86) which presented a farcical 1920s social elite focusing on a closeted gay male 'sissy' (Georgie Pilson) and a bombastic lesbian 'dyke' ('Quaint' Irene Coles). Increasingly gay characters would become stock types, essential in the construct of sit-com. This would involve a transition in later sit-coms such as *The Brittas Empire* (BBC 1991-94) set in a sports centre, and *Drop the Dead Donkey* (1991-94) set in a media news office, where the gay characters would become the most ordinary, and the *least* eccentric. In *The Brittas Empire* a gay male couple (Gavin and Tim) were the most normal characters, and in *Drop the Dead Donkey* a lesbian character (Helen) was one of the most rounded characters. These texts would offer a move away from associating gay people with outrageous stereotypes, by inverting expectation.

However, when Julian Clary produced the ironically titled *Terry and Julian* (Channel 4 1992) after the mainstream heteronormative sit-com *Terry and June* (BBC1 1979-87), camp returned to sit-com, but this time connected to an openly gay male potentially making political commentary. Julian Clary was an 'alternative' gay male entertainer who became famous in the 1980s. He expressed an elaborate and theatrical version of gay male sexuality, potentially to the degree of parodying the idea of effeminate behaviour. It's possible to argue that he employed camp in his stage persona and in the sit-com *Terry and Julian* as a type of 'Brechtian distanciation' (the audience reads the irony, and 'intellectualises' the issue). However, as Julian's delivery was more concerned with aesthetics, and bodily deployment (his glittering camp costumes and effeminate gait) this reading is ambiguous. As George W. Brandt (1998) argues, whilst Bertolt Brecht's 'alienation or estrangement effect' is connected to the Marxist ideology and resisting subjugation, he warns us that this becomes 'little more than a *stylistic flourish* when simply used as an *aesthetic*,

rather than a consciousness raising device' (my emphasis, 224). Hence
without the foregrounding of an obvious political ideology, camp may be
seen merely as a stylistic aesthetic, and possibly a distancing device:
thereby continuing the distance between identities. Similarly, later sit-
coms authored by gay people, which foregrounded stereotypes, would be
viewed with ambiguity. This is particularly evident in *Gimmie! Gimmie!
Gimmie!* (BBC1 and BBC2 1999-2001) and *Rhona* (BBC2 2000).

     Gimmie! Gimmie! Gimmie! was authored by celebrated gay male
writer Jonathan Harvey (playwright of *Beautiful Thing*, discussed above),
and also starred openly gay actor James Dreyfus. This sit-com became an
outrageous carnivalesque series in which the comic, inter-dependent
relationship of the 'fag hag' and the gay male was foregrounded.
Similarly *Rhona,* scripted by openly gay comedienne Rhona Cameron,
inverted   ideas   of   lesbian   romantic   activity   (loving   democratic
relationships) by presenting Cameron as not dissimilar to a heterosexual
male unable to commit to a dedicated relationship.

     In   this   way   both   *Gimmie! Gimmie! Gimmie!*   and   *Rhona*
expressed issues surrounding gay identity, but at the same time parodied
relationship ideas, in the former the heterosexual female/homosexual
male, and in the latter lesbian coupling. As texts scripted and acted by
non-heterosexuals,   they   potentially   present   a   viewpoint   which   is
transgressive. As Peter Stallybrass and Allon White (1986) have noted,
there exists a 'possibility of shifting *the very terms of the system itself* by
erasing   and   interrogating   the   relationships   which   constitute   it'   (58).
Through the removal of hierarchies which may form dominant cultural
ideology, we may experience the potential of 'a potent, populist, critical
inversion   of   ...   official   worlds   and   hierarchies'   (7).   Therefore   by
removing the hierarchy of male heterosexual order (there are no powerful
heterosexual males), and the parodying, and inversion of identity ideals
(identities are not fixed to dominant order), a carnivalesque world is
presented which offers scope for change.

     Whilst   both   soap   opera   and   situation   comedy   trade   in   the
ordering of dominant social identity, opportunities have occurred which
have allowed ground-breaking storytellers concerned for gay identity to
express new ideas. From political agency in *Brookside* and *Eastenders* to
contemporary representations in *Crossroads* and *As If,* soap opera has
progressed identity ideals revealing youth identity as a significant
influence. Similarly, from 'hidden yet hyper' identity in *Are You Being
Served?,* to 'apparent' normalisation in later texts, through to the
carnivalesque potential of self aware gay identity in *Gimmie! Gimmie!
Gimmie!* and *Rhona,* an advancement has occurred which alters the scope

for change. This degree of non-heterosexual self awareness is particularly apparent in *Tipping the Velvet* (BBC2 2003), and its impact and transgressive potential is partly enabled through British television audiences' interest in period adaptation, and quality drama.

Adaptation, Quality & Auteurs

Tipping the Velvet was adapted from Sarah Waters' ground-breaking novel, which explored the idea of lesbian sexuality and romance, and was set in late Victorian London. Whilst the sensation for its broadcast mostly focused on the tabloid press' interest in the titillation of lesbian sexuality (most notably *The Star's* anticipation of erotic sexuality), *Tipping the Velvet* may be viewed as a high quality drama which employed the representation of lesbian romance. Its appearance also follows a tradition in television concerning quality period drama which has accommodated the depiction of non-heterosexuals.

As Jane Arthurs (2004) has observed, '[q]uality drama is accorded the status of art despite its presence on a mass medium and as such is protected to some degree from censorship regimes that regulate the majority of television's output'(114). This has afforded those interested in depicting non-heterosexual desire an easier conduit for distribution. Therefore the early appearance of Daniel Massey (as a discontented homosexual) in the adaptation of Jean Paul Sartre's *Roads to Freedom* (BBC2 1970), marks not only the first openly sexualised gay male on British television, but also the beginning of a discourse in quality drama which would extend to later, more mainstream texts, and potentially engender change. Hence the appearance of upper class gay male desire in *Brideshead Revisited* in 1981 on ITV, and its address to large mainstream audiences represented a shift towards increased visibility. However, at the same time this signalled the continuing distance between non-heterosexuals and 'us', seen not only in the idea of forbidden sexuality, but also in the focus on a family grounded in Catholicism. Evidence of this is also seen in Alan Bennett's *An Englishman Abroad* (BBC1 1983) which focused on the exploits of the infamous upper class communist homosexual traitor Guy Burgess, whilst living in exile in Moscow. This continued a disconnection between heterosexual lower middle class worlds, and supposed homosexual upper class remoteness.

Later texts in this vein would close the class distance. This may be seen in dramas such as *The Buddha of Suburbia* by Hanif Khureshi (BBC2 1993) with the representation of a sexually ambiguous young Indian male on a journey of discovery within middle class and ethnic worlds, and *Oranges are Not the Only Fruit* by Jeanette Winterson (BBC2 1990) which focused on the difficult life of a young lesbian growing up trying to establish her identity within an un-accepting evangelical religious working class community. Whilst Arthurs (2004) argues that these texts 'could be read through a liberal humanist perspective, which values pluralism and freedom of speech while avoiding any sense of homosexuality as a politicised sexual identity' (p. 115), more contemporary texts such as *Tipping the Velvet*, have expressed political ideas mostly through the agency of openly gay authors and producers. In this way, the closing narrative of *Tipping the Velvet* (found lesbian love) is indicative not only of audiences' interest in non-heterosexual desire within 'distanced' quality formats, it is representative of the 'closeness' of openly gay media producers and writers who involve themselves in personal agency. This reflects Anthony Giddens' (1992) ideas of a 'transformation of intimacy' which focuses on the potential of citizens who openly express details of their personal lives, and this changes social worlds. As Ken Plummer (1995) observes, openly gay agents are expressing their identity as 'intimate citizens', creating new democratic orders through the stories they tell. We read Sarah Waters not just as a celebrated author writing within the genre of period drama addressing audience expectation, we experience her 'self reflexive' (Giddens 1991) visions of identity - played out through the genre of quality and period drama. This stimulation towards self reflexivity is not only the signature of Sarah Waters' work in *Tipping the Velvet*, it is a common theme which has stimulated change within television drama, largely engineered by gay writers and producers.

Conclusion

Tipping the Velvet, like *Queer as Folk* and *The Naked Civil Servant* became valued as a textual representation produced by non-heterosexual agents (Sarah Waters, Russell T. Davies, and Quentin Crisp respectively) reflecting their own lives, and working towards social change. This extends beyond the level of esteemed writers, and connects to a widening network of media producers interested in reflecting the diversity of non-heterosexual life. Evidence of this is seen in the valuable contribution of less well known contemporary media producers, such as Johnny Capps, and a variety of unknown scriptwriters.

Johnny Capps has involved himself in many ground-breaking texts, including not only *As If* (mentioned above), but also the serial drama *Sugar Rush* (Channel 4 2005) an adaptation of Julie Birchill's novel which depicts young lesbian sexual desire without shame. In addition he set this agenda in the drama series *Peak Practice* (ITV 1993-2002), with the representation of elder gay men in love, addressing the potential threat to homosexual coupling from family and authority in times of illness and death (without the legal security of marriage) (Capps 2001). Johnny Capps is an unsung hero, who alongside other numerous unnamed scriptwriters has engaged in the political contexts of gay identity. Evidence of this may be seen not only in the dramas, soap operas and sit-coms already discussed here, but also in a network of agency, continually reconfiguring and building.

The serial hospital dramas *Casualty* (BBC1 1986-present) and *Holby City* (BBC1 1999-present) have addressed the idea of including gay identity and have depicted same sex romance (including weddings), foregrounding this with equality to heterosexual experience.[29] This has been a constructive task, which supports regular non-heterosexual cast members. This often involves playing out discursive scenarios where value is quantified, and justified. This is not only apparent in representing same sex desire/romance, and the need for legal equality in relationship rights, but also in exploring the value of homosexual life. Evidence of this is vividly presented in an episode of *Holby City* (November, 2005) where the producers pose a debate about the worthiness of a homosexual man or a heterosexual female as recipient of a heart transplant (the gay man is considered on equal terms and he is ultimately the chosen recipient, despite his own expressed feelings of inequality and doubt). This focus on gay identity as valued within society is something which has been resisted: gay characters have been depicted as outsiders.

The location of gay characters as outside acceptance and equality has been a recurring motif in television drama. Although a large progression may be defined away from the early covert and stereotypical representation, towards the idea of inclusion - mostly stimulated by self reflexive writers hoping to display the connectivity between gay and straight experience, we are still only at a starting point. Groundbreaking texts such as *Victim, The Naked Civil Servant, Queer as Folk,* and *When I'm 64* (discussed in the introduction) do reach out and stimulate minds. However they are isolated events largely eclipsed by the mass of mainstream televisual representation. If we consider statistics collected by Stonewall in early 2006, television representations of non-heterosexual identity on BBC equated to less than one 16th of one percent of viewing

---

[29] *Casualty* and *Holby City* are related texts not only from a production point of view (BBC Bristol), but also from a textual perspective (they are both set in the fictional location of Holby City, and a number of the characters appear in both series).

time.[30]

There has been a distinct shift away from invisibility, and a 'silent revolution' is underway: ideas may change through stealth. Social paradigms are changing towards the inclusion of gay identity, mostly stimulated through personal agency on various levels, in complex networks of agency. I would argue that this is more effective than providing provocative moments in drama, alone. *Queer as Folk* may have been momentous, it may have stimulated change, it possibly altered ideas of perception, but essentially its resonance will continue to fade, and we will view it as an historical moment. While such moments are worthy, they are transient.

Perhaps we do not need more bright shooting stars of (queer) romance, but instead the illumination of the night sky revealing constellations of (non-heterosexual) domain.

Works cited

Arthurs, Jane (2004), *Television and Sexuality: Regulation and the Politics of Taste,* Maidenhead: Open University Press, 2004.

Avert,   http://www.avert.org/pictures/aidshistory2.htm,   5th   November 2005a.

Berube, Allan, *Coming Out Under Fire: The History of Gay Men and Women in World War Two,* New York: The Free Press, 1990.

Babuscio, Jack, *We Speak for Ourselves: The experiences of gay men and lesbians,* Revised edition. London: SPCK, 1988.

Bourne, Stephen, *Brief Encounters: Lesbians and Gays in British Cinema 1930-1971.* London: Cassell, 1996.

Clum, John M., *Still Acting Gay,* revised edition, New York: St Martin's Griffin, 2000.

Edwards, Tim, *Erotics and Politics Gay Male Sexuality, Masculinity and Feminism*, London: Routledge, 1994.

Ellis, John, *Seeing Things: Television in an Age of Uncertainty*, London: IB Tauris, 2000.

Foucault, Michel [1976], *The History of Sexuality Vol 1*, London, Penguin, 1998.

Freud, Sigmund [1901], *The Interpretation of Dreams*, London, Penguin,

---

[30] In early March 2006 a 'Stonewall study [examining one week's broadcasting] revealed that only 0.06% of BBC airtime was devoted to sexual diversity. The figures suggest that lesbian and gay lives were covered in just six minutes out of 168 hours of prime time television' (Schoffman 2006).

1991.
Giddens, Anthony [1991], *Modernity and Self Identity: Self and Society in the late Modern Age.* Reprint. Cambridge, Polity Press, 1992.
—. [1992], *The Transformation of Intimacy: Sexuality, Love and Eroticism in Modern Societies.* Reprint. Cambridge, Polity Press, 1995.
Hall, Stuart (ed), *Representation: Cultural Representations and Signifying Practices.* London: Open University, 1997.
Halliwell, Leslie with Phillip Purser, *Halliwell's Television Companion,* London: Grafton Books, 1986.
Harvey, Sylvia in Edward Buscombe (ed) *British Television: A Reader,* Oxford: Oxford University Press, 2000.
Howes, Keith, *Broadcasting It,* London: Cassell, 1993.
Kaeser, Gigi and Peggy Gillespie, *Love Makes a Family: Portraits of Lesbian, Gay, Bisexual, and Transgender Parents and Their Families,* Amherst: University of Massachusetts Press, 1999.
Kingsley Knight, Susan, *Gender and Power in Britain, 1640-1990,* London: Routledge, 1999.
Lucas, Ian, *Outrage,* London: Cassell, 1998.
Martin, Daniel, 'Street Crimes: What is Going Down on Coronation Street? *Gay Times,* August 2004.
Munt, Sally, 'Shame/pride dichotomies in *Queer as Folk'*, *Textual Practice* 14 (3), 2000. pp. 531-46.
Plummer, Ken, *Telling Sexual Stories: Power, Change and Social Worlds,*. London: Routledge, 1995.
Pullen, Christopher, unpublished master's dissertation, University of Bristol, 2000.
—. in James Keller and Leslie Strayner (eds) *The New Queer Aesthetic on Television: Essays on Recent Programming*, Jefferson: McFarland, (2005a).
—. unpublished doctoral thesis, Bournemouth University, (2005b).
—. *Documenting Gay Men: Identity and Performance in Reality Television and Documentary Film.* Jefferson: McFarland, 2006.
Russo, Vito, *The Celluloid Closet*, revised edition, New York: Harper & Row, 1987.
Sinfield, Alan, *Literature, Politics and Culture in Postwar Britain*, Oxford, Basil Blackwell, 1989.
Stallybrass, Peter and Allon White [1986], *The Politics and Poetics of Transgression*, New York: Cornell University Press, 1995.
Tibballs, Geoff, *Brookside The Early Years,* London: Boxtree, 1995.
White, Mimi, *Tele-advising,* Chapel Hill, 1992.
Wolfenden, Sir John (Chairman), *Report on Homosexual Offences and*

Prostitution, London: HMSO, 1957.
Vahimagi, Tise, *British Television*, Oxford: Oxford University Press, 1996.

Interviews

BFI, communication with Elaine Burrows of the British Film Institute 2001
Capps, Johnny, interview with Johnny Capps, 2001.
ITC (2001), communication with Mark Bell of ITC.

Websites

Avert (2005b) http://www.avert.org/pictures/aidshistory4.htm, Accessed 5th November 2005.
Carlton, http://www.carlton.com/crossroads/, Accessed 2nd September 2001
Johnh, http://www.imdb.com/title/tt0093269/, Accessed 5th November 2005.
Schoffman, Marc, 'Gay Media Monitor Launched',
   http://www.pinknews.co.uk/news/entertainment/2005-730.html,
   Accessed 16th March, 2006.
Wyatt, David (2005) 'Gay/Lesbian/Bisexual Television Characters' http://home.cc.umanitoba.ca/~wyatt/tv-char1990s.html. Accessed 10th October 2005.

CHAPTER SEVENTEEN

THE QUEER SUBJECTS OF TWENTY-FIRST
CENTURY TELEVISION DRAMA IN BRITAIN

TONY PURVIS

Synopsis

Today, more than 10 years later, one can't help wondering why so
much was made of the lesbian aspect of *Oranges Are Not The Only Fruit*.
The more powerful theme is the fight between the individual and a rigid
and repressive society, manifested in Jess's struggle to become her own
person, rejecting the strict control of her mother and of patriarchy, in the
form of the church and Pastor Finch. She emerges to find a new world of
possibilities - leaving home, her first proper job, a place at university. The
individual in this case wins out over society, making this a piece of
timeless drama just as relevant to modern audiences.

For audiences that have grown up with lesbian characters in most
of the main soap operas, the routine appearance of lesbian characters in
ITV and *BBC* dramas, and *Channel 4* pushing the boundaries of
'acceptable' British television with programmes like *Queer as Folk* (1999-
2000), *Oranges* seems quite tame when seen today.[31]

Querying the Situating of Television Drama

Discussion of sexuality and television drama will proceed in at
least two directions. On the one hand, there is the drama itself, allied as
this is to institutional contexts of broadcasting, production, scheduling,
audience reception, and ratings. On the other hand, discussion of

---

[31] British Film Institute: http://www.screenonline.org.uk/tv/id/589721/index.html
(Dec. 2005)

televisual output will also proceed in relation to how the drama has been examined against the backdrop of textual and cultural theory. Any discussion of the institutional contexts of drama is problematised from the outset as a result of the wider social and ideological settings in which sexualities and dramas are discursively shaped. Dramas dealing with heteronormative personal relationships, heterosexual romance, social class, 'Britishness', or gender, for instance, have not really been governed by the same kinds of structures, norms, and policies as dramatic output dealing with sexualities, though a clear exception to this is drama dealing with black and Asian cultures. Sarita Malik's survey of this work offers an important corrective (Malik 2000).

If television drama, as Lez Cooke has suggested, needs to be seen in the context of 'an increasingly cautious broadcasting industry' which produces 'safer, more formulaic drama which is designed to maximise audiences' (Cooke 2003: 190), then televisual output dealing with sexualities has invariably meant that the industry has been all the more cautious. Andy Medhurst's discussion of television personality Gilbert Harding notes how Harding's sexuality has a relevance which makes sense outside of television. For many queer subjects, sexuality was decoded in the context of 'the possibilities of blackmail at a time when homosexual acts between men were still illegal' (Medhurst 2000: 256). Joe Orton's plays, for instance, are encoded against such a backdrop, and the film *Victim* (1961) was in part made in response to widespread homophobia and criminal prosecution.[32] More recently, such caution has been legitimised by policies such as Section 28 of the Local Government Act (1988) in Britain and a more general if often unspoken homophobia which has marked British culture.[33]

The second area, critical work on television drama and queer representation, has moved in three main directions. Firstly, the dominant trajectory in television drama criticism in the UK either ignores queer representation altogether or provides only minimal coverage of matters relating to sexual subjectivity, over-relying on gender rather than sexuality as its analytic category. Work by George Brandt (1993), John Caughie (2000), Lez Cooke (2003), and Robin Nelson (1997) has been important in examining historical, technological, and formal developments in

---

[32] The film is both daring and prescient, a landmark in British film and cinema history. The film starred Dirk Bogarde whose character is gay and who is being blackmailed. Bogarde's own sexuality remained, at the time, very private.

[33] See important discussion of this period's racial-sexual politics in A-M Smith, *New Right Discourse on Race and Sexuality: Britain, 1968-1990* (Cambridge: Cambridge University Press, 1995).

mainstream, alternative and 'quality' dramas but tends to sidestep any
serious or prolonged discussion of sexual subjectivity and lesbian and gay
representation. Nelson's discussion of *Oranges Are Not the Only Fruit*
(BBC, 1990), for instance, is undertaken through the language of form,
realism, and what Nelson refers to as the 'routine and mechanical
representation[s] of human experience' (Nelson 1997: 136). Cooke's
discussion of *Queer As Folk* (Channel 4; Red Productions, 1999-2000)
addresses the drama's 'celebratory', 'shocking', and 'outrageous' tone
(Cooke 2003: 187-88). Similar epithets, when applied to the Channel 4
drama *Shameless* (2004-) do not resonate with the same heteronormative
connotations. His comments are set within the broader context of British
television drama's 'reinvention' in the period 1991-2002 and so it is
important that discussion of queer (self) representation has been woven
into Cooke's discussion. However, such discussion occurs, as with many
other critical works, only briefly, and at the end of the book. Moreover,
descriptors such as 'celebratory' and 'shocking' lend support to the
popular assumption that gay men are exceptionally happy or simply
outrageous in ways that others sexual subjects are not. Brandt and Caughie
tend to circumvent any discussion of sexual subjectivity altogether and
rely instead on analyses which attend to matters of canon formation
(Brandt), and realism and modernism (Caughie). Yet the very analysis of
representations of sexual subjectivity in television drama would surely
augment any discussion of canon formation, realism, or modernism. I
return to this discussion of form, canonicity, and taste by way of
Shameless later in the chapter.

   A second line of inquiry has tended to be either anti-homophobic
or 'pro-queer' in its analysis of both media representations and television
drama. Within this trajectory, a number of commentators have proposed
that lesbian, gay and queer representations in the media should be
examined with the same urgency and frequency as queers have been
examined in film and cinema studies. One of the most prominent critics in
the area of film and visual studies is Richard Dyer (1993), though criticism
by, amongst others, Paul Burston and Colin Richardson (1995), Alexander
Doty (1993; 2000; 1997) and Ben Gove (1997), and Sean Nixon (1997;
2003) has been important in establishing frameworks in what we might
refer to as queer media criticism. However, this work seems generally to
assume that the object of inquiry, namely sexuality or sexual subjectivity,
possesses some degree of transparency and obviousness, and is thus open
to critical analysis. If the sexual subject is contradictory, ambivalent,
obscure or simply queer, then its queerness, at least in the queer media
criticism trajectory, is also grounds for its valorisation and subsequent

analysis.

Doty and Gove argue that 'there has been some kind of queer representation on television from the late 1940s' (1997: 85) though their essay offers little discussion of the queer ontology which grounds their consideration of queer viewing strategies, narratives, characterisation, and forms of stero-typification. Nixon, in analysing images of masculinity, suggests that 'new man imagery' is important in 'sanctioning the display of masculine sensuality' and makes possible 'an ambivalent masculine sexual identity' (Nixon in Hall 1997: 328). Yet it is not quite clear in Nixon's argument why ambivalence is being valorised. In many ways, it serves to undermine the argument, after Foucault, that subjects are discursively constructed. Some queer-critical appropriations of Foucault's notion of 'technologies of the self', for instance, need to recognise that if the subject is discursively and historically situated, then it is surely the contingency and impersonality of the circumstances – and not the subject's sexuality – which is the ambivalent terrain. Discourse cannot at the same time construct the subject and then simultaneously undo the subject it shapes. Rather, if subjects are socially constructed (and again social constructionist theories of the subject are more complex than appropriations of Foucault contend[34]), then this is testimony to the stabilising as opposed to the dismantling force of the discourse.

A third strand of criticism has taken a more guarded approach in its understanding of queer representation in dramatic, fictional and filmic material. Drawing on post-structuralist and/or neo-Marxist theory, these critical routes have tended to suggest that the (queer) sexual subject be understood in one of two ways. In the case of post-structuralist critique, the sexual subject is formulated in terms of its textual and performative dimensions, and in neo-Marxist critique, sexuality is understood in relation to the structures of late-capitalism, consumption, visibility and commodification. John Champagne's *The Ethics of Marginality* (1995), Judith Halberstam's *Female Masculinity* (1995), and David Savran's *Communists, Cowboys and Queers* (1992) and *A Queer Sort of Materialism* (2003) draw on post-structuralist critique in their understanding of cultural output, and Rosemary Hennessy's *Profit and Pleasure: Sexual Identities in Late Capitalism* (2000) draws on materialist-feminist and Marxist theory. Work by Sally Munt (2000), and Sue Thornham and Tony Purvis (2005) draws on elements of both these trajectories in the theorisation of recent television dramas. In this work,

---

[34] Such complexity is acknowledged and debated in Butler's work, particularly *Gender Trouble* (1990) and *Bodies That Matter* (New York and London: Routledge, 1993).

the sexual subject of television drama is not one which is easily visualised, but nor is it one which is simply absent, intentionally misrepresented, or always filtered through the lens of sexual stereotype or the heteronormative gaze.

Queer Identifications

Perhaps, however, this work points to the need for a reconsideration of the structures which framework and represent sexuality. There is little doubt, for instance, that the work of the first group of critics has been important in establishing patterns and traditions in UK television drama. Their work, however, is interested in canon formation and it has often been underpinned by critical perspectives which leave heteronormative social and critical practices unquestioned. It is work which does not intentionally exclude discussion of sexuality so much as it assumes a particular *version* of sexuality to be more or less universal. The work of the second group of critics confronts sexuality as a key facet of human experience. In this work, heteronormative practices are either interrogated and their implicit homophobia exposed, or gay and lesbian lives are shown to be as 'normal' as any other. The work of the third group, but particularly that focused around post-structuralist critique, perhaps provides the grounds for a revised understanding of sexuality, television, and drama.

In this trajectory, sexuality is seen to be an always-already problematic category of analysis. Michel Foucault shows how sexuality is made into a 'truth', an identity and a life form (1976). Television and media output have been central in the on-going proliferation and making of sexual identities. More recently, Judith Butler, developing Foucault's work, and Tim Dean, working in the field of Lacanian psychoanalysis, show how the psychic, performative and discursive dimensions of sexual identifications cast doubt on the truth and the identity which an embodied sexuality is thought to express.[35] These are also problematisations which, in many ways, have been staged in television drama of the last ten years. If there is no truth as such to sexuality, and if sexuality makes sense in relation to the discourses and contexts in which it is constructed, then

---

[35] See Butler's most recent *Undoing Gender* (New York and London: Routledge, 2004), for a re-statement of her earlier work *Gender Trouble* (New York and London: Routledge, 1990). Dean's work, which runs counter to Butler's trajectory, represents an important intervention in the study and theorisation of sexuality and sexuation; see particularly his *Beyond Sexuality* (Chicago: Chicago University Press, 2000).

dramas which *appear* to deal more directly with sexuality (e.g. *Metrosexuality* (Channel 4 1999), *Oranges Are Not The Only Fruit, Queer As Folk*), are as much about the social, political, and *impersonal* forces which construct sexuality as a meaningful category as they are about homosexual specificity or personal identity. Alan Sinfield, for instance, in examining the structures of both homosexuality and homophobia, assumes by default that we know what *any* sexuality is, not least homosexuality. More specifically, his question, 'Is homosexuality intolerable?' (1994: 177) might be re-phrased as: 'Is any sexuality tolerable?'. In many ways, the tolerability of sexualities – as opposed to the intolerability of a singular homosexuality – is one of the underpinning questions which queer theory brings to the study of sexual futures (O'Rourke 2006). But it is not the only question. What, for instance, are the terms which allow sexuality to be considered? How might television drama contribute to an on-going critique which seeks to understand the identity which sexuality is thought to express? Or does all media output necessarily rely on a constant making and un-making of sexual identities in order to capture audience ratings?

To continue to ask what sexuality is, and to question its status as an identity category, are questions which are not being posed on some abstract, metaphysical plane. I would suggest that these are the sorts of questions which have also been central to those television dramas which have seemed, ostensibly at least, to be dramatising the experiences of lesbians and gay men rather than the experiences of social life as it is lived in relation to how desires are transcribed in the culture. On one very obvious level, dramas such as *Metrosexuality, Oranges Are Not the Only Fruit,* and *Queer As Folk* are concerned with the lives of lesbians and gays. However, how might queer-cultural theory help us reconsider the terms of reference and the questions which are asked? If these dramas are considered less in terms of their treatment of homosexuality and, following the critical directions of Foucault, Butler, and Dean, are instead reconceptualised in terms of their examination of the *impersonal* discourses of power, identity and object choice, how do the notions of drama and sexuality shift? Are we left with or without a notion of 'sexuality' (often figured in drama as a sexual person or sexual identity) which can actually be represented? Would it not be more profitable – at least in terms of queer futures – to dramatise the ways in which all sexualities are derivative and not original, textually constituted and not expressive? How might we critically move on from an analysis of representations whose analytic frames are grounded in a logic which seeks to re-establish the (past) ontology of sexual identity? Would it not be more useful to consider the metonymies of desires and identifications, more than the metaphors of identity, as the principal structuring devices which inform how social life is lived in the culture? Why has object choice been figured in personal terms? Is it not the limiting logic of metaphor which compels subjects to claim a sexuality?

An interpretation which explores these questions will view sexuality less as an inner truth to be explored or personalised (often in UK/USA theatre and television drama via forms of interiority, psychological depth, typification or exceptionality), and more as a category which the society requires its subjects to speak in order, in the Foucaultian sense, to contain and put under surveillance, its dissident citizens.[36] Television, one of society's principal means of surveillance, is also a medium which operates to constrain subjects on the basis of its popular, mass appeal. In this framework, representations of sexuality are not truths which the drama unveils but are forms of constraint. The drama's interpellations potentially limit the subject to hegemonic identities and identifications. However, and to slightly re-phrase Butler's most recent work, sexuality in much television drama is also in the process of being *un-done* Butler 2004). If television's earlier portrayals of lesbian and gay identities seem 'tame by today's standards', then perhaps this is not because programming is more radical or society more enlightened. Rather, if sexuality is formed in relation to psychic as well as discursive operations, then the subject's negotiation of the discourse will excite meanings which point to the limits as well as the limitations of the discourse in terms of social and psychic determination.

All three dramas mentioned above, for instance, have as their backdrop the heteronormative and dominant cultures of twentieth-century Britain. In the case of *Oranges*, the drama's complex portrayal of a young woman's same-sex desires makes sense in relation to a society constructed around secrecy and lies, in which the family, marriage, and Protestant fundamentalism structure how all sexualities are spoken. Here, all the attendant discourses which structure identity in the drama (Church, family, etc) are at the centre and at the edges of what sexual identity is also conceived to be. These are discourses which construct not just what seems like an identity ('this is what a lesbian looks like'; 'this is how a lesbian behaves'), but in addition audiences are offered a specific understanding of group identity as well. Discourses partly function on the basis of a self/other dichotomy, so that in *Oranges* the young heroine is always

---

[36] See John Champagne (1997) for a critique of 'images of' criticism. Champagne looks at the work of Richard Dyer as an example of this critical trajectory.

being defined in contexts of what she is not: she is not heterosexual, she is not like other girls, she is outside of the family, and so on. Lesbian and gay subjects are forced into visibility on the basis of a discourse which, because it is unable to set the terms of its own (heterosexual) invisibility, relies on the prior and thus over-determining textual force of the (homosexual) textual other. Even if female or male homosexuality is defined simply in terms of same-sex sexual desire, then it is increasingly clear that the range of lesbian (and gay) identifications which have been broadcast on UK television are more complex than the definition of homosexuality assumes. Jess in *Oranges* is only one girl among many: in that sense her exceptionality is no greater than any of the other characters. Situated in a longer broadcasting history, there are not one but many desires which might be 'lesbian'. Moreover, there is no reason why lesbian desires need be tied to biologically female bodies. Ranging from the early film-drama *Richard's Things* (BBC, 1980), through to *Out on Tuesday* (Channel 4 1989-92), to *Brookside* (Channel 4 1982-2003), and *Eastenders* (BBC 1984-), representations of female homosexuality in UK cultures cannot be assessed on the basis of an innate, unitary, empirically-observable sexual experience shared by all lesbians.

Is it important to know that Jess in *Oranges* is a lesbian if lesbianism is a more diverse category than much earlier dramas and drama criticism seems to imply? Is such diversity not simply a recognition of queerness? One of the themes regularly addressed in the study of lesbian and gay representations concerns the way in which homosexuality is associated with the language of secrecy and lies. In *Oranges* and in *Queer as Folk*, the dramatic devices of soliloquy, understatement, and silence can be seen to represent how *homo*sexuality is always figured as the open secret (See Sedgewick 1990). We want to know (something special, unusual, perplexing, eccentric, or queer!) about the lesbian or gay character because homosexuality, now an innate secret knowledge, is dramatically figured as the form if not the cause of desire. This is not a knowledge, however, which contains a truth. Rather, the epistemological status accorded more generally to sex and sexuality is an effect of the discourses which generate the promise of a truth. This truth, however, is always provisional and deferred, something which is open to a queerer future than some popular dramas of the past imagine. Whilst heteronormative institutions such as the church, the family and much of the mainstream media have historically buttressed one discourse of sexuality over another, this support can only occur on the basis of the simultaneous inclusion *and* exclusion of other sexualities. Heteronormative discourse sets the terms for the negatively-charged category of the homosexual (or the figure of the lesbian in the BBC version of *Oranges*), though the resulting hegemony of heterosexuality can only occur on the basis of the opposing sexuality. There is no specificity, at least not in any ontological sense, to Winterson's heroine's homosexuality because hers is a sexuality which is always being inscribed in relation to heterosexual discourse. This is also true of heterosexuality though heterosexuality remains uncontested, assured of its naturalised status in the culture.

Identifications and desires: *Tipping the Velvet; Queer As Folk; Shameless*

In BBC 2s dramatisation of Sarah Waters' *Tipping the Velvet* (BBC 2004), lesbianism makes sense against the wider backdrop of a society which inscribed erotic pleasure – far more than a discrete sexual identity as such – into every aspect of everyday life.   If lesbianism is conceived in feminine or female terms or in masculine and male terms (and there are no reasons why it should not be conceived in both ways at the same time (see Halbestam)), then these enactments of lesbian femininity or masculinity, whilst read in terms of bodily expression, are actually conventions which make sense in relation to the discourse which inscribes the lesbian as masculine or feminine in the first instance.   In *Tipping the Velvet*, the protagonists' desires are articulated in spaces which expose the extent to which the ordinary, the everyday and the mundane are already sexualised and eroticised. Alley ways, street corners, military barracks, bars, and music halls are the arenas for arousal, sexual satisfaction, and 'illicit' pleasure. Yet these illicit pleasures are also now very much public pleasures as well, dramatised on streets whose sexual theatres are the impersonal doorways, empty back lanes, and shopping arcades of Victorian England.

Although sexual relations between women and women historically have been marginalised and hidden from public view, *Tipping the Velvet* dramatises the ways in which erotic pleasures and satisfactions have always been inscribed into the discourses of the social sphere. Sexologists such as Richard von Krafft-Ebing and Havelock Ellis at the end of the end of the nineteenth and the beginnings of the twentieth centuries sought to prescribe a sexual identity to all subjects. However, their more radical contemporary, Sigmund Freud, showed how sexuality is written into the mundane and ordinary in ways which limit and subvert the definitional projects which the sexologists undertook. In Freud's *Three Essays* (1905) and in *Civilisation and Its Discontents* (1930), all subjects are to some degree polymorphously perverse and never easily categorised. Such 'normal' perversity is to some extent dramatised in Russell T Davies' *Queer As Folk*. This is a drama which is peopled by 'straight' characters who are queer (Vince's mother and her male house-partner-cum-husband), and by lesbian and gay characters who are 'straight' (Stuart, for instance, conforms to stereotypes of straightness far more than Vince's mother). It is not so much that the characters or indeed the text are open to these 'queer' readings. Rather, the drama itself cannot finally produce a determinate truth about sexuality on which to construct reliable models of sexual sameness and difference.

The drama's queerness can be observed in its attempts to move away from forms of characterisation grounded in notions of (sexual) authenticity. In the series, sexuality is not presented as a discrete identity, even if the drama does at times show how same-sex sexual identifications and relations run alongside the (gay-friendly and thus seductive) heterosexual and heteronormative mainstream. Rather, the series explores a much bigger, extra-sexual world when compared to those popular dramas of the recent past which made lesbians or gay men the 'outrageous' exception to the heterosexual norm. The queerness lies in part in the drama's attempt to situate sexual desires outside of the body and in those social spheres which will ultimately expose the fictions of the epistemology and the ontology of the gay closet. There are no gays or lesbians as such who await dramatic representation. In queer drama, desire is for anyone or anything rather than simply another 'person' – gay or straight.

In *Queer as Folk*, for instance, desire is imagined and represented in relation to clothes (Stuart), styles of walking (Nathan watching Stuart), cars (Stuart), internet chat rooms (all the gay men), mobile phones (Vince), specific music genres (each main character is assigned a tune), bars and clubs (straight and gay characters), magazines (Nathan), and *Dr Who* videos (Vince!) far more than it is realised in relation to same-sex object choice. Always inside and outside the mainstream of drama, gesturing to the shame of an awkward past but pointing as well to the pride of an imagined future in which sex no longer matters (see the last episode of Series Two, 2000), *Queer As Folk* deals with more than sexuality in its exploration of people's lives at the end of the twentieth century. Constructions and/or representations of obsessional behaviour, hysteria and the emotional extremes, drug addiction, 'under-age' sex, 'un-safe' sex, lesbian parenting, club cultures, criminality, racism, misogyny, white British-ness, and social class antagonisms are all woven into Davies' drama. Sexuality is situated in *all* these discursive spheres and thus takes some of its meaning in a language which resonates the (psychoanalytic) structures of pleasure and reality, suffering, pain, anger, and death. On the one hand, sexuality operates as the defining limit of the discourse (so that every event and relationship in the drama is sexualised or sexually motivated). On the other hand, the discourse serves to undermine any definitional coherence sexuality is thought to possess (so that the discourse maintains its impersonal and constraining hold regardless of sexuality). In Davies' drama, the wider discourses undercut the definitional integrity of sexuality even though discourses are themselves never simply asexual or outside of the sexual sphere as such. As a result of this dual operation, Davies' drama will not simply interpellate a gay, lesbian or straight audience but will address groups of viewers whose own queer or ambivalent desires resonate the conflicts and confusions which structure sexual identifications in the first instance.

His drama exposes how sexual subjectivity is not enacted in the claiming of a specific identity or the coming-out narrative, staged in the drama via high-school character Nathan and the confused supermarket manager, Vince. Rather, the drama shows layer upon layer of sexual *identifications* (interwoven with class, whiteness, northern-ness, gender, etc) more than it unveils what it means to claim a *homo*sexual identity. Older gay men live with straight women; couples remain in sexless heterosexual marriages; and the bonds among groups of gay and straight characters are often greater than the bonds between two lovers. In many respects, the series' real queerness is realised in its exploration and staging of social class, ethnic positionality, northern-ness, gender and youth via discourses of 'straightness'. Heterosexuals have to perform an identity as much as homosexuals; to be straight, or to be straight-acting, is to be as culturally marked and as textually inscribed as the camp or effeminate male homosexual subject of the past (Butler; Halberstam). In the way that white subjects are now conceived in terms of the ethnic positionality accorded to their own skin colour rather than chromatic invisibility or an absence of skin colour (Dyer 1997), so heterosexuals (are made to) lay bare the devices which have naturalised (which is to say made invisible) their own constructed status within the discourse. In *Queer as Folk*, all the characters are being 'dragged up'.

Lead (gay) character Vince, for example, convinces all his supermarket workmates that he is straight, and it is a straight-schoolboy 'chav', Christian, who is aroused by straight-acting 'twink' Nathan, whose closest sexual confidante is straight black (but queer-identified) schoolmate Donna. Vince's mother's sexual identifications are also interesting to the extent that she initially makes sense to the series' gay audience in the context of the straight/queer sub-cultural spaces peopled by fag-hags (See Madison 2001), spaces which are themselves derived from the once sub-cultural world of urban gay bars. But the former *Coronation Street* actor is also a catalyst for the series' straight mothers, establishing bonds between Nathan's and Stuart's mothers. These sexual identifications are structured around same-sex - though predominantly 'straight' - identifications far more than the opposite-sex sexual relations they have with their respective husbands. Finally Alexander, fresh back from a trip abroad, is frustrated by the macho world of the white and Western gay scene (it is too straight for him), and so he speaks a sexuality in relation to the diasporic lady-boy subculture of Thailand and South-East Asia. Alex displaces the straight-acting gay image and ironically reproduces the very straight-acting discourse which allows lady-boys to construct their own versions of masculinity-femininity. On Davies's stage, it is difficult to discern who is copying whom. At times, the only element of the drama which seems to have any stability is the city of Manchester in which the series is set.

The drama's key locations and settings (Harlo's supermarket, Nathan's school, the various workplaces, the respective family homes, and the journey to the US in the second series) are all far removed from Manchester's *gay* village. The drama, then, begins to make sense against the backdrop of Manchester and the north of England generally far more than the relatively small if vibrant world of Manchester's gay village around Canal Street. The suburban locations also matter in terms of where sexual identifications take place. The sexual identifications dramatised in *Queer As Folk* are constructed in relation schools (and therefore age), workplaces (and thus economic power), living- rooms (and thus domesticity), shopping malls and bars (and therefore profit, hedonism, and consumption).

These public-social spheres are queer (to the extent that they can't be defined simply in terms of homosexual or heterosexual geographies), and impersonal (because they are linked to desire in ways which exceed a specifically personal mark of a discretely sexed anatomy). 'If you fancy a threesome at the end of the night, you can't start getting choosy about which particular three', suggests Alexander. His refusal to be choosy can also be read as an attempt to displace an imagined homosexual space in which to articulate desire (a space similar to the gay village or sexual zone of the city) by one which imagines desire in more expansive, which is to say, less spatial terms. If Alexander really does desire a twosome or a threesome, isn't the space potentially enlarged on the basis of the radical, non-spatial cause of desire? Actor Anthony

Cotton's character is certainly one which will be decoded by some viewers in terms of the effeminacy, campness, and joviality associated in television history with characters such as Mr Humprhies (*Are You Being Served*, BBC 1972-1985) and 'Gloria' (*It Aint Half Hot Mum,* BBC 1974-1981). Similarly, straight-acting Stuart and Nathan seem on one level to function in relation gay rather than post-gay or queer identities. Although we get to know these characters in the contexts of gay bars, gay sexual relations, and gay male life styles, we are also confronted by their desires. These desires move beyond the spaces associated with gay male urban cultures and surreally dislodge the constraining grounds of identity. Such surreal flights (in the last episode the three gay lead characters), whilst they might reflect the freedom of living one's desires and fantasies also highlight how desire is manipulated under capitalism. Alternatively phrased, these are fantasies which also make sense in the economic context of late-twentieth century Western economies where desire is imagined in terms of consumer commodities. These are identities which consumer-capitalism constructs, exploits and outmodes. However, these are not identities which are the expression of deep-rooted inner core so much as they are effects that are discursively framed by capitalism's need to continuously commodify, compartmentalise and exploit the market in identities (see Alexandra Chasin 2001).

A similar movement away from the dramatisation of sexual identity to a focus on class, ethnic and sexual identifications is staged in Paul Abbott's *Shameless* (Channel 4). It shares much in common, in many respects, with *Queer As Folk*: it is set in the north of England; it in interested in 'extremes' of behaviour; and living and household arrangements make the drama post-familial and post-domestic. The drama's interrogation of traditional patterns of domesticity and family living is in many ways more challenging than much of the theoretical literature on sexual citizenship which has tended to see the family in its various transmutations as a unit which can ground (so-called) alternative gay and lesbian ways of living[37].

In *Shameless* there are no demands for rightful inclusion in the family or the 'community', particularly the idealised versions of the latter historically promoted by the church, municipal authorities, and the school.

---

[37] The debates surrounding gay/lesbian families and sexual citizenship are varied. Jeffrey Weeks' 'The Sexual Citizen', *Theory, Culture and Society*, 15: 3-4 (1998), 35-52 is one of the key articles promoting the case for sexual citizenship; see also *Same Sex Intimacies: Families of Choice and other Life Experiments* (with Brian Heaphy and Catherine Donovan) (London: Routledge, 2001); and see David Bell and John Binnie, *The Sexual Citizen: Queer Politics and Beyond* (Pluto, 2000).

Abbot's characters are suspicious of outsiders yet these are also characters who welcome those in need. The estate's residents are not the national government's model of the citizen, however. On the estate, criminality and crime are routineised and normalised; social class more than a sense of citizenship is the discursive lens through which sexual and ethnic identifications are explored. Class and whiteness in *Shameless* (more than *Queer As Folk*) are also filtered through the discourses of Irishness; and heterosexual identities and belongings are less of a concern in the series than sexual identifications. In whichever ways citizenship and families are theorised, both notions are invariably articulated via an underpinning endorsement of heteronormative discourse. Moreover, whenever family or home is conceived, it is mostly the case that monogamy, the couple and the private sphere are also being endorsed. Those not living in coupled and monogamous arrangements are often excluded from the protection afforded by 'family' or 'community'. Both these terms, however, are also associated with a 'good', which is to say heteronormative, image of the citizen. Bad citizens, or those who resist or refuse the privatised or coupled articulations of sexual identifications, are the ones explored in *Shameless*.

Alongside Abbot's challenging representation of citizenship is his depiction of 'the North'. However, his is a distinctly different representation of the North when compared with the 'other' northern dramas: *Queer as Folk*, *Coronation Street* (ITV1, 1960 -) and *The Royle Family* (BBC, 1998-200). The north of England setting, specifically the Chatsworth council estate (in extreme binary opposition to the actual stately home of the same name), signifies the drama's interest in understanding sexual identifications against the backdrop of an underclass. Gone are the minimalist office blocks and waterside apartments of the often idealised work and consumer culture of *Queer As Folk*; characters drink at the estate's 'local' (as opposed to Canal Street bars or *Coronation Street's* 'The Rover's Return'), Frank famously mixing his drinks with whatever drugs are available on the day; kitchens and living rooms become *boudoirs*, sites for S and M dressing-up rituals where older women, who are traditionally represented as frigid and 'past it', seduce younger men; and consumerism, which *Queer As Folk* explores in relation to the construction of late-capitalist identifications, gives way to the debt-ridden and criminal micro-economies of the council estate with its rule-governed systems of distribution and exchange.

The drama, importantly, also signifies in the direction of idealised English, Irish, and post-colonial Irish-diasporic cultures. The Gallagher family at the centre of Channel 4's series make sense in relation to 'extremes' of behaviour that have traditionally been made meaningful in an historical lineage which privileged and idealised English, and specifically white-English cultural, ascendancy (See Finnegan & McCarron 2000; Mac-an-ghaill 1999). Such 'white' middle-class hegemony makes the 'underclass' into an extreme or marginal group whereby under-class whiteness becomes an ethnicity. In *Shameless*, whiteness is given an 'Irish' name (Gallagher); the family (nominally) profess faith in an imported (Irish) religion (the first Roman Catholic priests after the Catholic Emancipation Act were mostly Irish); and the social networks with which they are associated are not the 'Brit-pop' ones of another (Noel and Liam) Gallagher family but the more recent 'charva' and 'scally' subcultures of contemporary white Britain. But Abbott also seems interested in examining how identities are always an idealised fantasy - a 'scotch broth' to use his own terms (see below) -- which suits the purposes of government more than 'community'.

Unlike the realism of some television dramas, where the genre often over-determines *what* can be said and *how*, *Shameless* explores working-class life in terms of the possibilities of stretching and mixing genres and, by implication, identities and identifications. Abbott seems more interested in considering what can be done with genres rather than allowing himself to be ruled by the apparent determinations of genre conventions. Whilst naturalism and social realism have been important in the dramatisation of class, gender, and social relations more generally, these forms have often blended keen insights into (idealised and homogenised representations of) working-class life with forms of characterisation grounded in personal pessimism or despair (See Nelson 1997 and Hill 1986). Moreover, heteronormative as opposed to plural sexual identifications have been given precedence in dramas which have often explored notions of culture and value far more than the inter-operation of the erotic and desire with the lived culture itself.

This theatrical and dramatic exposing of 'extremes of behaviour' has often been figured in relation to discourses of obscenity and pornography.[38]   Yet definitions of pornography and obscenity are themselves filtered through the language of class, taste and the official culture far more than the language of sex, sexuality and subcultures. If the sub-cultural spaces which make up the Chatsworth estate appear extreme, 'not like Eden' as the opening credits remind us, then this is consistent with Abbott's aim to show behaviour as it is lived according to

---

[38] E.g. this was the case with the Lady Chatterley trial of the early 1960s; and it beset the work of British playwright Joe Orton.

those discourses which turn some people into 'extremes' or underclasses. Abbott writes that *Shameless*

> is a real scotch broth of my experience, but it's not bleak or sentimental, it's the total opposite – just really funny and outrageous. I hung onto the title *Shameless* for its irony, the kind of accusation outsiders would have chucked at my family back in the 1970s. To observers we were a chaotic bunch of kids trying to bring ourselves up after both parents had walked. No doubt about it, we were a mess. But how were we to know that? [...] Ignorance being bliss was our most treasured human asset. We'd been loud, aggressive, primitive and anarchic. But I never once recall us feeling... Shameless.
> (http://www.channel4.com/entertainment/tv/microsites/S/shameless/intervi ews_2.html (June, 2006).

Reviews of *Shameless*, for instance, have discussed the drama in terms of a (Leavisite) moral-critical attention to canonicity, culture and form. Andrew Billen of the *New Statesman* writes how the drama series has a 'disregard for taste, sentiment and political piety'. This is a series which depicts the 'lowest rung of Mancunian society' (2006). The report accompanying the UK Film Council Seminar on the Cultural Value of UK Film in 2005 noted how the tone and ensemble stories of Channel 4's *Shameless* would not have been possible 'without the artistic precedent of Mike Leigh's work for cinema. Film established new ways of seeing and new approaches to storytelling'. (http://www.ukfilmcouncil.org.uk/usr/downloads/Cultural%20value%20re port.pdf (Dec.2005)..

Whilst this is a fairly accurate context in which to understand *Shameless* and similar television output, the report assumes much about 'culture', 'value', and 'aesthetics'. 'Culture' is deployed in the report to signify aesthetics rather than a way of life. As a consequence, culture is understood in terms of form and genre more than the activities, desires, and identifications of particular groups of people who compose the culture at any one historical moment. *Shameless* is interesting surely because it begins to consider those marginal spaces, the ones often visited by Government ministers,[39] which have often been though to threaten values, culture, and aesthetics. But *Shameless* is also interesting because of its attempts to move beyond those heteronormative structures which many canonical television drama texts - both in terms of form and content – have

---

[39] Michael Heseltine famously visited the northern city of Liverpool under Margaret Thatcher's period as Prime Minister, and Thatcher herself told Northerners not to be 'moaning Minnies'.

left un-interrogated.

The Channel 4 series examines structures of desire and the emotions formally/generically as well as through complex character identifications. It achieves this interrogation in three ways. Firstly, *Shameless*, whilst it might have its contextual roots in the work of Mike Leigh, nonetheless experiments more innovatively with form. Such innovation is seen in the drama's move away from an exclusive stress on character/identity to an experimentation with hybridised generic frameworks which show identifications taking place on a number of levels. In *Shameless* (as well as *Queer As Folk*), the inter-textual blending of modes associated with tragedy, soap opera, romance, comedy, documentary, social and psychological realism, melodrama, and naturalism means that the world is conceived differentially. The modes of soap opera, the romantic, the comedic and the tragic ensure that the stories concerned with mental illness, neuroses, sexual desires, unemployment, parenting, and housing are rendered in terms of the conflicting dimensions to which these modes avail themselves. The mixing of modes is also a way of suggesting that characterisation is always a matter of hybridity and dimension rather than generic wholeness and homogeneity. By incorporating the dramatic modes that it does, so *Shameless* complements those dramas which rely more on generic unity in their attempts to render emotional identifications and diversity.

A second feature is the drama's context and setting. Abbott attempts to show an 'other' culture, one which is at odds with the moral(ising) tradition which views the 'full rich life' (Hoggart) through the moral-critical legacy of Matthew Arnold and F R and Q D Leavis.[40] The drama alludes, ironically, to Eden and paradise, the golden age imagined in many English literary works from Spenser to Eliot. Yet dramas such as *Shameless* also mix the pastoral and Arcadian with the gargantuan, carnivalesque, the common, and the vulgar in order to explore the sexual and the erotic in conflicting ways. But these are sexual identifications which in part structure the underclass culture which the series attempts to represent. Rather than gesturing to a golden age, either for the sake of the drama or the culture, as ground for meaning, dramas such as *Shameless* and *Queer As Folk* expose the past as deeply

---

[40] See Matthew Arnold, *Culture and Anarchy* (London: Cambridge University Press, 1960 (1869)); Richard Hoggart, *The Uses of Literacy* (Harmondworth: Penguin, 1990 (1957)); F R Leavis, *Mass Civilization and Minority Culture*, Minority Pamphlet No. 1, Gordon Fraser, The Minority Press: Cambridge, 1930; Q D Leavis, *Fiction and the Reading Public* (London: Chatto and Windus, 1978 [1932]).

heteronormative and conservative, a past which has not always bequeathed the best that has been 'thought or said' (Arnold), and a past which is as multiple and as disputatious as the present. Abbot's 'reading public' do not quite read the same fictions which the Leavises imagine.

A third feature is the series' (Freudian-psychoanalytic) exploration of how sexual identifications mark all aspects of other social identifications. *Shameless* shows how polymorphous sexual identifications are not enacted in some private compartment off-stage or off-screen. Rather, these very visible identifications are precisely what the drama is not ashamed to explore. In *Shameless*, there is nothing outside of the world of these identifications that could possibly shame the people or the action. Consider, for instance, Channel 4's website details on Shamelesss's depiction of sexual identifications.

Episode Two:

And there's another voracious sexual appetite on the estate when Kev's sister, Kelly-Marie, starts lodging at Frank and Sheila's house. While Sheila delights at the sound of Kelly's loud sexual antics and uses it to fuel her and Frank's lovemaking, Frank is suspicious of the string of boyfriends paying her visits. When it transpires that Kelly-Marie is charging all these men for the privilege, Frank and Sheila have to take drastic action

Episode Five:

Carol, meanwhile has found herself a new gentleman-friend, Norman Owens. He seems to be a perfect gent and exactly what she's been searching for, until he joins the family for breakfast, in the nude (http://www.channel4.com/entertainment/tv/microsites/S/shameless/three_two.html (June 2006).

There is only shame when one form of identification is seen as better or superior than another. Rather than allowing the family and heterosexual identifications to be seen as normative, *Shameless* shows how all relations are oedipally and psychically motivated to the extent that adult-child relations are marked by desires structured around love, passion, and hatred. The private space of the family, alongside the attendant discourse of heterosexual romance, are unable to sustain their private, shame-filled visions of sexual pleasure. Desires are inscribed in all other social identifications, seen particularly in the story of fifteen-year old character Ian Gallagher (played by Gerard Kearns).

His attempts to keep his (same-sex) identifications private are rendered impossible. Whilst a gay identity is something you might want to keep very hidden on the Chatsworth estate, the social space is one which sees all sexual identifications being lived very publicly. The open

sexual secrets that crisscross all the networks on the estate suggest that
there are in fact *no* sexual secrets. Ian's relationship with Kash (Chris
Bisson) is one which is ultimately sanctioned by the leading players on the
estate, not least the Gallagher family.   Indeed, the biggest open secret of
all is that 35-year old Kash, the hard-working manager of the local mini
mart is also the married, Muslim father of two who is having a love affair
with 'under-age' shop assistant Ian. But these identifications emanate not
on the basis of gay or indeed straight identities waiting to be expressed.
Rather, these are *identifications* which emerge from the in-between spaces
of an estate where the warmth of the bonds facilitated by sexual intimacy
seem to offer some protection from the impersonal forces of
unemployment, poor housing, and poor social amenities. Sexual identity
in such contexts will be less important than the identifications which the
social space permits, identifications which emerge in and around the
estate's homophobia, misogyny, and racism.

Curtain Call

        I have argued in this chapter that one of the areas which is often
left out of discussions of television drama are the operations of sexual
desires and identifications, both in the criticism and in the theory which
informs the criticism. Television dramas which have treated queer
sexualities in more than cursory ways (*Metrosexuality, Oranges Are Not
the Only Fruit, Queer As Folk, The Buddha of Suburbia, This Life, Tinsel
Town*, and *Shameless*), have also been interesting because of a more
general questioning of binary sexual frameworks as well. Desire, I have
suggested, is more than simply heterosexual or homosexual and shifts on
the basis of social class, ethnicity, and age as much as it is apparently
triggered, in essentialist arguments, by an innate homosexual core. As a
consequence, sexual desire, far from being a straightforward expression of
personal or internal desire of one person for another is actually
impersonal, something which makes sense outside of the drives thought to
motivate (dramatic) personae. Perhaps drama which has been described as
'queer' is not simply because it deals with non-heterosexual
representations of desires. Rather, the drama might be queer because it
cannot situate the specificity of sexuality.
        In *Shameless*, for instance, desire makes sense not in terms of one
person's love for another (same-sex or otherwise). Nor does sexuality
assume meaning on the basis of an erotic desire which emanates from one
subject to another. Following Foucault and more recently Butler and
Dean, this chapter has argued that there is only truth to bodily sex or desire

on the basis of discourses situated outside of the sexuality of person in question. Often, the discourse has constructed sexual subjects (and sexual objects) which have been shamed by and ashamed of the name of that sexuality. Rather than being staged or thought in personal terms, I contend that *Shameless* dramatises desire always in the context of the social and psychic conditions in which subjects live their daily - which is to say sexual, ethnic, gendered, class, and economic - lives. Popular British television drama, framed as it is around notions of the personal, the domestic, and the familial, is forced to structure desire in terms of persons and people rather than the impersonal discourses of the culture in which desire is made to appear personal. The BBC's dramatisation of *Tipping the Velvet*, and Channel 4's *Queer as Folk*, whilst in many ways radical in terms of their representations of the confusions of sexual desire, nonetheless appear to position sexual desire as emanating from characters Nan and Kitty, or Stuart and Nathan. Yet these dramas, including *Shameless*, are unable to settle desires which seem all the time to exceed the subjects in question. For desire to mean what it does amongst audiences, desire will have to be understood outside of that which seems – often transparently though in my view, erroneously – personal. I would argue, following Dean,[41] that sexual desire, alongside the sexual object, are mistakenly figured when they are understood exclusively in terms of people, persons, or bodies. I would argue that desire is dispersed and not, as is often assumed, located in the subject. As a consequence, *it* (the object cause of desire, the desire of the subject) is something which is without shame. Shameless!

Works cited

Arnold, Matthew [1869]. *Culture and Anarchy* London: Cambridge University Press, 1960.

Bell, David and Jon Binnie, *The Sexual Citizen: Queer Politics and Beyond,* London: Pluto, 2000.

Brandt, George, *British Television Drama in the 1980s,* Cambridge: Cambridge University Press, 1993.

---

[41] For a more detailed appraisal of Dean's work, see Tony Purvis, ''All you get from an imaginary relation is an ego and lots of trouble: From psychology to sexuality to desire and the unconscious', in Journal for the Centre of Freudian Analysis and Research', Issue 14, Spring 2004, 90-100.

Burston, Paul and Colin Richardson (eds), *A Queer Romance: Lesbians, Gay Men and Popular Culture*, London and New York: Routledge, 1995.

Buscombe Edward (ed), *British Television: A Reader*, Oxford: Oxford University Press, 2000.

Butler, Judith, *Gender Trouble: Feminism and the Subversion of Identity* New York and London: Routledge, 1990.

—. *Bodies That Matter: On the Discursive Limits of Sex*, New York and London: Routledge, 1993.

—. *Excitable Speech: A Politics of the Performative*, New York and London: Routledge, 1997.

—. *Undoing Gender*, New York and London: Routledge, 2004.

Caughie, John, *Television Drama: Realism, Modernism, and British Culture,* Oxford: Oxford University Press, 2000.

Champagne, John, *The Ethics of Marginality: New Approach to Gay Studies,* Minneapolis: University of Minnesota Press, 1995.

Chasin, Alexandra, *Selling Out: The Gay and Lesbian Movement Goes to Market,* Basingstoke: Palgrave Macmillan, 2001.

Cooke, Lez., *British Television Drama: A History,* London: BFI, 2003.

Dean, Tim, *Beyond Sexuality.* Chicago: Chicago University Press, 2000.

Doty, Alexander, *Making Things Perfectly Queer: Interpreting Mass Culture,* Minneapolis: University of Minnesota Press, 1993.

—. *Flaming Classics: Queering the Film Canon*, New York and London: Routledge, 2000.

Doty, Alexander and Ben Gove, 'Queer Representation in the Mass Media', in Medhurst, Andrew and Sally Munt, (eds), 1997.

Dyer, Richard, *The Matter of Images: Essays on Representation,* London and New York: Routledge, 1993.

—. *White: Essays on Race and Culture*, London: Routledge, 1997.

Finnegan, Richard and Edward McCarron, *Ireland: Historical Echoes, Contemporary Politics,* Boulder, Colorado: Westview, 2000.

Foucault, Michel, [1976], *History of Sexuality: Volume I: An Introduction,* trans. R Hurley, New York: Random House, 1978.

Freud, Sigmund, *Three Essays on the Theory of Sexuality*, Standard Edition: London: Hogarth, 1905.

—. *Civilization and Its Discontents*, Standard Edition: London: Hogarth, 1930.

Halberstam, Judith, *Female Masculinity*, Durham: Duke University Press.

Hall, Stuart. (ed.), *Representation: Cultural Representations and Signifying Practices,* London, Thousand Oaks: Sage, 1997.

Hall, Stuart (ed), *Representation: Cultural Representations and Signifying*

Practices. London: Open University, 1997.

Hennessy, Rosemary, *Profit and Pleasure: Sexual Identities in Late Capitalism*, New York and London: Routledge, 2000.

Hill, John, *Sex, Class and Realism: British Cinema, 1956-1963,* London: BFI, 1986.

Hoggart, Richard, [1957], *The Uses of Literacy,* Harmondworth: Penguin, 1990.

Leavis, Frank. R., *Mass Civilization and Minority Culture*, Minority Pamphlet No. 1, Gordon Fraser, The Minority Press: Cambridge, 1993.

Leavis, Queenie. D., [1932], *Fiction and the Reading Public,* London: Chatto and Windus, 1978.

Mac-an-ghaill, Mairtin, *Contemporary Racisms and Ethnicities: Social and Cultural Transformations*, Basingstoke: Palgrave, 1999.

Madison, Stephen, *Fags, Hags, and Queer Sisters: Gender Dissent and Heterosocial Bonds in Gay Male Cultures,* Basingstoke: Palgrave Macmillan, 2001.

Malik, Sarita, *Representing Black Britain: Black and Asian Images on Television*, London, Thousand Oaks: Sage, 2000.

Medhurst, Andy, 'Every wart and pustule: Gilbert Harding and television stardom', in Buscombe E. (ed) *British Television: A Reader*, Oxford: Oxford University Press, 2000.

Medhurst, Andy and Sally Munt (eds), *Lesbian and Gay Studies: A Critical Introduction.* London: Continuum International, 1997.

Munt, Sally, 'Shame/Pride Dichotomies in Queer as Folk', in *Textual Practice*, 14:3, 2000: 531-546.

Nelson, Robin, *Television Drama in Transition: Forms, Values and Cultural Change*, Basingstoke: Palgrave Macmillan, 1997.

Nixon, Sean, *Advertising Cultures: Gender, Commerce, Creativity,* London, Thousand Oaks: Sage, 2003.

—.'Exhibiting Masculinity' in Hall (ed), *Representation: Cultural Representations and Signifying Practices.* London: Open University, 1997.

Smith, Anne-Marie, *New Right Discourse on Race and Sexuality: Britain, 1968-1990*, Cambridge: Cambridge University Press, 1995.

O'Rourke, Michael, *Autoimmunity, Messianicity, Futurality*, Paper presented at FUTURE/QUEER Conference, University College Dublin, June 30 2006.

Purvis, Tony, '"All you get from an imaginary relation is an ego and lots of trouble": From psychology to sexuality to desire and the unconscious', in *Journal for the Centre of Freudian Analysis and Research,,* Issue 14, Spring, 2004. 90-100.

—. 'Sexualities', in Waugh, Patricia. (ed), *The Oxford Guide to Literary Theory*, Oxford: Oxford University Press, 2006.

Savran, David, *Communists, Cowboys, and Queers: The Politics of Masculinity in Arthur Miller and Tennessee Williams*, Minneapolis: University of Minnesota Press, 1992.

Savran, D., *A Queer Sort of Materialism: Recontextualising American Theatre*, Ann Arbor: University of Michigan Press, 2003.

Sedgwick, Eve. K., *Epistemology of the Closet,* Berkley and Los Angeles: University of California Press, 1990.

Sinfield, Alan, *The Wilde Century: Effeminacy, Oscar Wilde, and the Queer Moment*, London: Continuum, 1994.

Thornham, Sue and Tony Purvis, *Television Drama: Theories and Identities,* Basingstoke: Palgrave, 2005.

Waugh, Patricia. (ed),, *The Oxford Guide to Literary Theory*, Oxford: Oxford University Press, 2006.

Weeks, Jeffrey (1998), 'The Sexual Citizen', in *Theory, Culture and Society*, 15, 1998.

Weeks, Jeffrey., with Brian Heaphy and Catherine Donovan, *Same Sex Intimacies: Families of Choice and other Life Experiments*, London: Routledge, 2001.

Newspaper reviews

Billen, Andrew, *New Statesman*, 6 February, 2006.

Websites

http://www.channel4.com/entertainment/tv/microsites/S/shameless/three_two.html (June 2006).

SECTION III:

THEATRES OF DIFFERENCE

CHAPTER EIGHTEEN

GREY SILHOUETTES: BLACK QUEER THEATRE ON THE POST-WAR BRITISH STAGE

VICTOR UKAEGBU

Synopsis

This essay interrogates post-war black queer theatre in the UK, exploring its history, aesthetics, and the ambivalent reception surrounding it. The essay will also attempt, and only to a degree, a panoramic reading of black queer theatre through the works of three of its prominent practitioners: Jackie Kay, Paul Boakye, and Valerie Mason-John.

I. Introduction

Black queer theatre is almost invisible on the post-war British stage. This is due firstly, to the cultural ambivalence that made black British communities for a long time, to deny the existence of gay, lesbian, transgendered and bi-sexual sexualities in their midst. The second reason is the historical under-representation of black people in British history, in art and in culture, despite their sojourn on the island dating back to a time before the transatlantic slave trade (Godiwala 2006 & Osborne 2006). The third factor is cultural and derives from the first two. This is the tendency for black gay and lesbian performers to distinguish between their art and sexuality and between their sexualities and racial identities.

In effect, historical and cultural forces collude in the presentation of gay and lesbian images on post-war British stage, especially in denying performers what Balme (1999) describes as cultural space. This is the only space that authenticates the personal experiences of queer performers and recognizes their art as inseparable from their sexualities. Black gay icons, Valerie Mason-John, a.k.a. 'Queenie', Co-artistic Director of Pride Arts

Festival, Jackie Kay, Paul Boakye, Megan Radclyffe, Inge Blackman, and the existence of theatre groups, Theatre of Black Women and the Gay Sweatshop highlight the diversity of gay and lesbian performance materials in UK black communities. Despite routine denials and rejection by their communities, queer performers and work have been in existence among black peoples as they do among other races. Isaac Julien's 1989 film, *Looking for Langston*, revolutionized how black communities viewed them but black queer performers had always featured in fringe theatres though marginalised in mainstream British theatres. Film may have increased the range and diversity of materials on black queer sexualities in the UK but it merely followed in the paths long charted by theatre.

The terms, gay and lesbian, are generally used in binary relationship or in opposition to heterosexuality. Martin Banham argues that occasionally 'gay theatre' 'includes lesbian drama and theatre' (Banham 1992:381) but the terms subscribe to different gender constructs that exclude the other and that distinguish them from bisexuals and transgender discourse. There are good reasons for Banham's inclusive agenda but because this essay is not about hegemony and sexuality, I will not debate the differences between sexualities. However, I use the words gay and lesbian synonymously with queer, a description that is 'more capacious than *lesbian and gay*' and which 'always includes gays and lesbians and often functions as a metonymy for *lesbian and gay*' (Marcus 2005:196).

Queer is used in the context of this essay to describe plays and performances that speak specifically to and about non-heterosexual identities and politics, and about the diverse issues embraced by queer discourse itself. The term is thus employed as an inclusive narrative trope that denotes a binary relationship with heterosexuality and that signifies the different cultural ideologies behind gay, lesbian, bisexual and transgender performers and art, all of which exist in binary relationship with heterosexual art. In any case, queer is widely accepted and has been used in black settings (Kay 1988) where it has generated its own discourse, spawned its own internal nomenclature and dynamics, and also played its part in race relations between black and non-black gay people (Mason-John 1999).

II. Contexts and Contents

(i) Sexuality and Identity in Jackie Kay's *Chiaroscuro*

In 1988 Jackie Kay's aptly-titled *Chiaroscuro* was published by Methuen having started off as *The Meeting Place* (Kay 1988). It features four women from different cultural backgrounds; Aisha, Beth, Opal, and Yomi who explore their sexuality through dance, songs, music, and symbolic props that are used to instigate individual stories and to denote the commonality of the women's experiences. The play explores the women's first meeting and how their friendship became their main support system in a world of insecurities, rejection, and prejudice. It analyses the cultural biases, fears and stereotypes surrounding lesbianism but is most effective for exposing the lack of debate between sections of this subculture, the lack of acknowledgement and documentation, and the need for lesbians to do away with divisive internal frictions. As the women's experiences show, their prejudices and the things that separate them are less important than the things that unite and their need for a common front:

> OPAL: I don't like that word – lesbian...
> OPAL: We don't need a name....
> AISHA: ....(To Opal) She first thought she might be a lesbian at school....
> None of the textbooks mentioned her name....She was still alone.... (p. 66)

The play presents a balanced picture of queer subculture. The women share stories, not in the confines of a domestic setting but in a public forum where they reveal their common bonds and the patriarchal hegemony beneath the seemingly innocuous cultural practice of giving names. Each character takes the audience through the painful journey of self-discovery, through the cultural bias that lesbians and gays generally face on domestic and public fronts in different societies. Although each woman's tale is unique, they share common features and differ only in their inconsequential externals as Kay indicates through the play's highly symbolic costumes, images, and stage directions. In the end, the women rise above personal idiosyncrasies, they unite and face the future on a more certain footing:

> ALL: Time changes light
> light changes time
> ... trying to find the words....
> AISHA: This is how we got where we are. My name is Aisha, remember, I was called after my grandmother on my mother's side....

YOMI: My name is Yomi…. Remember her? (p. 81)

All four characters wear identical costumes and add only a few oddments to these in order to suggest changes in narrative, in specific cultural settings and to show advances in plot development. Every aspect of the women's lives, their personal experiences and identity are linked to their sexuality irrespective of their culture. The characters are neither divided by class nor by culture but mainly by sexuality, their narratives are similar to those in Franca Rame's and Dario Fo's *Same Old Story* and *A Woman Alone*, two plays in which women are subjected to patriarchal narratives whose constraining influences demand their attention if they are to present themselves in their own gaze and create their own liberating narratives. Kay dispenses with elaborate exploration of theme and subject matter. In its place, she employs symbolic props and music to supplement the dialogue and to advance the plot. The resulting drama does not simply present readers with an array of different complex characters with whom they empathize, some of the props such as the wooden chest and mirror are used to interrogate conventional constructions of sexuality and to challenge stereotypical representations of lesbianism.

Chiaroscuro is a dialogic debate with mainstream sections of society. It is simultaneously expository and presentational. These features and the play's symbolic props and images give the women the evocative, powerful voices to trace their personal journeys to lesbianism. Kay's deployment of Brechtian distancing to the presentation of subject matter and her interrogation of every characters motive are features that Mason-John uses years later in *Brown Girls in the Ring* (1999). In Kay's hands, these strategies achieve the candour and directness of literary discourse without the radical polemics that Mason-John employed later. This approach was by 1988 a departure from the tangential treatment that queer sexuality received in plays written during and soon after the end of censorship (Sinfield 1999) as we see in Delaney's *A Taste of Honey* (1958) and Mart Crowley's *The Boys in the Band* (1968).

(ii) Love and Angst in Paul Boakye's *Boy with Beer*

Paul Boakye's *Boy with Beer* (1995), is a play about gay love between two black men, one African the other, West Indian, and the wider cultural relationship between these two sections of the black Diaspora. It focuses on Karl's search for love and the discovery of this love, not within his own circle of Africans but in the most unexpected quarters, in Donovan, an Afro-Caribbean. The play also interrogates the tense relationship between Africans and black people of West Indian origins, focussing especially on differences in cultural attitudes and perceptions. In the play Donovan visits Karl, an artist and photographer in his plush studio flat following their first meeting in a gay club. Karl's astute observations about the black gay scene reveal the class divide between the two men and highlights the insecurity, the betrayals and the suspicions that characterize black gay relationships. The social gulf between the two is evident. However, this pales to insignificance when compared to the insincerity and denials that Karl objects to and rails against but to which Donovan subscribes to the extent of masking his sexuality in an unfulfilling heterosexual relationship with the unsuspecting Susan.

The two start off like people checking out an opponent in a mental duel. Karl discovers that Donovan's thoughts are as mixed as his sexuality yet his needs for re-assurance and validation are no different from Karl's. Karl is after the security and fulfilment of non-manipulative gay love while for Donovan, these consist of acceptance within his cultural circle and the socially constructed respectability he thought was only possible in a heterosexual relationship, even if, as in his own case, such a relationship is false. Although the suave, much more mature Karl is thrown together with the ideologically naïve Donovan, he feels duty-bound to rescue him from self-deceit. Theirs' is a tense, yet tender relationship in which Karl plays both sides successfully. Karl's sensitivity does not stop him from exploiting his lover's vulnerability. As the tension between them erupts in violence, he forces the insecure Donovan to confront and acknowledge his true sexuality as the first step in asserting his real identity. In the end Donovan breaks out of the shadows, he rejects pseudo heterosexuality and with Karl, begins a journey into the uncertain terrain of gay love:

KARL: We'll see how it goes. One day at a time....
DONOVAN: I liked you from time, man. It's just me, ennit? Call it progress, if you wanna. (p. 37)

Karl's approach to gay sex in *Boy with Beer* seems casual but his actions merely demonstrate the extents he is prepared to defend the gay love he believes is devalued by Donovan's insincerity and quest for heterosexual respectability. His unprotected sex with Donovan, now frightened he might be infected with HIV, is not suicidal. It highlights the trust that lovers require of each other if gay love is to be a meaningful, fulfilling relationship that satisfies everything gay men seek in heterosexual affairs.

(iii) Mason-John and Lesbian Radicalism in *Sin Dykes*

In the 'Publish and be Damned' section of the treatise accompanying her monologue, *Brown Girl in the Ring* (pp. 11-40), Valerie Mason-John advises lesbians to link their sexuality to ideological determinism and to avoid the culture bias that breeds separatism in their ranks. *Sin Dykes* explores the contentious issue of race relations. It draws lesbians of different races into a wider ideological framework in which their survival depends on celebrating difference and on accepting other people whose sexuality and preferences do not necessarily mirror their own. This postmodernist take on race and sexuality challenges the insularity and exclusion that lesbian separatism espouses. Mason-John sees the successes of former political struggles like racial equality as a template for establishing a queer subculture in which there are no stereotypes and in which interracial relationships are neither uncommon nor viewed as disrupting the boundaries of sexuality and race.

In the play six friends, three of Caribbean and African extraction and the others of different white British backgrounds; Trudy, Gill, Kat, BD, Clio, and Trace meet in a club for queers. In a background of sex games during which the boundaries of stereotypes are challenged and disrupted, the characters confront their fears and prejudices about how lesbians ought to relate with other lesbians, with gay men, and heterosexuals of different races. Mason-John challenges the ghettoisation inherent in separatism, using Clio's belief in sleeping with anyone irrespective of colour, gender or sexuality to de-stabilize stereotypes. The ensuing debate enables Clio and Trudy, like the other characters in the play, to traverse racial and ideological boundaries. Starting tentatively but growing in confidence, Clio and Trudy learn more about each other. Both confront the *unknown,* relying much more on historical evidences and on *nature* than on cultural conditioning. Their awareness of the implications of their sexuality is tantalising, frightening and fascinating them simultaneously. The characters rise above cultural prejudice and personal insecurities with Trudy in particular, undergoing what amounts to a 'second outing':

TRUDY: All I know is that the same thing which turns me on, is the same thing which scares me....
CLIO: But you can always be in control.... That is the exciting thing about sex, talking, exploring fantasies....
TRUDY: I can't, black girls don't do your type of sex.
CLIO: Be-ave. What am I? A snowflake in disguise?...
TRUDY: You are different.

CLIO: The only difference is that I don't pretend. I sleep with who I want
to…. And I've ad my fair share of black girls who 'ave taught me a thing
or two. (p. 88) ….
TRUDY: I'm Romeo and you're Juliet… I'm Tom
CLIO: I'm Jerry…. (p. 90)

Like other writings of Mason-John's, *Sin Dykes* employs very
explicit, graphic language. The play reads like a political pamphlet, a
radical manifesto with deliberate propagandizing intentions. This is a
dramaturgical shortcoming but *Sin Dykes*, more than any other play,
projects black lesbianism to the forefront and Mason-John pushes its
discourse further than many other black writers.

III. An Abbreviated History of Black British Queer Theatre (BBQT)

Historically black societies in Africa and in the diaspora have
generally denied the existence of non-heterosexuals in their midst. In the
UK, gay and lesbian issues were denied the kind of recognition that race
and cultural politics enjoyed in black studies and performances. Some
communities that recognized the achievements of their gay and lesbian
members refused to acknowledge their sexuality, let alone celebrate them.
At this time, queer black performers could be classified into three main
categories; those whose sexualities were rejected by black cultural
institutions, those who concealed their sexuality or denied it altogether,
and those that asserted their sexual identity robustly whilst being
stigmatized by their communities.

From the late 1970s and 1980s legislative acts began to transform
attitudes to gay and lesbian rights. International events like gay pride
parades in mostly Western Europe and the US became a public platform
for black gays and lesbians from different walks of life. In the combined
influences of queer political activists and anti- discrimination regulations
led to the UK parliament legalizing gay civil unions in 2005. Despite these
developments, large sections of black British society remain awkward and
uncomfortable about queer sexualities.

Deb Price (1995) recalls two significant comments by Essex
Hemphill, the late African-American poet, novelist, essayist, gay rights
activist and performance artist, about the marginalisation of gay and
lesbian issues from mainstream black race discourses. Hemphill claimed
that he 'started writing about and addressing' his 'homosexuality because
it wasn't there in the black text' pointing out specifically that he 'needed
something to be there to validate that' his 'experience was real for' him (in

the internet article 'Deb Price: Discovering the Voice of Black Gay Men'), the same complaints that Jackie Kay's Aisha makes in *Chiaroscuro*. Hemphill was adamant that 'the silence surrounding black gay and lesbian lives is being meticulously dismantled.... Every closet is coming down— none are sacred....'
(http://www.qrd.org/qrd/www/culture/black/articles/essex.html).

His spotlight on the tokenistic representation of black gay men and lesbians throughout history and their marginalisation in global discourse came at a time the UK queer scene was defining its own internal dynamic and people like Megan Radclyffe, Valerie Mason-John and Jackie Kay were contesting its pre-occupation with inter-racial relations (Davis 1988).

A lot has happened in the UK since the '80s but black gay performances are still few in mainstream theatres and are hardly indicative of the growing work by black performers. Materials on black British queerness have been out there but have either been ignored or left un-documented by black studies and communities. This means that while black gay performances have been flourishing underground and the literature on them growing steadily, the discourse is still disparate as Hemphill asserted.

IV. Problems and Challenges for Black Queer Theatre

The reception for black queer presentations in post-war mainstream British theatre is muted when compared to the volume of work by heterosexual performers. Most often, queer black performers appear on the stage but these are often less about their sexuality than they are about their culture and the colour of their skin. Television and Radio have done better in this regard. In a BBC Radio Four documentary on Thursday 11 November 2004, 'Black, Muslim and Gay', Jaheda 28-year old British Asian, Rumi, Asian of East African origin and 40-year old G, policeman of Nigerian and Jamaican parentage shared their experiences as gay people, speaking of the pains of rejection, about their isolation and frequently having to defend their lifestyles before their families and public. Despite the advance publicity, that the complaints the Radio Four programme generated in certain Muslim quarters reveal the complexity of the problems still facing the struggling, but steadily emergent black British queer theatre (BBQT).

Black plays abound in the UK but black queer theatre is yet to define itself through its own materials. It has some very powerful, ideological materials but the problem is not limited to access to performance material, the theatre is just beginning to forge an aesthetic that articulates its position in mainstream black theatre and society. These conditions are important for the theatre and ought to be satisfied since the aesthetic of a theatre depends, first and foremost, on a supporting ideological framework and secondly, on a discourse that acknowledges and 'emphasizes affinity and solidarity over identity' (Marcus, 2005:196). Black queer theatre has to define itself on its own needs and visions within general cultural discourse. Such a posture is necessary condition if it is to fashion the kind of sustainable aesthetic on which theatres of all cultures and ideologies are built.

The presence of 'black' performance materials and performers for whom presentations are ideological and indicate affinity with their sexuality and identity are key conditions for a sustainable performance aesthetic. These parameters need to be satisfied if we are to accept the ironic but truthful suggestions made by Smith, Parks and McCauley *et al* (2005) that a black 'play' or performance material for that matter 'should wittingly, or unwittingly, raise social questions and controversies'' in the black community' (p. 573) and that as a matter of cultural necessity, that they 'should, like the black church, have social and political significance' (p. 573). One can only add here that a black British queer play or performance should at least attempt to do for its performers and audiences alike, what Smith, Parks and McCauley *et al's* (2005) black play is designed to do. Essex Hemphill warned about this condition as events continue to prove that

> [t]he Black homosexual is hard pressed to gain audience among his heterosexual brothers; even if he is more talented, he is inhibited by his silence or his admissions. This is what the race has depended on in being able to erase homosexuality from our recorded history.

(http://www.qrd.org/qrd/www/culture/black/articles/essex.html)

V. Black Queer theatre and the Search for Socio-cultural Identity

Black British gay theatre has for long been trapped in the nebulous region between fact and fiction; fact because queer has always been a whispered presence in black communities and fiction, because of the cultural denial that surrounded them for a long time. Unlike their white counterparts who also faced rejection but managed to create an ideological framework on which to contest their sexuality, the absence of affirmation and the validation of their experiences within black communities denied queer performers a voice. Black queer subculture had never had an effective platform or organ prior to the first black lesbian conference in 1985 (Mason-John 1999) and the setting up in 1995, of the black list, a grouping and document comprising of openly queer black artists, writers, politicians and thinkers. The list was the brainchild of cultural activists within the management of the Black History Month (BHM) committee in America who realised that while BHM has grown in stature, it had been insensitive to the struggles of its queer community.

The theatre neither has an 'official', documented history nor acknowledged presence before World War 2 even though the notions of a black play had been articulated in the US as far back as 1927 by drama critique Theophilus Lewis (Krasner 2005). There are no documents to suggest that black queer acts graced the British stage prior to WW2, during, and immediately after censorship ended in Britain. The matter of their sexuality did not factor in performances by Langston Hughes. Any assumptions about the existence of a black queer theatre during these periods lacks credible support given the social position black people occupied in the British Isle and the suspicion with which they were viewed. Although this was when avant-garde forms flexed their muscles, influential black gay artists did not challenge black political and cultural establishments on gay issues along the cultural lines that gave rise to Black History Month activities.

Culturally British queer theatre is white, not black and though tolerant of black performers, like its mainstream counterpart, it hardly serves black concerns (Mason-John 1999). The state of the theatre may be due to historical factors and the hegemonic relations between black and white cultural institutions but it is also true that the socio-demographic changes that took place in black communities in the mid-decades of the 20th century left queer sexuality behind and only began to countenance it in the early 1980s. Black queer was and to a large extent remains separated from white queer, prompting Mason-John's assertion that to be black and queer 'meant socialising in separate spaces, where the culture of an event is specifically geared towards' black people's 'music, food, and entertainment tastes' (1999:15). Mason-John, herself a lesbian, decries the absence of a vibrant black queer scene and the cultural imbalance that makes black lesbians to abandon their familiar cultural tastes, submerge themselves in mainstream culture, or find alternative spaces.

The ambivalence in black communities meant that as a form, queer theatre lacked the means and cultural backing to renew itself through constant re-enactments. So unlike white queer theatre that could at least, trace its roots to an event like the trial of Oscar Wilde, black queer theatre had no such historical landmark on which to establish itself on the cultural landscape. The historical links to Oscar Wilde and his work are what Joe Orton exploited in his resistance against heterosexual conventions and official censorship. After Wilde and Orton white queer theatre could only go up but this is a battle the black queer theatre is still waging in its own cultural constituencies.

McCauley argues that culturally 'playing black also, of course, pushes buttons' (2005: 584) but for black performers in the UK, this has required pushing against the boundaries of cultural attitudes as well as against mainstream and alternative theatres. The problem has persisted simply because the very acts of defining and staging black theatre are not only political issues, 'playing black' can also 'mean "in your face"' (Hatch 2005:597). Many sections of black British society accommodate the whispered presence of gays and lesbians in their midst and close circles but uncomfortable and insecure with the assertiveness and self-assurance that '*in your face*' fosters in people. Queer black performers do not only battle racial stereotypes, they have to also contend with the ambivalence that their sexuality arouses within the wider black cultural communities.

VI. Rainbow Hues: Development of Black Queer Theatre Aesthetics and Identity

Mason-John suggests that from the first ever black lesbian conference at Tindlemanor, Featherstone Street, in October 1985, 'a black lesbian subculture has evolved, in order to maintain specific racial and cultural identities' (1999:19). The fact however, is that this subculture has long been in existence but quietly and unnoticed. Such a scene is a necessary condition if black queer theatre is to define its own aesthetics and ideology. Culturally black theatre draws from different artistic expressions; from music, poetry, dance, storytelling, etc, and as the plays in this essay demonstrate, such an aesthetic is neither determined by nor is it subservient to *text* alone. The plays draw their content and from black British society, their aesthetics are all about queers envisioning and depicting the theatre that problematizes their experiences. This is the theatre's way of avoiding a definition that is based on a binary relationship with its white counterpart and the unfortunate misrepresentation that happens whenever 'the image and name to which people identify is mobilized under the gaze of the Other' (Roysdon 2004:125). Representation is primarily about how people articulate 'their lived social realities, as well as imagined possibilities' (Wandor 2001:21). What the three playwrights have done is to define the codes and images by which black queer sexuality is represented since representation by *others* creates the kind of 'slide that destabilizes and pleads for reiteration' (Roysdon 2004:125) simultaneously.

In 1958 Shelagh Delaney's *A Taste of Honey* broke new ground as the first British play with a strong gay sentiment even though it has no clearly defined messages (Taylor 1969) about queer sexuality. The play's reference to homosexuality is not directed at Nigerian-born sailor but to Geof, a white, young man still negotiating the uncertain terrain of his sexuality. After this came Mart Crowley's *The Boys in the Band*, another play about being homosexual and white with a solitary black gay man, Bernard. Despite the iconic stature of both plays, the playwrights' attempt at inclusiveness falls into the stereotypical pattern of acknowledging without problematising what it is to be black and gay. A black queer play such as Paul Boakye's *Boy with Beer* (first staged in 1992) accomplishes more than this; it pushes ideological buttons (McCauley 2005) within black communities and its narrative and images are about being black and gay.

In effect what plays like Mason-John's *Sin Dykes*, Kay's *Chiaroscuro*, and Boakye's *Boy with Beer* and many others do is more than destabilize stereotypes, they are unequivocal about defining the content and gaze of black queer theatre. The results are plays in which stage action is neither about the singularity of ideas nor about specific views of homosexuality and lesbianism. The three plays explore specific stories yet each offers a multilayered image of black queer sexuality. Their dramaturgies are both about steering the action and facilitating debate. They offer a discourse in which there is neither hierarchy nor do contesting views occlude each other. Prior to, but much more so since the 1985 conference that Mason-John alludes to, black playwrights have articulated the inextricable links between their sexuality and art. Like political agitators of the past, queer playwrights now realise that 'theatre can be an important tool to enable victims/survivors to voice their views' (Taylor 2003: xxix). All three plays deal with the problems of ambivalence but more importantly, they steer away from the fetishism and *objectification* associated with naked black bodies in historical race discourse.

Despite its many difficulties black British queer theatre has an identity that is both old and *new*. Its writers have followed Marcus' dictum that 'those writing queer histories of the past and present often need to construct their own archives through oral history, personal testimony, and participant observation' (Marcus 2005:201). The theatre's *new* identity can be traced back to 1968, to Bernard, the first black gay character in Mart

Crowley's *The Boys in the Band*. Crowley casts Bernard as a fully independent member of the *band* who experiences the frustrations surrounding his sexuality on two fronts, on his class and racial background. *The Boys in the Band* was ground-breaking in its day but it was still reductionist. Bernard achieves limited cultural significance as a type and sole representative of black gay men in a play that the New York Times described as 'a homosexual play, and ... the first to accept homosexuality as an ordinary fact of life, and then go on to explore the hates, doubts and agonies of love between men' (1969, back cover UK Penguin edition).

Since *The Boys in the Band* and up to the 1980s, aesthetic developments in black British queer theatre were closely linked with events in other areas of queer culture and media especially films such as Neil Jordan's *Mona Lisa* (1986), Isaac Julien's *Looking for Langston* (1989) and Gurinder Chadha's taboo-breaking *Bhaji on the Beach* (1993) to mention a few. These films disrupted conventional constructions of sexuality, a factor that black queer theatre has drawn upon in its development of an aesthetic based on black cultural praxis and settings. Black queer theatre has developed through identifying with other theatres of its genre and by drawing from an ever-increasing queer social scene that performs itself as acts of affirmation and resistance. It has benefited from ideological solidarity with the increasing numbers of queer programmes on television, film and radio. One of such benefits is changing the pre-war imagination that perceived queer sexuality and racial *others* 'as threats (Duggan, 2000:27) to mainstream cultures.

VII. The Rise of Black Queer Performance Material

In her introduction to *Lesbian Plays* (1988) Jill Davis decried the small number of lesbian plays in print in the UK. At the time, there were perhaps few other lesbian plays beside Jacqueline Rudet's *Basin* (Davis 1988) that addressed the concerns of black women specifically. The disruption of closet mentality and the limited exposure of black gay performers on the UK stage were on their own, insufficient to generate a body of work or mention in any forum. For instance, none of the reference guides to British, European and world theatres such as Banham's *Cambridge Guide to Theatre* (1995) and Chambers' *Continuum Companion to Twentieth Century Theatre* (2002) mentions black gay and lesbian plays, playwrights and theatre companies. Banham and Chambers cite 1960s and 1970s respectively as the probable dates for the beginning of gay theatre, a form that can be traced to Oscar Wilde's trial and his play

The Importance of Being Earnest (1895). The Gay Sweatshop that started in 1975 and had done work involving black gay and lesbian performers and the Theatre of Black Women were already in existence. Also on the scene prior to 1988, 1995 and 2002 were black queer theatre icons like James Baldwin and David Warren Frechette (in the US), Paul Danquah, Inge Blackman, Jackie Kay, Paul Boakye, and Valerie Mason-John. The latter in particular was already beginning to make huge waves but all *managed* to elude mention in these academic references.

The situation changed in the last two decades of the 20th century as black performers realised that 'queer lives are performative, often by choice, but also as a result of occupying the position of outsider or other, in the web of signifier / signified' (Roysdon 2004:126). The contexts of black plays have also expanded to include all aspects of being black in Britain, from immigration to racial identity and social inclusion; from health matters and racial discrimination to family tensions. The availability of materials and the growing visibility of the theatre are due to the pioneering works of Mason-John and Blackman whose sexuality was always inseparable from their theatre and art. Discourse on the theatre is also growing; playwrights, writers and cultural activists continue to instigate debate with Yvonne Brewster's three edited collections of black plays including queer plays and making performance materials more accessible. On reflection when many black queers denied their sexuality, masked it, or straddled the sexuality divide, there seemed to be little stomach for a robust black queer theatre and discourse. The dramatic characters created by non-blacks lacked both the cultural authenticity and the contagious *joie de vivre* that *Boy with Beer*, *Chiaroscuro* and *Sin Dykes* have created.

Unlike mainstream British and European theatre discourses in which *queers* have always featured (see Smith's (1991) *Homosexual Desire in Shakespeare's England*) from Homers accounts through to the Renaissance (see Goldberg's (1994) *Queering the Renaissance*) black theatres have ignored the subject. If anything, black queer is mostly 'sustained by private ritual, by ways of speaking and behaving which constitute a private replacement for a real social milieu in which they can be themselves' (Wandor 1987:67). The need to bring black queer theatre out of the shadows of their white counterparts and black mainstream culture is one of the main things that the newer plays and the steadily emergent discourse have been about.

Works cited

Banham, Martin (ed), *The Cambridge Guide to Theatre* (new ed.), Cambridge: Cambridge University Press, 1995.

Balme, Christopher, *Decolonizing the Stage: Theatrical Syncretism and Post-Colonial Drama*, Oxford: Oxford University Press, 1999.

Boakye, Paul, *Boy with Beer*, In Yvonne Brewster (ed.) *Black Plays 3*. London: Methuen, 1995.

Brewster, Yvonne (ed), *Black Plays: Two*, London: Methuen
—. (ed.) (1995) *Black Plays 3*, London: Methuen, 1989.

Chambers, Colin (ed), *The Continuum Companion to Twentieth Century Theatre*, London: Continuum, 2002.

Crowley, Mart, *The Boys in the Band*, London: Penguin, 1968.

Davis, Jill (ed), *Lesbian Plays*, London: Methuen, 1988.

Duggan, Lisa, *Saphic Slashers: Sex, Violence, and American Modernity*, Durham, North Carolina: Duke University Press, 2000.

Godiwala, Dimple, 'Editorial Introduction: Alternatives Within the Mainstream: British Black and Asian Theatre', in Dimple Godiwala and Peter Thomson (eds) *Studies in Theatre and Performance*, Vol. 26, No. 1, 2006. pp. 3 – 12.

----. *Alternatives within the Mainstream: British Black and Asian Theatres*, (ed) Dimple Godiwala, Newcastle: Cambridge Scholars Press, 2006.

Goldberg, Jonathan (ed), *Queering the Renaissance*, Durham, London: Duke University Press, 1994.

Harris, Keith M., 'Untitled': D' Angelo and the Visualisation of the Black Male Body' in Harris (ed.) *Wide Angle*. Vol. 21 No. 4, 1999. pp. 62 – 83

Kay, Jackie, *Chiaroscuro* in Jill Davies (ed) *Lesbian Plays*, London: Methuen, 1988.

Krasner, David, 'What Have We Learned? : Forum on Black Theatre', in. Harry J. Elam Jr (ed) *Theatre Journal*, Vol. 57, Number 4, December 2005. pp. 585 – 587.

McCauley, Robbie, 'The Struggle Continues' Forum on Black Theatre', in Harry J. Elam Jr (ed) *Theatre Journal*, Vol. 57, Number 4, December 2005. pp. 583 – 585.

Marcus, Sharon, 'Queer Theory for Everyone', in Sandra Harding and Kathryn Norberg (eds) *Signs: Journal of Women in Culture and Society*. Vol. 31 No. 1 Autumn 2005. pp. 191 – 218.

Mason-John, Valerie, *Brown Girl in the Ring*, London: Get a Grip, 1999.
—. *Sin Dykes* in *Brown Girl in the Ring*, London: Get a Grip, 1999.

Clintock, Anne, *Imperial Leather: Race, Gender and Sexuality in the
Colonial Contest*. London & New York: Routledge, 1995,
Osborne, Deidre, 'Writing black back: an overview of black theatre and
performance in Britain' in Dimple Godiwala and Peter Thomson (eds)
Studies in Theatre and Performance. Vol. 26 No. 1, 2006. pp. 13 – 31.
Rame, Franca & Dario Fo, *A Woman Alone: & Other Plays*, London:
Methuen Drama, 1991.
Roysdon, Emily,. 'Democracy, Invisibility, and the Dramatic Arts', in
Vaccaro, Jeanne (ed) *Women and Performance: A Journal of Feminist
Theory,* Issue 28, 14: 2, 2004. pp. 123 – 126
Sinfield, Alan, *Out on Stage: Lesbian and Gay Theatre in the Twentieth
Century*, London and New Haven, Conn.: Yale University Press, 1999.
Smith, Anna D., 'Black Plays', in Harry J. Elam Jr (ed) *Theatre Journal*.
Vol. 57, Number 4, December 2005. pp. 571 – 576.
Smith, Bruce R., *Homosexual Desire in Shakespeare's England: A
Cultural Poetics*. Chicago;   London: University of Chicago Press,
1991.
Smith D. A., Parks, S-L, McCauley, R. *et al*, 'A Forum on Black Theatre:
The Questions: What is a Black Play and/ or What is Playing Black?'
(ed) Harry J. Elam Jr., *Theatre Journal*. Vol. 57, Number 4, December
2005. pp. 571 – 616,
Taylor, Philip, *Applied Theatre*. Portsmouth, N.H.: Heinemann, 2003.
Wandor, Michelene, *Look Back in Gender: Sexuality and the family in
Post-war British Drama*, London: Methuen, 1987.
—.*Post-War British Drama: Looking Back in Gender*. London: Routledge,
2001.

Filmography

Bhaji on the Beach, Directed by Gurinder Chadha. 101 mins. Channel 4
Films & Umbi Films, 1994.
Mona Lisa, Directed by Neill Jordan. Handmade Films, 1986.

Websites

BBC MMVI *Black, Muslim and Gay* [online]
London: British Broadcasting Corporation (BBC) News, 2004.
Available from:
http://newsvote.bbc.co.uk/mpapps/pagetools/print/news.bbc.co.uk/1/hi/
magazine/4001447.stm . Accessed 1 June, 2006.
British Film Institute (BFI) *Looking for Langston*

[online] London: British Film Institute, 2006. Available from:
http://www.bfi.org.uk/booksvideo/video/details/langston/. Accessed 4
April, 2006.
Price, Deb, *Discovering the Voice of Black Gay Men* [online] USA: Chuck
Taver, 1995. Available from:
http://www.qrd.org/qrd/www/culture/black/articles/essex.html.
Accessed 4 April, 2006.

CHAPTER NINETEEN

A VISITOR'S GUIDE TO 'GLASGAY!'

DEIRDRE HEDDON

Synopsis

Launched in Glasgow in 1993, Glasgay! has proved to be an enduring lesbian, gay, bisexual and transgender arts festival. Given the surprising longevity of Glasgay! it seems imperative that this important queer festival, whose survival is always precarious, is documented. 'A Visitor's Guide to Glasgay!' is part of that documentation, offering an account of the festival from each of its producers and mapping their different aims and agendas, alongside their shared frustrations.

*****

In 1993, the lesbian and gay cultural landscape of Glasgow was changed dramatically with the launch of the first Glasgay! festival. As I write this, plans are well underway for the launch of Glasgay! 2006. It is unlikely that co-founders Cordelia Ditton and Dominic D'Angelo could have predicted the longevity of the festival when they began planning the first one in 1991, particularly given the sustained political and financial obstacles that each festival producer has had to face. The survival of Glasgay! seems a necessary act of wilful obstinacy, a refusal to counter the possibility that the festival has (ever) had its proper time and place. I very much hope that in 2016, someone else (or even an older me) is recording the continued history of Glasgay!

The 'record' that follows is primarily produced from interviews with each of the directors/administrators. These oral histories are dictated by the vagaries of memory as well as the influences of the interviewer and the questions that I posed. 'The writing of history', as Ludmilla Jordanova reminds us, 'is about the transmission of memory' and 'the practice of history is [...] a highly specialised form of commemoration' (Jordanova 2000: 138). This re-membering takes place in the present, allowing a retrospective rewriting of events helped with the benefit of hindsight. As Andreas Huyssen puts it,

> The mode of memory is the *recherche* rather than recuperation. The temporal status of any act of memory is always the present and not, as some naïve epistemology might have it, the past itself, even though all memory in some ineradicable sense is dependent on some past event or experience. It is this tenuous fissure between past and present that constitutes memory, making it powerfully alive and distinct from the archive or any other mere system of storage and retrieval. (Huyssen 1995: 13)

Rather than being cautious of memory's uncertainties, we should rather embrace and recognise it as 'a valuable historical resource' (Cvetkovich 2003: 8), a form of local knowledge.

My practice of history, here, also inevitably inscribes and gestures my location and perspective; from the outset I admit more than a passing acquaintance with, and investment in, Glasgay! In 1993, I volunteered to assist at one of the venues hosting Glasgay! events, becoming a general dog's body, fetching sandwiches and cups of tea for various artists including (to my delight) Jude Winter from Dorothy Talk Theatre Company and Lois Weaver and Peggy Shaw from Split Britches. In 1994, I helped Cordelia Ditton organise a one-night benefit for Glasgay! 1995. Between 1996 and 1998 I became a Board member, responsible for much of the programming and delivery of the 1997 event, 'Waiting for Glasgay!'. Moving to Exeter in the autumn of 1998, my relationship with Glasgay! inevitably became more distanced, though throughout 1998 and 1999 I continued to recommend theatre and live art events that I saw in the South of England, and in 2002 participated in a panel discussion on the oeuvre of Annie Sprinkle. Throughout its history, I have remained a committed spectator. Such involvement no doubt gives my line of vision a distinctive colour (or rainbow of colours). Different reporters, looking at the landscape from a different place, asking different questions of different people and utilising different sources would undoubtedly produce a different history. I do not intend this one to be singularly authoritative. However, since at present no documented history of Glasgay! exists in the public domain it seems imperative that this important queer festival takes up some space in a published history of British queer cultural production, not least because Glasgay! has, since its inception, nurtured, encouraged and promoted many queer British artists.

Beginnings 1993 - 1995: Cordelia Ditton and Dominic D'Angelo

Glasgay! launched itself on Saturday 30th October 1993. This lesbian and gay arts festival was the innovation of Cordelia Ditton, herself a new resident to Glasgow having moved recently from London. Ditton, well known in the London arts scene as a performer, writer, and co-director of Gay Sweatshop felt that the gay and lesbian community in Glasgow, in the early 1990s, was much less visible than in London.[42] There, the introduction of Section 28 in 1988 had, in Ditton's opinion, galvanised a whole new era of political and public agitation,[43] best epitomised by the founding in 1989 of the influential national lobbying group Stonewall. Ditton herself had been involved in the Section 28 campaign, and was on the steering group of the arts lobby. Her impressions of Glasgow were that, in contrast to London, gay men and lesbians were mostly hidden (although Ditton recognised that important local organisations such as the Glasgow branch of Switchboard already existed). Given her own background, and continuing involvement in the arts, Ditton struck upon a lesbian and gay arts festival as a means to render the lesbian and gay communities of Glasgow more visible, to say 'look, we're here' (Ditton, 2006). At the end of 1991, she joined forces with Glasgow-based freelance arts administrator Dominic D'Angelo to produce an arts festival that would

> celebrate something. We wanted to show gay lifestyles and performers and work in a very very positive light. We wanted to change public opinion about gay people. And we wanted to show the wealth of amazing work

---

[42] I am aware that the concept of 'community' is problematic and contested (see Heddon, 2004), and use the term here with hesitation. However, since my agenda here is simply to make public the 'history' of Glasgay! rather than to explore the inter-relationship between Glasgay! and notions of 'community', I will risk critical approbation in this instance. Similarly, I use 'gay and lesbian' and 'queer' interchangeably in this text since the purpose of this article is not to propose the extent to which Glasgay! is a 'queer' festival, or even how that interpolation might apply to Glasgay! I leave such critical enquiries to future commentators.

[43] The Local Government Act of 1986 was amended in 1988 with Section 2a, which provided that 'A local authority shall not (a) intentionally promote homosexuality or publish material with the intention of promoting homosexuality; (b) promote the teaching in any maintained school of the acceptability of homosexuality as a pretended family relationship'. Section 28 was finally repealed in Scotland in 2000 (but not without virulent homophobic campaigning), and in England in 2003.

that was out there. (Ditton, 2006)

This dual and imbricated strategy of celebration and revelation was very much located in a cultural context of invisibility and of a certain backlash against sexual minorities signalled by both Section 28 and by the fear surrounding the supposed 'gay disease', AIDS.

Over the course of eight days, Glasgay! 1993 attracted a staggering 23,000 people. The success of this first festival was due in no small part to Ditton and D'Angelo's aspirations to ensure it was popular in its appeal. Strategically scheduled at a time in the year that offers opportunities for specific 'celebrations' (Halloween, Samhain,[44] and Guy Fawkes or Bonfire night), Glasgay! capitalised on the calendar by hosting spectacular parties and events, alongside theatre, performance and dance shows, workshops, literary readings and discussions. For Ditton, the parties were as important as the more easily identifiable 'arts' events; the strategic aim was that they would pull in people not typically attracted to 'arts' events, but who would then be encouraged to attend those as they were part of the same overall Glasgay! programme. Ditton recalls, 'We wanted something that was big, and bold, and inclusive'. Specifically,

> we wanted to make it popular. That was a very deliberate choice. We did not want to make it cutting edge. Queer Up North was doing that. And we had a very different agenda. That would work in Manchester. We felt Glasgow needed popular stuff. (Ditton, 2006)

Attention is drawn here to the cultural specificity of Glasgow; though Manchester founded the first British gay arts festival in 1992, the fact that this was launched in a city with an already visible gay (sub)culture and neighbourhood in Canal Street arguably made that act less radical than launching a lesbian and gay arts festival in a Scottish city where the lesbian and gay presence was far from recognised or even tolerated. Against the backdrop of a city ingrained in national popular imagination as 'hard' or 'mean' (in spite of various re-branding exercises) , and a city where the Catholic and Protestant churches have remained powerful, we might consider Ditton's and D'Angelo's vision as naively utopian in spirit. Alternatively, however, we could argue that this context made their proposition all the more necessary. We should also recognise that prior to Glasgay!, a cultural renaissance of Glasgow had already been attempted in the guise of European City of Culture in 1990. The rhetoric of the arts being a tool of regeneration had already become common-place;

---

[44] Samhain is a Celtic festival held on 1st November, marking the end of one year and the beginning of the next.

to extend that rhetoric to the arts being used as a tool to change social attitudes towards sexuality was perhaps not so far fetched.

Though Glasgay!'s primary target audience were lesbians, gay men and bisexuals, the directors were always clear that the festival was not just for gay people but was, rather, an arts festival intent on showcasing the best in gay arts. Only a week in duration (the approach was to pack a lot into a short space of time, in order to generate excitement), the programme included national and international, amateur and professional theatre, dance, comedy, literature and films. Ditton and D'Angelo also worked hard to reach out to the gay and lesbian community (or diverse communities that coalesce around those identity labels), by programming a range of workshops intended to develop new skills, ranging from writing workshops to a Brazilian Street Samba workshop. Recognising the potential for an arts festival to act as a platform for or bridge into other areas, this first festival also convened a number of important open discussions on issues felt pressing, including discrimination in education. Finally, sitting comfortably beside the art offerings were the club nights and special events, such as *Appetites at the Arches*, the most lavish women's club that Glasgow had ever seen; *A Show for Glasgay!*, which included appearances by Ian McKellan and Michael Cashman; and the uniquely Scottish *Samhain: Keltic Clyde Firewitch*, a pyrotechnic extravaganza which also launched the UK's first women's drum band, *Sheboom*.

The diversity of the programme not only helped attract a diverse range of people to the festival, it also succeeded in forging collaborations between Glasgay! and the majority of cultural venues and producers operating in the city, ranging from the more mainstream, such as The Citizens, to the more experimental, including the CCA. Given the small amount of funding that the festival received, this collaborative structure was pragmatic. With little money to actually commission or programme its own events, Glasgay! acted as a broker between venues/producers and 'products', matching the two.

The funding of Glasgay! since its inception, has been a fraught affair. Initially, Ditton and D'Angelo had to confront the challenges made in the wake of Section 28, which stipulated that an authority could not 'intentionally promote homosexuality or publish material with the intention of promoting homosexuality'. The wording of the clause is open to interpretation; when might an action or a representation be deemed as the 'promotion' of homosexuality? Section 28 provided the incentive, if any was needed, for the Council to reject any funding application made by Glasgay! Ditton records having to attend many Council meetings and bearing witness to homophobic reasons as to why the Council would or could not meet Glasgay!'s funding needs. In Ditton's opinion, the reason that the Council eventually agreed to provide some funding was that Glasgay! had the unequivocal support of Stonewall; that the Council could pay the funds through D'Angelo's business account rather than directly to Glasgay!; and finally, though the Council were anxious that Section 28 would be used against them, Ditton subsequently learnt that an anonymous business person had financially underwritten this risk. In addition to the funding finally given by the city Council, Strathclyde Regional Council pledged other small amounts of funding for very specific events; finally, a few local sponsors were persuaded.

Whilst funding might have been lacking, the will of the community was much more forthcoming and Ditton and D'Angelo astutely recognised that to involve members from the gay and lesbian community was to engender a sense of shared ownership and therefore a shared desire to see the festival succeed. With no money to pay people, Glasgay! depended on a raft of volunteers who committed their time and energy to any number of different tasks. Without the invaluable assistance of the voluntary Coordinator, Natalie Wilson, Ditton and D'Angelo would not have been able to mount the festival. Other volunteers organised specific events, hosting artists, and leafleting and fundraising in the gay bars and clubs in the weeks leading up to the festival and throughout it. As Ditton puts it, 'so many people got involved in it, and owned it' (Ditton, 2006). Of course, these people were not only helping to make Glasgay! happen on a practical level; they were also the audience for Glasgay! and in turn brought in other audience members (friends, family, etc.).

Ditton and D'Angelo were careful to ensure that the festival was recognised as being a festival with equal attraction for lesbians and gay men, a point stressed by Ditton when she insists that Glasgay! is a lesbian and gay arts festival (not a gay and lesbian arts festival). Run by a lesbian and a gay man, this model of equality was promoted in the organisational structure from the start, and consciously embedded in the entire event. Ditton and D'Angelo took it in turns to speak to the press and attend interviews; both a man and a woman jointly programmed each art form, as in the case of literature, where Toni Davidson and Ellen Galford were equally responsible. In the programme itself, there was a deliberate balance of male and female performers, and events specifically for men and women. Even the launch of the programme, fronted by Michael Cashman and Horse MacDonald, promoted this gender equality alongside a sensitivity towards the local and the national, a position also reflected throughout the entire festival.

Though aiming for a 'big splash' (Ditton, 2006), Ditton and D'Angelo were very much stepping into untested waters and could not know, at the outset, whether they would succeed. Managing to bring many of the best international lesbian and gay artists to Glasgow, many for the first time, suggests that their vision was realised. Though 'efficacy' is always difficult to measure, the attendance record of 23,000 certainly proposes the 'success' of the first Glasgay!. Given that Glasgay! had been such a huge unknown, in terms of outcomes, at its inception there was no discussion of Glasgay! being an annual or bi-annual festival. As Ditton reports, 'We hadn't decided anything. A lot of it was jumping in the deep end and not knowing what was happening' (Ditton, 2006). However, the achievement of Glasgay! 1993 nevertheless meant that there was a huge impetus to do another one; also, as Ditton acknowledges, there was a need to capitalise on the mood that Glasgay! had perhaps helped form. In Ditton's opinion, 'there had been a huge change, I thought, starting to happen, in the way we were being regarded. I wasn't a politician, but I did think, this is a way to get people's attitudes to alter' (Ditton, 2006). Glasgay! also arguably shifted the attitudes of some gay men and lesbians too, 'because people did get involved and they were proud of being involved' (Ditton, 2006).

Though D'Angelo, having taken over Gay Scotland, was no longer able to be a co-director, Ditton felt that her newly acquired experience, alongside her now-realistic expectations, would enable her to take on the mantle of Festival Director. Again, she drew extensively on the support of gay men and lesbians from the community, each of whom had their own areas of expertise and skills to offer; in addition, Ditton employed two 'Events Co-ordinators', although one of these was hired only in the run-up to the event. The second festival was launched in 1995. Given that D'Angelo and Ditton began working on the 1993 festival in 1991, Ditton (who was also pursuing a degree at this time) was realistic in allowing a two-year planning period, thereby implicitly proposing Glasgay! as a bi-annual festival. The aim of this second festival was largely one of consolidation, placing it more securely within a national (UK) frame. Where the scale and impact of the first festival had taken cultural commentators by surprise, the national media seemed more prepared for the second festival, dedicating an increased amount of coverage to it nationally.

Running from the 27th October to the 5th November Glasgay! 1995 was billed as 'Europe's biggest and brightest lesbian and gay arts festival'. The programme developed the model of the first festival, mixing the local with the national and international, the professional with the amateur, and art, dance, theatre, performance, film, music and literature with celebratory club and special events, and pertinent discussions and forums alongside workshops. As with Glasgay! 1993, Glasgay! 1995, though commissioning a number of its own events, relied largely on the commitment of other city venues to be part of the Glasgay! programme.

On reflection, Ditton considered the second festival, in terms of delivery, more problematic than the first, partly because she felt that people had already begun to expect it, and therefore to have certain expectations of and assumptions about it. In Ditton's view, there was a mood of complacency, of taking the festival for granted.[45] The cultivated sense of shared ownership perhaps also placed a greater strain on Ditton in terms of programming events; the diversity of the so-called 'gay community' in reality makes it difficult to please all of the people all of the time. If one of the aims of Glasgay! had been to render the gay and lesbian population of Glasgow more visible and to encourage those people to have a voice, then a side-effect of such empowerment is that the voice also becomes more vocal inside the 'community'. Finally, the 'success' of the first Glasgay!, because the event was such an untested quantity, had been unanticipated. For the 1995 festival, businesses orientated towards the gay and lesbian consumer were more prepared to capitalise on Glasgay!. Although some of these did become sponsors of the festival, Ditton nevertheless identified something of an 'internal market' that had not been present at the first festival. Clubs and bars in the city began to compete with each other, and with Glasgay!, hosting their own 'special events' during the festival and reaping the financial rewards generated by the festival without fully supporting it in economic terms. Events programmed by Glasgay!, which should have brought financial returns for Glasgay! were, in effect, now in competition with other commercial businesses whose market was the same constituency. As Ditton reflects, 'It got to me that the clubs were competing with each other and trying to compete with us rather than think, "no actually, this is to everybody's benefit"' (Ditton, 2006).

---

[45] A number of the producers stated that the attendance figures of 23,000 for the first festival have never been matched. However, it is difficult to measure 'success' in terms of attendance figures, since well-attended events can skew the overall picture. For example, a well-known show at a large theatre, such as Alan Bennet's *The History Boys* at the Theatre Royal, which played for a number of weeks, will result in a festival attendance record of thousands, even if other shows did not sell particularly well. Moreover, as *The History Boys* was a Theatre Royal production, not a Glasgay! commission, it might be difficult to claim this as a Glasgay! success.

Continuing to secure only limited funding and funding-in-kind Glasgay! again relied on the support and will of Ditton and her team of volunteers. Though utilising the expertise and resources of the 'community' to co-ordinate certain aspects, as the only paid worker Ditton was ultimately responsible for the organisation (albeit supported by a Board of directors). By the end of the 1995 festival, Ditton admits to being 'completely burnt out' (Ditton, 2006). For the festival to remain viable and to develop, Ditton felt that it needed to have considerably more funding – a sentiment we will hear repeated by each successive producer. In Ditton's opinon, 'we had really proved we could do something special and the funding was not at the level it should have been and it never has been since' (Ditton, 2006). Having established the festival as a successful bi-annual event in Glasgow's calendar, Ditton felt that it was in a position to be passed on:

> I just thought, there's enough people here, there's a good legacy here, people can pick this up, they can take it in a different direction, they can do what they like with it, but there's good PR being done, there's a lot of good will, everybody's on the map, everybody knows about it. (Ditton, 2006)

Transitions 1996 - 1999: The Glasgay! Board

At a public meeting held at the Lesbian, Gay, Bisexual and Transgender (LGBT) Centre, Ditton tendered her formal resignation; a new Board was constituted, and a new administrator, Jill Scott, appointed. Established as a bi-annual festival, Scott was working towards the delivery of the next festival scheduled for 1997. However, according to Board member David Peutherer, Scott failed to lodge funding applications with the Scottish Arts Council and Glasgow City Council, leaving the organisation with less money than it had ever had. The subsequent departure of Scott also left Glasgay! without an administrator. With no money to replace her, the Board were faced with a decision; either they would work collectively to produce Glasgay! or the company would cease trading. Opting for the former, the Board also realistically acknowledged that Glasgay! 1997 would necessarily be a much smaller festival than the two that had preceded it. However, sensitive to the impact of momentum and legacy, they thought it imperative that some event took place given that the last festival had been in 1995. Prior to her departure, Scott had secured some programming commitments from a number of venues in the city. These commitments provided the main structure for what would become 'Waiting for Glasgay', around which the Board built other events, many of which drew on the resources of the Board itself and which therefore entailed very little financing.

Given the financial and organisational situation, the fact that 'Waiting for Glasgay!' happened at all was remarkable. Peutherer recollects that the total funds available to Glasgay! were in the region of three thousand pounds. All of the Board, other than Peutherer, had full-time jobs or other commitments. Unable to pay for an office, the organisation was run from Peutherer's living room. One asset the Board did have was a plethora of different experiences, including working for a local authority, setting up theatre companies, and applying for funding, all of which would be essential to Glasgay!'s survival. Following 'Waiting for Glasgay', the Board submitted applications to the various councils for the 'full' Glasgay! 1998 festival. The decision was also made at this point that if Glasgay! were to endure, then it would need to become an annual event in spite of the enormous amount of energy and effort required to mount it. As Peutherer explained, 'We recognised that if you were not an annual festival, then you were going to drop out of the funding stream and you were going to have to struggle to get grants next year because somebody else would have to get squeezed out to let you in' (Peutherer, 2006).

The funding applications that the Board submitted were successful to the extent that the company could again afford to employ a part-time administrator, Gillian Garrity, to assist with Glasgay! 1998. The Board remained responsible for programming the festival, and making artistic decisions. As with the previous festivals, Glasgay! 1998, still operating with limited financial resources, combined commissioned events with events programmed by other city venues. The company also managed to secure its largest sponsorship deal to date, provided by Gordon's Gin, to cover the cost of a dedicated visual art space programmed entirely by Glasgay!. Glasgay! 1998, much larger than 'Waiting for Glasgay!', produced 40 events over ten days. Emulating previous programmes in terms of its mix, it nevertheless appears to have been more local in scope, with the emphasis on producing and supporting local talent. This might be explained by the limited finances rather than indicating any ideologically motivated strategy. Peutherer admits to having worried that the festival looked nepotistic, with the same people being programmed each year. However, he also recognises that

> at the end of the day, these were the people who were willing to do things for nothing or for very little money, and we couldn't afford to pay anybody. We had no choice. (Peutherer, 2006)

Between 1998 and 2001, the Board had defined some very clear objectives which included

> i) to premiere new work
> ii) to bring the best of lesbian and gay arts to Glasgow, which people would not otherwise have access to
> iii) to provide a platform for local artists
> iv) to help reduce discrimination through attracting a 'straight' audience as well as a gay one
> v) to facilitate community involvement
> vi) to attract new audiences for the arts. (Peutherer, 2006)

In Peutherer's opinion, the Festival did remarkably well in achieving the majority of these. However, the one area where he felt they failed was in bringing the best of work to Glasgow, simply because the organisation could not afford to bring the best, and for that reason, Glasgay! was more likely to support local artists than programme or commission international artists.

In March 1999, Lindsay Mitchell replaced Gillian Garrity as administrator. Since applications had already been made to the funding councils, and the Board had an outline of ideas for the programme, Mitchell's intended role was to take forward the work that had already been planned, and to secure further sponsorship. Billed as 'the biggest and best gay and lesbian arts festival in Britain this year', the ten-day festival showcased work from New Zealand, Portugal, Canada and Ireland. In addition to Mitchell being hired as administrator, it is worth noting that Robert Thomson was also hired to look after the press aspects, although he is credited in the brochure as 'Programme Co-ordinator', signalling a formal shift that was soon to take place within the structure of the organisation. Not since Cordelia Ditton's leadership in 1995 had one person taken responsibility for the general shape of the programme; rather, the Board had collectively fulfilled this function. Mitchell felt this to be an untenable and inefficient model, as well as a cause of frustration. Moreover, she found the programme limited in scope with the festival 'looking quite stereotypical' (Mitchell, 2006). Where the founders of Glasgay! had been careful to ensure a gender balance in both structure and programme, the Board at this time was male dominated which was perhaps reflected in the 1999 programme. It is also to be noted that Glasgay! was now billed as a gay and lesbian arts festival, where Ditton had been careful to describe it as a lesbian and gay arts festival.

Though appointed as an administrator for the 1999 festival,

Mitchell's presence at the initial planning stages of the 2000 festival enabled her to press for greater autonomy in relation to programming the entire event. Given that the Board were all necessarily unpaid volunteers, most of whom had full-time jobs and other priorities, it made sense that Mitchell took over the role of determining the festival programme. Committed though the Board were, Mitchell knew from experience that often unrealistic ideas would be proposed, without then being followed through, leaving her in the difficult situation of having to ask, 'well, what is the programme?', and then rather frantically putting one together. Taking responsibility for the programme would enable a more coherent and systematic approach to planning and delivery.

Glasgay! 2000 – 2001: A Producer's Festival

Appointed as Festival Producer for the 2000 Festival, Mitchell's aim was to 'widen the scope of the festival a bit more' and to develop the audience profile by ensuring a greater diversity of work (Mitchell, 2006). For Mitchell, a primary agenda was to appeal to people who would come to the festival because it presented good art, not simply because it was a lesbian and gay festival. In Mitchell's words, the challenge was 'how to attract the thousands of gays and lesbians who didn't see the scene as the be all and end all, and who didn't necessarily want to identify with a gay festival' (Mitchell, 2006). This perspective reveals how far the aims of the festival had shifted from its inception in 1993, where the agenda had been to announce and celebrate the presence of lesbians and gay men in the city. By 2000, that presence was more or less recognised (not least because of the heavily publicised furore over the repeal of Section 28). For Mitchell, the celebratory aspect of Glasgay! was its celebration of good quality arts by lesbian and gay artists.

Though the 2000 and 2001 programmes displayed an eclectic and diverse mix of art forms, again ranging from the international to the national to the local, and from the professional to the amateur, funding continued to restrict the scope and vision of the festival. In fact, in 2000, the Festival received its biggest threat to funding to date as Mrs Strain, supported by the Christian Institute, brought a lawsuit against Glasgow City Council claiming that it had violated Section 28 by funding events 'promoting' homosexuality. The Council, though supportive of the festival, nevertheless froze its grant as a precautionary measure, later reinstating it.

During Mitchell's leadership, in spite of the visible success and popularity of Glasgay!, core funding remained the same, a situation which was inevitably frustrating given the desire to develop and expand the programme and the quality of the programme. Unsurprisingly, by the end of her third festival, Mitchell had become exhausted, mentally and creatively:

> I was struggling to see how I could develop things on the same kind of budget. Struggling to see how we could secure different funding without more input from other people with creative ideas, or ideas for commissions. [...] The money wasn't there. We did a lot of applications, but the third festival we spent a lot more time doing applications, trying to find funding, which is pretty frustrating. (Mitchell, 2006)

Peutherer, who resigned from the Board at the same time Mitchell resigned as Festival Producer, echoes Mitchell's sentiments:

> I couldn't face another year of going through [...] basically the same. The same procedure. Applying for more money, not getting it. Applying for sponsorship. Not getting it. Starting with all these ideas; having to ditch them all. Having the same kind of programme, the same size of audience, and I just thought, I don't want to do it again. (Peutherer, 2006)

Like Mitchell, Peutherer, who had been on the Board since 1996, felt that the Festival now needed to move up a gear, but he did not know how it could achieve that without securing more money; and in turn, he did not know how the organisation could increase its financial revenue. Repeated attempts to attract larger sponsorship deals had failed, even though one of the Board members worked for the Association for Business Sponsorship of the Arts. Whilst much has been made of the so-called 'Pink Pound' since the 1990s, the LGBT community of Glasgow did not appear to hold much appeal for businesses. The annual process of applying for funding, and not knowing how much you would receive, further limited the extent to which the organisation could forward plan, prohibiting collaborations with other creative organisations such as theatre companies. At no point could Mitchell operate as a commissioner or even a co-producer with companies working on projects to be realised over more than twelve months. This seriously limited the type of commissions and collaborations that Glasgay! was able to generate or facilitate, leading to a festival programme that, despite Mitchell's inclusion of live art events, was in danger of appearing repetitive – a situation that Mitchell had precisely been hoping to challenge.

Glasgay! 2002 – 2003: 'A Multi-Arts Festival For Multi-Sexual People & Their Friends'[46]

Following Mitchell's resignation, in January 2002 David Leddy was appointed as the new Festival Producer, charged with delivering Glasgay! 2002. Leddy recognised in Glasgay! a product that was already successful and internationally renowned. One of his priorities was to announce this success more confidently since Glasgay! had 'been too modest' about its considerable achievements (Leddy, 2006). Like all the previous producers, Leddy felt that Glasgay! was seriously underfunded, given the level of programme it delivered on an annual basis. The Scottish Arts Council had, since the festival's inception in 1993, awarded it only five thousand pounds per annum; while Glasgow City Council's level of funding was between fifteen and seventeen thousand pounds. Moreover, even these sums of money were never guaranteed and had to be applied for each year. A consultation with Arts Officers revealed that part of the difficulty in attracting funding was that the quality of the programme was felt to be uneven; some of the work was professional and internationally acclaimed, while other contributions to the festival programme were amateur. Leddy, aiming to achieve a more consistent quality that would, he hoped, release more funding, chose to withdraw the amateur strands of the festival. In fact, the Arts Council raised their contribution only marginally in 2002, committing nine thousand pounds. However, producing a Festival with a more visible concentration of professional work also fed into Leddy's agenda of transforming Glasgay! into a more confident festival. For Leddy, this confidence was based on its quality, rather than on notions of size or quantity. Having made the decision not to include amateur work, Leddy further decided that, rather than replacing such events with additional professional work (an impossible task, perhaps, given the funding limitations), he would instead produce a smaller festival, with an overall higher standard. Leddy's first programme contained only 26 events, compared with the 45 programmed by Mitchell the preceding year. Leddy's hope was that this smaller programme would prevent the festival from cannibalizing itself; instead of deciding between two events presented on the same night, spectators could go to both, over two nights (Leddy, 2006). In terms of content, Leddy did not so much change the type of professional work being programmed as make it more visible to the potential audience by refocusing the marketing material. The alphabetical or chronological brochure design was replaced with one that

---

[46] Strapline taken from the Glasgay! programmes 2002 and 2003.

capitalised on the 'big names' appearing at Glasgay! The head of Annie Sprinkle, for example, was displayed prominently on the front cover of 2002's brochure, while her performance, *Herstory of Porn: Reel to Real*, was advertised on the first page.

Glasgay! 2002 was subtitled 'The UK's largest multi-arts festival for multi-sexual people & their friends', a strapline that would also appear on the 2003 publicity. Leddy acknowledges that this was intended to be 'quite arch and a bit tongue in cheek', since it deliberately avoided saying that the festival was a 'gay, lesbian, bisexual, transgender and intersex' arts festival (Leddy, 2006). Poking gentle fun at the diversity of identity labels now deemed necessary within the 'sexual minority' sector this subtitle also openly confronted the anxiety that funding bodies felt when considering an application for a lesbian and gay arts festival; they would much rather support 'a gay festival that's for everyone' (Leddy, 2006). The strapline did also suggest Leddy's own ideological position in relation to lesbian and gay identity, and his political aspirations for the festival. Like Mitchell, he aimed to challenge the assumptions about sexual identity and the stereotypes that frequently accompany them. In Leddy's words, he wanted the festival to be

> as open and discursive as possible. The work that interested me the most was work that was troubling the notions of what gay and lesbian is, particularly the notion that gay culture is gay male culture and is camp and drag. (Leddy, 2006)

Leddy hoped to surprise people with his programme, offering events that were unexpected and unusual, and sometimes challenging, such as Diamanda Galás's *Frenzy*, a concert dedicated to Aileen Wuornos, and Russell Barr's *Transphobia*, concerning the murderous attack of a drag queen. Signalling yet another shift from its inception, Leddy perceived the festival as being less a platform for celebration, than a means to explore the problematics internal to 'gay identity' and to any so-called 'gay community'.

> We needed to move forward from those things. That actually the time has passed that we have to have a celebration, a big party, and we have to say how great it is to be gay, we're all proud to be gay, it's really great. And actually, within our own gay cultures we need to start looking for how to move forward. (Leddy, 2006)

As Leddy acknowledges, people were questioning the whole notion of a 'gay culture' and 'gay identity', whilst also recognising the very real experiences of marginalization and oppression. For Leddy, gay culture is not always, and not for everyone, 'great'. In the same vein, Leddy was less concerned with using the festival as a platform for persuading a 'straight' dominant culture that 'we're all really nice' (Leddy, 2006). In his opinion, by 2002 there was not that same need for gay men and lesbians to prove themselves (Leddy, 2006), although the representation of 'minorities' remained an issue – outside but also within the festival itself. Like Mitchell and Ditton, Leddy worked hard to ensure a balance of representations from different constituencies of the 'community', whilst admitting the difficulty of achieving this.

> You get into this horrible chicken and egg situation, of saying, well there's not really many lesbian artists who are good, doing good work of the standard you want, and then the reason they're not there is because no-one books them, but when you do book them the audience don't go and see them because no-one's developed the audience because there's no work... and you go round in circles. (Leddy, 2006)

Having programmed two festivals, Leddy, like Mitchell, felt exhausted. Securing adequate funding remained a constant battle, even though the amount of money available to Glasgay! during Leddy's leadership rose from £45 thousand to £110 thousand (including sponsorship raised by Mitchell). Though the Arts Council increased its grant marginally, Leddy realised that Glasgay! still did not receive substantial financial support commensurate with other national festivals. According to Leddy, a major stumbling block for the Arts Council was Glasgay!'s multi-arts form, since it did not comfortably fit into any department's remit (and therefore responsibility), falling between stools; it was neither a drama festival, nor a music festival, nor a visual art festival. As a result of its multiplicity, Glasgay! was positioned under a community-arts umbrella, where awards were capped at a much lower level. As Leddy records,

> As far as [the Scottish Arts Council] were concerned, it was a purely administrative problem but they were unwilling to solve it. [...] I think that fundamentally they didn't believe that a gay festival could be culturally relevant and important to a wide degree. (Leddy, 2006)

Though Glasgow City Council had supported Glasgay! over the years, their own limited resources meant that they did not have many funds to distribute. While Mitchell had been successful in securing a sponsorship deal from Northern Rock in 2001, by 2003 they had changed their funding area and withdrawn support from all Scottish organisations. Leddy had also made a successful application to the Lottery Fund, but subsequent changes to criteria prohibited any future applications being submitted. As Leddy admits, 'in the end, like all arts organisations, you then come back to the Arts Council and the City Council' (Leddy, 2006).

In the same unenviable position as his predecessors, the limited amount of funding meant that Leddy was the sole full-time employee of Glasgay!, fulfilling the roles of artistic director, administrator, funding manager, and marketing manager. Revealingly, Leddy stresses that

> it's still a really hard job, and needs someone willing to do all those jobs. [...] It's a job that burns you out very quickly. You need someone brilliant to do each of those jobs well. Which is why only four people applied [for the vacancy]. (Leddy, 2006)

Glasgay! 2004 – 2006: 'Scotland's Annual Celebration of Queer Culture'[47]

Taking over the role of Festival Producer from Leddy when he resigned after Glasgay!'s tenth festival, Steven Thomson was already connected with the organisation through his role as a Board Member. Though admiring the quality of Leddy's programming, and his success at turning it into a visibly more confident festival, Thomson's aim was to reshape both the programme and the business structure of Glasgay!. In this latter respect, Thomson's leadership has been the most radical to date.

As noted, since its inception Glasgay! has, largely due to financial constraints, remained something of a broker between other producers, venues and artists. The majority of the Glasgay! programme has therefore been built on a co-production relationship, with Glasgay! taking sole responsibility for only a small number of presentations. Leddy provides a useful example of the model employed during his leadership, although stresses that the relationship was different with every venue and every show.

> With the Tron, often what happened is that they would pay the fee of the artist, Glasgay! would pay the artist's travel and accommodation, and then we'd split the box office, 70% to the Tron, 30% to Glasgay! (Leddy, 2006)

Taking on the mantle of Festival Producer, Thomson was acutely aware that much of his predecessors' time was taken up with 'micromanagement', negotiating the minutiae of details with other producers and venues, for very little financial return (Thomson, 2006). In

---

[47] Strapline taken from the Glasgay! programmes 2004 and 2005.

Thomson's words,

> it seemed to me that it was the wrong way round and that maybe Glasgay!
> needed to take more ownership of its product, take more risks in some
> ways, but also earn some money. (Thomson, 2006)

From 2004 Thomson began to radically change the working model of
Glasgay! by hiring venues and directly commissioning/programming the
work for those spaces. As a result, the box office returns all came to
Glasgay!, rather than being split between producers. The risk of this
strategy, of course, is that there has to *be* substantial box office returns in
order for Glasgay! to meet the larger outgoing costs.

In terms of the artistic agenda, Glasgay! seems to have travelled
full circle under Thomson's reign. His primary aim is to reshape the
public's perception of Glasgay! by transforming it (or reforming it) into a
popular, celebratory event.

> My mantra became, entertain first, educate second. Get the audience
> through the door, make them feel a product is accessible, make them feel
> that it has recognisable qualities.   (Thomson, 2006)

Thomson's sentiments echo Ditton's and D'Angelo's, and the
festival's subtitle, 'Scotland's Annual Celebration of Queer Culture',
again places the word 'celebration' at the heart of the programme, this
time literally. Sensitive to the cultural context of Glasgow, in Thomson's
opinion Glasgay! is 'absolutely rooted in a popular, ever so slightly
working-class audience. It's rooted in a mainstream audience' (Thomson,
2006). Perhaps responding to the increasing prevalence of work that might
be considered experimental in Mitchell's and Leddy's programmes,
Thomson is keen to reconnect with what he considers more mainstream
culture, albeit a 'gay' culture.

> What's the basic meaning of what we're doing here. It's show business.
> It's celebration. We're celebrating gay culture. (Thomson, 2006)

Struggling with the same lack of funding experienced by all
Glasgay! producers, Thomson's tactic has been to make the festival even
more visible on a national and international scale. In his words, 'I thought
the only way I would get true recognition from the funders was to grow to
a certain size, and to develop partnerships right across the city' (Thomson,
2006). While his first festival was fourteen days in length, the most recent
festival in 2005 had grown to an entire month, running from the 20th
October to the 20th November. Also new to Glasgay! 2005 was a dedicated
gallery space, Q! Gallery, run and programmed entirely by Thomson

throughout the year.

Though Thomson's stated aim is a more popular programme, in fact his line-up to date has been as eclectic and mixed as those that preceded it, ranging from self-evidently 'camp' events such as *Lypsinka! The Boxed Set*, to the mainstream hit of Alan Bennett's *The History Boys*, to the more performance-oriented work of Annie Sprinkle and Adrian Howells (although admittedly even these latter pieces might be considered intimate and celebratory, rather than politically challenging or confrontational). Thomson also admits that the place of politics remains crucial. The image for the 2005 brochure encapsulates this necessity – barbed wire running along the centre of the page. Again in Thomson's words,

> We are biting the barbed wire in many ways. Equal rights means a lot more than just getting the rights to live with someone. It's about a recognition of a number of different levels of society and our right to be recognised, not just people saying 'yes, we recognise you', but that being enshrined within policy. (Thomson, 2006)

For Thomson, the 'politics' embraced and represented by Glasgay! should extend beyond the local and national, and also beyond issues relating solely to sexuality since gay artists have important political contributions and perspectives to offer on international affairs. As Thomson stresses, the artists represented by Glasgay! are 'not just a bunch of cabaret acts' (Thomson, 2006).

Glasgay! The Past and the Future

Cordelia Ditton and Dominic D'Angelo began working on the first festival in 1993, as a response to Ditton's perceptions that the gay and lesbian community of Glasgow was largely invisible, both on stage but also within the city in general. This first Glasgay! not only placed cultural representations of gay men and lesbians literally in the city's spotlight, it also, through its extensive networking, community involvement, and marketing, brought 'real' gay men and lesbians into city centre spaces. This collectivization of 'sexual minorities' served to render them present in the whole city, rather than ghettoized in the 'scene'. Twelve years on, and the question is begged as to whether such a festival is still needed. Indeed, many 'advances' must now be recognised; in 2000, Section 28 was removed from the Scottish statute books; in 2003, it became illegal for employers to discriminate against someone because of their sexuality; in 2005, gay men and lesbians gained the right to civil partnerships; in 2006, under the Equality Act, it will be illegal to discriminate on the basis of sexuality in the provision of goods, facilities and services. Mainstream representations of gay men have also proliferated (many of them imported from the USA), from the saccharine *Will & Grace* to the banal *Queer Eye for the Straight Guy.* (Lesbians admittedly remain largely invisible, with the exception of *The L Word.*)

We might applaud such shifts. However, whilst gay men and lesbians now have the right to civil partnerships, they do not have the right to marriage; and the split in the various churches over this 'right' serves to reveal the extent to which 'homosexuality' remains unacceptable. Whilst Section 28 might have been removed from the Statute books, the vitriolic 'Keep the Clause' campaign staged in Scotland in 2000 made very clear the extent of fear, hatred, and disgust still felt by many of Scotland's citizens towards gay men and lesbians. Stagecoach tycoon Brian Souter, in an attempt to block the repeal of Section 28, funded his own private referendum. In his poll, more than a million people – 87% of the total who voted – voted to keep Section 28. Mori Scotland, arguably a more legitimate indicator of opinion, produced similar results in the same year. Thirty-three per cent of those polled agreed with Cardinal Winning's description of homosexual relationships as 'a perversion'; 14 per cent indicated that if schools were to be allowed to discuss homosexuality, they should 'teach children that homosexuality is wrong, and should not be tolerated as a way of life'; while 24 per cent responded that schools should 'teach children that homosexuality is wrong, but should be tolerated as a way of life'. Adding up these responses, we are confronted with the fact that more than one in three people in Scotland, at the start of the twenty-first century, believed that 'homosexuality is wrong'.[48] Is it possible that in the space of only five years, such attitudes have changed? In March 2003, the *Sunday Herald* refer to a report by Greater Glasgow Health Board, which recorded that 80% of lesbian, gay, bisexual or transexual young people had reported discrimination in 2002, while approximately '40% of lesbian and gay pupils had experienced a violent attack at school and nearly a fifth had contemplated suicide as a result of attitudes to their sexuality'.[49] In 2004, the Herald also reported that homophobic incidents in Strathclyde had increased by 60% in one year.[50] Meanwhile, a recent

---

[48]. www.mori.com/polls/2000/sh000121.shtml, 16 November 2003.

[49]. http://www.sundayherald.com/31978, 20 May 2006.

[50]. http://www.findarticles.com/p/articles/mi_qn4156/is_20041114/ai_n12591517, 20 May 2006. Such an increase might well be due to an increase in those willing to report such incident; however, the point remains that the experience of homophobia remains common.

national (UK) survey by Gay Times and Diva Magazine found that 'one in eight lesbians and one in 10 gay men questioned for the Out Now 2005 survey said they were harassed at work in the past 12 months because of their sexuality, despite legislation that came into force in 2003 banning discrimination'.[51]

Given the continuing oppression of lesbians and gay men, it is unsurprising that each of the respective producers of Glasgay! continues to support the festival. For David Peutherer, Glasgay! 'portrays a very positive image of the LGBT community, we contribute a lot to the arts, we contribute to the city by organising an important festival, we bring visitors in, we bring money in, we put bums on theatre seats, and we do it without going bankrupt' (Peutherer, 2006). Peutherer recognises that, following the homophobic baiting encouraged by the 'Keep the Clause' campaign, it would be impossible to deny the existence of a LGBT community in Glasgow. The aim of the festival, then, is not so much to do with visibility as continuing to provide positive role models for a marginalised community that is persistently discriminated against by the dominant culture. As well as looking outwards, Glasgay! continues to play an important internal function; 'There's a large section of the community that has a very negative self-image' (Peutherer, 20096). This aspect is also iterated by Cordelia Ditton; Glasgay! remains crucial for the isolated young man or woman, disowned by family and friends. In addition, Glasgay! provides a forum for some internal debates, debates that Ditton feels are crucial to these times, including discussion around 'what our place is now?', 'what it is to be gay'? (Ditton, 2006).

The vitriol that surfaced during the repeal of Section 28 served to bring home to Mitchell the fact that 'things haven't moved on that far' (Mitchell, 2006). Mitchell also continues to question the extent to which queer culture or gay and lesbian identity is represented in venues throughout Glasgow, throughout the year. Against such a backdrop, 'there is still a need to have someone championing that kind of work' (Mitchell, 2006). For Mitchell, Leddy and Thomson, Glasgay! continues to serve an important function in rendering visible the diversity of LGBT experience, beyond the stereotypes. Whilst gay men might have made it onto mainstream television networks, unsurprisingly the majority of shows do not represent the everyday, complex lives of gay men, tending to render gay characters in still-stereotypical guises; either the asexual, sensible, professional gay man, such as Will (who lives with a straight woman), or

---

[51]   http://www.findarticles.com/p/articles/mi_qn4156/is_20060122/ai_n16015911, 20 May 2006.

the campy, irresponsible, sluttish Jack (a figure of fun with whom it would be hard to identify). While *Queer Eye* has five 'gay characters', each one inhabits a dominant stereotype – the butch handy-man, the philosophical cook, the sensitive personal coach, the campy stylist, the trendy hairdresser. None are allowed to transgress their particular boxes, shift identities, or inhabit multiple locations; instead, each is a one-dimensional cartoonish cut-out. Though Leddy acknowledges that we 'now have a degree of wider visibility with out gay celebrities', he also admits 'that we're still very limited', and that 'we're not going to get the sort of discussions of gay culture that we saw in [Russell Barr's] *Transphobia* from Elton John' (Leddy, 2006). Significantly, Leddy also draws attention to the continuing specific cultural marginalisation of representations of lesbians, a lack of visibility that Glasgay! needs to respond to and address. Thomson, meanwhile, recognises that 'no matter how mainstream our lives become, no matter how much we get public celebrations of our lives, our relationships, there's still a need for […] queer lifestyles to be presented on stage' (Thomson, 2006). Understanding Glasgay! as a lobbyist, Thomson adds,

> If we rely on mainstream culture to keep us well represented, we'll starve of oxygen. That's Glasgay!'s job. We're front line ambassadors for that underground world that needs positive representation rather than marginalising. That's what I see my job as; I'm a conduit for that and what I try to do is make sure that all of those flavours and tastes are represented. (Thomson, 2006)

In spite of their different aims and agendas, then, each producer of Glasgay! shares a keen political awareness of the necessity to represent the diversity of the LGBT culture, a culture that is located within a local, national and international context. What each producer also shares is the frustrating and ongoing battle to secure funding; and while this persists, the future of Glasgay! remains under constant threat. Whether Glasgay! is needed is perhaps the wrong question to ask in such a context. A more pertinent one might be whether Glasgay! is wanted, a question to be proposed to, and answered by, Creative Scotland when it replaces the Scottish Arts Council in 2007. Creative Scotland must, in the words of Thomson, 'have the notion of cultural rights enshrined in their status', which will in turn 'guarantee that our audience have representation' (Thomson, 2006).

Works cited

Cvetkovich, Ann, *An Archive of Feelings: Trauma, Sexuality, and Lesbian Public Cultures*, Durham and London: Duke University Press, 2003.

Glasgay! 1993 Brochure Update.

Glasgay! 1995 Brochure.

Glasgay! 1998 Brochure.

Glasgay! 1999 Brochure.

Glasgay! 2000 Brochure.

Glasgay! 2001 Brochure.

Glasgay! 2002 Brochure.

Glasgay! 2003 Brochure.

Glasgay! 2004 Brochure.

Glasgay! 2005 Brochure.

Heddon, Deirdre, 'Performing lesbians: constructing the self, constructing the community', in *Auto/biography and identity: Women, Theatre and Performance*, Maggie B. Gale and Viv Gardner (eds.), Manchester: Manchester University Press, 2004.

Huyssen, Andreas, *Twilight Memories: Marking Time in a Culture of Amnesia*, New York: Routledge, 1995.

Jordanova, Ludmilla, *History in Practice*, London: Arnold, 2000.

Interviews

Ditton, Cordelia, (3 February 2006), interview with Dee Heddon.

Leddy, David (20 January 2006), interview with Dee Heddon.

Mitchell, Lindsay (15 March 2006), interview with Dee Heddon.

Peutherer, David (25 March 2006), interview with Dee Heddon.

Thomson, Steven (20 January 2006), interview with Dee Heddon.

Websites

www.mori.com/polls/2000/sh000121.shtml. Accessed 16 November 2003.

http://www.sundayherald.com/31978, 20 May 2006.

http://www.findarticles.com/p/articles/mi_qn4156/is_20041114/ai_n12591 517. Accessed 20 May 2006.

http://www.findarticles.com/p/articles/mi_qn4156/is_20060122/ai_n16015 911. Accessed 20 May 2006.

CONTRIBUTORS

Selina Busby teaches at Central School of Speech and Drama, University of London. Her work focuses both on applied drama and contemporary theatre. Currently she is researching the representation of chosen families and network communities within British Theatre of the 1990s.

Dr Paul T. Davies is Senior lecturer and course leader of BA (Hons) Performing Arts at Suffolk College. His teaching covers acting techniques, writing and directing for performance, issues of identity, performance analysis, and he is the director of productions. He has directed at the Sherman Theatre, Cardiff, at the Edinburgh Festival Fringe, and at the New Wolsey Theatre, Ipswich, in both main house and studio theatres.

Sarah Jane Dickenson is a Lecturer in Drama at The University of Hull, UK. She specializes in applied drama, radio drama, and the structure of written drama. She has published articles on subjects ranging from adaptation to pantomime and is regularly commissioned to write plays for young people to perform in a variety of situations and for a variety of purposes.

Dr Kate Dorney is the Curator of Modern and Contemporary Performance at the V&A Theatre Collections, the National Museum of Performing Arts. She previously worked with the AHRC British Library Theatre Archive Project at the University of Sheffield reclaiming scripts missing from the British Library's Modern Plays Archive, researching and sorting the archive of Sir Ralph Richardson , and collecting oral history testimony from theatre-goers and workers between 1945 and 1968. She has also worked with the Liverpool Everyman Theatre Archive collecting oral history testimony from those who created and worked in the theatre. She has published articles on Beckett, Joe Orton, post-war British theatre and the aftermath of theatre censorship in Britain. She has a study of the life and career of Ralph Richardson in press.

Dr Stephen Farrier teaches at Central School of Speech and Drama, University of London. His work focuses on gender, queer reading and experimental theatre. His previous work includes conference papers on Queer Praxis as well as using queer to read soap opera as in his 'Ga[y]zing at soap' in *Frames and Fictions on Television,* Llewellyn Jones, M. and Carson, B. (London: Intellect 2000).

Dr Dimple Godiwala has taught at various American and British Universities in England. She has written widely in the fields of feminist, performance and postcolonial theory. Godiwala is the author of the monographs *Breaking the Bounds: British Feminist Dramatists Writing in the Mainstream since c. 1980* (New York & Oxford: Peter Lang, 2003), and *Queer Mythologies: the Original Stageplays of Pam Gems* (Bristol & Portland: Intellect, 2006). She has edited a critical anthology *Alternatives within the Mainstream: British Black and Asian Theatres* (Newcastle: Cambridge Scholars Press, 2006).

Dr Deirdre Heddon is a Senior Lecturer in the Department of Theatre, Film and Television Studies at the University of Glasgow. She has published widely in various journals and anthologies. An article on the Glasgay! show *Fingerlicks*, 'Performing Lesbians: Constructing the Self, Constructing the Community' has been published in *Auto/biography and identity: Women, Theatre and Performance*, eds. Maggie B. Gale and Viv Gardner (Manchester: Manchester University Press 2004).

Kathy McKean is a postgraduate researcher at Kingston University, London. She is an AHRC Doctoral Award holder and is writing a PhD entitled '"If you sit in the dark long enough something scary's bound to happen": The ghosts of Phyllis Nagy.'

Catherine McNamara is the Course Leader of the MA Applied Theatre (Drama in the Community & Drama Education) at the Central School of Speech and Drama, University of London. Recent research includes: 'When a Girl becomes a Man: Female-to-Male Narratives in Performance', a paper given at the Women's Writing for Performance: Process and Practice International Symposium, Lancaster University, April 2006, and 'Re-inhabiting the Uninhabitable Body: Interventions in Voice Production with Transsexual Men' paper given at Theatre and Performance Research Association, University of Manchester, September 2005. Catherine is the Project Co-ordinator for the Wellcome Trust funded project 'Sci:dentity - What's the Science of Sex & Gender?' which works with transgendered and non-transgendered young people to explore relationships between lived experiences of gendered identity, and scientific and medical discourses around the body. She also founded the ongoing TransVoices Project which began in June 2004 and works with trans men doing practical voice work which aims to develop resonance, range and healthy voice use, particularly for those who are undergoing hormone treatment.

Simon O'Corra is a writer, visual artist and film maker. His writing focuses on Human Rights issues, including lesbian, gay, bisexual and transgender rights. Simon explores issues of gender in his work *Get Me Out Of This,* a visual/performance arts project exploring the social control exemplified by the fashion industry. He has made a range of short films one of which, *Queer Fear in Iraq*, about the plight of lesbians and gay men in Iraq, was premiered in 2007. Simon is also a Reiki Master and Life Enhancer.

Dr Christopher Pullen is Senior Lecturer in Media, Gender and Performance at Bournemouth Media School, Bournemouth University. He has published a number of articles on gay identity and reality television, and has forthcoming work on French queer cinema and contemporary AIDS narratives in documentary. Also he is the author of a progressive new book titled *Documenting Gay Men* (McFarland, 2006) which explores how gay people as teens, devoted couples, parents, and influential producers have contributed to the progression of gay identity within domestic arenas.

Dr Tony Purvis is part of the Media and Culture team in the Faculty of Humanities, Arts and Social Sciences, University of Newcastle. He teaches and researches television, media and cultural theory, and psychoanalysis. His book publications include the co-authored (with Sue Thornham) *Television Drama: Theories and Identities*, and *Media and Cultural Studies* (Edinburgh: Edinburgh University Press). He is currently completing a monograph on media and sexuality (Edinburgh University Press).

Ian Spiby was the Head of the Performance Studies Division at the University of Northampton for sixteen years. He has written and presented many programmes on drama for BBC Radio 3 and 4 and has published a number of books, including contributions to *Shakespeare's World and Work*, and *Drama 7 – 11* for Routledge. At present he works with the company *art and life* producing dramas for radio.

Dr Kathleen Starck is Junior Professor for cultural studies at Osnabrueck University. Her research interests include contemporary drama, postcolonial/transcultural studies, and gender in British and American literature and film, as well as British and American films of the Cold War. She is the author of *'I Believe in the Power of Theatre.' British Women's Drama of the 1980s and 1990s*. Trier: WVT, 2005.

Dr Ashley Tellis was most recently Adjunct Assistant Professor in English at Hunter College, City University of New York. He is completing his manuscript *Productive Contaminations: Same-Sex Politics in Contemporary India* and editing an anthology of essays on the possibilities of joint activism by the immigrant and queer rights movements in contemporary United States.

Dr Victor Ukaegbu is a Senior Lecturer and Field Chair for Drama, University of Northampton. He is a performance practitioner and academic with a wide range of research and practical performance interests including intercultural theatre, postcolonial performances, applied theatre and theatre adaptations. His most recent publications include 'Mythological and Patriarchal Constraints: The Tale of Osofisan's Revolutionary Women' in *Portraits for an Eagle: Essays in Honour of Femi Osofisan* edited by Sola Adeyemi, 2006; 'The Problem with Definitions: An Examination of Applied Theatre in Traditional African Context(s) in *National Drama*, Volume 3, 2004; and 'Performing Postcolonially: Contextual Changes in the Adaptations of Wole Soyinka's *Death and the King's Horseman* and Femi Osofisan's *Once Upon Four Robbers* in *World Literature Written in English (WLWE)* Vol. 40, No 1, 2002. This is his second publication on Black British theatres.